Biographical Memoirs

NATIONAL ACADEMY OF SCIENCES

NATIONAL ACADEMY OF SCIENCES
OF THE UNITED STATES OF AMERICA

Biographical Memoirs

VOLUME XLIV

NATIONAL ACADEMY OF SCIENCES
WASHINGTON, D.C. 1974

INTERNATIONAL STANDARD BOOK NUMBER 0-309-02238-X

LIBRARY OF CONGRESS CATALOG CARD NUMBER 74-7654

Available from

PRINTING AND PUBLISHING OFFICE, NATIONAL ACADEMY OF SCIENCES
2101 CONSTITUTION AVENUE, N.W., WASHINGTON, D.C. 20418

PRINTED IN THE UNITED STATES OF AMERICA

CONTENTS

PREFACE	vii
CHARLES HASKELL DANFORTH BY BENJAMIN H. WILLIER	1
THOMAS FRANCIS, JR. BY JOHN R. PAUL	57
DONNEL FOSTER HEWETT BY JAMES GILLULY	111
WILLIAM VERMILLION HOUSTON BY KENNETH S. PITZER AND HAROLD E. RORSCHACH, JR.	127
HOWARD BISHOP LEWIS BY WILLIAM C. ROSE AND MINOR J. COON	139
ROBERT HARRY LOWIE BY JULIAN H. STEWARD	175
WINTHROP JOHN VANLEUVEN OSTERHOUT BY L. R. BLINKS	213

THEODORE WILLIAM RICHARDS BY JAMES BRYANT CONANT	251
RUDOLF RUEDEMANN BY JOHN RODGERS	287
EDWARD ARTHUR STEINHAUS BY E. F. KNIPLING	303
CHESTER HAMLIN WERKMAN BY RUSSELL W. BROWN	329

PREFACE

The *Biographical Memoirs* is a series of volumes containing the biographies of deceased members of the National Academy of Sciences and bibliographies of their published scientific works. Each biographical essay has been written by a fellow member of the Academy familiar with the professional career of the deceased, with only occasional exceptions. These volumes, therefore, provide a record of the lives and work of some of the most distinguished leaders of American science as witnessed and interpreted by their colleagues and peers.

The National Academy of Sciences is a private, honorary organization of scientists and engineers elected on the basis of outstanding contributions to knowledge. Established by a Congressional Act of Incorporation on March 3, 1863, and supported by private and public funds, the Academy works to further science and its use for the general welfare by bringing together the most qualified individuals to deal with scientific and technological problems of broad significance.

Biographical Memoirs

VOLUME XLIV

CHARLES HASKELL DANFORTH

November 30, 1883–January 10, 1969

BY BENJAMIN H. WILLIER *

CHARLES HASKELL DANFORTH left not only a published record of sixty years (1907–1967) of scientific articles but also an autobiographical sketch (a typewritten copy of thirty pages dated March 1948 which was deposited in the files of the Home Secretary of the National Academy of Sciences) that tells the story of "facts not usually printed in biographical reference books," for example, such items as home life and occupations, schooling, and development of special interests. This sketch was written merely for "atmosphere," and so that his "possible biographer need do little more than condense and paraphrase—which somehow reminds me of one of my earliest observations that it takes many buckets of sap to make a small cup of syrup." It is of interest here to note that, in a fire which destroyed the Danforth home in 1939, there was lost "a notebook in which I began during high school days to develop, point by point, what I hoped would be a satisfactory and integrated philosophy and code for living."

---

* Dr. Willier died December 3, 1972, before the processing of his manuscript had been completed. The final version of this memoir owes a good deal to the constructive criticisms and/or valuable comments of Leslie C. Dunn, Roman O'Rahilly, Curt Stern, and Sewall Wright, the last named providing the evaluation of Danforth's pioneer paper on frequency of mutation in man. Special credit is due Curt Stern who assumed the responsibility for the final editing of the memoir.

No one who knew Charles Danforth personally and has visited the region of his birth in his native state can imagine for him any other birthplace. He was born on the last day of November 1883 on "a farm just over the Oxford line and about three miles from Norway village" in Maine, the Pine Tree State ("Old Dirigo"). The natural environment in and around Norway to the horizon is a typical postglacial landscape near the southern margin of the Wisconsin Continental glacier, a result of the last great ice age (10,000–15,000 years ago) in the Pleistocene epoch. It is a picturesque region made up of forests, freshwater lakes and ponds, hills and valleys, and springs and streams interspersed with agricultural farmlands. The many forests are of mixed character, with white pine and other conifers, and deciduous trees such as white birch, sugar maple, and oak. And there is the poet's rhodora whose "beauty is its own excuse for being." The hills, seven of them, range in height from Pikes Hill (870') to Merrill Hill (1,243') in the town of Norway. Indeed, our biographee had a gentle face and personality akin to the landscape of the gentle hilltops, beloved forest green, quiet lakes and rippling brooks, and rustic simplicity of the farmland. Such was nature's scenic area that played a role in Danforth's development as a naturalist.

ANCESTRY

In telling words Danforth wrote: "Most New Englanders of colonial stock have much the same ancestral background and my own is quite typical of the group as a whole." So far as he had been able to learn it seemed probable that all of his immigrant ancestors were exclusively British (English, Scottish, Welsh, and possibly Irish). All of them reached America during the first half of the seventeenth century, some coming in the *Mayflower* and some in various small vessels. They spread along the coast from Plymouth to what is now southwestern Maine (Oxford, York, and Cumberland counties). The largest early concentrations of them were around Boston, Billerica, Salem, and Falmouth. Of these early arrivals a few may have returned to England; the majority, however, lived and died within two hundred miles of Boston. Danforth "thinks" that every one of his native American ancestors was born and died within the same radius. He writes: "As a group they were fairly representative of the large middle class whose members rarely distinguished themselves by any very appreciable deviation from the norm of their time and locale." Danforth lists fifty-seven names of these ancestors. Among them are Danforth (grandfather), Frost (maternal grandmother), Reed (grandmother), and Haskell (grandfather and mother). Further, "there are more names than there are chromosomes in a human germ cell, so it is quite possible that some of these lines are ancestral in name only." He was surprised to find only a low degree of consanguinity among his direct ancestors. To establish descent Danforth became a member of the Society of Mayflower Descendants about 1930.

The last of his ancestors to go from Massachusetts to Maine was his paternal grandfather, Asa Danforth, who having been licensed at Boston in 1820 to "practice physick and surgery" moved shortly thereafter to Norway, Maine, and there married a descendant of a *Mayflower* passenger, Abigail C. Reed, daughter of the first postmaster of the town. Asa Danforth practiced his profession in Norway for nearly sixty years and seems to have been a typically beloved old-time country doctor. It is said that he built the first woolen mill in the state and was engaged in a variety of town affairs. His fellow citizens evidently respected and trusted him, for he served a term in the state legislature. The couple had nine children, of whom James Danforth was the eighth child, the father of Charles, his brother (Francis) and two sisters (Ann and Śara). James Danforth's occupation included being a farmer, a commercial traveler, and caretaker of his father's property interests. He had considerable interest in ancient and colonial history as well as an appreciation of good writing. Moreover, in personal relations with his son Charles, James Danforth "employed good psychological techniques or perhaps better just normal common sense."

Charles Danforth's maternal grandfather was Charles Henry Haskell, a native of Westbrook, Maine, whose ancestors arrived on the *Mayflower*. He married Laura Diantha Frost, a descendant of the first settlers of the town of Norway, also passengers on the *Mayflower*. This grandfather was a farmer, and at times an agent for a cracker company, a road surveyor, and a minor town official. The couple had five children, all girls, the eldest of whom was Mary File Haskell, the mother of Charles. His mother had the usual high school education of that period and taught school for a while. Throughout her life she took an active interest in the local schools, participated in the activities of a literary club, and frequently served as chairman of church and other organizations. She "did not seek responsibility but took it seriously when it did come her way." As a mother she was sympathetic and solicitous—inclined to "drive" rather hard in the intellectual field. She had a sound but aggressive interest in the schools where Charles was a pupil.

By contrast, his grandmother Haskell "had the most 'character' in the group." A good voice, a good sense of humor, and a good memory made her interesting and stimulating. She had "angles," however, that were to be merely tolerated—her attitude toward life was more defiant than humble.

On June 24, 1914, Charles Haskell Danforth married Florence Wenonah Garrison, a teacher of science and a member of the Daughters of the American Colonists and the Society of Daughters of the American Revolution, who was a writer of delightful historical articles on the Smithsonian Institution.* The couple had three sons, Charles Garrison (biologist), Alan Haskell (lawyer), and Donald Reed (engineer). Mrs. Dan-

* See *American Heritage*, 15 (1963):26–27.

forth died in May 1968 about eight months prior to the demise of her husband, who himself died in the hospital on the Stanford University campus on January 10, 1969.

TO BE OR NOT TO BE—A NATURALIST

The total environment comprising wild nature and intellectual climate provided a setting into which Charles was born and developed into a young man. His first eight and a half years were spent mostly on the farm of his parents. As he grew older, he participated "at least vicariously" in most of the common activities of a typical agricultural farm, such as making hay and maple syrup and weeding the garden. More attractive, however, were "my abundant and very pleasant memories of this period [that] have rather strong emotional components [of] mingling evening twilights with slightly eery calls of frogs and whip-poorwills, the boom of nighthawks and lowing of distant cattle, the exhilaration of morning with sunshine on the tree tops, and myriad things of interest through the whole day." These early interests and observations appertained to each and every living thing whether plant or animal. Seemingly not one was overlooked—ranging from the speckled lily *(Lilium canadense)* and partridge berries to nighthawks and thrashers. "Seeing my first humming bird was an event, dampened a little by learning it was not a queen bee."

At seven years of age he entered primary school in Norway village where he lived with his grandparents, the Haskells—going home for weekends. Of this period he writes: "School matters do not loom large in my memories. It is the 'farm' and not the 'village' around which my memories center most vividly."

The aggregate of environmental conditions affecting his life and development changed for Charles in 1892. In that year his father sold the farm and took over the home and other holdings of grandfather Haskell in Norway, a village of "perhaps 2000 people." There was a "little island in the brook" on the old farm, however, that took a long time before "I became reconciled to relinquishing" it.

From this time on to 1897, a period of five years of "early days in Norway," his environment combined the main features of farm life, though on a reduced scale, and of life in a small manufacturing town. He participated in the work of the former as he did on the old farm and in "the diversion" of the latter. Charles did not lose any of his natural curiosity and deep interest in living objects. In fact, at about twelve years of age while botanizing in Norway, he found plants of the saxifrage family—known commonly as foam flower or false miterwort—that vary in color of the anthers, which is either a bright yellow or an orange red. This discovery of a clear-cut variation of a single character was either held in memory for ten years or, more likely, recorded in his notebook. It was not until 1911, three years after graduation from college, that this early observation was published under the title of "A Dimorphism in *Tiarella cordifolia.*"

Although love of nature was primary, great books and distinguished naturalists were also influential in his decision whether or not to be a naturalist. Of singular influence were the famous volumes of Darwin, as the following quotation shows:

"A particularly memorable evening occurred in the summer of my eleventh or twelfth year. Several of us boys were rolling hoops around the square during a long summer twilight when my uncle Frank Danforth, passing by, called me to the sidewalk and gave me two books that he thought I 'might like to have.' They were the two volumes of Darwin's *Animals and Plants under Domestication* and the inscriptions on their flyleaves showed that they had long ago been presented to my grandfather Danforth by A. E. Verrill. These volumes proved fascinating reading and probably influenced me more than any other books I have ever read. They dealt with things with which I was familiar, and in a way that made a strong appeal to my imagination. The close observation and the type of reasoning displayed in the chapters, especially those dealing with the pigeon and dog, were highly stimulating. I read them with intense interest, reflected much on their contents, and observed my own animals more closely. My father, who had apparently not noticed these volumes before, also read them, but my mother mildly disapproved.

"Although at this time I had never heard of the National Academy of Sciences, three of its members were well known to me by name. They were C. O. Whitman, Sidney I. Smith, and A. E. Verrill, all of whom had attended the Norway High School ('Liberal Institute') with my father. Throughout life, my father's most intimate friend was the brother of Professor Smith and brother-in-law of Professor Verrill. So with a feeling of easy familiarity I wrote to Professor Verrill telling him that I expected to be a naturalist and asking for suggestions. He replied, in effect, 'Don't unless you can't help it.' At thirteen I thought I couldn't help it. How much of my subsequent history is due to the strength of this assumption, and how much to chance or lack of imagination, I can not say."

But why did Professor Verrill, a distinguished naturalist, discourage young Charles from becoming a naturalist? In an attempt to answer this question it is perhaps of significance "to recall that Verrill lived through practically the entire history of zoology in America, from the coming of Louis Agassiz in 1847, to the experimental period of the present century." The vogue in zoology had changed from taxonomy to comparative anatomy, then to adaptations and other zoological disciplines, and at the beginning of the twentieth century to experimental fields. Moreover, "Verrill maintained to the end of his life the importance of taxonomy as a necessary preliminary to this more specialized biological work," that is, to genetics and other experimental fields.*

At the age of fourteen another change came about for Charles—a move to a house on Pleasant Street where he was to live with his family for six years. The move in itself introduced no radical change in his life. His work consisted of the usual chores such as delivering milk, caring for lawn and garden, and all the usual phases of farming such as plowing, hoeing, and harvesting crops. These activities were commonly shared with his father. "I never received any pay for my work nor any explicit allowance—boys of my age and background felt themselves as much a part of their family in responsibilities as in other respects." There was no sense of oppression or lack of freedom. Charles took a special interest in selecting the best seeds for flower and vegetable gardens. He introduced into his neighborhood the then new strain of chickens known as "Rhode Island Reds." Experience in breeding them led him to conclude, "In general a poor specimen of a good strain is to be preferred to a good specimen of a poor strain (to which I might now take some exception)."

The change had decided advantages, for it made his contact with woods and fields even easier than before. Behind the house was a wooded tract belonging to his uncle and beyond that the lake, the "Great Pond" or Pennesseewassee Lake, streams, pastures, and swamps stretching off toward wilder, more alluring country.

Charles entered a high school with a long and distinguished background in promoting the "cause of education" and culture of the mind. In his life sketch Charles refers to his high school as "the lineal descendant of the Norway Liberal Institute." This phrase has unusual significance, since the Institute at the time

* See Biographical Memoir of Addison Emery Verrill, by Wesley R. Coe, National Academy of Sciences, *Biographical Memoirs*, 14 (1929):39.

of its greatest vigor was highly respected for its excellence. (Many such Liberal Institutes were established by the people in western Maine—in 1852 there were six of them in Oxford County and ten in York County. The purpose of their founding was "for promoting religion and morality, and for the education of the youth in such languages, and such of the liberal arts and sciences as the said Trustees shall direct.")

During its eighteen years of existence the Norway Liberal Institute was " a college-fitting school" of very high rank with "a brilliant record." Many of its students entered colleges and universities where they often graduated with high honors. Of its early graduates three were members of the National Academy of Sciences who were active pioneer leaders in the development of the life sciences in our universities. C. O. Whitman was the first director of the Marine Biological Laboratory at Woods Hole, Massachusetts, and first chairman of the Department of Zoology, University of Chicago; Addison E. Verrill was the first Professor of Zoology, Yale University; and Sidney I. Smith was Professor of Comparative Anatomy, Yale University. To this trio of distinguished Academicians the name of Charles H. Danforth was added in 1942—a grand total of *four* Norway Liberal Institute naturalists.

The Norway Liberal Institute was opened in 1847 as a self-supporting academy; it started with 174 pupils, a principal, and a corps of teachers of much ability and enterprise and was incorporated June 25, 1849. About 1865 "the village district purchased the Institute building and changed the name of the school to the one it bears today." *

Whether the Norway High School at the time Charles entered it was equal in educational capability to the Institute, he does not say, yet the influence of its forerunner remained strong for several decades. He tells of choosing the "classical

---

* See Charles F. Whitman, *A History of Norway, Maine, from the Earliest Settlements to the Close of the Year 1922* (Lewiston, Maine, 1924).

curriculum" without giving the choice any special thought. The courses included Latin, Greek, English, and mathematics. Of these, Latin and Greek were "especially pleasant." "The *Aeneid*, more than any other book, awakened an appreciation of epic sequences and lyric associations." While a passage of the *Aeneid* was running through his mind one morning as he was feeding the cows, it suddenly occurred to him that a part of the beauty of passages written in foreign languages is "that the words are not overladen with connotations and so stimulate rather than hinder the imagination."

Charles retained an interest in the classics in his high school years. In addition, these years were naturally ones of expanding interests and a time during which new acquaintances of influence were being made. One of the most important of these was apparently his teacher Walter Bacon. In his fifteenth or sixteenth summer Charles wrote: "While walking near the pond one day, I saw a man crouching on the shore and intently looking into the water. As I approached cautiously, he remarked that he was watching two hornpouts *(Ameiurus)* swimming about in a school of polywogs." Charles adds, "I showed him his 'polywogs' were young hornpouts," and explained the breeding habits of this species (a catfish). Although Bacon, who was the man, was shown to have made an erroneous observation, he and Charles became and remained good friends and frequent collaborators in the study and identification of "a difficult moss, a puzzling carex, the call of a night bird or an intricate crossword puzzle." Finding the answer was Bacon's one all-absorbing goal. Moreover, he was like Rafinesque (a distinguished taxonomist) in his broad interests and untiring energy, yet without a trace of a desire to assign names or receive credit. Charles writes, "I learned much from his intense objectivity, quite unhampered by a highly imaginative and poetic side of his nature."

Only a few days after finding a collaborator Charles showed him "a bird's nest containing a foreign egg which I suspected was that of a cuckoo." Walter Bacon identified the owners of the nest as indigo buntings. Together they visited the taxidermy shop of J. Waldo Nash, who had an egg collection, and decided the foreign egg "was indeed that of a cuckoo (a very unusual find)." On the same day Charles learned for the first time of several books on birds available in the public library of Norway. On that same day, therefore, he was introduced to two stimulating naturalists as well as to the works of Baird, Coues, Maynard, and Chapman. From these it was but a short step to Asa Gray's *Manual of Botany,* Jordan's *Manual of Vertebrates,* and other volumes which he soon owned. Charles writes: "Before long, I was aspiring to know, at least by name, all living things about me. It was easy to learn the Latin names of new species as I identified them, and I caught up on old acquaintances by getting a few names in mind each morning and noon and rehearsing them while I worked." Charles had acquired one of the distinctive qualities of a naturalist—the knowledge of plants and animals by their Latin names.

At about this time his grandmother Haskell, not to be outdone by all this learning from nature, decided to give "us children" another demonstration of how things were done in earlier days—this time on how cheese was made and on how to cut a forked stick on which to dry a calf's stomach from which rennet was to be obtained and used in the curdling of milk.

Influences outside of high school continued to affect his way of life and thought. The most influential of these were contacts with citizens prominent in Norway affairs, among whom were George Howe and George Noyes, two members of old Norway families, each about forty years of age. Howe, a graduate of Tufts College, was a well-known naturalist and philosopher, and Noyes was a naturalist, artist, and wit. Charles had for a long time wanted to know them but, "with an ineptitude which has always been rather characteristic," he failed to meet either one of them personally until a special event opened the way.

Having written an article in defense of hawks and owls, he submitted the manuscript to the Norway *Advertiser,* the local newspaper, and then went to call on Mr. Howe, "ostensibly to ask about the approved pronunciation of scientific terms." How excited Charles must have been; Howe "invited me to his rooms where I was amazed at the beauty and wealth of his collections, especially his minerals and insects."

Thus what may be regarded as a naturalist club in miniature had its beginning for Charles. George Howe, who during the day worked sporadically in his father's insurance office or took long walks, at night held forth in his study, which was a mecca for nature lovers and visitors of many sorts. Noyes, the naturalist, was almost invariably there and before long Charles became a regular visitor himself. The group that met in evenings with Howe and Noyes were all familiar with the surrounding country and with much of its animal and plant life. Charles emphasized that they, as did his close friend V. Akers, knew its mineral and artistic resources better than he. All of them regarded Thoreau as a kind of intellectual patron inasmuch as he used "our language and had much the same outlook and humor." "In these respects Emerson on the whole fell a little short." "This was in the days before Thoreau had been 'rediscovered' and when popular nature study was in its infancy." The discussions were so lively and stimulating that Charles returned home "rather guiltily along the silent street" on many a winter evening "as late as 9:30 or even 10 o'clock."

The number of naturalists in Norway and its environs was most unusual for a small country town of about 2000 people. At the age of about thirteen years Charles knew personally as many as six able and knowledgeable amateur naturalists. Moreover, Charles adds to the list the names of his father and grandfather in these words: "Without any special technical training he [his father] was a keen observer and had many of the instincts of a field naturalist as, apparently, had his own father."

Thus the large number of devoted naturalists had the effect of producing an intellectual climate highly colored with a strong interest in things of nature. Charles had no other course to follow than to be a naturalist.

Just when he first acquired the idea of becoming a naturalist, however, is uncertain—possibly during the early days on the old farm. A relevant incident cited by Charles has a bearing on this matter. In looking at pet snakes he kept in a barrel, two adult cousins exclaimed, "I guess he is going to be a naturalist." "That was in fact just what I would be," Charles thought. Then he writes, ". . . throughout my whole life I never seriously entertained any other thought."

Somewhat frequently the evening discussions in the Howe study dwelt on matters more or less philosophical. Those of an agnostic or frankly atheistic tenor at first distressed Charles greatly. During his boyhood he had been active "in a kind of diffident way" in church and had "taken the Universalist religion for granted, despite an accumulating volume of complexities." With this religious background his first impulse was to do some "missionary" work against the view of agnosticism. His own thinking had in a manner conditioned him so much that conversion to agnosticism became, in his words, "inevitable but not easy." He wrote, "In due time I acknowledged to myself the absence of proof for the things I had believed and recognized an attitude of agnosticism as probably the only tenable one." The transition involved many restless nights of despair and groping. But in due time "a scarcely less harrowing ordeal was the attempt to build something satisfying and dependable to replace the religion I had lost." After struggles day and night with relative intangibles until a satisfactory and workable basis could be achieved, he finally came to hold the belief that "absolute finality is not an attainable goal and oriented my thinking accordingly—in the end, the new approach offered a better basis for 'serenity' than I had previously experienced."

A few years later at college he observed with satisfaction, "I was amazed at the number of students who were thrown into mental turmoil by aspects of philosophy which then left me quite undisturbed." Also, although he had never read them before, "Descartes and Kant were to appear almost as old friends and fellow seekers for the same goal." He adds, "Nevertheless 'philosophy' (except as I built up my own!) always seems to me particularly sterile, and so did formal logic."

Less than a week before he graduated from high school his mother died quite suddenly on Memorial Day. Almost within the hour of her death she had asked Charles to rehearse his graduation essay. Later that morning he "went up on the hill and looking across acres of blooming rhodora in the valley below recalled a couplet from one of Emerson's poems which she had often quoted.

> If eyes were made for seeing
> Then beauty is its own excuse for being.

The rhodora became a recurring symbol of enduring love for his mother and for nature. (*Rhodora canadensis,* a shrub related to rhododendron, has delicate pink flowers produced before or with the leaves in the spring. It is characteristic of the New England countryside.)

A NATURALIST PREPARES FOR COLLEGE

At the time of graduation from high school in the spring of 1903 Charles had "no expectation whatever of going to college." For nearly two years prior to graduation he had many protracted arguments with his parents on the subject. Contrary to the wishes of his parents he reached the decision that "going to college would be a useless, expensive and disturbing interruption of the simple life I had chosen to live."

As a consequence, Charles remained at home (at the Haskell house on Main Street) "leading a life that must have appeared most unpromising." He continued to participate in routine work of the farm and garden. His free time was spent in the field observing nature and in reading books both "stimulating and broadening." These included *The Descent of Man* by Darwin, *Cosmic Philosophy* by John Fiske, and *Riddle of the Universe* by Haeckel, as well as many controversial books and articles of the late nineteenth century. Once again his grandmother Haskell took an interest in him, this time in broadening his social life by giving him money for dancing lessons. To her annoyance he purchased among other things a copy of Preston's *Theory of Light*. The avowed reason for the purchase was to be able to honor a request to serve as physicist in the organization by George Howe of the local science forum. "I tried to do so, but with no great enthusiasm."

During the year after graduation, which he characterized as "Transitional Year 1903–1904," Charles wrote a diary or autobiographical sketch of "my first twenty years," which unfortunately was lost. In the sketch written when he was sixty-five, however, Charles saw himself "in a clearer light now [1948] than I could then [1904]." His self-analysis is set forth below in his own words.

"From my earliest days, I have been to a degree unsocial. I have not disliked people, but have always felt a kind of social inadequacy, on the one hand, and a personal self-sufficiency, on the other, that has made it easy to be alone. I enjoyed friends, games of strength and skill, but for an all-day trip in the summer or a snowshoe hike in the woods on a cold winter night I preferred to be alone. Because of some notion that 'nature' represented the highest state of perfection, man the enemy of nature seemed of all animals least interesting. I enjoyed music but was never able to carry a tune (a definite hereditary deficiency), and I never learned to dance. Failure to cultivate some of the social graces was in part genuinely due to a greater interest in other things and in part, no doubt, to rationalization of my inherent deficiencies. By the time I finished high school (the lineal descendant of the Norway Liberal Institute) I was far better acquainted with the local fauna and flora than most boys of my age but in comparison with Verrill, and perhaps Whitman, at a comparable age and graduating from the same school, I was woefully deficient. But for all that, and in spite of despairing of ever having a memory such as Professor Smith's, I still planned to be in effect a naturalist, though probably not a professional one. My attitude toward nature was somewhat reflective and at this time I though it not impossible that ultimately I might arrive at some important generalization, even as Darwin had done."

Of this year Charles wrote, "This was one of the best years of my life." In the spring of that year he decided to try at least one year of college and "drew up columns of pros and cons for Yale (Smith and Verrill), Harvard (Shaler, whom I had never met) and Tufts (fewer entrance requirements and less expensive)." The balance finally fell in favor of Tufts College, to which he went secretly in June for entrance examinations and entered in September 1904 as a freshman. Upon leaving Norway that autumn, he wrote in his notebook "with prophetic insight, a warning not to drift thoughtlessly into conventional ways of life. As it happened, I did just that, and then drifted on to baccalaureate and advanced degrees."

A NATURALIST AT COLLEGE

When Charles entered college he was nearly two years older than the average freshman student and accordingly thought of himself as much more "adult" than many classmates and in other respects "intellectually younger than most of them." From the very first he made fairly rigid rules not to study after ten o'clock at night and to set aside some time each week for a trip into the country, to such places as Lexington, Concord, and Walden ("not yet made a resort"); more especially to nearby Middlesex Falls and Mystic Lakes, where "I sought eagerly for *Potamogeton mysticus,*" a plant of the pondweed family. The many species of this family commonly have floating leaves that often differ greatly in shape from the submerged leaves. Moreover, the floating leaf is borne on a stalk that permits the leaf blade to rise and fall with the level of the water. In addition, the leaf is waterproofed on its exposed surface. Apparently he had previously concentrated on other families of aquatic plants, such as the water plantains (the *Alismacea*) and the water nymphs (the *Naiadaceae*) and was eager to see a potamogeton in its natural habitat. There is an illustration of a mind that was able to discern fine structural differences of significance among plants and among organisms in general.

Of broader appeal was the rural village of Concord and nearby Walden Pond, a region that boasted an unusual concentration of distinguished original thinkers—poets, philosophers, and/or naturalists. Charles had long been familiar—ever since as a boy of high school age he became a member of Howe's naturalist club—with *Nature,* a book by Ralph Waldo Emerson, and *Walden; or, Life in the Woods* by Henry D. Thoreau. Both books aroused sympathetic feelings in Charles. However, of the two authors, Thoreau the naturalist was more fully understood and appreciated by Charles the naturalist. To both Charles and Thoreau, intimacy with nature was vital and supreme.

Most of the courses in the humanities and arts at Tufts were found to be of interest by Charles. Of one subject after another he thought that, if it were not for biology, this or that subject would be a fascinating one to follow. At this time, which was a romantic period with such authors as Keats looming large, and under the influence of his professors of English and fine arts and of his classmate and closest friend, Clinton J. Masseck, Charles was deeply impressionable—so much so that "I wrote a little." It must have been more than a little since in his third year he was made associate editor of the college literary magazine. Later he was elected to Phi Beta Kappa—"a complete surprise, the more so since I had some poor grades in both German and trigonometry."

His formal training in biology consisted on the whole of pretty much the orthodox morphology of the late nineteenth and early twentieth centuries. The main subjects included comparative anatomy of vertebrates and plant morphology, the former taught by J. S. Kingsley, the well-known comparative anatomist, and the latter by F. D. Lambert, the botanist. Supplemental training included laboratory instruction in elementary biology and participation in a seminar on "Mendelism" by which he acquired a general point of view and an interest in the "genetic basis for racial differentiation." Because of the proximity of the Harvard University campus, he was able to listen to lectures by Professor William E. Castle, the geneticist, and other distinguished scientists and to attend meetings of seminars and the Biology Club. He became a member of the New England Botanical Club and frequently attended meetings of the Boston Society of Natural History.

With a natural bent for the theoretical and having been previously influenced by Darwin and Louis Agassiz, Danforth was prepared to seek knowledge of the processes by which life develops from an egg and thus gain an understanding of nature in general. With this objective in mind, early in his freshman year he sought permission to obtain eggs for a study of chick embryology. Instead of having this request honored he received an assignment to work on pteropods (wing-footed snails) which Dr. Kingsley had collected, fixed, and preserved in alcohol at South Harpswell, Maine. With "much supervision" the results of this study were published in 1907 under the title "A new pteropod from New England" (with four plates of his own drawings). By way of contrast he published in his senior year (1908) an article on numerical variation in a daisy, of which he was justly proud.

WASHINGTON UNIVERSITY, 1908-1922

The summer after graduation from Tufts was characterized by a series of dramatic changes that led step by step to a professorial career of distinction in biological research. Early that summer he fully expected to return in the fall to his alma mater on a fellowship. Moreover, he was at work on the morphology of the head of the 20-mm embryo of the catfish *(Ameiurus)*, a study that began in 1907 at Dr. Kingsley's suggestion and that had continued during his senior year. (It may be noted here that nothing came of this work until later, when it served as the dissertation for the master of arts degree awarded to him in 1910 by Tufts College.) Then, quite suddenly Danforth received from Professor R. J. Terry an offer of an instructorship in the Department of Anatomy at Washington University Medical School in St. Louis at a salary of $800 a year.

The decision was an important, yet a very difficult, one to make. Danforth pondered long and hard. In going to Washington University, he reasoned, "I could make substantial payments on my indebtedness [to his father] and still have my summers free of the necessity of earning money." Moreover, "this fortunate situation" would permit him to spend a number of successive seasons at the Harpswell Laboratory on the seacoast of Maine, which was chiefly a Tufts enterprise under the direction of Dr. Kingsley. There was an added inducement: He "could continue to work on fish," as Terry promised in the offer.

The advantages seemed to outweigh any disadvantages (none mentioned), and he decided to accept the offer. In making this decision "I automatically gave up the idea I had been toying with during the summer of going into botany rather than zoology."

In September 1908 Danforth arrived at St. Louis in the mood of a pioneer in the far west, that is, one venturing beyond the Allegheny Mountains. The romantic old city of St. Louis opened up new vistas to him. Moreover, the countryside, the people, and their activities "all differed appreciably from those to which I had been accustomed" in New England, especially in Norway and in the metropolitan environment of Boston. Professor Terry, a doctor of medicine, a native and long-time resident of St. Louis, took a special interest in the newly acquired naturalist on his staff. He gave generously of his time in introducing Danforth to historic restaurants and other old places in the city, and to caves and cliffs and Indian mounds. Danforth commented, "Medicine seemed to be the best field in which Terry could cultivate his interest as a naturalist." On Sundays, as had been his custom of old, Danforth usually explored alone in the many outlying regions of the countryside. However, there was a difference from earlier explorations in that little or no comment on plants or animals was made in his autobiographical sketch.

He soon began, at Terry's suggestion, the study of Polyodon, commonly known as paddlefish, a fish peculiar to the Mississippi River. His interest in a habitat study of Polyodon took Danforth to the lakes and muddy streams in the bottomlands of the Missouri and Illinois rivers, branches of the big Mississippi. By 1912, these explorations had been extended to Reelfoot Lake (Tennessee) in search of the elusive eggs and young of Polyodon.

As time moved on he became a member and secretary of a "flourishing biological club" in St. Louis, composed of naturalists and medical men. He was likewise a member and secretary of the St. Louis Academy of Sciences. Further, he was occasionally invited to the meetings of the distinguished

"Twelve Apostles," a group comprising an ornithologist, an archaeologist, a herpetologist, and nine other scientists. The fine personalities in these organizations led Danforth to have "a sincere respect for the amateur naturalists of St. Louis, among whom there was a mellow atmosphere of goodwill that seems to have been largely lost in these harsher times" (written in 1948). The foregoing lines again show evidence of Danforth's joy in being a naturalist and being among men of similar interests.

In the Department of Anatomy he was both an instructor and a student for a doctoral degree. His immediate superior, Victor E. Emmel (later Professor of Anatomy, University of Illinois), and Danforth had the joint responsibility of organizing and developing courses in embryology, histology, and neurology. The available study material for these courses was meager, so it was necessary to work many evenings at the old laboratory at Eighteenth and Locust to keep ahead of the students. Danforth's "necessary association with recently dead bodies" was so repugnant to him that it took time before he "could think of no better final dissolution than being dissected by two eager medical students."

The question of a doctoral degree naturally arose soon after he entered the university. It seemed desirable to prepare for either an M.D. or a Ph.D. degree, or the combination, as Dr. Terry urged. Danforth reasoned that while his attitude toward "man" had undergone great changes since his pre-college days, he still would have preferred farming to the practice of medicine. So he decided to take the Ph.D. degree, with the inclusion, however, of self-imposed provisions for attaining a breadth of knowledge of other disciplines in the medical curriculum. This enabled him to be "on the inside of medical education." His major subject was anatomy; his dissertation was on the anatomy of Polyodon, a fish of unusual interest in the evolution of teleosts. His minor subjects included human physiology and special investigations in animal and plant physiology. He was awarded the Ph.D. degree in 1912 by Washington University.

It seemed quite natural that Danforth, having a good understanding of the general genetics of animals and plants and having the anatomy of man as the main subject of his study, should take an interest in human heredity. Somehow his view of man had changed from what it was in 1903–1904 (see p. 15). To this end in the summer of 1913 he went to Cold Spring Harbor where he took a course in eugenics given by Charles B. Davenport and H. H. Laughlin. He also became acquainted with the work of the Eugenics Record Office, an institution then devoted to the study of human heredity, factors of race betterment, and improvement of the inborn traits of the race. Thereupon he became active in the study of human heredity, as his record of publication shows, and offered a course in heredity for medical students. More perhaps than in any other field of biology he obtained the highest recognition for his original contributions in general and developmental genetics.

That summer the most beautiful of all events in his life took place. Riding on the bus from the railroad station to the laboratory at Cold Spring Harbor, Danforth noticed a young woman who was also obviously making the trip for the first time. It so happened that Danforth was assigned to the same table as she in the dining room. She was Florence Wenonah Garrison, a teacher of science in a high school of Wilkes-Barre, Pennsylvania, who had come to the laboratory for further work in biology. They soon took boat rides together across the moonlit harbor and enjoyed corn roasts on the old Sand Spit; as with many another couple having mutual biological interests, a romantic association developed. Charles and Florence were married on June 24, 1914, exactly one year after their first meeting. Most naturally they went to an oasis of gentle wilderness in the Maine woods for their honeymoon.

In the fall of 1914, when it became apparent that the United

States would be drawn into World War I, Danforth joined with many others and applied for assignment to an officers' training camp. Although in due time he received instructions to report, he was kept at the medical school to continue teaching medical students. What could an anatomist do to further the war effort? Through a questionnaire he became impressed with possibilities in the field of physical anthropology. Thus began an interest that brought him into local and national organizations. He subscribed to the very first volume of the *American Journal of Physical Anthropology,* founded in 1918 by Ales Hrdlicka, and later served on the editorial board of that journal. He was one of the charter members who helped organize the American Association of Physical Anthropologists. He subscribed to *Genetics* "in advance to help insure launching of the project" proposed by George H. Shull.

It was not until the summer of 1919 while Danforth was at Cold Spring Harbor with his family (wife and two small children) that Dr. Charles B. Davenport persuaded him to participate in an anthropometric study of demobilized soldiers. Leaving his family at Cold Spring Harbor he went to Washington, consulted Dr. Hrdlicka on plans for several camps, and then went to Camp Dix where he took charge of the anthropometric work, leaving in time to return to teaching in the autumn.*

In the summer of 1917 he taught a course in ornithology at the Biology Laboratory of the University of Montana at Yellow Bay on Flathead Lake. The summers of 1920 and 1921 were spent at the Marine Biological Laboratory at Woods Hole, where he worked on the problem of human populations, a subject that had interested him for many years. The resulting article turned out to be "my best mathematical effort" (for appraisal, see p. 32). Toward the end of each summer he and

---

* For comment on frequency of syndactyly in soldiers stationed at Camp Dix, see *Eugenics, Genetics and the Family,* Vol. 1. (Baltimore, Williams & Wilkins Company, 1923), p. 121.

his family returned to the Norway country that he loved so much as a boy.

Sometime during the year 1921 he was invited by Dr. A. W. Meyer to join the staff of the Department of Anatomy of Stanford University. After fourteen years on the faculty at Washington University, the decision to leave was not an easy one. It meant interrupting several research projects well under way, one of which was a study of hypertrichosis in the human (which he entered into reluctantly with a surgeon through whom a research fund had been provided). This study was left for Danforth's doctoral student and research assistant, Mildred Trotter. To break a close association with a colleague, Edgar Allen, the discoverer of the ovarian follicular hormone, was disheartening. Danforth tells of aiding and encouraging Allen in his very first success in producing estrus in a spayed mouse. Despite the multitude of ties in St. Louis, "we embarked cheerfully on the new venture."

STANFORD UNIVERSITY, 1922–1969

Except for a period of fourteen years at Washington University, Danforth's professional life was connected with Stanford University. In the fall of 1922 he entered Stanford as an Associate Professor of Anatomy and was promoted to full professorship in 1923. Fifteen years later (1938), upon the retirement of Arthur W. Meyer, Danforth succeeded him as executive head of the Department of Anatomy, a position he held until his retirement in 1949, a span of eleven years. After official retirement he remained active in research for many years, as the list of his publications testifies.

In entering upon his duties at Stanford he was impressed by Dr. Meyer's forceful approach to the teaching of gross anatomy, which, owing to Meyer's emphasis on functional and pathological aspects, was made "interesting and stimulating." To Danforth the ideal combination would be the Meyer approach and an interpretation of human anatomy in terms of the evolution of organ systems, a field in which he had extensive training. On this matter Danforth wrote in 1948: "I have never been willing to concede that anatomy should be regarded as other than an absorbing subject in its own right, by no means a mere stepping stone. I consider it almost axiomatic that an interest in normal structure and function should be characteristic in any branch of medicine, and that has been the real, if not always expressed, attitude of most of the outstanding clinicians with whom I have come in contact."

Most of his teaching of gross anatomy was highly personal, conducted through conversation with individuals or small groups of students in the laboratory. With a breadth of knowledge, enthusiasm, and patience Danforth was able to kindle interest among medical students in learning anatomy. As one student put it, "He made the dullest things alive." In a similar way he encouraged the faltering student.

His scholarly interests in the heredity of man and the human body and its parts, which, as noted above, reached a turning point in 1913, continued to dominate his thinking and teaching. The course on human heredity, which he first organized and gave to medical students in 1914 at Washington University, was offered each year from 1926 to his retirement at Stanford. The course dealt with the facts and problems of heredity in relation to the individual and the population as a whole. He also offered a course on physical anthropology, in which the lectures laid emphasis on anatomical variation and heredity in man. His lectures have been characterized as showing comprehensive knowledge of the subject matter as well as a depth of understanding. The search for "true knowledge" was a characteristic of them.

As executive head of the Department of Anatomy, Danforth was capable of winning and holding the trust of his faculty colleagues in the department. Without seeming to do so, he administered in a quiet and patient way. Moreover, he had the steadiness of purpose to serve as a focusing center of group enthusiasm by arousing enthusiasm for research and teaching among staff members and students. Occasionally he was privately nettled by discourtesies or by any attempt to take advantage of his generosity. He could suffer in silence.

With respect to university affairs at large he soon found the atmosphere of the campus, with its large number of departments representing a wide variety of disciplines, very agreeable and intellectually stimulating. However, inasmuch as the clinical departments were not established on the campus until later, he missed the everyday contact with clinicians and their problems that he had had at the medical school of Washington University. At Stanford he entered more fully into university life through the years, serving on a multitude of committees and as president of Phi Beta Kappa; he was a member of a research club and others of a like nature. He had adopted Stanford as his own.

In addition to his professional activities on campus he was a member of and often participated in both state and national professional societies. The number of them is legion. Among them are the American Philosophical Society, American Eugenics Society, American Society of Naturalists (president, 1941–1943), American Society of Zoologists, California Academy of Sciences, California Academy of Medicine, Genetics Society of America, Society for Developmental Biology, and Society for the Study of Evolution. In 1942 Charles Haskell Danforth was elected to the National Academy of Sciences.

SCIENTIFIC WORK—AN APPRAISAL

Among the first publications by Danforth were those concerned with the morphology of a marine snail (a study of a new species) and the comparative anatomy of Polyodon. These papers represented fields that fitted in with his teacher's research specialty. The articles on Polyodon listed in the bibliography satisfied the thesis requirement for the Ph.D. degree awarded by Washington University. Together they present a thorough and detailed knowledge of the anatomy of an ancestral fish, then commonly known as a ganoid fish and now regarded as an aberrant chondrostean survivor. The work on Polyodon served to strengthen his qualifications as an anatomist. There were, however, fields of even greater interest to him and more in keeping with his talent as a naturalist.

Three of these early publications deal with questions of variation and speciation; they represent ideas that probably came to him in reading Darwin at twelve years of age. The first of these papers, published in 1908 while he was a senior in college, dealt with the number of florets (tiny flowers) in the flower head of the common daisy, a composite plant. By comparing the number of ray florets of plants from three different geographical regions, Danforth was able to show a relation between mode (number of ray florets) and the external environment. The paper represents, as he stated in 1948, "my natural 'approach' as anything I have written quite independently." Another observation made at about the same age was on the occurrence of a color variation in two forms of plants of the same species of the foam flower. In using the term "dimorphism" in the title he remained noncommittal as to the cause of the variability. Yet he anticipated a Mendelian interpretation by noting that the two forms of plants occurred together in all places in which he found the species and that they might be useful in "cytological and Mendelian" analysis.

In 1909–1910, while he was studying for the doctoral degree, Danforth's curiosity was aroused over the question of factors controlling periodicity in the appearance of reproduction phases in many algae. Although algal periodicity was a matter of common observation, there was little experimental evidence on whether it was due to an inherent tendency or was environmentally induced. On this question W. Benecke had postulated, on the basis of his work on growing *Spirogyra communis* in different media, that the loss of ammonium salts—removed from water by the growth of angiosperms—would induce conjugation under natural conditions. Danforth wondered whether the absence of ammonium salts could be taken as a specific stimulus. He repeated the experiments of Benecke, using other species, five different ones of *Spirogyra*. Danforth obtained results showing specific differences in the reaction of filaments and zygospores in the five species. Indeed, it is possible that *Spirogyra* "is inherently periodic in its functions, although its periodicity may be extensively influenced by its environment."

Very soon Danforth turned away from problems of variation and speciation in plants—never to return to them—to the field of human heredity, a field in which he was to excel as a contributor of new knowledge. As an anatomist and a teacher of anatomy, Danforth intuitively felt morally obligated to include man among his own investigations. To him almost any structural variation from the normal became a problem for exploration. It became just as natural for him to study any anatomical variation in the human body as it was to study variation in the number of ray florets in a common daisy. The human body became for him a part of nature about the time (1912) he acquired the Ph.D. in anatomy. In the summer of the next year he studied eugenics, which in part led him to formulate a program of study of anatomical variations from the standpoint of genetics, not only of man but likewise of birds and mammals. Progress was rapid. In one year (1914) his first paper on a dominant mutation for cataract was published, and by 1921 he had publised articles on a variety of hereditary traits or mutations in man. Among these are such significant ones as (*a*) suppression of the palmaris longus muscle, apparently a dominant trait, and (*b*) the complete absence of hair from the middle segments of the digits, a recessive trait (see p. 49).

As Danforth customarily worked on a variety of problems at the same time, he early saw the suitability of studying family histories of man in which pairs of twins occur, in order to elucidate the hereditary tendency for twin production, and also in order to investigate the degree of resemblance between members of a pair of twins, particularly where the sex is the same.

Two classes of twins have long been recognized, monozygotic twins and dizygotic twins. It has been commonly assumed that twins of opposite sex are necessarily dizygotic while those of the same sex may belong in either class. Dizygotic twins may sometimes resemble each other closely and monozygotic twins may be quite different. Moreover, absolute identity is never attained. How may these classes be distinguished? Is the relation of the fetal membranes (amnion and chorion) in which the twins develop a reliable criterion for the recognition of monozygotic or dizygotic origin of twin pairs?

If a pair of twins of the same sex at birth is enclosed in a single set of membranes, they have arisen from a single ovum. However, when surrounded by separate sets of membranes, they are not necessarily dizygotic. By reasoning from a study of Simon Newcomb's data of 37,621 pairs of twins (born in Germany and France), Danforth in 1916 pointed out that 29+ percent of all twin cases are monozygotic, whereas the number of monozygotic twins given in textbooks of obstetrics is about 15 percent when based on the relations of fetal membranes. The difference between 15 percent and 29+ percent represents the number of cases in which monozygotic twins develop in separate sets of fetal membranes. Here is a discrepancy that was generally overlooked. Thus, by number of twins and reasoning, Danforth deduced that fetal membranes in which twins develop have only a limited value in the diagnosis of their zygotic origin. Danforth was "the first to use the similarity diagnosis [phenotypes of twins] as a check of the diagnosis based on the afterbirth [number of placentas and chorions]." *

In a study of resemblance and difference in twins Danforth

---

* See Curt Stern, *Principles of Human Genetics*, 3d ed. (San Francisco, W. H. Freeman & Company, 1973), p. 642.

(1919) asked why there are differences in twins known or assumed to be monozygotic. Why are such twins not actually identical? In seeking an explanation of the differences Danforth argued that since each member of a twin pair represents but one half of a single zygote, there is little reason to expect them to resemble each other more closely than do the two lateral halves of a single individual. Moreover, the two sides of the same single individual are by no means identical; for example, right and left sides of the face are rather frequently asymmetrical. Whatever may be the cause of variation between the two sides of the body when they develop as a single individual, it is reasonable to expect that they will be equally effective when each half of the primary formative cell-mass develops as a separate individual. It might therefore be predicted that monozygotic twins would differ from each other in the same respects and to the same degree as two sides of the body differ in ordinary individuals.

The theoretical considerations discussed by Danforth serve to account for most of the resemblances and differences actually observed among twins; also they aid in understanding why monozygotic twins are not absolutely identical and why dizygotic twins are very often closely similar. Such features "seem to be due more to the inherent constitution of the germ plasm than to influence of the environment."

Thus, Danforth has brought to the forefront a problem of supracellular organization, namely, that of the nature and developmental origin of asymmetry. It is well known to anatomists that man and many other vertebrates are inherently bilaterally asymmetrical and not strictly bilaterally symmetrical as is popularly thought. Furthermore, asymmetrical organization manifests itself in the fertilized egg and/or the embryonic cell-mass from which two growth centers arise, each developing into a distinct individual. Twins derived from a single zygote may be thought of as parts of a single system of asymmetrical organization, each half of which upon separation undergoes a reorganization, that is, a reordering of symmetry pattern of cells. Each half is a germ whose developmental history is peculiar to it. By such a view one may account for mirror-image duplicates of hair whorls and other dissimilar features in like twins.

Danforth also carried out an analytical study of structural anomalies of the foot of the common domestic fowl in which he was concerned with the kinds of factors that have a "determining influence" on the ontogeny of brachydactyly. He presented evidence (1919) on the bases of breeding tests and correlations in developmental morphology that brachydactyly (shortening of digit IV), syndactyly (formation of two digits from digit number I), and ptilopody (feathers on the tarsus and toes of the foot) constitute an "heredity complex," that is, they are primarily associated in heredity and are primarily caused by a single gene.

The foregoing seven years of pioneer explorations may be characterized as a period of intensive study of mutations in man as well as in the common fowl. The record when scrutinized shows that he had acquired an excellent command of the literature on the phenomena of mutation and theory—including the relevant works of H. S. Jennings, Sewall Wright, Kristine Bonnevie, and others. As his factual knowledge and his understanding increased, his thoughts and ideas tended to focus on the question of mutation frequency in the human population. He was thus admirably well prepared for a quantitative study of mutation frequencies, as will immediately become apparent.

From about the year 1913 onward, Danforth (as noted above) eagerly participated in promoting the science of human heredity and the study of eugenics during their early history. It was a natural bent for Danforth to feel he "ought to do something" for the oncoming Second International Congress of Eugenics to be held in New York City on September 22–28, 1921. He worked at Woods Hole much of the summer of 1921 in preparing a manuscript entitled "The Frequency of Mutation and the Incidence of Hereditary Traits in Man." This was a result of his thought on the problem of human population genetics, in which he had been interested for many years.

This paper is a highly original attempt to determine the mutation rates of dominant human genes under the assumption of a steady equilibrium in large populations between the effects of recurrent mutation and adverse selection. Such an equilibrium is to be expected because mutation, recurring at a given rate, tends to increase the frequency of the gene in question in proportion to the frequency of its normal allele and thus practically uniformly as long as it is rare, while selection tends to reduce its frequency in proportion to its own frequency. There must be a certain frequency at which these processes balance. Danforth noted that the number of generations through which an individual mutant gene persists in the population is the reciprocal of its selective disadvantage. His estimate for the mutation rate per generation of a particular gene was thus the ratio of its estimated equilibrium frequency to its average persistence (in generations).

From a study of pedigrees, he estimated the average persistence for the dominant traits polydactyly and syndactyly to be about three generations in both cases. The estimated gene frequency being about one in two thousand in both, his estimates for the mutation rates were both about one in six thousand. He noted, however, the likelihood that this estimate of persistence from pedigrees was less than the actual persistence, so that the true mutation rates might be considerably less than one in six thousand.

This pioneer contribution was overlooked for many years. As noted by L. C. Dunn in his *Short History of Genetics* (1965), this method of estimation of mutation rates for dominants, given in Danforth's address in 1921 and published in 1923, preceded use of the same idea by J. B. S. Haldane and by L. S. Penrose by fourteen years. Moreover, none of those who later used it attributed its origin to Danforth. In a similar vein, Curt Stern comments: "His pioneering paper remained without consequences and the same method had to be reinvented in 1935 by Haldane and by Penrose (see Gunther and Penrose)." *

In 1950, however, H. J. Muller, who had listened to Danforth's address at the 1921 Congress of Eugenics, called attention to Danforth's pioneering role and used his principle extensively in developing his concept of "genetic load" with special reference to man.

The long period of neglect poses a question as to the reason. At my request, Sewall Wright has commented as follows:

"Danforth's address in 1921 and publication in 1923 probably did not attract much attention at the time because few geneticists were then actively interested in the subject. Its fate was that of many pioneering papers which are not actively followed up by their authors. The few who were interested probably took equilibrium in itself for granted since it is merely the negative aspects of the principle of natural selection as applied to gene mutation: The rare favorable mutations tend to become established, while the unfavorable ones tend to be held at low levels of frequency. With respect to Danforth's particular formula, they probably questioned whether the average number of generations of persistence of a mutation could be determined sufficiently accurately for valid estimates.

"Most pedigrees involve only a few generations because of lack of knoweldge about remote ancestors. Thus the estimated average number of generations found in pedigrees is unlikely to exceed three by much, even though the real average is more than a hundred. Moreover, many dominant traits of which polydactyly is a notable example, show incomplete penetrance and thus manifestation often skips one or more generations. Another complication is that the same condition may arise from mutations at more than one locus.

* Curt Stern, *Genetic Mosaics and Other Essays* (Cambridge, Mass., Harvard University Press, 1968), pp. 3, 7.

"Haldane [*Proc. Camb. Phil. Soc.,* 23 (1927):838–44] was the next author to give quantitative expression to the idea of equilibrium. According to his formula, the mutation rate for a gene is the product of its equilibrium frequency and its selective disadvantage, which in principle requires merely comparison of the reproductive successes of affected individuals and their normal siblings. Haldane, however, used it merely as an aspect of his theory of evolutionary dynamics on which he wrote a series of papers between 1924 and 1934, including a book (1930) which attracted much interest.

"As noted, it was not until 1935 that new estimates of human mutation rates were made by Haldane himself and by Gunther and Penrose. These estimates (2×10^{-5} for sex-linked hemophilia, 10^{-5} for dominant epiloia) were more than an order of magnitude smaller than Danforth's estimate for polydactyly and syndactyly.

"Whatever the difficulties in using his particular formula, Danforth's paper should clearly be credited with being the first to point out the possibility of using the principle of equilibrium in calculating human mutation rates."

His work on the frequency of mutation in man was only one phase of a broader program of investigations. In fact, he was simultaneously at work on a miscellany of specific problems that apparently were of even greater interest and appeal to his fertile mind. The problems had a common objective, that of investigating the role of genes in the ontogenetic processes of structural mutations. From the very first he was concerned with the kind of factors that play a role in the developmental anatomy of brachydactyly, polydactyly, and the like in the domestic fowl and later with their role in the production of polydactyly in the domestic cat.

Polydactyly, when considered as a "genetic and morphological entity," provides excellent material for the analysis of the role of the genes and other factors in the morphogenesis of supernumerary digits of the foot, that is, in the matter of extra toe production. By a long-range research program comprised of breeding tests and an extensive study of the embryology and morphology of the normal and polydactylous foot, Danforth discovered that polydactyly in the cat is a trait controlled by a single dominant gene.

Moreover, he suggests that the chief effect of the gene is to "incite" an excess of digit-forming tissue in the preaxial part of the limb bud. Indeed, the excess digital tissue may be the only "direct function of the causative gene." At first it is a bulge of unorganized tissue. The excess of unorganized tissue is viewed as disturbing the normal balance of developmental processes in such a way as to change the size and/or number of digital lobes produced. The amount of digitogenic tissue present at a given *critical moment* during the organization of the limb bud material is postulated as determining the grade of polydactyly.

Thus Danforth has brought the subject of polydactylous limb development to the very threshold of contemporary embryological formulation. His idea that excess digital tissue is the direct function of the dominant gene is in consonance with the discovery of E. Zwilling (1956) that a typical polydactylous limb develops from the combination of mutant mesoderm and normal ectoderm in chick embryos. Mutant mesoderm appears to be the equivalent of Danforth's "digital tissue" [mesoderm] in that both are endowed with polydactylous potentialities, which, however, can only be realized through interaction with specialized ectoderm.*

---

* It is now firmly established that limb morphogenesis in the chick embryo is the resultant of reciprocal interactions of an ectodermal thickening (ectodermal ridge) and underlying mesoderm. A similar pattern of ectoderm–mesoderm interactions is characteristic of the limb bud of the mouse in which correlation between structural and/or cytochemical changes in areas of thickened ectoderm and in the underlying mesoderm take place—properties that are maintained to the tip of each digital bud [J. Milaire, in Robert L. DeHaan and Heinrich Ursprung, eds., *Organogenesis* (New York, Henry Holt, 1965)]. Moreover, the limb buds of many mammals are characterized by an area of thickened ectoderm at their tips. Such an ectodermal specialization serves as a marker or clue to the onset of reciprocal interactions with the underlying mesoderm [see O'Rahilly, Gardner, and Gray, *J. Embryol. Exp. Morph.*, 4 (1956):254].

To Danforth "the hair follicle * is a kind of 'biological microcosm' in which almost any problem relating to growth, differentiation, decline and rejuvenescence of tissue can be studied to advantage." The study of such a wide variety of problems was initiated in an auspicious manner. While riding on a streetcar in Wilkes-Barre one summer, Danforth observed, in his words, that "a man in front of me draped his arm over the back of the seat and I noticed that while his arm was very hairy the middle segments of his fingers were free of hair and so, I observed, were my own; but I knew this was not generally true." So far as he was aware, no one before had recognized this variation as possibly hereditary. This was to Danforth a fertile source of inspiration. He at once began an extensive study of hair on the digits of man that showed the presence or absence of hair on the dorsal aspect of the middle phalanx (mid-digital hair) is genetically determined, the presence of hair being dominant. Danforth (1921) was apparently the first to record these conclusions.

Moreover, the functioning of the individual follicles of the human pilary system shows a remarkably high degree of autonomy in the length of successive cycles. Such autonomy is maintained over long periods and is not readily disturbed by external factors. Each follicle has its own individual rhythm which is relatively constant and frequently does not synchronize with the rhythms of neighboring follicles. How are these characteristics and potentialities acquired? Danforth searched for the answer in the developmental arrangement of hair follicles in the neonatal mouse, that is, before hair papillae are visible. The hair papillae were found to arise in an orderly manner in the skin of the back of the mouse, from which Danforth reasoned that the skin at first has a generalized capacity for forming hair papillae (follicles in certain regions of the skin show specializations which suggest a form of embryonic predetermination).

* At the base of the follicle is the hair papilla, which comprises a dermal component covered with epidermal cells from which the hair is generated.

Each papilla during its development creates a negative zone (conceived of as having inhibitory forces) immediately surrounding it. A few papillae would then arise at the intersection of negative zones. Danforth in this speculation touched upon a contemporary view that the embryonic determination of the spatial pattern in the distribution of hair papillae and/or of feather papillae is the resultant of inductive interactions between the dermis (mesoderm) and epidermis (ectoderm) and alignment of forces in the dermal cells and a lattice of collagen fibers.

With his expert knowledge of comparative anatomy and of human heredity, Danforth raised the question of homologies of hair, the "most distinctive characteristic of mammals," the "highest" class of vertebrates. From a thorough analysis of observations bearing on homologies of hair, he was able to present a thought-provoking new theory. Generalizing from the new data, he pointed out that there is no one-to-one correspondence between hairs and any of the structures (e.g., scales of a common reptilian ancestor) from which they are supposed to have been evolved, nor between the hairs of one mammal and those of another. These facts, together with the ontogeny of hair, are interpreted by Danforth (1925) to mean that the number and character of hairs that appear are determined by factors which come into play during development. In general these factors have a hereditary basis. The resemblance between hairs and their supposed homologous structures may be explained on the grounds that several structures owe their development to the action of groups of factors, some of which are in common with those that produce hair. It is in the causal factors themselves that the real basis of homology is to be sought. Homology between hair and a related structure is dependent upon the similarity of genetic factors involved in their production. These concepts make it possible to arrive at a more satisfactory meaning of homology of hair in relation to its forerunner structures.

Danforth maintained a deep interest in the biology of human

hair and its ramifications over a period of many years, with the result that we now have a broad and secure foundation of developmental morphology and physiology of the hair follicle (1925 and 1939). His synthesis of new and old facts stimulated new ideas and concepts that will serve as a challenge to future investigators interested in questions of determination, differentiation, and functional rhythmicity.

The antecedent of Danforth's extensive work on mice was a leave of absence granted by Washington University in order that he could spend a year (1910–1911) in the anatomy department of Harvard Medical School. Professor C. S. Minot gave him the "job of adding fertilization and segmentation stages of a mammal to the Harvard Embryological Collection." The mouse was chosen, and in carrying out the assignment Danforth gained experience in the breeding of this mammal, which is such a highly suitable animal for the study of heredity. He writes, "The initiation of my work with mice thus dates from 1910." Upon returning to St. Louis, he soon established a colony of mice and organized a full laboratory course in embryology based entirely on mammalian material, probably the first to do so. On research productivity with mice, Danforth facetiously remarked: "Few, I think, have raised more mice and kept more extensive pedigrees in proportion to their published papers."

At the outset Danforth envisaged the value of using mice for the study of mutations under controlled conditions. More specifically, he had in mind a study of the genetic makeup of the anomalous individual and the embryonic development of its structural anomalies. In this way new insights may be gained on the developmental processes and potentialities.

Although he started to build a colony of mice at St. Louis, it was in 1923, one year after his arrival at Stanford University, that he discovered the *first* anomalous specimen from a stock that had been inbred for several generations. Having this anomalous mouse, it was possible to isolate a strain in which about 20 percent of the living young showed some degree of posterior duplication, ranging from typical cases of *duplicitas posterior* to individuals that scarcely deviated from the normal (Danforth, 1925 and 1930). In mice with posterior duplicity may be found four hind legs, two urogenital openings, four kidneys, four gonads, etc.

To Danforth the posterior doubling (double monsters) provided valuable material for a study of the developmental process. There is evidence, he pointed out, of some direct and determining influence of one region upon another, through an impulse exerted directly with an intensity proportional to distance. This was a phenomenon akin to the "organizer effect" of H. Spemann, which is especially evident in the developing limb bud. Danforth fully realized that a more complete picture of the embryology of these posterior doubles is essential before any light can be thrown on morphogenetic processes.

It is clear from the foregoing considerations that Danforth fully recognized the value of posterior duplications and of other abnormal variants in their bearing on the nature of developmental and/or morphogenetic processes. As will be immediately apparent, he did not continue the challenging problems that he initiated.

In October 1936, Danforth, in a most generous act, sent four short-tail mutants (2 ♂ + 2 ♀) of the posterior duplication stock to Professor L. C. Dunn of Columbia University. In January 1938, Dunn and S. Glueksohn-Schoenheimer (*Genetics*, 23: 146) published an abstract which states: "Short-tailed mice found by Prof. C. H. Danforth among descendants of the posterior duplication stock have been tested and found to contain a new mutant. The short-tailed ones proved to have a new allele with dominant effect on skeleton and some other structures (e.g., kidneys) and a recessive lethal effect shortly before birth. . . . We named it 'Short-Danforth' with symbol *Sd*. *Sd* homozygotes were found to have no kidneys, no excretory openings, and no vertebrae posterior to the lumbars and this proved to be useful in studying several embryological problems such as the relation between the development of the ureter and the differentiation of the metanephros. Moreover shortness of tail is due to absence of posterior part of the notochord. *Sd* was an important tool in one stage of developmental genetics."

To Danforth, mice and men and birds went "hand in hand" as implements for testing ideas by thoughtful observation or by experimentation. For certain kinds of problems, however, birds were uniquely suitable among vertebrates. They were selected as especially suitable animals for the exploration of what Danforth had in mind, namely, the role of genetic and hormonal factors in the phenotypic characterization of plumage. Sex in birds is commonly reflected in striking plumage differences in feather structure, color, and color pattern, that is, the phenomenon of sexual dimorphism is displayed in plumage.

When in 1922 Danforth arrived in Stanford he brought with him "some bantams." The bantams were bred *inter se* and became the center about which he assembled many diverse breeds of the domestic fowl and of exotic birds ranging from specimens of red and gray jungle fowl to Reeves's pheasants and even to Brewer's blackbirds. At one time, in 1939, the collection gave the writer the impression of an aviary in miniature.

The common domestic fowl, owing to racial differences in feather color and/or color pattern, afforded excellent material for analyzing the interplay of developmental factors in feather differentiation. For such an analysis Danforth used the very simple technique of grafting pieces of skin from one newly hatched chick to another of different breed. The site of interchange of skin pieces between chicks of different breed was the lumbosacral region where sexual dimorphism in the feathers is most clearly expressed. The graft (covered with down feathers) became either permanently incorporated as an integral part of the host or after varying periods of normal growth and activity underwent regression and was lost. Since regression did not occur in autografts, the observed regression was regarded as a consequence of tissue incompatibility—a host vs. graft reaction. (When skin grafts persist, it is now believed that the host has actively acquired tolerance to the foreign graft and hence develops under the influence of its genes.)

Furthermore, the potentialities of the chick skin were already fixed at the time of hatching; that is, the grafted skin and its individual feather germs produce contour feathers (replacing down feathers) not only characteristic of the donor breed but also tract specific (lumbosacral). In some instances feathers (at the edge of the graft) had mosaic patterns comprised of donor and host colors or a barred pattern, as, for example, in a Barred Rock graft on a Rhode Island Red host. These mosaic patterns were correctly interpreted as genetic mosaics. Danforth, however, was somewhat puzzled as to their mode of origin, largely because at the time (1927) little or nothing was known about the migration of pigmentoblasts (melanoblasts). He did recognize the possibility of some migration of pigment-forming cells from one feather follicle to another. Twelve years after it was discovered that the melanin pigmentation of feathers is a phenomenon dependent on highly autonomous migratory pigmentoblasts, Danforth concluded that these feather mosaics are truly pigment-cell mosaics, the product of two pigment cells that differ in genotype.

Another fixed potentiality in the skin at hatching is the responsiveness of the feather germ to sex hormone; for example, if the host is genetically male, the graft feather germ produces a contour feather that is structurally male, a form brought about by a hormonally altered type of morphogenesis.

The experimental production of genetic mosaics is the prototype of an extensive series of experiments designed to analyze the relative role of genes and hormones in the production of sex differences in feather pattern that is peculiar to each of the many well-defined races of the domestic fowl and to certain selected species of birds. Many racial traits are represented in the feathers—more properly in the feather follicles themselves, of whose reactions the fully developed feather is an index.

Several types or kinds of feather follicles (each bearing a papilla) * have been described by Danforth with respect to hormonal vs. genotypic regulation in the production of shape, color, and markings of feathers. The diversity of types of response is briefly characterized as follows: (a) feather follicles of either sex that produce sex differences in plumage by genic regulation without hormonal action (dove); (b) feather follicles that react to either male or female sex hormones; feathers produced in skin grafts follow the breed of the donor but the sex of the host (all breeds of the common domestic fowl—nine tested); (c) a feather follicle of each sex genotype that responds in its own way to both male and female humoral complexes; sex characteristics of the plumage are dependent on simultaneous action of both genic and hormonal factors (Reeves's and Ring-necked pheasants); and (d) a feather follicle of a hen-feathered genotype *(HH)* that produces a hen-feathered feather on a male Leghorn host (Silver Campine; no sexual dimorphism). A single gene difference is decisive for divergent reactions to hormone in two races, Campines and Brown Leghorn.

These four types of reaction of adult feather follicles to genes and hormones represent ways in which different forms of "protoplasm" (or tissues) respond to genetic and hormonal factors. The potentialities of protoplasm † are already fixed in

* At the base of the follicle is the feather papilla (or feather germ), a body comprised of a vascularized dermal component around which is a collar of epidermal cells from which the feather is generated.

† To Danforth the site of hormonal action is protoplasm, a term which to this writer is here equivalent to the prospective epidermal cells of the feather germ—cells that synthesize the protein keratin and provide the structural framework of the feather.

the skin transplant at hatching or, as stated by Danforth, "its future manifestations are rigidly pre-determined by hatching"; that is, protoplasm is under the control of intrinsic factors (genes, embryological factors such as interaction of tissue components). Genetic factors govern the course of fixation of the feather germ and seemingly the feather germ does not become fixed in regard to its sex. It is only later (toward sexual maturity of the host) that racial sex differences of the feathers are mediated by the endocrines. The feather germs have been prepared by gene action to respond to the hormone. Danforth emphasizes that responsiveness resides in the feather germ and not in the hormone. For example, in one kind of hormonal environment the feather germ produces a hen feather, in another kind a cock feather. The ability to respond to the hormone resides in the specific properties of the follicle papilla and not in the hormone.

As one of his finest contributions to developmental genetics, Danforth pioneered in establishing basic conditions for an understanding of the mechanisms for the production of sex differences in the plumage of birds. Of primary import is the concept that genes give character to the cytoplasm (of the feather germ) or "condition" it; that is, they determine the diversity of response in accord with racial differences in the genetic constitution of the bird. During development, a new adjustment comes about in the feather germ which imparts to it the capacity to utilize hormones in the making of sex differences not only in form but also, if genotype permits, in color marking of feathers.

As to the site of hormonal action, Danforth had little to say, save that hormones act as "activators or stimulators" and "produce their final effect only through such protoplasm as will respond to them." Moreover, the specificity of most hormone–tissue reactions is more properly an attribute of the tissue than of the hormone—it is largely a question of whether or not the tissue will utilize the hormone if available. To refer to hormones as chemical "messengers" is "more figurative than our present concepts should permit." Moreover, Danforth would agree that the term "target organ" should be replaced by a more appropriate term, the receptor organ (a functionally integrated unit) —better still, an interaction between hormonal molecules and receptor organ—a mutual fitting together of hormonal molecules and prospective epidermal cells, cells that synthesize keratin as they "build" the framework of the definitive feather. From this standpoint of original thought and interpretation, no one has excelled Danforth in presenting the characteristic features associated with feather follicles in the form of concepts that are not only original but still sound today.

On the question of the evolution of follicle types in birds having a sexual dimorphism of plumage, Danforth regarded the four types characterized by him as not corresponding to any particular evolutionary sequence; they do show, however, the kind of diversity that would provide for the evolution of special types of response. The phylogeny of the hormones presents a fascinating problem on which Danforth liked to think that the evolution of tissues had rendered hormones as necessary for their normal development and function.

In the foregoing appraisal, Danforth's scientific work has been centered on five major subjects: human heredity, the hair follicle, mouse genetics and mutation, genetic mosaics in birds, and the role of genes and hormones in feather characterization. An examination of his bibliography will reveal many papers on diverse subjects somewhat unrelated to the above major subjects. Many of these are singularly important yet only a few pages or a single paragraph in length. In his autobiographical sketch he wrote: "I suspect there may be those who would say that as an anatomist I am something of a geneticist, others who might think as a geneticist I am an amateur endocrinologist, and so on, but to me *all of my work seems to have a definite unity*" (italics mine). He points out further that the largest proportion of his projects never reached publication, for some were failures and some were just not completed. Danforth regarded the loss as slight, "for what one biologist does not do, some other one will" (a paraphrase of a saying by Professor Herbert S. Jennings of The Johns Hopkins University).

In an "epilogue" to his autobiographical sketch Danforth comments on research interests and motivations: "My natural inclination has been strongly toward leisurely *observation* (vs. exploration or experiment), and I have always aspired to put myself sufficiently *en rapport* with nature so that facts and relations would be perceived naturally (not 'logically'). Distant mountains, far streams and rare plants have a strong appeal, but there is even greater satisfaction in a more intensive study of what is within easy reach of a selected 'station,' whether near or far. In pre-college days I got a great deal of satisfaction out of studying various 'second crops' in plants but, despite some insight, I failed to recognize the full significance of the 'length of day' factor. For many years I observed conditions influencing venation in Sagittaria leaves, but never brought any study of the subject to completion. Every summer for over forty years I have given attention to the arrangement of leaves and floral parts in plants—with a good deal of intellectual satisfaction. . . . Despite a marked deficiency in musicality, I have a better 'ear' for bird notes than many of my friends who persist in trying to hear birds in terms of human musical notation, and I have gotten much enjoyment out of detecting varietal differences at the vocal level of, for example, the warbling vireos in different parts of the country. . . . I had early intended to devote myself to things like these, and to the profound enjoyment of such deeply spiritual beauty as there is in the notes of a hermit thrush projected against a background of receding thunder, or a chorus of white-throated sparrows singing in a spring twilight, with occasional interludes marked by the faint notes of a woodcock high in the evening sky. But while my orientation was basically to the out-of-doors, I early began studying nature in-doors, and have in a measure suffered the fate that Agassiz predicted for those that do so."

What was the fate that Agassiz predicted for those who study nature indoors and that Danforth, at the age of sixty-five, avows he had in a measure suffered? Louis Agassiz, the noted apostle of the *Great Book of Nature,* admonished his students to "read Nature not books," and explained to them, "If you study Nature in books, when you go out-of-doors you cannot find her." *

"You cannot find her" is a form of punishment that would have been very disquieting to Danforth. Actually, as noted above, his observations of nature continued throughout his life. Only in the sense of not having contributed significantly to the outdoors variety of natural history would he have been troubled. Occasionally he pondered on whether he would have arrived at some generalization broad in its scope had he remained an out-of-doors naturalist instead of an indoors naturalist.

The writer of this memoir now ventures to speak less formally, in the name of all Charles Haskell Danforth's friends, dead or living. We loved and respected him. What impressed us most, I think, was his quiet integrity. Had he been only a successful teacher and investigator, the writer does not think we would have responded so positively to his personality. But Danforth was different. He had both a mind and a heart. He was a

---

* See James D. Teller, *Louis Agassiz, Scientist and Teacher,* Graduate School Studies, Education Series No. 2 (Columbus, Ohio State University Press, 1947), p. 85. I am greatly indebted to a colleague of Charles Danforth, Dr. David Perkins of Stanford University, for his friendly interest and his thoughtful and painstaking research in locating the Agassiz quotation on which Danforth's comment is based. The quotation fits perfectly with Danforth's comment on his "natural inclination" to study nature outdoors. Also it is a distinct pleasure to acknowledge my indebtedness to Dr. Edward Lurie of the Milton S. Hershey Medical Center, Hershey, Pa., an authority on Louis Agassiz, for his keen interest and bibliographic aid in my search for the source and/or basis for the "in-doors–out-of-doors" philosophy of Danforth. In reading several publications on or by Agassiz suggested by Lurie, I was led by the key phase "you cannot find her."

devoted naturalist who built solid structures out of ideas. What he built will be consciously treasured in the memories of those who knew him. As Ralph Waldo Emerson said at the funeral of another naturalist, Henry David Thoreau:

> Wherever there is knowledge,
> Wherever there is virtue,
> Wherever there is beauty,
> He will find a home.

BIBLIOGRAPHY

KEY TO ABBREVIATIONS

Am. J. Anat. = American Journal of Anatomy
Am. J. Ophthalmol. = American Journal of Ophthalmology
Am. J. Phys. Anthropol. = American Journal of Physical Anthropology
Am. Naturalist = American Naturalist
Anat. Record = Anatomical Record
Arch. Dermatol. Syphilis = Archiv für Dermatologie und Syphilis
J. Exp. Zool. = Journal of Experimental Zoology
J. Heredity = Journal of Heredity
J. Morphol. = Journal of Morphology
Proc. 6th Internat. Congr. Genet. = Proceedings of the Sixth International Congress of Genetics
Proc. Soc. Exp. Biol. Med. = Proceedings of the Society of Experimental Biology and Medicine

1907

A new pteropod from New England. Plates 1–4. Proceedings of the Boston Society of Natural History, 34:1–19.

1908

Notes on numerical variation in the daisy. Botanical Gazette, 46: 349–56.

1910

Periodicity in *Spirogyra,* with special reference to the work of Benecke. Twenty-first Annual Report, Missouri Botanical Garden, 21:49–59.

1911

A 74 mm. Polyodon. Biological Bulletin, 20:201–4.
A dimorphism in *Tiarella cordifolia.* Rhodora, 13:192–93.

1912

The heart and arteries of Polyodon. J. Morphol., 23:409–52.

1913

The myology of Polyodon. J. Morphol., 24:107–46.

1914

Some notes on a family with hereditary congenital cataract. Am. J. Ophthalmol., 31:161–72.

1915

The structural relations of anterior hepatic arteries. Anat. Record, 9:72–73.

1916

Some aspects of the study of hereditary eye defects. Am. J. Ophthalmol., 33:65–70.
The inheritance of congenital cataract. Am. Naturalist, 50: 442–48.
Is twinning hereditary? J. Heredity, 7:195–202.
The relation of coronary and hepatic arteries in the common ganoids. Am. J. Anat., 19:391–400.
The use of early developmental stages in the mouse for class work in embryology. Anat. Record, 10:355–58.

1918

Observations on brachydactylism in the fowl. Anat. Record, 14: 33–34.

1919

An experimental test of the possibility of differential selection of germ cells (in the fowl). Anat. Record, 16:147–48.
Resemblance and difference in twins. J. Heredity, 10:399–409.
A comparison of the hands of a pair of polydactyl Negro twins. Am. J. Phys. Anthropol., 2:147–65.
The developmental relations of brachydactyly in the domestic fowl. Am. J. Anat., 25:97–115.
An hereditary complex in the domestic fowl. Genetics, 4:587–96.
Evidence that germ cells are subject to selection on the basis of their genetic potentialities. J. Exp. Zool., 28:385–412.

1921

Bufo fowleri Putnam in Missouri. Transactions of the Academy of Science, St. Louis, 24:1–8.
Distribution of hair on the digits of man. Am. J. Phys. Anthropol., 4:189–204.
With J. W. Thompson and J. McC. Batts. Hereditary and racial variation in the musculus palmaris longus. Am. J. Phys. Anthropol., 4:205–18.

1922

The question of digital homology. Anat. Record, 23:14–15.
With Mildred Trotter. The distribution of body hair in white subjects. Am. J. Phys. Anthropol., 5:259–65.
With Mildred Trotter. The incidence and heredity of facial hypertrichosis in white women. Am. J. Phys. Anthropol., 5:391–97.

1923

The status of unilateral variation in man. Anat. Record, 25:125.
The frequency of mutation and the incidence of hereditary traits in man. In: *Eugenics, Genetics and the Family,* Vol. 1, pp. 120–28. Scientific Papers of the Second International Congress of Eugenics, New York, September 1921. Baltimore, Williams & Wilkins Company.

1924

The theoretical distribution of hereditary traits in man. Am. J. Phys. Anthropol., 7:291–98.
The heredity of unilateral variations in man. Genetics, 9:199–211.
The problem of incidence in color blindness. Am. Naturalist, 58:447–56.
The question of homology as related to hair. Anat. Record, 27:180.

1925

Adiposity and doubling as constitutional traits in the mouse. Anat. Record, 29:354.
The cycling activities of hair follicles. Anat. Record, 29:381–82.
Hair in its relation to questions of homology and phylogeny. Am. J. Anat., 36:47–68.
Hereditary doubling suggesting anomalous chromatin distribution in the mouse. Proc. Soc. Exp. Biol. Med., 23:145–47.
The number of brothers and sisters of selected individuals. Science, 61:17–18.
Studies on hair with special reference to hypertrichosis. I. The phylogeny of hair. Arch. Dermatol. Syphilis, 11:494–508.
Studies on hair with special reference to hypertrichosis. II. The hair of mammals. Arch. Dermatol. Syphilis, 11:637–53.
Studies on hair with special reference to hypertrichosis. III. General

characteristics of human hair. Arch. Dermatol. Syphilis, 11: 804-21.
Studies on hair with special reference to hypertrichosis. IV. Regional characteristics of human hair. Arch. Dermatol. Syphilis, 12:76-94.
Studies on hair with special reference to hypertrichosis. V. Factors affecting the growth of hair. Arch. Dermatol. Syphilis, 12:195-212.
Studies on hair with special reference to hypertrichosis. VI. Aberrant forms of hair growth. Arch. Dermatol. Syphilis, 12:212-32.
Studies on hair with special reference to hypertrichosis. VII. Hypertrichosis. Arch. Dermatol. Syphilis, 12:380-401.
Studies on hair with special reference to hypertrichosis. VIII. General aspects of the hair problem. Arch. Dermatol. Syphilis, 12: 528-37.
Hair with Special Reference to Hypertrichosis. Chicago, American Medical Association. 152 pp. (Chapters published serially in Archives of Dermatology and Syphilology from April to October 1925).

1926

Alcohol and the sex ratio in mice. Proc. Soc. Exp. Biol. Med., 23:305-8.
The developmental arrangement of hair follicles. Anat. Record, 32:230-31.
The American race. J. Heredity, 17:94-96.
The hair. Natural History, 26:75-79.
The interaction of genes in development. Proc. Soc. Exp. Biol. Med., 24:69-71.

1927

A gynandromorph mouse. Anat. Record, 35:32. (A)
The problem of adaptation. J. Heredity, 18:125-31.
Hereditary adiposity in mice. J. Heredity, 18:153-62.
The nature of homology in muscles *(extensor carpi radialis)*. Anat. Record, 35:32. (A)
With S. B. de Aberle. Distribution of foetuses in the uteri of mice. Anat. Record, 35:33.
Feather production by skin grafts in the fowl. Anat. Record, 37: 182.

With S. B. de Aberle. The functional interrelation of certain genes in the development of the mouse. Genetics, 12:340–47.
With Frances Foster. Skin transplantation as a means of analyzing factors in production and growth of feathers. Proc. Soc. Exp. Biol. Med., 25:75–77.

1928

A case of alopecia in the fowl. J. Heredity, 19:546–50.
Skin transplantation in ducks and pigeons. Proc. Soc. Exp. Biol. Med., 25:717.
Cause of hen-feathering in campine and bantam males. Proc. Soc. Exp. Biol. Med., 26:86–87.
The reaction of transplanted skin in the fowl. Anat. Record, 38:10.
With S. B. de Aberle. The functional interrelation of the ovaries as indicated by the distribution of foetuses in mouse uteri. Am. J. Anat., 41:65–74.

1929

The effect of foreign skin on feather pattern in the common fowl (Gallus domesticus). Archiv für Entwicklungmechanik der Organismen, 116:242–52.
Genetic and metabolic sex-differences. The manifestation of a sex-linked trait following skin transplantation. J. Heredity, 20:319–22.
Bantam genetics: distribution of traits in a Sebright-Mille Fleur cross. J. Heredity, 20:572–82.
Two factors influencing feathering in chickens. Genetics, 14:256–69.
With Frances Foster. Skin transplantation as a means of studying genetic and endocrine factors in the fowl. J. Exp. Zool., 52:443–70.

1930

Chorio-allantoic grafting followed by direct transplantation in the chick. Proc. Soc. Exp. Biol. Med., 27:1066–67.
Developmental anomalies in a special strain of mice. Am. J. Anat., 45:275–87.
The nature of racial and sexual dimorphism in the plumage of campines and leghorns. Biologia Generalis, 6:99–108.
Numerical variation and homologies in vertebrae. Am. J. Phys. Anthropol., 14:463–81.

Some racial and hereditary characteristics of hair. Eugenical News, 15:35–37.

1931

Persistence of contra-sex skin grafts in the fowl. In: *Proceedings of the Second International Congress for Sex Research,* ed. by A. W. Greenwood, pp. 171–72. London, August 1930. Edinburgh, Oliver & Boyd, Ltd.
Predetermined and fortuitous features in the development of a gland (lacrimal gland of a mouse). Anat. Record, 48:41, Supplement.

1932

Artificial and hereditary suppression of sacral vertebrae in the fowl. Proc. Soc. Exp. Biol. Med., 30:143–45.
Family size as a factor in human evolution. Third International Congress of Eugenics. J. Heredity, 23:385.
Genetics of sexual dimorphism in plumage. Proc. 6th Internat. Congr. Genet., 2:34–36.
Hereditary posterior duplication in the mouse. Proc. 6th Internat. Congr. Genet., 2:253.
Racial and sexual traits revealed by skin transplants. Proc. 6th Internat. Congr. Genet., 2:257.
A new hereditary feather deficiency in the fowl. Proc. 6th Internat. Congr. Genet., 2:257–58.
The interrelation of genic and endocrine factors in sex. In: *Sex and Internal Secretions,* ed. by Edgar Allen, pp. 12–54. Baltimore, Williams & Wilkins Company.
Three views of evolution. J. Heredity, 23:405–9.

1933

Genetic factors in the response of feather follicles to thyroxin and theelin. J. Exp. Zool., 65:183–97.
Racial differences in the reaction of developing feathers to artificially administered hormones. Anat. Record, 55:52–53, Supplement.
The reaction of dominant white with yellow and black in the fowl. J. Heredity, 24:301–7.

1934

Genetics and anthropology. Science, 79:215–21.

1935

With John B. Price. Failure of theelin and thyroxin to affect plumage and eye-color of the blackbird. Proc. Soc. Exp. Biol. Med., 32:675–78.

With Jerome K. Fisher. Inability of testicular hormone to masculinize plumage and eye-color of female Brewer's blackbird. Proc. Soc. Exp. Biol. Med., 32:1115–17.

Testicular hormones and Sebright plumage. Proc. Soc. Exp. Biol. Med., 32:1474–76.

Different potentialities of male and female skin in Reeves's pheasants. Proc. Soc. Exp. Biol. Med., 33:291–92.

Genetic mosaics in the feathers of the common fowl. Transactions on the Dynamics of Development, 10:339–44. (Part in Russian)

1936

Genetics of sex differences in plumage *(Syrmaticus reevesi)*. Am. Naturalist, 70:46.

1937

Artificial gynandromorphism and plumage in *Phasianus*. Journal of Genetics, 34:497–506.

Some genetic implications in dissecting room material. Anat. Record, 67:12–13.

Interaction of hormones and genotypes in pheasants. Anat. Record, 67:60, Supplement.

Pigment cells in heterogenous feathers. Anat. Record, 68:461–68.

Responses of feathers of male and female pheasants to theelin. Proc. Soc. Exp. Biol. Med., 36:322–24.

An experimental study of plumage in Reeves's pheasants. J. Exp. Zool., 77:1–11.

1939

Relation of genic and endocrine factors in sex. In: *Sex and Internal Secretions,* 2d ed., ed. by Edgar Allen, C. H. Danforth, and E. A. Doisy, pp. 328–50. Baltimore, Williams & Wilkins Company.

Genic and hormonal factors in biological processes. Harvey Lectures, 34:246–64.

Direct control of avian color pattern by the pigmentoblasts. J. Heredity, 30:173–76.

With Gunnar Sandnes. Behavior of genes in intergeneric crosses. Effects of two dominant genes on color in pheasant hybrids. J. Heredity, 30:537–42.
Physiology of human hair. Physiological Reviews, 19:94–111.

1941

With John B. Price. A persistent mutation in the California quail. Condor, 43:253–56.

1942

Sex inversion in the plumage of birds. Part II. In: *Hormonal Factors in the Inversion of Sex.* Biological Symposia, ed. by Jacques Cattell, Vol. 9, pp. 67–80. Lancaster, Pennsylvania, Science Press.

1943

Gene *H* and testosterone in the fowl. In: *Essays in Biology in Honor of Herbert M. Evans,* written by his friends, pp. 159–67. Berkeley, University of California Press.
Hair. In: *Dictionary of Biochemistry and Related Subjects,* ed. by W. M. Malisoff, pp. 288–97. New York, Philosophical Library.

1944

Relation of the follicular hormone to feather form and pattern in the fowl. Yale Journal of Biology and Medicine, 17:13–18.

1945

With others. Should the BNA be abolished? Anat. Record, 92:105–7.
With others. How much modification of the BNA is desirable? Anat. Record, 92:197–200.

1946

Physiological aspects of genetics. Annual Reviews of Physiology, 8:17–42.

1947

Heredity of polydactyly in the cat. J. Heredity, 38:107–12.
Morphology of the feet in polydactyl cats. Am. J. Anat., 80:143–71.

1948

Biographical Memoir of Charles Vincent Taylor, 1885–1946. In: National Academy of Sciences, *Biographical Memoirs,* 25:205–25. New York, Columbia University Press.

1949

With Victor Schwentker. Snowball: a repeated mutation in the cotton rat. J. Heredity, 40:252–56.

1950

Evolution of plumage traits in pheasant hybrids, *Phasianus* × *Chrysolophus*. Evolution, 4:301–15.

1953

With Elizabeth M. Center. Development and genetics of a sex-influenced trait in the livers of mice. Proceedings of the National Academy of Sciences, 39:811–17.

Free and unequal: the biological basis of individual liberty. American Journal of Human Genetics, 5:402–4.

1954

With Elizabeth M. Center. Nitrogen mustard as a teratogenic agent in the mouse. Proc. Soc. Exp. Biol. Med., 86:705–7.

1955

Delayed effects of mutagenic agents. Science, 122:874.

1958

With Elizabeth M. Center. The occurrence and genetic behavior of duplicate incisors in the mouse. Genetics, 43:139–48.

Gallus sonnerati and the domestic fowl. J. Heredity, 49:167–69.

1967

With Elizabeth M. Center. Genetical and embryological basis of the *duplicitas posterior* manifestation in the mouse. Genetics, 56:554.

THOMAS FRANCIS, JR.

July 15, 1900–October 1, 1969

BY JOHN R. PAUL *

THOMAS FRANCIS, JR., was born in Gas City, Indiana, on July 15, 1900, the son of Thomas and Elizabeth Anne (Cadogan) Francis. His father had emigrated from Wales shortly before Thomas, Jr., came into the world. He was the third of four children, but the first to be born in this country.

Thomas Francis, Sr., had studied for the ministry as a young man, but had decided later to join his father in the tin mills of South Wales. He had married Elizabeth Anne Cadogan, a graduate of a Salvation Army Training School in London. It is said that she kept "her Salvation Army ideals" throughout her entire life. At least she strove to do her part in supplying a firm religious background to her brood of four children.

In 1897 the Francis family had been persuaded to visit America. Their destination was a small colony of Welsh families which had settled in and about Gas City, Indiana. For a while this venture was considered to be temporary, but when the family moved to New Castle, Pennsylvania, and Mr. Francis became associated with the steel mills of that town, it became permanent. After Thomas Francis, Sr.'s, retirement from the steel mills he turned again to religious ideals and became or-

---

* Prior to his death, the author asked Dr. Dorothy M. Horstmann of the Yale School of Medicine to make certain revisions in this memoir. The final version of the memoir owes a great deal to Dr. Horstmann's careful and constructive review, as well as to the faithfulness with which she adhered to the author's style.

dained as a lay minister. Henceforth he was known as the Reverend Thomas Francis. For several years he preached at a small New Castle church.

Both parents had very definite ideas about the home life of the Francis family: what it should be and how the children were to act. There were strict rules of behavior, and yet, in spite or because of them, the family life was a happy one. As a boy, Tommy led the normal existence of a lad in a small town environment in which his natural inclinations included fishing and baseball. At the local high school he became quite active in dramatics, which, according to his sister, were usually of the Shakespearean variety.

With regard to the rest of Tommy's immediate family, I shall not dwell, although they all enjoyed successful lives. His younger brother, Herbert, graduated in medicine from Yale. The bulk of Herbert's professional career was spent at the School of Medicine, Vanderbilt University, as professor and chairman of the roentgenology department and also as a consultant to the Institute of Nuclear Studies at Oak Ridge, Tennessee.

With high school over, where all records maintain that Tommy was an able student, he attended Allegheny College at Meadville, Pennsylvania, and received the B.S. degree in 1921. He entered medical school the following fall. I am not aware of the reason why he made the decision to study medicine but he told me often about his choice of a medical school. In this he was influenced by a brother-in-law (a successful surgeon, Dr. Edgar R. McGuire of Buffalo, New York), whose views he had sought during his last years at college. He was advised to consider seriously the idea of applying for admission at the rejuvenated Yale University School of Medicine, which had been completely overhauled by Yale's new President, James R. Angell, who had recently come from the University of Michigan, and by the new Dean of the Medical School, Dr. Milton C. Winternitz, who was also a newcomer at Yale from Johns Hopkins.

Although the Yale medical school was a venerable school of medicine as far as this country was concerned, having been founded jointly by the Connecticut State Medical Society and Yale College in 1810, it had never achieved its hoped for goals during the nineteenth and early twentieth centuries. Indeed, prior to World War I, it was definitely a second-rate school with only a handful of students. And yet, oddly enough, in 1915 it had on its faculty an unusually distinguished group of men: Yandell Henderson, as professor of physiology, and Lafayette Mendel, of vitamin fame, in biochemistry, both members of the National Academy of Sciences; and two very able and wise clinicians, George Blumer and Wilder Tileston, in internal medicine, both members of the Association of American Physicians.

But luckily the school made a sudden rightabout-face when in 1917 Winternitz arrived from Baltimore to assume the position of chairman of the Department of Pathology. He had previously been an associate professor of pathology at the Johns Hopkins medical school under that dean of pathologists, medical educators, and medical historians, Dr. William H. Welch. Dr. Welch had been a loyal graduate of Yale College and his hope was to do something along the lines of a salvage operation for the Yale School of Medicine. Winternitz was an able emissary to perform this duty. His move to Yale had come just at the time when the medical schools of this country were undergoing a state of ferment. The cause of this was the recent issuance, and the recognition of the worth, of the Abraham Flexner *Report on Medical Education in the United States and Canada*, which introduced a timely reform that was to go into sharp reverse within the next fifty years. Flexner's report was beginning to have its effect in 1917 and Winternitz was quick to take advantage of this. The recommendations concerned, in part, the introduction of the full-time system into the clinical departments of the medical schools of North America—an idea that heretofore had been foreign to the rank and file of American physicians, academic or otherwise.

Within two years of Winternitz's coming to Yale, the medical faculty, sensing that here was no ordinary professor of pathology, elected him dean. His plan for Yale was modeled to a certain extent along the lines that made the Johns Hopkins School of Medicine great, that is, close personal contact between scholars and carefully picked students, and a devotion to research. So Winternitz, having made his decisions, went about his first task, which was that of gathering together the best young medical scientists and physicians that he could lay his hands on to fill the recently created full-time professorships in the clinical departments: Dr. Francis G. Blake, John P. Peters, and William T. Stadie from the Hospital of the Rockefeller Institute in internal medicine, all three of whom were subsequently to become members of the National Academy of Sciences; and Dr. Edwards A. Park in pediatrics.

It was at this stage, in 1921, coincident with Dr. Blake's arrival at the school as chairman of the Department of Internal Medicine, that the young Francis, having submitted his application, was accepted, and entered the newly rejuvenated Yale University School of Medicine as a first-year student. He was taking a chance not to have chosen one of the *established* and better known medical schools of this country. But, as it turned out, it was a chance worth taking. The reason for dwelling so long in this memoir on his academic background is that I am convinced that the training the young Thomas Francis received at Yale opened up a vista of new paths and new opportunities which he eagerly followed.

All accounts testify that he was a fun-loving, attractive, and able student, quick to learn and quick to appreciate the idea that the Yale school was supposed to do something out of the ordinary—and to act as a spearhead in a movement of reform in medical education for the nation and for Yale University.* Most of the members of the clinical faculties, especially those in internal medicine and pediatrics, whose combined members in the 1920s could not have amounted to more than fifteen or eighteen, had put their hearts and souls into making the new scheme work. They were determined to put the Yale school on the map and to establish beyond peradventure that the organization of the clinical departments on a full-time basis was not a theoretical pipe dream.

The young Thomas Francis became keenly aware of the intimate attention that was being bestowed on this first small group of medical students who had been admitted under the new regime. He soon fell under the spell of the newly appointed faculty members, who besides being clinicians were inspiring and high-minded teacher: men such as Francis G. Blake † and James D. Trask in medicine, and Edwards A. Park and Grover F. Powers in pediatrics. Dr. Blake was especially quick to recognize Francis's ability and his early grasp of what the school was supposed to do. As a result, a mutual respect developed that lasted throughout their lives.

With Dr. Blake he had almost a filial rapport. He admired Francis Blake as an astute diagnostician, a wise teacher, a physician and medical scientist of complete integrity, and an able clinical investigator. Besides, Blake had something akin to an epidemiological instinct long before that science had received the attention in this country that it deserved. This last characteristic accounted for Blake's being chosen as the first president to head the Army Epidemiological Board (AEB) during the years of World War II and for some years afterward.

---

* The few instructors in the Department of Medicine in the Yale University School of Medicine of the 1920s who are living today all testify to this estimation of his character.

† See memoir of Francis G. Blake, by Dr. J. R. Paul, in National Academy of Sciences, *Biographical Memoirs,* 28 (1954):1–29.

Some of these qualities must have rubbed off on the young medical student who was eventually to become Dr. Blake's successor as president of the AEB [subsequently the AFEB (Armed Forces Epidemiological Board)] in the years 1958–1960.

When Dr. Francis graduated as an M.D. in 1925, he was immediately appointed as an intern on the medical service of the New Haven Hospital, the next year as resident, and the next as an instructor in Blake's Department of Internal Medicine. This was a prime example of the apprenticeship type of instruction in which the professor did not have to preach but resorted instead to imparting the principles of clinical medicine by personal example. As a result, the young Dr. Francis was inspired to set his sights to emulate Dr. Blake, who in turn recognized that his pupil, having fulfilled his post of house officer and instructor admirably, had also begun to show signs of promise as a clinical investigator. Blake's early estimate of Francis's talents was not far wrong, for sixteen years later Francis was to become the president of the American Society for Clinical Investigation.

In any event, Blake decided that here was no ordinary young physician—indeed, Thomas Francis was one who might go far. So he advised him to prepare himself further by a period of training at the best contemporary institution that was available for this kind of instruction, namely, the Hospital of the Rockefeller Institute. Blake had no hesitancy in recommending Dr. Francis to Rufus I. Cole, the director of this hospital, as a promising candidate. Francis was a young man who possessed all the talents of an able house officer and the qualifications of a budding research worker (assets which were highly sought after by Dr. Cole in any candidate he was to take on as a junior member of his staff). This sophisticated center of learning and research was a far cry from New Castle, Pennsylvania.

Had Francis pursued this course of in-service training to its obvious end, it should have led him straight down the path of an academic career in internal medicine—to an assistant, then associate, and eventually a full professorship at one of the full-time medical schools in this country. But other career goals eventually proved more attractive to him.

Among the group which Dr. Cole had assembled on the Rockefeller hospital staff at this time were included Drs. Thomas M. Rivers, William T. Tillett, Oswald T. Avery, Donald D. Van Slyke, Alfred E. Cohn, Homer F. Swift, and several others whose names were to rank high during the 1930s—an era which is understandably considered by some as *the* age of the flowering of American Medicine—spelled with a capital M.

It was during this period that the young Thomas Francis began to gain a feeling of confidence that he had arrived as a person to be reckoned with in the field of full-time clinical investigation. Besides his qualifications as an investigator, his clinical abilities as a young physician also came to the fore on the the wards of the Rockefeller hospital. He often told me that he must have been appreciated as "a doctor" at this time. Among his prominent "private patients" were members of the Rockefeller family, and for a time he almost rated as their private physician.

Indeed, during the first half of his long and distinguished career, he did not relinquish the hope that he might be considered as a suitable candidate for a position as chairman of the Department of Medicine in one or another of the country's leading medical schools. This hope was not based on the fact that he possessed a knowledge of medicine that was of encyclopedic nature, but he felt the important thing was that he had acquired from his parents and his respected teachers—Drs. Blake and Cole—the altruistic principles of a physician, as well as the ideals of clinical medicine and, incidentally, of clinical investigation—and this was enough. Talents which Dr. Francis had developed at this time were those that had to do with both clinical and experimental medicine in infectious disease, microbiology, and epidemiology. He could have filled an academic position in any of these various fields, as well as a professorship in internal medicine.

On arrival at the Hospital of the Rockefeller Institute, Dr. Francis pursued the line of work that he had started under Dr. Blake at Yale. His interest had been aroused by studies which had to do with the various types of the pneumococcus, both rough and smooth varieties, and with the respiratory diseases including lobar pneumonia, a subject of great interest in that pre-antibiotic age. In an article written immediately after Dr. Francis's death, Colin M. MacLeod said:

"On coming to Avery's laboratory, Francis and William Tillett worked together on cutaneous and serological reactions to products of pneumococcus, particularly the specific capsular polysaccharides and the 'C' or somatic carbohydrate, now known to be a constituent of the bacterial cell wall. Over the three-year period of their collaboration two remarkable findings came forth.

"The first of these was that there occurs in the blood of patients with many acute infections a new substance, not an antibody in the usual sense, which reacts specifically with the 'C' carbohydrate of pneumococcus to give a precipitation reaction. During recovery from the disease the 'C-reactive protein,' as it came to be known, diminishes in amount and within a few days disappears entirely. This is an enigmatic reaction whose function in man and animals is still unknown but which provides a useful clinical test to measure the activity of a variety of infectious processes, for example the activity of the inflammatory process in rheumatic fever.

"Francis and Tillett also discovered that minute amounts of specific capsular polysaccharides of pneumococcus injected intracutaneously in man cause the development of specific antibodies and that the antibodies are protective. . . .

"While Francis was in Avery's laboratory, Dubos and Avery

had developed their famous studies on an induced enzyme obtained from a soil bacterium which specifically hydrolyzes the capsular polysaccharide of pneumococcus Type III whether the latter is in solution or attached to the living, virulent pneumococcus." *

Dr. MacLeod went on to say: "Francis, with Terrell, devised methods for producing Type III pneumonia in monkeys and published meticulous studies of its clinical course. In collaboration with Dubos and Avery they then went on to demonstrate in this experimental disease of primates, which simulates pneumococcal pneumonia in man, that the S III enzyme has striking curative properties. Unfortunately, test of the therapeutic effect in man was never carried out."

Discontinuance of this line of investigation was due to Dr. Francis's departure from the pneumonia service when he entered upon his work on influenza. But Francis must have derived not a little satisfaction from his early work at the Rockefeller hospital, for in recounting the memory of it some forty years later in his address entitled "Moments in Medical Virology," presented at the First International Congress for Virology in Helsinki, Finland, he recalled events that had occurred while he had been working enthusiastically on the transformation of pneumococcus types. He said:

"So I spent the mornings in the laboratory learning of these phenomena and the afternoons in the library and on the tennis court developing a model of the double fault. Being convinced that the induced change of pneumococcus types in the animal host was a true bill, I began very primitive efforts to obtain transformation in the test tube. (It is worth noting that a healthy air of skepticism surrounded the entire phenomenon—that probably some live organisms were persisting in the heated, supposedly, killed preparation.) It became clear that the

* Colin M. MacLeod, "Thomas Francis, Jr., 1900–1969," *Arch. Environmental Health,* 21 (1970):226–29.

capsular polysaccharide, with all its divine properties, was not the effective agency. But then it seemed likely that whatever the transforming principle was, it needed special care and I began making extracts by freezing and thawing organisms in the cold under relatively anaerobic conditions so as to avoid an enzymatic destruction of the principle. One day at noon I thought I was all alone in the lab. I was occupied with the tedious procedure of freezing and thawing. I had put my head down on my arms on the desk. Unexpectedly, a quiet voice said, 'What's the matter, boy?' Startled, I said I hated to see another pneumonia season start with the great time and attention required for clinical work; that I thought what was in these flasks was more exciting. Then I received a very sharp lecture from Dr. Avery reminding me that we were physicians; that the major concern of this laboratory was lobar pneumonia and that what was done here was in effect to understand the disease and to lick the pants off the pneumococcus—a theme that was developed under Avery and Dubos with the Type III decapsulating enzyme. This is a true view of Avery's intellectual commitment to the clinical problem.

"New lines of effort were freely allowed even if they were not always enthusiastically supported. I found this when I studied transformation of the rough Type III to virulent in rabbits; there was a lot of specificity involved and much work, but it never was published until later (by others). . . . Things were apparently dormant for 10 years.

"Then came the epochal study by Avery, MacLeod and McCarty in 1944. . . .

"Somewhere in these early days I rode on the train from New York to Princeton, New Jersey, with two leaders in virology, Thomas Rivers and Christopher Andrewes, to see a third, Dick Shope. In those days, virology had not yet descended to the level of the common man and I listened, as the privileged young man, to their sage and effete comments on viruses and their behavior. The conversation turned to pneumococcus transformation and the nature of the principle. In my immaturity I asked if it were not like a virus—but this did not fit. Again today with the many accumulations of knowledge on many sides, one can still ask is it not a virus?—call it what you like in reply. It is a major part of virology—reactivation—recommendation and all."

It was during the period when he was on the staff of the pneumonia service at the Rockefeller hospital that he married Dorothy Packard Otton, in 1933. The Francises had two children: Mary Jane and Thomas Francis III ("T"). Francis used to tell me over the years, with some wonderment and great interest, of the growth and development of their offspring. Theirs was a closely knit family.

He had begun at this early stage in his career not only to take an interest in literature but to match wits with critical minds in adroit and articulate conversation. He derived great pleasure from sitting among his friends talking about abstractions and the scientific fields with which he was acquainted; discussing personalities and what made men do the things they did, and indeed the affairs of the world in general. He developed early in life the characteristic of combining seriousness with an excellent sense of humor, but at the same time he was a tough and resilient opponent. At college he had been an amateur boxer and he never lost the opportunity of being combative—on occasions.

After his withdrawal from the pneumonia service at the Hospital of the Rockefeller Institute his work became concentrated solidly on the newly discovered influenza virus which Smith, Andrewes, and Laidlaw had turned up in London in 1933. Francis was almost the first microbiologist in this country to take advantage of the discovery. He proceeded to make what was the first isolation of influenza virus on this side of the Atlantic—the PR-8 strain. In July 1934, an outbreak that had all the earmarks of influenza had occurred on the island of Puerto Rico, and Francis was considering a trip to that island (by boat) to try to isolate the virus. He was debating with himself and others (actually at the lunch table one day) whether the virus would withstand this prolonged travel and whether he could bring it back alive. Francis had to forgo the trip but he had gotten the idea that his objective could be achieved by a simpler method. Thus the proper specimens for virus isolation were obtained by the process of mailing some bottles containing a mixture of saline solution and glycerin to Puerto Rico for collection of sputum specimens from patients suffering from influenza-like symptoms in the current epidemic there. The bottles were then mailed back to New York. The use of glycerine to stabilize viruses present in clinical specimens had been introduced only a few weeks previously as an effective means of transporting and preserving poliovirus present in oropharyngeal washings obtained from patients suffering from poliomyelitis. This was before the days of dry ice and freeze-drying.

Together with his colleague Dr. Stuart-Harris (eventually Sir Charles Stuart-Harris) of England, Francis and his team were to make many a contribution in the field of experimental influenza using ferrets as the test animal. Indeed this work precipitated Francis promptly into a position of authority and leadership in the field of influenza in the United States, much as Flexner had found himself in a similar position in the poliomyelitis field when the news of Landsteiner's discovery of poliovirus had come across the Atlantic in 1908, and been confirmed at the Rockefeller Institute. Influenza being the kind of disease that it is, and with the 1918 pandemic fresh in almost everyone's mind, Dr. Francis was pitched forcibly into the field of epidemiology. I shall not attempt to describe all or even part of the work done by Dr. Francis and his colleagues in the experimental laboratory. Many of their contributions were fundamental developments and of these several descriptions are contained elsewhere.* Those accounts may be familiar enough by this time, but they were excitingly new in the late 1930s.

In the words of Sir Charles, written some thirty-five years after he had collaborated with Dr. Francis in New York:

"Of all the achievements for which Dr. Thomas Francis will be remembered, none surpasses his contributions to the elucidation of the problem of influenza. As the first American to recover and to study influenza virus in the laboratory, Dr. Francis lit in his own hand the torch of discovery which still burns brightly in the hands of others. When the first evidence of antigenic variation of the influenza A viruses was published in 1936 by Dr. Thomas Magill and Dr. Francis, it was received with incredulity by the London team of influenza workers of the Medical Research Council, Dr. Christopher Andrewes, Wilson Smith and Patrick Laidlaw. The latter, however, examined their viruses by neutralization with a hyperimmune horse serum whereas the Rockefeller workers used a more specific rabbit serum. On such apparently small differences may turn matters of great moment, and the great importance both epidemiologically and immunologically of the antigenic diversity of both influenza viruses A and B is now recognized universally.

"Dr. Francis's demonstration that subcutaneous immunization with influenza vaccine can protect against epidemic influenza was an equally significant finding. The reasons why vaccine has yet to provide control over the disease [has been the source of constant argument]. . . . In truth the pioneer observation was but the end of the beginning, and much hard work and faith is required even now after 26 years. The inspiration of such men as Dr. Francis lives on in the lives of those whom

* The Thomas Francis, Jr., Memorial Festschrift, *Arch. Environmental Health*, 21 (1970):225–474.

they have influenced, and I count it a privilege and a source of pride to have been an assistant to Dr. Francis many years ago at the Rockefeller Institute, New York." *

It was inevitable that the talents of Thomas Francis were such that he should become a desirable choice for a chair in many a prominent U.S. medical school. His qualifications were so varied that he could command a professorship in any one of the fields in which he had been active. So, it was no surprise when he was offered and accepted in 1938 the chairmanship of the Microbiology Department at New York University College of Medicine, which carried a supplementary appointment as visiting physician at New York City's Bellevue and Willard Parker Hospitals. Dr. Francis had requested that he be allowed to pursue his clinical interests on the wards of these New York hospitals, and the authorities at N.Y.U., recognizing his clinical ability, had had no hesitancy in granting him hospital privileges. He was only thirty-eight years old at the time.

During his short period at N.Y.U., Dr. Francis continued to pursue influenza work with vigor. He had plenty of irons in the fire by this time and he had begun to make his influence known throughout the nation. He had many loyal students. One, in particular, was the bright young Jonas E. Salk, who in due time was to become a junior colleague and a devoted admirer.

A characteristic feature of Dr. Francis's long and variegated career was that he did not consider himself a specialist in any field, even in microbiology, the field in which he held a professorship. He had started out as a clinical investigator in the field of experimental medicine, an area in which he had already excelled. Although he branched out in many directions, he was always sympathetic to this—his most rewarding line of work. He was to be associated with the activities of various

* C. H. Stuart-Harris, "Control of Influenza. Lack of Knowledge versus Lack of Application of Knowledge," *Arch. Environmental Health,* 21 (1970):276–85.

specialty societies; for example, as an active Fellow of the American Public Health Association, in which he served on numerous important committees; as a member of the Society of American Bacteriologists, of which he served as president in 1947; and as a member of the American Epidemiological Society, and its president in 1954–1955. But what is more remarkable, he identified himself continuously with clinical societies besides. Not only did he keep up with old friends at the annual Atlantic City meetings of the American Society for Clinical Investigation, of which he was president in 1945–1946, but of the Association of American Physicians—and he got tremendous pleasure out of these contacts. They provided a chance to renew old ties with friends who had continued in clinical medicine. To have maintained loyalty and a sustained interest in all of these variegated groups would have seemed well-nigh impossible. But Francis not only continued to attend an astronomical number of meetings—a fearfully time-consuming activity in itself—but he entered into the spirit and discussions of many of these gatherings with enthusiasm. Perhaps that was what made him such an excellent epidemiologist.

After three years at New York University, Francis changed his location in 1941. He had been invited by Dr. Henry F. Vaughan, the former Commissioner of Health in the city of Detroit, and the first dean of the newly established School of Public Health at the University of Michigan, to become Professor of Epidemiology and chairman of that department there. For twenty-eight years Francis was to administer this truly great department. It became for him more than just a department where the statistical methods of epidemiology were taught; it was a place where the whole philosophy of epidemiology was constantly explored. During this period he was to train such men as F. M. Davenport, his successor, Jonas E. Salk, and Gordon C. Brown, to mention but a few.

As early as 1941 his pioneer studies on influenza virus were about to be put to a severe trial. Such a test would have probably come about in due time, but it was hastened by this country's precipitation into World War II. At this time the 1918 pandemic of influenza of World War I was still fresh in everyone's mind. That disastrous epidemic had taken a toll of U.S. servicemen (46,992) almost equal to those who had died of wounds received in combat (50,385). The Preventive Medicine Service in the Surgeon General's Office, Department of the U.S. Army, was determined, if it could do anything about it, not to let such a catastrophe happen again. Accordingly, the Board for Investigation and Control of Influenza and other Epidemic Diseases in the Army, soon to be shortened to the Army Epidemiological Board (AEB), was brought into being.* It had been created by the newly appointed chief of Preventive Medicine Service in the Surgeon General's office, Col. (later Brig. Gen.) J. S. Simmons, M.C.; Dr. Francis G. Blake was its first president, and Col. (later Brig. Gen.) S. Bayne-Jones served as its first executive officer. Among these three men (Simmons, Blake, and Bayne-Jones) there had been no difficulty in selecting Thomas Francis, Jr., as director of the Board's first Commission on Influenza. Thus the happy relationship with Dr. Blake was renewed.

Fortunately the assignment was one that carried a minimum of the usual red tape and strict military responsibilities that might have ensued. Had it not been for the leaders who guided its course, this Board might well have had a pedestrian life. But all of those whose names have been mentioned had a reputation throughout the length and breadth of the land of fairness, scientific integrity, and an ability to get things done.

Soon Dr. Francis was to realize that not only had he been put in charge of the important task of protecting against in-

---

* Bayne-Jones, "Board for the Investigation and the Control of Influenza and other Epidemic Diseases in the Army," *U.S. Army Med. Dept. Bull.*, 64 (1942):1–22.

fluenza the largest wartime army that had ever been assembled by the United States, but that his control measures would be followed eagerly and soon imitated or rejected by the U.S. Public Health Service—as well as the country at large. He had been the elected leader of a program of momentous importance. It was enough to have struck terror into the hearts of lesser men. But with his customary courage he rose to meet the challenge. He had not only the timely knowledge but the fortitude to take on such a responsible assignment.

The emergency posed by wartime conditions brought him the necessary confidence and also gave a boost to his own program on human vaccination against influenza, experiments which had been going on slowly heretofore. But now the way was open not only to improve technical methods in the preparation of influenza vaccines but to streamline the logistics of their administration as well. Also he was in a position that enabled him to devise tests of the effectiveness of his vaccines, paying particular attention to statistical adequacy in the design of the trials. To many members of the AEB commissions it had come as a surprise that here was an opportunity to conduct experimental trials on a scale hitherto impossible. No large body of men, no population of comparable age, had ever submitted to such controlled conditions. For these influenza trials had a decided advantage because they could be carried out under military jurisdiction, with the vaccinees being followed closely and compared with a matched control group of unvaccinated men.

Results of these early tests of 1943 conducted by the Commission on Influenza (AEB) were reported in a series of seven papers.* As was practically inevitable, revisions in the conduct of the trials were made as work proceeded. New strains of influenza virus had to be incorporated into the vaccine as they

---

* Members of the Commission on Influenza, Board for the Investigation and Control of Influenza and other Epidemic Diseases in the Army, Office of the Surgeon General, U.S. Army, *Am. J. Hyg.*, 42 (1945):1–105.

came along; and the addition of Freund's adjuvant was introduced as one of the best methods of enhancing the immune response to vaccine preparations of uncertain potency and for prolonging the protective effect of those vaccines of established value. And, as a useful procedure, frequent serum surveys spaced at intervals up to a year and more could occasionally be made to determine levels of antibodies which had been actually produced and retained by the vaccinees.

During subsequent postwar years, the work of the Influenza Commission was published promptly in a second series of papers. The fact that Salk's name headed the list of authors in one of these is a measure of his early accession to a position of leadership.

Salk's ability to design the vaccine trials and to carry them through to completion was of great help to Francis. The experience was also of signal help to the young Jonas Salk when it came later to the designing of his own experimental trials of the inactivated poliovirus vaccine. Interesting as the whole influenza vaccine story is and the part that the Commission on Influenza played at the very start, there is not room to include it here. It has been extensively reviewed in Francis's Festchrift volume.*

On one feature, however, it is necessary to dwell, and that is the antibody response induced by the whole heterogeneous family of influenza viruses. There were infinite complexities, for it was found that when an individual became infected sequentially with a variety of different strains of influenza virus, apparently each one left its footprint, whether heavy or light. Francis, with Davenport and other collaborators, made the astute observation that it made a difference what the order of previous exposure to various strains of influenza had been. In other words, the individual's first influenza experience determined what his subsequent responses were to be and shaped

* *Arch. Environmental Health,* 19 (1970):267–92.

the influenza antibody pattern of that particular individual. This was the doctrine of "original antigenic sin," as Francis was wont to call it. It was a subject that never ceased to fascinate him.

During the war years he was busy enough with matters pertaining to the study and control of influenza. But he did not spend all of his time on laboratory problems having to do with influenza viruses and the composition of vaccines: As a restless and inquisitive fieldworker he visited places far and near to see how the various vaccines were working. Incidentally, he branched out to try his talents on other virus diseases at this time, among which was infectious hepatitis.

In 1946, with the war over, he took a third viral disease under his wing—poliomyelitis. By this time the National Foundation for Infantile Paralysis (NFIP) had been in existence a dozen years, and Francis felt that here was an organization with which he could establish a firm relationship. As long as Thomas M. Rivers, his old colleague at the Hospital of the Rockefeller Institute, was its scientific mentor, he was willing to throw in his lot with the National Foundation. In the poliomyelitis field, after a few faltering steps, he quickly became an accomplished worker, and soon slid easily into a position of leadership.

It was during the period of the late 1940s and early 1950s that the NFIP had begun to change its image from that of an essentially philanthropic organization, operating in much the same way as The Rockefeller Foundation, to an organization that dominated to a certain extent the whole field of poliomyelitis. The NFIP had received an enormous and justifiable boost in confidence to do just this—as a result of the successful operation with an *ad hoc* interuniversity group which had set up a collaborative project and proved beyond doubt that the poliovirus family could be broken down into three types—I, II, and III. This early and important step in developmental research ultimately led to the control of the disease by vaccination. The success of the typing program strengthened the NFIP's view that it could solve many problems by fostering cooperation among its interuniversity grantees—the leverage being that of continued financial support. To promote this scheme and to signify the confidence that the NFIP placed in Dr. Francis, in 1953 he was called upon to administer the truly colossal task of conducting a field trial on the Salk-type vaccine—the largest trial to test the effectiveness of any vaccine that had ever been attempted anywhere.

But here I should retrace my steps to indicate that by midcentury Thomas Francis had reached a stage in his career when he had branched out beyond being a specialist in influenza or in the two other diseases he had investigated to date—poliomyelitis and infectious hepatitis. In reality he had become an epidemiologist capable of covering the whole broad field of medicine.

By this time most of his old friends had become medical administrators or full-time clinicians. But his bond with clinical medicine was so strong that he was ready to take his place among clinical societies and hold his own among the discussions, be they ever so erudite, even though over the years the sheer number and variety of these meetings had taxed him beyond endurance. And yet he always was ready to discuss a question which in any way touched his heart.

An episode which occurred at the Atlantic City meetings provides an indication of his devotion to clinical medicine and to the old clinical days in New York that represented his first love. Thus, some five or more years after he had settled in Ann Arbor, he sprang to his feet to engage in a discussion on the floor. I believe the occasion was a meeting of the Association of American Physicians. His first words through the microphone were: "Francis, of New York City." It was a Freudian slip due, I believe, to an attempt to retain the image of the old days when he had combined his eager clinical interest in infectious disease and in experimental medicine; in this combination lay the makings of a great epidemiologist.

When Francis became president of the Armed Forces Epidemiological Board (during the period 1958–1960), his ability to understand this group of clinicians, lately turned amateur epidemiologists, was where much of his strength lay. As was his wont, he fought frequent bitter battles with these clinicians, particularly over the question of their innate disparagement and disregard of the use of biostatistics. But he was nonetheless able to understand them, for he had been brought up with them. By keeping abreast of clinical medicine through attendance at various meetings he bridged the gap between the specialty of epidemiology and the whole broad field of the medical sciences. This ability enabled him to take the change in emphasis from infectious diseases to noninfectious diseases in his stride.

But to return to the year 1953. During September, while on sabbatical leave from the University of Michigan, Tommy Francis had been attending a meeting in Geneva of the World Health Organization's (WHO) Expert Committee on Viruses—a meeting which had been called to discuss not only poliomyelitis in general but the impending vaccination trials. Subsequently he made his way gradually through northern Italy, visiting the art treasures and galleries in Florence and other Italian cities.

Tommy recounted to me several times how he became saddled with the huge job of directing the NFIP's 1954 field trial on the inactivated Salk-type poliovirus vaccine. It was about Thanksgiving time, 1953, as he was visiting friends in London, that he received a telephone call from Hart Van Riper in New York putting the question abruptly to him as to whether he would consider an assignment as director of the field trial. This was shortly after Dr. Joseph Bell (of the National Institutes of Health) had submitted his resignation from this difficult position.

The upshot was that, after a bit of soul-searching on Francis's part and a number of conferences including a session with Professor Bradford Hill, the eminent biostatistician at the London School of Tropical Medicine and Hygiene, he came to New York about Christmastime and there laid down in no uncertain manner the only terms under which he would accept the responsibility of running such a trial. These included the crucial point that an equal or greater number of children than those who were to receive the vaccine should receive an injection of an inert solution (the placebo controls), so that the two groups could be followed in exactly the same manner. He also insisted on noninterference on the Foundation's part. Not until all these conditions were agreed to did he accept the assignment. Thus the Poliomyelitis Vaccine Evaluation Center was quickly established in early 1954 at the University of Michigan.

It was anticipated that the field trial would begin in the latter part of March 1954 and would be concluded in early June, that is, before the beginning of the poliomyelitis season. The collection and testing of matched samples of sera from the vaccinees and their fellow schoolmates who acted as placebo controls was a huge task. Had not the field trial had excellent planning by Dr. Francis and had it not been carried out under such carefully controlled conditions, it probably would not have succeeded. As it was, the experiment did not escape criticism. But probably never in the history of medicine has a new public health measure been tested on such a wide scale and so thoroughly. It was risky doing so many vaccinations with an unknown product that might be potentially dangerous, but as events turned out, the trial came through without mishap. The venture had proved to be eminently worthwhile.

During a period of seven or eight months the nation waited expectantly to see what results would be forthcoming in the widely heralded field trial. Inevitably as the trial drew to its close, interest in the public press, which had been alerted to the fact that "big news" was in the offing, mounted accordingly. Dr. Francis often recounted to me how repeated attempts were made by several news agencies to obtain a release—a preview of results—before he or anyone else was ready, even before a comparison of the results in vaccinees and controls had been completed. One news agency is reported to have announced sometime in late February or early March 1955 that it had learned "from an unimpeachable source that the vaccine had proved 100 per cent effective." Immediately thereafter other newspapers began to storm Dr. Francis's office by telephone for a verification or a denial. Accordingly Dr. Francis's words to the reporter on the wire were: "I have absolutely nothing to say. If I said: Yes, it is true; or if I said: No, it is not true, my statement would be taken as if I had something to say, but to tell you the honest truth I *really* have nothing to say. If you are so anxious for news at this point, I advise you to go back to that unimpeachable source from whence the rumor originally came."

The field trial had been inadvertently taken out of its proper setting as a scientific experiment and had emerged as a prime dramatic spectacle. Perhaps it was inevitable, for by this time a far larger audience than the medical profession had been aroused. More than 1,800,000 children throughout the length and breadth of the land had participated in the great "experiment," and all were anxious about the results.

Describing the day of the news release, April 12, 1955, Dr. Francis had occasion some years later to write:

"It may be worthwhile to visualize the circumstances which prompted the undertaking. Just think: after years of theoretical consideration, of investigating and speculating, here was a vaccine which was a natural development of accumulated technical advances and experimental demonstrations that antibody is directly correlated with protection against poliomyelitis. Here was substantial evidence that children receiving the material developed significant levels of antibody without harmful effect. Here was an agency, headed by a forceful imaginative administrator, possessing the financial resources, the staff, the nationwide organization, the public support and the desire to subject the material to a critical test of effectiveness. Moreover, it was highly desirable to determine for the guidance of future research whether or not the currently accepted hypotheses of pathogenesis and immunity to poliomyelitis were sound. . . . This was the situation in December 1953, when the proposal was made that the evaluation be conducted at the University of Michigan." *

For a time it seemed appropriate that the news of the outcome of the trial be made public at a meeting of an important scientific society. The annual meeting of the National Academy of Sciences was suggested as a place where the report might have at least a slim chance of being discussed dispassionately. The annual meeting of the American Epidemiological Society was considered, but the body was excluded as being too small an organization to handle such big news. Gradually the forces of publicity and sensationalism took over and since the Poliomyelitis Vaccine Evaluation Center had been established at the University of Michigan, it seemed that this university had the right to capitalize on the project which had become such a national issue. Furthermore, the university had an appropriately large hall to accommodate the army of newsmen that was expected to be on hand to hear the momentous announcement. A full-dress meeting was therefore set to be held in Ann Arbor on April 12, 1955, which incidentally turned out to be the tenth anniversary of President Franklin D. Roosevelt's death.

The abbreviated report which Dr. Francis gave at the meet-

* T. Francis, Jr., et al., *Evaluation of the 1954 Field Trial of Poliomyelitis Vaccine; Final Report* (Ann Arbor, Mich., Edwards Brothers, Inc., 1957), p. xxvii.

ing, unequivocally established the product developed by Dr. Salk and further tested by Dr. Francis as an effective vaccine for the prevention of poliomyelitis. The latter stressed that he was not presenting a preliminary report but a summary of objective analyses of valid data from records that were essentially complete. No one can say that the result was not a triumph. History had indeed been made. The inactivated Salk-type vaccine eventually was to have a tremendous effect in reducing the rate of paralytic poliomyelitis in this country and around the world.

And yet the circumstances under which the report was released proved to be a temporary disaster for American science. Dr. Francis, who had done his work with such care and scientific integrity, was unhappy to have it so exploited. One witness described the scene as being set to the tune of "the rockets' red glare and flash bulbs bursting in air." The information which had been gathered so painstakingly at the Evaluation Center and at such an expense of time, money, and energy by Francis and his earnest staff of workers, did not deserve to be so cheapened by the hysterical outburst that ensued. It is said that one excuse for the response was that it was "the American way of doing things." In any event, the triumphant manner in which the news was announced to a waiting public was almost bound to have a backlash. And when one came just fifteen days later in the form of the Cutter incident, which involved a number of cases of vaccine-induced paralysis due to a faulty lot of vaccine, the accident led fortunately to only a temporary upset in the program, although the setback might have proved to be a major tragedy. The publicity-minded exploiters of the situation had practically asked for it.

And yet, although his scientific reputation had been jolted, through it all Tommy Francis kept his head. He had not been responsible for the manner in which his excellent field trial had been downgraded, or for events which had followed close upon the heels of the spectacular news release. He had performed his colossal task with an adroitness and a thoroughness that characterized his whole professional career.

The strenuous life that he led nevertheless took a toll. Early in his career Tommy Francis had begun to suffer from recurrent symptoms of peptic ulcer, an affliction that was to plague him for the rest of his life and was eventually to be responsible for his death. As he took on an increasing load of major tasks and responsibilities, symptoms had increased; but once he had achieved the confidence that comes from dealing with extensive projects, he felt he could get on with them, come what may.

At about the time of the completion of the vaccine trial, Francis, having sensed the fact that epidemiology did not deal exclusively with infectious diseases, made the decision to branch out and consider more important, and certainly more prevalent, noninfectious diseases, that is, ailments which were to prove a major plague to mankind during the second half of the twentieth century; they were very different ones from those of the first half. As Sigerist, the medical historian, had said: "Every civilization makes its own diseases." It was such a philosophy that enabled Francis to make the transition easily from microbiology and the epidemiology of infectious diseases to the epidemiology of the whole broad field of noninfectious conditions, such as heart disease, cancer, and other chronic illnesses including mental illness. After all, for the epidemiologist the shift was not to a different field but was just a matter of applying epidemiological methods to other conditions.

His immediate approach to this wider field was to select a town population (the town of Tecumseh, Michigan) and to initiate there a continuing study. Its objective was to observe, as a doctor observes his patient, the diseases or illnesses that various segments of the population suffer—in other words, what happens to the life of that community and various sections of it in the ordinary passage of time.

Well do I remember when Francis first brought up the subject for discussion before one granting agency. The reaction of certain individuals was: "Surely, this is not epidemiology." And his application was immediately voted down. But Francis persisted. He knew that it "was the latest and most forward looking kind of epidemiology." The members of the Tecumseh staff, to whom the project had been entrusted, wrote some twenty years later:

"It was toward the understanding of fundamental disease processes that his [Dr. Francis's] deep interest and concern was primarily directed. His plan for a comprehensive study of health and disease in what he called a 'natural community' evolved in the late 1940s and early 1950s. The great vision was to observe people of all ages, as individuals, members of families and various social groupings, to determine the factors which preserve health and predispose to disease." *

The study, in which the emphasis was on cardiovascular disease, had been a model for many another epidemiological project. It also has become an integral part of the teaching program of the Department of Epidemiology of the School of Public Health at the University of Michigan.

Yet not content with large and small projects close to home, he embarked on another one which was to take him on frequent trips halfway round the world. Whenever and wherever, in either the western or the eastern hemisphere, the opportunity arose to deal with a project that appealed to him, and was important enough, he must have a look at it. Such was the impetus behind his contribution to the work of the Atomic Bomb Casualty Commission (ABCC).

* F. H. Epstein *et al.*, "The Tecumseh Study Design, Progress and Perspective," *Arch. Environmental Health*, 21 (1970):402–7, p. 402.

When President Harry Truman issued a directive in 1946 requesting the National Academy of Sciences–National Research Council to initiate and conduct a study of the delayed effects of radiation on the survivors of the bombings which had taken place over Hiroshima and Nagasaki, Japan, he probably had little awareness of what a tremendous time-consuming and expensive undertaking such a study involved. During the subsequent twenty-five years, in the words of Dr. Keith Cannon, it has been "a story of a continuing struggle to pursue intellectually valid investigative goals in the face of uncontrollable variables and in the changing winds of recruitment of investigators, of national economic policies, and of international relationships. Work has been continuous for 22 years and the end is not yet in sight. . . .

"There were, however, no adequate rosters of survivors nor were there means to establish a physical estimate of the amount of radiation to which each survivor was exposed. Japanese estimates indicated that there might be as many as 300,000 survivors. If acceptable epidemiologic principles were to be applied, it would be necessary to seek out each one of these individuals, record his current residence, his medical history, his exact location at the time of the bomb, and the kind of shielding from radiation that was afforded by his surroundings."

Dr. Francis's report on this colossal survey was, in the words of Dr. Cannon, "a blueprint for a 'Unified Study Program' for ABCC. It was based on a broad strategy of detection designed to be sensitive to the emergence of diseases that might be uniquely associated with exposure to ionizing radiations, but designed also to record significant alterations in the incidences of and in the natural histories of, known diseases and changes in physiological status not detected in evidences of overt diseases." *

---

* R. K. Cannon, "Contribution to the Work of the Atomic Bomb Casualty Commission (ABCC)," *Arch. Environmental Health*, 21 (1970):263–66.

This investigation would not be accomplished in a year or two. Indeed, it was only through the resolute leadership of George B. Darling, D.P.H., director of ABCC since 1957, that the study continued and achieved important results. Dr. Francis laid down the rules. His contribution to this venture is remarkable in its enduring quality.

Over and above supplying the necessary leadership of his department at the University of Michigan, Francis developed a new interest which continued during the latter part of his professional career. In 1963 he became a member of the Board of Scientific Advisors of the Jane Coffin Childs Memorial Fund for Medical Research. This is a granting agency, established in association with the Yale University School of Medicine, concerned with cancer research. The field was new for him, but even then he never felt at a loss to tackle something new. How he had gotten into it in the first place is partially explained by his great friendship with Dr. Richard Shope of the Rockefeller University, also on the Childs Fund Board. Shope was a great friend and his path had constantly intertwined with that of Dr. Francis from the early days on. As a measure of his success in this venture, Francis became the director of the Board from 1965 to 1969.

Perhaps his interest in the subject of neoplasms had been stimulated as far back as the 1950s, when Francis recorded a great moment in his varied career. This event occurred after lunch one day at the Rockefeller Institute when he encountered Dr. Peyton Rous, and Rous asked if he could talk to him briefly.

"He seemed a bit agitated and I thought he wanted some medical advice. We went to the library where he told me they had just found that a number of rabbits they had kept for a long period after inoculation with the Shope papilloma had developed genuine cancers. I'm told he had been in England for three months, and one didn't work in summers. It was clear that he was not just agitated, but really excited. So was I. Moreover, it was quite surprising that he decided to tell me. His reason, he said, was that he believed we observed and thought in similar ways—very complimentary—but I believe I was the first one he ran into." *

And so we have but skimmed over briefly the career of this remarkably able, knowledgeable, and friendly man. Not that he was unable to be tough at times, and indeed he could drive people sometimes to the brink of distraction. But in the words of Dr. Myron E. Wegman, who succeeded Henry Vaughan as the dean of the Michigan School of Public Health: "Everyone knew that he never drove anyone else harder or farther than he would have driven himself, and that Tommy would be as pitilessly critical of the work of his most senior associate colleague as he was of the junior associate." †

That was the characteristic that made him in constant demand on important government and international committees. There he was a combination of articulateness, humor, wisdom, and sound criticism—yoked to friendliness. He was at his best in discussions where he was both sharply critical of what he considered to be wrong and equally generous of what was right.

When he came to New Haven in the later years of his life to attend a meeting of the Board of the Childs Fund, he seldom forgot his old friends. Although I had retired from Yale University and was living some fifteen miles in the country at this time, he almost always called me up, and on occasion visited me.

On these visits our talks used to range widely—over the current state of the political and social scene—and even in general about what was good for mankind; but most of all about the good friends we had known in the past, and what had made them do what they did. We shall miss him sorely.

* *Op cit.*, "Moments in Medical Virology," pp. 226–28.
† Myron E. Wegman, "Thomas Francis Jr.: An Appreciation," *Arch. Environmental Health*, 21 (1970):230–33.

IN WRITING this memoir I have drawn heavily upon the Thomas Francis, Jr., Memorial Festschrift Number of the *Archives of Environmental Health,* 21 (Sept. 1970):225–418. This issue contains many articles describing in detail Dr. Francis's career and scientific achievements.

I am also greatly indebted to Mrs. Thomas Francis, Jr., and Mrs. Arthur J. Lacey (widow and sister, respectively, of Dr. Francis), for their accounts of the background of the Francis family.

CHRONOLOGY

1900	Born July 15, Gas City, Indiana
1921	B.S., Allegheny College
1925	M.D., Yale University School of Medicine
1927–1928	Instructor in Medicine, Yale University School of Medicine
1928–1936	Hospital of the Rockefeller Institute
1933	Married June 29 to Dorothy Packard Otton; children: Mary Jane, Thomas Francis III
1936–1938	Member of staff of International Health Division, The Rockefeller Foundation (in charge of influenza research)
1938–1941	Professor of Bacteriology and Director of Bacteriological Laboratories, New York University College of Medicine
1938–1941	Visiting Physician, Bellevue Hospital; Third Medical Division, New York University
1940–1941	Visiting Physician, Willard Parker Hospital, New York City
1941	D.Sc. (Hon.), Allegheny College
	M.S. (Hon.), Yale University School of Medicine
1941–1969	The Henry Sewall University Professor of Epidemiology and Chairman of the Department of Epidemiology, School of Public Health, University of Michigan
1941–1969	Professor of Epidemiology, Department of Pediatrics and Communicable Diseases, University of Michigan Medical School
1961–1968	Director, Center for Research on Diseases of the Heart, Circulation, and Related Disorders, University of Michigan
1968	University of Freiburg, Germany, Dr. Med. (Hon.)

MILITARY SERVICE

1941–1955	Director of the Commission on Influenza, Armed Forces Epidemiological Board, Department of Defense; Member, from 1941 onward
1955–1967	Member, Armed Forces Epidemiological Board, Department of Defense; President, 1958–1960

1955–1967
(Continued)
        Lecturer, Tropical and Military Medicine, Army Medical School, Washington, D.C., during World War II
        Overseas missions to Natousa, Etousa, Antilles, and Pacific area during the war

HONORS AND DISTINCTIONS

AWARDS

1946	Medal of Freedom, United States Army
1947	Lasker Award for influenza research, American Public Health Association
1952	Howard Taylor Ricketts Award and Medal, University of Chicago
1953	James D. Bruce Memorial Lecturer for 1953 and Medal in Preventive Medicine, American College of Physicians
1953–1954	Henry Russell Lectureship, University of Michigan
1955	Phi Delta Epsilon Fraternity, Annual Award of Merit
1955	Wolverine Frontiersman Award
1956	SPHINX, Honorary Society, Junior Class Honorary Society, University of Michigan
1960	Faculty award for distinguished achievements, Development Council of the University of Michigan
1961	Michigan Health Council Hall of Fame in Health
1967	Outstanding Civilian Service Medal, U.S. Army
1967	The Memorial Medal and Badge of the Gamaleya Institute of Epidemiology and Microbiology, Academy of Medical Sciences of the USSR, for recognition of his contribution in advancing biological research
1969	ABCC, NRC Commemorative Medal for distinguished service

MEMBERSHIPS IN PROFESSIONAL, HONORARY, AND LEARNED SOCIETIES

Harvey Society (Secretary, 1938–1941)

Society of American Bacteriologists (Chairman, Medical Section, 1940; Editorial Board, *Bacteriological Reviews;* Vice President, 1946; President, 1947)

American Society for Clinical Investigation (Editorial Board, 1940–1944; President, 1945–1946)

Society for Experimental Biology and Medicine (Editorial Board, *Proceedings,* 1941–1946)

American Medical Association

American Public Health Association, Fellow (Member of the Governing Council; Chairman, Committee on Research and Standards, 1947–1950; Chairman, Epidemiological Section, 1951; Chairman, Subcommittee on Diagnostic Procedures; Editor,

Diagnostic Procedures for Virus and Rickettsial Disease, 1st edition, 1948)
American Association of Immunologists (Editorial Board; Councillor; President, 1949–1950)
American Academy of Microbiology
American Epidemiological Society (President, 1954–1955)
American Philosophical Society (Committee on Membership, Class II, Geological and Biological Sciences)
American Society of Experimental Pathology
Association of American Physicians
Association of Schools of Public Health
Constantinian Society
Central Society for Clinical Research
History of Science Society
National Academy of Sciences, elected 1948 (Member of the Governing Council, 1958–1961; Member of the Executive Committee and Member at Large of the Division of Medical Sciences, 1960–1963; Member of the Kovalenko Fund, 1954–1959; Chairman, Section on Pathology and Microbiology, 1963–1966; Chairman, Marsh Fund Committee, 1963; Editorial Board, *Proceedings,* 1958–1961)
New York Academy of Medicine
New York Academy of Sciences
American Academy of Arts and Sciences, Fellow, 1960
American Heart Association, Fellow in the Council on Epidemiology, 1965

BIBLIOGRAPHY

KEY TO ABBREVIATIONS

Am. J. Hyg. = American Journal of Hygiene
Am. J. Med. Sci. = American Journal of Medical Sciences
Am. J. Public Health = American Journal of Public Health
Am. Rev. Resp. Diseases = American Review of Respiratory Diseases
Ann. Internal Med. = Annals of Internal Medicine
Ann. N.Y. Acad. Sci. = Annals of the New York Academy of Sciences
Brit. J. Exp. Pathol. = British Journal of Experimental Pathology
Bull. N.Y. Acad. Med. = Bulletin of the New York Academy of Medicine
Bull. World Health Organ. = Bulletin of the World Health Organization
J. Am. Med. Assoc. = Journal of the American Medical Association
J. Clin. Invest. = Journal of Clinical Investigation
J. Exp. Med. = Journal of Experimental Medicine
J. Immunol. = Journal of Immunology
J. Infect. Diseases = Journal of Infectious Diseases
J. Lab. Clin. Med. = Journal of Laboratory and Clinical Medicine
J. Mich. Med. Soc. = Journal of the Michigan Medical Society
Med. Clin. N. Am. = Medical Clinics of North America
Milbank Mem. Fund Quart. = Milbank Memorial Fund Quarterly
Oral Surg., Oral Med., Oral Pathol. = Oral Surgery, Oral Medicine, Oral Pathology
Proc. Soc. Exp. Biol. Med. = Proceedings of the Society for Experimental Biology and Medicine
Trans. Assoc. Am. Physicians = Transactions of the Association of American Physicians
Univ. Mich. Med. Bull. = University of Michigan Medical Bulletin
Yale J. Biol. Med. = Yale Journal of Biology and Medicine

1928

Studies on pathogenesis and recovery in erysipelas. J. Clin. Invest., 6:221.

1929

With W. S. Tillett. Cutaneous reactions to the polysaccharides and proteins of pneumococcus in lobar pneumonia. J. Exp. Med., 50:687.

1930

With W. S. Tillett. Serological reactions in pneumonia with a nonprotein somatic fraction of pneumococcus. J. Exp. Med., 52:561.
With W. S. Tillett. Cutaneous reactions in pneumonia: the development of antibodies following the intradermal injection of type-specific polysaccharide. J. Exp. Med., 52:573.

1931

With W. S. Tillett. Cutaneous reactions in rabbits to the type-specific capsular polysaccharides of pneumococcus. J. Exp. Med., 54:587.

1932

The identity of the mechanisms of type-specific agglutinin and precipitin reactions with pneumococcus. J. Exp. Med., 55:55.

1933

The value of the skin test with type-specific capsular polysaccharide in the serum treatment of type I pneumococcus pneumonia. J. Exp. Med., 57:617.

1934

Antigenic action of the specific polysaccharide of pneumococcus type I in man. Proc. Soc. Exp. Biol. Med., 31:493.

With T. J. Abernethy. Cutaneous reactions in pneumonia to the somatic ("C") polysaccharide of pneumococcus. J. Clin. Invest., 13:692.

With E. E. Terrell. Experimental type III pneumococcus pneumonia in monkeys. I. Production and clinical course. J. Exp. Med., 59:609.

With E. E. Terrell, R. Dubos, et al. Experimental type III pneumococcus pneumonia in monkeys. II. Treatment with an enzyme which decomposes the specific capsular polysaccharide of pneumococcus type III. J. Exp. Med., 59:641.

Transmission of influenza by a filterable virus. Science, 80:457.

1935

Immunological relationships of strains of filterable virus recovered from cases of human influenza. Proc. Soc. Exp. Biol. Med., 32:1172.

Diagnosis and management of pneumonia in the United States. Ugeskrift for Laeger, 24:639.

Recent advances in the study of influenza. J. Am. Med. Assoc., 105:251.

With T. P. Magill. Rift Valley fever: a report of three cases of laboratory infection and the experimental transmission of the disease to ferrets. J. Exp. Med., 62:433.

With T. P. Magill. Immunological studies with the virus of influenza. J. Exp. Med., 62:505.
With T. P. Magill. Cultivation of human influenza virus in an artificial medium. Science, 82:353.
Localization and development of the lesion in experimental pneumonia. Archives of Pathology, 19:860.

1936

Etiological and immunological aspects of influenza. Health Examiner, 5:13.
With T. P. Magill. Vaccination of human subjects with virus of human influenza. Proc. Soc. Exp. Biol. Med., 33:604.
With R. E. Shope. Neutralization tests with sera of convalescent or immunized animals and the viruses of swine and human influenza. J. Exp. Med., 63:645.
With T. P. Magill. The incidence of neutralizing antibodies for human influenza virus in the serum of human individuals of different ages. J. Exp. Med., 63:655.
With T. P. Magill. Studies with human influenza virus cultivated in artificial medium. J. Exp. Med., 63:803.
With R. E. Shope. The susceptibility of swine to the virus of human influenza. J. Exp. Med., 64:791.
With T. P. Magill. Antigenic differences in strains of human influenza virus. Proc. Soc. Exp. Biol. Med., 35:463.

1937

Studies in influenza. Pennsylvania Medical Journal, 40:249.
With T. J. Abernethy. Studies on the somatic C polysaccharide of pneumonococcus. I. Cutaneous and serological reactions in pneumonia. J. Exp. Med., 65:59.
With T. P. Magill. The antibody response of human subjects vaccinated with the virus of human influenza. J. Exp. Med., 65:251.
Epidemiological studies in influenza. Am. J. Public Health, 27:211.
With T. P. Magill. Direct transmission of human influenza virus to mice. Proc. Soc. Exp. Biol. Med., 36:132.
With T. P. Magill. Direct isolation of human influenza virus in tissue culture medium and on egg membrane. Proc. Soc. Exp. Biol. Med., 36:134.
With T. P. Magill. The action of immune serum on human influenza *in vitro*. J. Exp. Med., 65:861.

With M. D. Beck, T. P. Magill, et al. Studies with human influenza virus during the influenza epidemic of 1936–1937. J. Am. Med. Assoc., 109:566.
With T. P. Magill, E. R. Rickard, et al. Etiological and serological studies in epidemic influenza. Am. J. Public Health, 27:1141.
Rift Valley fever. In: *Practitioner's Library of Medicine and Surgery,* ed. by G. Blumer. New York, Appleton-Century Company.
Recent advances in our knowledge of the etiology of influenza. In: *Practitioner's Library of Medicine and Surgery,* ed. by G. Blumer. New York, Appleton-Century Company.

1938

With E. R. Rickard. The demonstration of lesions and virus in the lungs of mice receiving large intraperitoneal inoculations of epidemic influenza virus. J. Exp. Med., 67:953.
The immunology of epidemic influenza. Am. J. Hyg., 28:63.
With T. P. Magill. A flocculation phenomenon with human sera and suspensions of the virus of epidemic influenza. Proc. Soc. Exp. Biol. Med., 39:81.
With T. P. Magill. An unidentified virus producing acute meningitis and pneumonitis in experimental animals. J. Exp. Med., 68:147.
With T. P. Magill. Antigenic differences in strains of epidemic influenza virus. I. Cross-neutralization tests in mice. Brit. J. Exp. Pathol., 19:273.
With T. P. Magill. Antigenic differences in strains of epidemic influenza virus. II. Cross-immunization tests in mice. Brit. J. Exp. Pathol., 19:284.
With C. H. Stuart-Harris. Studies on the nasal histology of epidemic influenza virus infection in the ferret. I. The development and repair of the nasal lesion. J. Exp. Med., 68:789.
With C. H. Stuart-Harris. Studies on the nasal histology of epidemic influenza virus infection in the ferret. II. The resistance of regenerating respiratory epithelium to reinfection and to physico-chemical injury. J. Exp. Med., 68:803.
With C. H. Stuart-Harris. Studies on the nasal histology of epidemic influenza virus infection in the ferret. III. Histological and serological observations on ferrets receiving repeated inoculations of epidemic influenza virus. J. Exp. Med., 68:813.

1939

Quantitative relationships between the immunizing dose of epidemic influenza virus and the resultant immunity. J. Exp. Med., 69:283.

The diagnosis of virus diseases. Minnesota Medicine, 22:807.

Epidemic influenza. Studies in clinical epidemiology. Ann. Internal Med., 13:915.

1940

Intranasal inoculation of human individuals with the virus of epidemic influenza. Proc. Soc. Exp. Biol. Med., 43:337.

Influenza. In: *Modern Medical Therapy in General Practice*, ed. by D. P. Barr, Vol. 2, pp. 1597–1605. Baltimore, Williams & Wilkins Company.

Inactivation of epidemic influenza virus by nasal secretions of human individuals. Science, 91:198.

With C. C. Stock. The inactivation of the virus of epidemic influenza by soaps. J. Exp. Med., 71:661.

With A. E. Moore. A study of the neurotropic tendency in strains of the virus of epidemic influenza. J. Exp. Med., 72:717.

With J. E. Salk and G. I. Lavin. The antigenic potency of epidemic influenza virus following inactivation by ultraviolet radiation. J. Exp. Med., 72:729.

A new type of virus from epidemic influenza. Science, 92:405.

Differentiation of influenza A and influenza B by the complement-fixation reaction. Proc. Soc. Exp. Biol. Med., 45:861.

1941

The problem of epidemic influenza. Transactions of the College of Physicians of Philadelphia, 8:218.

The significance of nasal factors in epidemic influenza. In: *Problems and Trends in Virus Research*, Vol. 1, pp. 41–54. Philadelphia, University of Pennsylvania Press.

Epidemic influenza. Bull. N.Y. Acad. Med., 17:268.

With M. V. de Torregrosa. The intracerebral infection of mice with *Haemophilus influenzae* as an index of strain virulence and the protective value of immune serum. J. Infect. Diseases, 68:59.

With I. J. Brightman. Virus-inactivating capacity of nasal secretions in the acute and convalescent stages of influenza. Proc. Soc. Exp. Biol. Med., 48:116.

1942

Present trends in the study of epidemic influenza. Advances in Internal Medicine, 1:169.
With A. E. Feller, L. B. Roberts, and E. P. Ralli. Studies on the influence of vitamin A on certain immunological reactions in man. J. Clin. Invest., 21:121.
Factors conditioning resistance to epidemic influenza. Harvey Lectures, 37:69–99, 1941–42.
With B. Eddie. Occurrence of psittacosis-like infection in domestic and game birds of Michigan. Proc. Soc. Exp. Biol. Med., 50:291.
With B. A. Friedman. Gall formation by *Phytomonas tumefaciens* extract and indole-3-acetic acid in cultures of tomato roots. Phytopathology, 32:762.
With L. E. Farr and W. C. McCarthy. Plasma amino-acid levels in health and in measles, scarlet fever and pneumonia. Am. J. Med. Sci., 203:668.
With C. E. Krill, J. A. Toomey, *et al.* Poliomyelitis following tonsillectomy in five members of a family: an epidemiologic study. J. Am. Med. Assoc., 119:1392.
An epidemiological study of poliomyelitis following tonsillectomy. Trans. Assoc. Am. Physicians, 57:277.
Epidemic influenza. In: *Nelson New Loose-Leaf Medicine,* ed. by W. W. Herrick, Vol. 1, pp. 583–617. New York, Thomas Nelson & Sons.
With J. E. Salk. A simplified procedure for the concentration and purification of influenza virus. Science, 96:499.

1943

A rationale for studies in the control of epidemic influenza. Science, 97:229.
With C. C. Stock. The inactivation of the virus of lymphocytic choriomeningitis by soaps. J. Exp. Med., 77:323.
Epidemiology of influenza. J. Am. Med. Assoc., 122:4.
With H. E. Pearson, E. R. Sullivan, *et al.* The effect of subcutaneous vaccination with influenza virus upon the virus-inactivating capacity of nasal secretions. Am. J. Hyg., 37:294.

With C. C. Stock. Additional studies of the inactivation of the virus of epidemic influenza by soaps. J. Immunol., 47:303.
With R. C. Rendtorff. Survival of the Lansing strain of poliomyelitis virus in the common house fly. *Musica domestica* L. J. Infect. Diseases, 73:198.
With E. Herrarte. Efforts toward selective extraction of poliomyelitis virus. J. Infect. Diseases, 73:206.

1944

Virus pneumonia. Canadian Journal of Public Health, 35:49.
With J. E. Salk and W. J. Menke. Identification of influenza virus type A in current outbreak of respiratory disease. J. Am. Med. Assoc., 124:93.
With J. E. Salk, H. E. Pearson, *et al.* Protective effect of vaccination against induced influenza A. Proc. Soc. Exp. Biol. Med., 55:104.
A clinical evaluation of vaccination against influenza. Members of the Commission on Influenza, Board for the Investigation and Control of Influenza and Other Epidemic Diseases in the Army, Preventive Medicine Service, Office of the Surgeon General, United States Army. J. Am. Med. Assoc., 124:982.
With J. E. Salk, H. E. Pearson, and P. N. Brown. Protective effect of vaccination against induced influenza B. Proc. Soc. Exp. Biol. Med., 55:106.
With H. E. Pearson, J. E. Salk, *et al.* Immunity in human subjects artificially infected with influenza virus, type B. Am. J. Public Health, 34:317.
Comments on immunity to virus diseases. Yale J. Biol. Med., 16:401.

1945

With M. V. de Torregrosa. Combined infection of mice with *H. influenzae* and influenzae virus by the intranasal route. J. Infect. Diseases, 76:70.
With G. C. Brown. The virus-neutralizing action of serum from mice infected with poliomyelitis virus. J. Exp. Med., 81:161.
With H. E. Pearson, G. C. Brown, R. C. Rendtorff, and G. M. Ridenour. Studies of the distribution of poliomyelitis virus. III. In an urban area during an epidemic. Am. J. Hyg., 41:188.

Influenza: methods of study and control. Bull. N.Y. Acad. Med., 21:337.
The development of the 1943 vaccination study of the Commission on Influenza. Am. J. Hyg., 42:1.
With J. E. Salk and W. J. Menke, Jr. A clinical epidemiological and immunological evaluation of vaccination against epidemic influenza. Am. J. Hyg., 42:57.
With J. E. Salk, H. E. Pearson, et al. Protective effect of vaccination against induced influenza A. J. Clin. Invest., 24:536.
With J. E. Salk, H. E. Pearson, and P. N. Brown. Protective effect of vaccination against induced influenza B. J. Clin. Invest., 24:547.
With G. C. Brown and H. E. Pearson. Rapid development of carrier state and detection of poliomyelitis virus in stool 19 days before onset of paralytic disease. J. Am. Med. Assoc., 129:121.
With J. E. Salk, H. E. Pearson, P. N. Brown, and C. J. Smyth. Immunization against influenza with observations during an epidemic of influenza A, one year after vaccination. Am. J. Hyg., 42:307.

1946

With A. W. Frisch and J. J. Quilligan, Jr. Demonstration of infectious hepatitis virus in presymptomatic period after transfer by transfusion. Proc. Soc. Exp. Biol. Med., 61:276.
With J. E. Salk and W. M. Brace. The protective effect of vaccination against epidemic influenza B. J. Am. Med. Assoc., 131:275.
The progress of research in poliomyelitis. Ohio Medical Journal, 42:838.
With J. E. Salk. Immunization against influenza. Ann. Internal Med., 25:443.
Biological beachheads. J. Clin. Invest., 25:906.
A consideration of vaccination against influenza. Trans. Assoc. Am. Physicians, 59:197.

1947

Dissociation of hemagglutinating and antibody-measuring capacities of influenza virus. J. Exp. Med., 85:1.
A consideration of vaccination against influenza. Milbank Mem. Fund Quart., 25:5.

Control of virus infections. J. Mich. Med. Soc., 46:566.
Apparent serological variation within a strain of influenza virus. Proc. Soc. Exp. Biol. Med., 65:143.
With G. C. Brown. Studies on the relation of wild rats to poliomyelitis. J. Infect. Diseases, 81:55.
With J. E. Salk and J. J. Quilligan, Jr. Experience with vaccination against influenza in the spring of 1947. Am. J. Public Health, 37:1013.
The present status of vaccination against influenza. Am. J. Public Health, 37:1109.
Mechanisms of infection and immunity in virus diseases of man. Bacteriological Reviews, 11:147.
With G. C. Brown. The neutralization of the mouse-adapted Lansing strain of poliomyelitis virus by the serum of patients and contacts. J. Immunol., 57:1.
Respiratory viruses. Annual Review of Microbiology, 1:351.
With J. J. Quilligan, Jr. Serological response to intranasal administration of inactive influenza virus in children. J. Clin. Invest., 26:1079.
Infectious hepatitis. In: *Handbook of Communicable Diseases*, 2d ed., ed. by F. H. Top. St. Louis, The C. V. Mosby Company, Medical Publishers.

1948

With G. C. Brown and J. Ainslie. Studies of the distribution of poliomyelitis virus. V. The virus in familial associates of cases. J. Exp. Med., 87:21.
Viruses as agents of disease. Oral Surg., Oral Med., Oral Pathol., 1:153.
The prevention of virus diseases. Oral Surg., Oral Med., Oral Pathol., 1:160.
With G. C. Brown. Studies of the distribution of poliomyelitis virus. IV. In rural schools following an epidemic. J. Infect. Diseases, 82:163.
With G. C. Brown and L. R. Penner. Search for extrahuman sources of poliomyelitis virus. J. Am. Med. Assoc., 136:1088.
With J. J. Quilligan, Jr., and E. Minuse. Homologous and heterologous antibody response of infants and children to multiple injections of a single strain of influenza virus. J. Clin. Invest., 27:572.

With E. Minuse. Influence of saliva upon hemagglutination by influenza virus. Proc. Soc. Exp. Biol. Med., 69:291.
Parasitism and disease. In: *Bacterial and Mycotic Infections of Man*, ed. by R. J. Dubos. Philadelphia, J. B. Lippincott Company.
Response of the host to the parasite. In: *Bacterial and Mycotic Infections of Man*, ed. by R. J. Dubos. Philadelphia, J. B. Lippincott Company.
With C. Armstrong, D. Bodian, A. B. Sabin, and J. R. Paul. A proposed provisional definition of poliomyelitis virus. Science, 108:701. (Committee on Nomenclature of the National Foundation for Infantile Paralysis.)

1949

With G. C. Brown and J. D. Ainslie. The incidence of poliomyelitis virus in cases of mild illness during a severe urban epidemic. Am. J. Hyg., 49:194.
Immunity in poliomyelitis. Phi Chi Quarterly, October, 1949. (First Annual Dr. Eben J. Carey Memorial Lecture, Omaha.)
With G. C. Brown. Evaluation of the effect of Darvisul upon infection with SK strain of virus in mice. Proc. Soc. Exp. Biol. Med., 70:535.
With J. J. Quilligan, Jr., and E. Minuse. Resemblance of a strain of swine influenza virus to human A-prime strains. Proc. Soc. Exp. Biol. Med., 71:216.
With J. J. Quilligan, Jr., and E. Minuse. Reactions to an influenza virus in infants and children. American Journal of Diseases of Childen, 78:295.
The family doctor: an epidemiologic concept. J. Am. Med. Assoc., 141:308.
Immunization Contra Influenza, Vol. 3. (One of a series of medical articles prepared exclusively for the physicians of Peru by distinguished authorities of the United States.)
With K. Penttinen. The failure of Merodicein to modify influenza virus infections. J. Immunol., 63:337.

1950

Immunity and vaccination in influenza. In: *Handbuch der Virusforschung*, ed. by R. Doerr and C. Hallauer, pp. 66–86. Vienna, Springer-Verlag. II. Ergänzungsband.

With J. J. Quilligan, Jr., Richard J. Rowe, et al. The action of Terramycin on the growth of strains of influenza, herpes simplex, and rabies viruses in chick embryos and mice. Ann. N.Y. Acad. Sci., 53:407.

With H. B. Kurtz. The relation of herpes virus to the cell nucleus. Yale J. Biol. Med., 22:579.

With W. W. Ackermann. Some biochemical aspects of herpes infection. Proc. Soc. Exp. Biol. Med., 74:123.

The significance of multiple immunological types of influenza virus. Cincinnati Journal of Medicine, 31:97.

With others. An agglutination-inhibition test proposed as a standard of reference in influenza diagnostic studies. J. Immunol., 65:347. (Committee on Standard Serological Procedures in Influenza Studies.)

Immunology and preservation of the norm. J. Immunol., 65:437.

With J. J. Quilligan, Jr., and E. Minuse. Identification of another epidemic respiratory disease. Science, 112:495.

With J. D. Ainslie and J. L. McCallum. Failure to demonstrate antibody in feces of monkeys vaccinated with poliomyelitis virus, Lansing strain. Proc. Soc. Exp. Biol. Med., 75:699.

1951

With F. M. Davenport. A comparison of the growth curves of adapted and unadapted lines of influenza virus. J. Exp. Med., 93:129.

With J. D. Ainslie and P. K. Stumpf. Serum alkaline phosphatase in monkeys and man during poliomyelitis. Am. J. Hyg., 53:58.

Immunity in virus diseases. Cornell Veterinarian, 41:190.

Plan for the evaluation of vaccination against influenza. Am. J. Public Health, 41:62.

With J. D. Ainslie and G. C. Brown. ACTH in experimental poliomyelitis in monkeys and mice. J. Lab. Clin. Med., 38:344.

1952

With G. C. Brown, J. D. Ainslie, A. G. Gilliam, and A. R. Zintek. Studies of the distribution of poliomyelitis virus. VI. In a small community in an epidemic area. Am. J. Hyg., 55:49.

Distribution of poliomyelitis virus in the epidemic community. Trans. Assoc. Am. Physicians, 65:176.

Distribution of poliomyelitis virus in a community. In: *Polio-*

myelitis, pp. 355–63. Proceedings of the Second International Poliomyelitis Conference. Philadelphia, J. B. Lippincott Company.

Developing a philosophy for the Committee on Research and Standards. Am. J. Public Health, 42:85.

Significance of antigenic variation of influenza viruses in relation to vaccination in man. Federation Proceedings, 11:808.

Parisitism and disease. In: *Bacterial and Mycotic Infections of Man,* 2d ed., ed. by R. J. Dubos, pp. 68–74. Philadelphia, J. B. Lippincott Company.

Response of the host. In: *Bacterial and Mycotic Infections of Man,* 2d ed., ed. by R. J. Dubos, pp. 98–118. Philadelphia, J. B. Lippincott Company.

1953

Research in poliomyelitis at Michigan. Michigan Alumnus Quarterly Review, February.

Influenza: method of Thomas Francis, Jr. In: *Current Therapy,* ed. by H. F. Conn. Philadelphia, W. B. Saunders Company.

With K. E. Jensen. Antigen–antibody precipitates in solid medium with influenza virus. J. Immunol., 70:321.

Vaccination against influenza. Bull. World Health Organ., 8:725.

Influenza: the newe acquayantance [sic]. Ann. Internal Med., 39:203.

With L. W. Chu. The interaction *in vitro* between poliomyelitis virus and nervous tissue. In: *Proceedings of the Sixth International Congress of Microbiology,* Rome, Italy, 1953. Vol. 8, p. 162. (A)

With A. V. Hennessy, E. Minuse, and F. M. Davenport. An experience with vaccination against influenza B in 1952 by use of monovalent vaccine. Am. J. Hyg., 58:165.

Correlations in clinical and epidemiological investigation. Am. J. Med. Sci., 226:376.

With G. C. Brown and J. D. Ainslie. Poliomyelitis in Hidalgo County, Texas, 1948: poliomyelitis and Cocksackie viruses in privy specimens. Am. J. Hyg., 53:310.

With K. E. Jensen. The antigenic composition of influenza virus measured by antibody-absorption. J. Exp. Med., 98:619.

With F. M. Davenport and A. V. Hennessy. Epidemiologic and

immunologic significance of age distribution of antibody to antigenic variants of influenza virus. J. Exp. Med., 98:641.

1954

The teaching of epidemiology. In: *Proceedings of the First World Conference on Medical Education,* London, 1953. London, Oxford University Press.

With W. W. Ackermann. Characteristics of viral development in isolated animal tissues. Advances in Virus Research, 11:81.

With E. Minuse and J. J. Quilligan, Jr. Type C influenza virus. I. Studies of the virus and its distribution; II. Intranasal inoculation of human individuals. J. Lab. Clin. Med., 43:31.

Evaluation of gamma globulin in prophylaxis of paralytic poliomyelitis in 1953: summary of the Report of the National Advisory Committee for Evaluation of Gamma Globulin. J. Am. Med. Assoc., 154:1086.

Immunological and epidemiological problems. Proceedings of the Royal Society of Medicine, 47:561.

With L. R. Penner and G. C. Brown. Some observations on the ecology of a North American chigger *Trombicula (Eutrombicula) lipovskyana,* Wolfenbarger, 1952, in a Tennessee community. Journal of the Kansas Entomological Society, 27:113.

With G. C. Brown and A. Kandel. Effect of fluoroacetate upon poliomyelitis in monkeys. Proc. Soc. Exp. Biol. Med., 85:83.

With K. W. Cochran and G. C. Brown. Antiviral action of a mold filtrate on experimental poliomyelitis in cynomologus monkeys. Proc. Soc. Exp. Biol. Med., 85:104.

The teaching of epidemiology. Journal of Medical Education, 29:15.

1955

Approach to control of poliomyelitis by immunological methods. Bull. N.Y. Acad. Med., 31:259.

With R. F. Korns, R. B. Voight, *et al. An Evaluation of the 1954 Poliomyelitis Vaccine Trials; Summary Report.* Ann Arbor, Michigan, Poliomyelitis Vaccine Evaluation Center, University of Michigan. 50, 63 pp. (Sponsored by the National Foundation for Infantile Paralysis.) Also in Am. J. Public Health, Vol. 45, May, Part II, special issue.

With R. F. Korns. Evaluation of 1954 field trial of poliomyelitis vaccine: synopsis of summary report. Am. J. Med. Sci., 229:603.

Poliomyelitis issue. Univ. Mich. Med. Bull., 21:153–55.
Evaluation of the 1954 poliomyelitis vaccine field trial: further studies of results determining the effectiveness of poliomyelitis vaccine (Salk) in preventing paralytic poliomyelitis. J. Am. Med. Assoc., 158:1266.
The current status of the control of influenza. Ann. Internal Med., 43:534.
With F. M. Davenport, A. V. Hennessy, and C. H. Stuart-Harris. Epidemiology of influenza: comparative serological observations in England and the United States. Lancet, 2:469–74.
Summary and review of poliomyelitis immunization. Ann. N.Y. Acad. Sci., 61:1057.
Virus problems in medicine. Illinois Medical Journal, 108:257.
With A. V. Hennessy and F. M. Davenport. Studies of antibodies to strains of influenza virus in persons of different ages in sera collected in a postepidemic period. J. Immunol., 75:401.
With D. Bodian, C. Larson, et al. Interim report, Public Health Service Technical Committee on Poliomyelitis Vaccine. J. Am. Med. Assoc., 159:1444.

1956

With K. W. Cochran. Antiviral action of helenine on experimental poliomyelitis. Proc. Soc. Exp. Biol. Med., 92:230.
With J. F. Enders, J. A. Bell, J. H. Dingle, et al. Adenoviruses: group name proposed for new respiratory tract viruses. Science, 124:119.
With K. E. Jensen, F. M. Davenport, and A. V. Hennessy. Characterization of influenza antibodies by serum absorption. J. Exp. Med., 104:199.
Approaches to the prevention of poliomyelitis. Univ. Mich. Med. Bull., 22:433.
With J. Napier and F. M. Hemphill. Poliomyelitisschutzimpfung. Münchener Medizinische Wochenshrift, 98:1349–55.

1957

Symposium on controlled vaccine field trials. Poliomyelitis. Am. J. Public Health, 47:283.
With K. E. Jensen and E. Minuse. Serologic comparisons with lines of influenza virus isolated and serially transferred in different experimental hosts. J. Immunol., 78:356.

Epidemiology and the future of medicine. University of Tennessee Record, Vol. 60, No. 6.
With L. Blair, M. Jacobs, et al. The role of the physical therapist in the evaluation studies of the poliomyelitis vaccine field trials. Physical Therapy Review, 37:437.
With F. M. Davenport and A. V. Hennessy. Influence of primary antigenic experience upon the development of a broad immunity to influenza. Trans. Assoc. Am. Physicians, 70:81.
Mobilization against influenza. Science, 126:1267.
Vaccination against Asian influenza: basis for recommendations and a preliminary report on efficacy. Members of the Commission on Influenza of the Armed Forces Epidemiological Board, Office of the Commission on Influenza, School of Public Health, University of Michigan, Ann Arbor. J. Am. Med. Assoc., 165:2055.
With J. A. Napier, R. B. Voight, et al. *Evaluation of the 1954 Field Trial of Poliomyelitis Vaccine; Final Report.* Ann Arbor, Michigan, Edwards Brothers, Inc. xxxi + 563 pp.
Facts and perspectives of a large-scale field trial. Special Publications of the New York Academy of Sciences, 5:99.

1958

A New Year's fantasy. Univ. Mich. Med. Bull., 24:1.
With K. G. Kohlstaedt, M. Moser, et al. Panel discussion on genetic and environmental factors in human hypertension. Circulation, 17:728, Part II.
Immunization. J. Mich. Med. Soc., 57:742.
Immunity to virus diseases. In: *Symposium on Viruses: Current Advances with Clinical Applications,* p. 123.
Influenza. In: *Communicable Diseases: Preventive Medicine in World War II,* ed. by E. C. Hoff, Vol. 4, pp. 85–128. Washington, D.C., Department of the Army, Office of the Surgeon General.
With D. E. Craig. Contact transmission of poliomyelitis virus among monkeys. Proc. Soc. Exp. Biol. Med., 99:325.
Frederick George Novy 1864–1957. Trans. Assoc. Am. Physicians, 71:35.
Viral inhibition. In: *Poliomyelitis,* pp. 361–65. Proceedings of the Fourth International Poliomyelitis Conference. Philadelphia, J. B. Lippincott Company.

1959

Influenza. In: *Viral and Rickettsial Infections of Man,* 3d ed., ed.

by Thomas M. Rivers and Frank L. Horsfall, Jr., pp. 633-72. Philadelphia, J. B. Lippincott Company.
With F. H. Epstein, W. D. Block, and E. A. Hand. Familial hypercholesterolemia, xanthomatosis and coronary heart disease. American Journal of Medicine, 26:39.
Adventures in preventive medicine: the Founder's Day address. Allegheny College Bulletin, June.
Influenza. Med. Clin. N. Am., 43:1309.
Serological variation. In: *Animal Viruses,* Vol. 3 of *The Viruses: Biochemical, Biological, and Biophysical Properties,* ed. by F. M. Burnet and W. M. Stanley, pp. 251-73. New York, Academic Press, Inc.
The epidemiological approach to human ecology. Am. J. Med. Sci., 237:677.

1960

Research in preventive medicine. J. Am. Med. Assoc., 172:993.
Preventive medicine in 1985 and a re-emphasis on the preservation of health. What's New, 220:26.
On the doctrine of original antigenic sin. Proceedings of the American Philosophical Society, 104:572.

1961

Influenza in perspective. Am. Rev. Resp. Diseases, 83:98.
Biological aspects of environment. Industrial Medicine and Surgery, 30:374.
Aspects of the Tecumseh study. Public Health Reports, 76:963.
With W. D. Peterson and F. M. Davenport. A study *in vitro* of components in the transmission cycle of swine influenza virus. J. Exp. Med., 114:1023.
Problems of acute respiratory disease. Yale J. Biol. Med., 34:91, 1961-62.

1962

With G. C. Brown. Incidence of heterologous antibodies in virus-confirmed cases of poliomyelitis. New England Journal of Medicine, 266:642.
With B. J. Neff, W. W. Ackermann, and F. H. Epstein. Inhibition of vaccinial hemagglutinins by sera of patients with coronary heart disease and other chronic illnesses. Circulation Research, 10:836.

With E. Minuse, P. W. Willis III, and F. M. Davenport. An attempt to demonstrate viremia in cases of Asian influenza. J. Lab. Clin. Med., 59:1016.

With B. J. Neff, G. L. Brady, and F. H. Epstein. Serologic and pathologic changes in rats on atherogenic diets. Journal of Atherosclerosis Research, 2:306.

1963

Epidemic influenza. Am. Rev. Resp. Diseases, 88:148.

1964

With A. V. Hennessy, F. M. Davenport, R. J. Horton, and J. A. Napier. Asian influenza: occurrence and recurrence, a community and family study. Military Medicine, 129:38.

With F. M. Davenport, A. V. Hennessy, J. Drescher, and J. Mulder. Further observations on the relevance of serologic recapitulations of human infection with influenza viruses. J. Exp. Med., 120:1087.

Ernest William Goodpasture (1886–1960). In: *American Philosophical Society Yearbook 1964*, pp. 111–20. Philadelphia, American Philosophical Society.

1965

A portrait of Henry F. Vaughan. University of Michigan Medical Center Journal, 31:100.

With H. F. Maassab. Influenza virus. In: *Viral and Rickettsial Infections of Man*, 4th ed., ed. by F. L. Horsfall and I. Tamm, pp. 689–740. Philadelphia, J. B. Lippincott Company.

In honor of Richard E. Shope. In: *Perspectives in Virology IV*, ed. by M. Pollard. New York, Hoeber Medical Division, Harper & Rowe, Publishers.

With F. H. Epstein, N. S. Hayner, *et al*. Prevalence of chronic diseases and distribution of selected physiologic variables in a total community, Tecumseh, Michigan. American Journal of Epidemiology, 81:307.

Genetics and epidemiology. In: *Genetics and the Epidemiology of Chronic Diseases*, ed. by J. V. Neel, M. W. Shaw, and W. J. Schull. Public Health Service publication 1163. Washington, U.S. Govt. Print. Off.

With F. H. Epstein. Tecumseh, Michigan. Milbank Mem. Fund Quart., 43:333.

With F. H. Epstein, L. D. Ostrander, Jr., B. C. Johnson, M. W. Payne, N. S. Hayner, and J. B. Keller. Epidemiological studies of cardiovascular disease in a total community. Ann. Internal Med., 62:1170.

Standards for research in new drug testing. In: *Proceedings of the Fourth International Congress of the International Federation for Hygiene and Preventive Medicine,* 2d ed. Vienna, May 1965. Vienna, Wiener Medizinishe Akademie.

With G. C. Brown, H. F. Maassab, and J. A. Veronelli. Detection of rubella antibodies in human serum by the indirect fluorescent antibody technique. Archiv für die Gesampte Virusforschung, 16:459.

With L. D. Ostrander, N. S. Hayner, et al. The relationship of cardiovascular disease to hyperglycemia. Ann. Internal Med., 62:1188.

Standards required in vaccine field trials. In: *Proceedings of the Cholera Research Symposium,* Honolulu, January 24–29, 1965, publication 1328, pp. 352–54. Washington, U.S. Govt. Print. Off.

With N. S. Hayner, M. O. Kjelsberg, and F. H. Epstein. Carbohydrate tolerance and diabetes in a total community, Tecumseh, Michigan. Diabetes, 14:413.

With N. S. Ling and T. Krasteff. Transcholesterin, a cholesterol-binding globulin: serological demonstration of a specific interaction between cholesterol and serum globulin. Proceedings of the National Academy of Sciences, 53:1061.

With E. Minuse, J. L. McQueen, and F. M. Davenport. Studies of antibodies to 1956 and 1963 equine influenza viruses in horses and man. J. Immunol., 94:563.

1966

The polyvalent vaccine: reasons for inclusion of earlier virus prototypes and contemporary virus strains into current and future vaccines. (Read before Division of Biologics Standards Conference on Formulation of Influenza Virus Vaccines. National Institutes of Health, October 1966.)

1967

With L. D. Ostrander, Jr., B. J. Neff, W. D. Block, et al. Hyperglycemia and hypertriglyceridemia among persons with coronary heart disease. Ann. Internal Med., 67:34.

Summary. In: *Working Conference on Smallpox Rapporteurs' Reports*, pp. 23-26. Sponsored by the U.S.-Japan Cooperative Medical Science Program, Office of International Research, National Institutes of Health.

Epidemic influenza: immunization and control. Med. Clin. N. Am., 51:781.

Immunization of selected population groups against influenza. Archives of Environmental Health, 14:747.

With T. O. Anderson, F. W. Denny, et al. *Epidemiologic Studies for Vaccine Development*. U.S. Department of Commerce, PB 176 814, National Bureau of Standards Institute of Applied Technology.

1968

Transcholesterin titers and their biological significance in experimental atherogenesis in rats. Proc. Soc. Exp. Biol. Med., 128:197.

Experience with vaccines: general comments. In: *Conference on Cell Cultures for Virus Vaccine Production*, Bethesda, Maryland, November 1967. National Cancer Institute Monograph 29.

1969

Faktoren der Immunität gegen respiratorische Infekte. Deutsche Medizinische Wochenschrift, 94:355.

With F. M. Davenport, E. Minuse, and A. V. Hennessy. Interpretation of influenza antibody patterns of man. Bull. World Health Organ., 41:453.

With A. S. Monto, F. M. Davenport, and J. A. Napier. Effect of vaccination of a school-age population upon the course of an A_2/Hong Kong influenza epidemic. Bull. World Health Organ., 41:537.

With H. F. Maassab, F. M. Davenport, *et al.* Laboratory and clinical characteristics of attenuated strains of influenza virus. Bull. World Health Organ., 41:589.

Moments in medical virology. In: *International Virology, 1,* ed. by J. L. Melnick, p. 224. Proceedings of the First International Congress for Virology. Basel, Switzerland, S. Karger, A.G.

DONNEL FOSTER HEWETT

June 24, 1881–February 5, 1971

BY JAMES GILLULY

Donnel foster hewett lived a long, fruitful, and satisfying life that impinged on many fields of science and many persons. He was alert and productive almost to the day of his death at the age of eighty-nine; in fact, two of his papers were in the press at that time. And he had the satisfaction, granted to few, of participating constructively in the evolution of economic geology as a profession during a period of explosive technologic progress and of being everywhere recognized for his contributions to these developments.

Foster Hewett was born June 24, 1881, at Irwin, Pennsylvania, son of George C. Hewett and Hetty Barclay Foster Hewett. Both his father and his paternal grandfather were highly successful mining engineers; his maternal grandfather had served as a Congressman from Pennsylvania and had once been a candidate for the governorship. Hewett's mother died when he was only three years old, and for more than ten years he was reared in the household of his mother's sister, Mrs. Frank A. Hopper, in Washington, D.C. He attended elementary schools in Washington until 1895 when his father remarried and established a family home in Atlanta, Georgia, where he was then employed by the Southern Railway Company. Young Foster had visited his father in some of the western mining areas during vacations and had become something of an amateur mineralogist; now rejoined with his engineer father, Foster was taken as a companion on many mine examinations in Alabama and Georgia—experiences that surely influenced his own final choice of a profession.

At fourteen young Hewett entered the Georgia School of Technology where he remained for a year and a half before dropping out to attend a business college. In the fall of 1897, when he was sixteen years old, he was employed as a stenographer and typist for several months. By this time he had decided on an engineering career, so he entered the National Capitol University School in Washington in order to prepare for college.

In the fall of 1898 Hewett enrolled at Lehigh University at Bethlehem, Pennsylvania, as a student of chemistry, metallurgy, and mining. Something of his outgoing personality is revealed by his election to the presidency of his class. He was graduated with high honors in 1902 as Bachelor of Metallurgy. He remained on at Lehigh for a year as an instructor in mineralogy and metallurgy and became one of the most skillful determinative mineralogists of his time. At Lehigh he had come under the influence of Joseph Barrell, one of the ablest geologists of his generation, and acquired the enthusiasm for geology that remained with him through life.

In 1903 Hewett entered the employ of the Pittsburgh Testing Laboratories as a mining engineer. This firm was at that time one of the largest consulting organizations in the mineral industries and the twenty-two-year-old Hewett, fresh from the classroom, was given flattering responsibilities from the beginning—responsibilities he quickly showed he was fully able to meet. Between 1903 and 1909 Hewett examined, mapped, and reported on scores of mines in widely scattered parts of the United States, Mexico, Canada, and Peru. The commodities sought ranged widely over the field of economic geology: arsenic, coal, gold, lead, silver, vanadium, and zinc.

In 1906 Hewett was primarily responsible for the discovery of the largest vanadium deposit in the world, at Mina Ragra, Peru. This was a fantastic ore deposit, from which nearly a dozen minerals new to science have been described. Hewett's skill as a chemist enabled him to recognize that the minerals of the ore body, though previously unknown, were rich in vanadium.* The world supplies of vanadium had previously been insufficient to justify any of the steel manufacturers venturing into the commercial production of vanadium steel, though its superiority for many uses had been recognized. Hewett realized, after mapping the surface ore, that he had before him a probable ore body that might revolutionize the steel industry, as indeed it has. He reported his findings to his principals in Pittsburgh, urging their immediate consideration. They had enough confidence in the judgment of this twenty-five-year-old engineer to act immediately on his recommendations. Their long-term reward was many millions of profits.

During these exciting and broadening experiences, Hewett became more and more convinced of the need for applying detailed geologic studies to the search for ores in a much more intensive way than was usual at the time. He decided, therefore, to undertake graduate studies in geology. In 1909 he enrolled in the Yale Graduate School to study with his old friend and counselor, Joseph Barrell. Although Hewett had originally planned to remain for only one year, a gift from the now prosperous Vanadium Corporation of America in acknowledgment of his work at Mina Ragra enabled him to finance a second year and thus to complete the residence requirements for the doctorate. His thesis and the award of the degree were delayed, however, until 1924.

The appeal of the scientific aspects of economic geology was so great that Hewett was now more attracted to the research

* Of the new minerals found at Mina Ragra, hewettite and metahewettite were named in his honor.

program of the United States Geological Survey than to the more directly economic work he had hitherto carried on. Accordingly in the spring of 1911 he took the three-day examination then required for a Civil Service appointment. He attained a high score and entered on duty as a Junior Geologist in the Geological Survey on June 1, 1911. Except for two brief periods of leave, he was to continue in the Survey until his death, more than fifty-nine years later.

Hewett's first assignment was to the coal fields of the Big Horn Basin of Wyoming, in association with C. T. Lupton. He quickly made significant contributions to the stratigraphy of the region and discovered the Heart Mountain thrust, still one of the most interesting and provocative structural features in the United States. He also discovered, and demonstrated convincingly, that bentonite, so widely distributed in the Cretaceous strata of the West, is an alteration product of volcanic ash. His elucidation of the systematic tilting of the anticlines of the Big Horn Basin was later of considerable value to the petroleum producers of the region. Few two-year field projects have produced so much.

Later assignments were to Oklahoma for studies of petroleum and manganese—the beginning of his lifelong interest in manganese minerals and their origin; to Oregon, where he studied the gold deposits of the Blue Mountains in conjunction with Joseph T. Pardee; to Cuba, for studies of manganese and iron. After nearly ten years of such miscellaneous assignments, Hewett entered upon his most productive mapping program, the study of the geology and ore deposition of the southern Great Basin. Though often interrupted by other duties, this project, under various titles, was to occupy him as long as he could do strenuous fieldwork; his other main scientific interest, the study of the emplacement of manganese, could be pursued even after arduous fieldwork was no longer possible.

Hewett began his Great Basin work in the Goodsprings mining district, in southern Nevada. Goodsprings was not and never has been a major mining area, but it became famous after Hewett, in 1924, announced the discovery there of the close association of dolomitization with the deposition of lead and zinc ores; an association that, soon recognized, was used the world over as a guide to such ore deposits. Most of the leading petrologists of the early twenties were agreed that magnesium is an element early fixed in magmatic rocks and that it could have little association with the more soluble and readily mobilized elements of ore deposits such as those of lead and zinc. Hewett's careful mapping and detailed observations in Nevada showed this viewpoint to be entirely wrong. In a few weeks in 1926 he showed that some of the classic ore districts of Europe (in Sicily, northern Italy, and Poland) were similarly encased in hydrothermal dolomite like that at Goodsprings. But he likewise showed that this association is by no means universal; the famous mines of Laurium have no such dolomitic mantles. As with most geologic phenomena, a common association is not necessarily an invariable one.

Goodsprings was also the scene of Hewett's recognition of the large thrust faults that characterize the southern Great Basin. He recognized that, while some of the thrusts were of Tertiary age, many were older. When he completed the Goodsprings study he expanded his fieldwork to include the much larger area of the Ivanpah Quadrangle. Here he demonstrated the continuity of a great section of Precambrian rocks in complete conformity with the overlying Paleozoic rocks—one of the few places in the world where the Cambrian–Precambrian boundary does not record a break.

Hewett's other main geological interest was the study of manganese mineralogy and ore deposition, a field in which he came generally to be recognized as the world leader. His interest in this subject began early, but was strengthened almost to the point of total absorption by his assignment during World War I to the evaluation of manganese deposits within the United States. This study was necessitated by the submarine campaign that threatened to cut off our normal imports from South Africa and Brazil. During the next two decades he personally visited virtually every significant deposit of manganese minerals in the United States.

Hewett's breadth and tact caused his assignment to many delicate intragovernmental tasks. Perhaps the most interesting was his study, along with Geoffrey Crickmay of the Georgia State Geological Survey, of the hydrology of the Warm Springs of Georgia, famous for their supposedly therapeutic effects in the treatment of poliomyelitis. President Franklin D. Roosevelt, although a self-admitted layman, was thoroughly convinced of the value of the springs and strongly urged a complete study, which he thought would show some peculiarity of the water to account for its supposed helpful qualities. The careful two-year study by Hewett and Crickmay revealed that the springs were not unusual in any way, except for their slightly higher than normal temperature; their volume was precisely what would be expected from deep circulation of the normal rainfall tributary to the watershed; the chemical composion, density, and gaseous content precisely what would be expected of the groundwater of the region. An amusing element in this study was that a German "expert" on therapeutic spas, one Dr. Paul Haertl, Managing Director of Bad-Kissingen, who had been brought over to advise on the development of both Saratoga Hot Springs in New York and Warm Springs, Georgia, insisted that the value of these springs largely depended on the fact that the gas bubbles contained were cubical rather than spherical and thus more stimulating to the skin! With this sort of advice to the authorities of the Warm Springs Foundation, it can be readily understood that Hewett had to walk warily; he did so, and though his report must clearly have been disappointing to the enthusiasts operating the resort, it was never challenged.

Hewett was made Chief of the Section of Metalliferous Geology of the Geological Survey in 1935 and continued in this position until 1944. Although this administrative position seriously interfered with his scientific work, it was of utmost value to the country during World War II. Hewett was a man of great foresight and was thoroughly familiar with a broad spectrum of mineral affairs. From his experience in World War I he early saw the threat of a wartime cutoff of many mineral products of which this nation has an insufficient supply. There can be little doubt that he was one of the dozen or so men best informed as to the mineral industry who by dint of constant pressure finally persuaded the administration to prepare for the war by building up supplies of "strategic minerals"—minerals whose domestic production is too low to support the needs of industry. He was able to get some support for this program as early as 1938, but full recognition of the crisis and the development of a strong Strategic Minerals Program did not begin until 1940.

Hewett recruited a staff of mostly young geologists until it was large enough to evaluate to some degree nearly every mineral showing of possible value in the country. Before the war ended the nation was producing from many small deposits and a few large ones most of the minerals in short supply. Notable progress was made, for example, in the production of tungsten, mercury, manganese, quartz crystals, mica, and bauxite, though in none of these was the country ever fully self-sufficient. Had it not been for Hewett's success in arousing the administration and the mineral industry to the potential crisis, the country's war effort would have been far more severely handicapped than it was.

After the war Hewett was relieved of his administrative duties and made "Special Scientist," in which position he was free to choose the area of research he would follow. He transferred from Washington, D.C., to Pasadena, California, where the California Institute of Technology offered him laboratory space, and from this base he returned to his studies of the mineral deposits and tectonics of the Nevada–California border region.

In 1949 Foster made a second discovery of a unique mineral deposit. He was the first to recognize the great deposit of rare earth elements at Mountain Pass, California. Here he identified and established the abundance of the mineral bastnäsite, a mineral elsewhere rare, but here in sufficient concentration and tonnage to constitute an ore. Hewett's skill in chemistry and mineralogy was dramatically demonstrated for the second time— and at an age approaching that of full retirement for most men.

But in 1951, when Foster reached the statutory retirement age, an unsolicited executive order returned him to active duty without terminal date; Foster was able to continue for many years his productive scientific career. When he was no longer able to do strenuous fieldwork, he continued his laboratory studies of manganese mineralogy, shifting his headquarters to the Menlo Park, California, office of the Geological Survey, where the support of many specialists was available to him. Here he worked until a few weeks before his death, a record of production few men of eighty-nine attain.

Hewett's foresight, already remarked on, extended to private matters. For example, he was one of the few who recognized, during the late twenties, that the paper prosperity of Wall Street was basically unsound. He sold his modest holdings of stocks in late 1928, knowing that prices had not yet peaked, and put the money into government bonds, then selling at very considerable discounts. In 1934, after the collapse of the market, he sold the bonds, then at par, and bought "blue-chip" stocks at the prevailing low prices. Few others were as farseeing.

His foresight was not so evident when he was behind the wheel of an automobile. Here he would become so interested in the passing scene or in some topic of conversation that he would often have narrow misses. Some of his passengers would, as one remarked, start a trip as bare acquaintances and after an hour's drive find themselves in each other's arms! While he never had a severe accident, Foster's passengers had many a thrill they would rather have gone without.

Foster was a man of medium height, broad-shouldered and appearing squat. His energy, so well displayed in his work, was evident in his every move. He walked with springy stride until he was past eighty, and his conversation was both quick and thoughtful. An interesting and stimulating companion, he had almost complete recall of events many years in the past and a fund of current information that was truly astounding.

Hewett was married in January 1909 to Mary Amelia Hamilton, of New Castle, Pennsylvania, his companion in the field and at home for more than sixty-two years, who survived him by less than a year. Mary Hewett was a delightful reader; one of the most pleasant occasions for their friends was to be included in a small group in the Hewett home for an evening of reading and discussion. Mary would read—usually political or philosophical works—and all were free at any time to interrupt either to agree or to disagree with the author. Sometimes the reading would stop for an hour as one listener after another had his or her comments to make. Foster's were always among the most thoughtful.

Although the Hewetts were childless, they became literally "foster" parents to a host of junior associates—secretaries, clerks, aspiring young geologists and their wives—whoever was privileged to work in close association with Foster. Later they took much satisfaction in aiding needy students in half a dozen colleges and universities; no one knows how many.

In any company Foster Hewett was a leader. His impress on the work of the Geological Survey was surely greater than that of any of his contemporaries; the present prestige of the organization is in large part due to his foresight in the matter of strategic minerals and the sound basis he then established for a wide spectrum of work. Few men have made so great a contribution to a scientific or governmental enterprise.

HONORS AND DISTINCTIONS

PROFESSIONAL SOCIETIES AND OTHER MEMBERSHIPS

Fellow, Geological Society of America (Councillor, 1931–1933; Vice President, 1935, 1945)
Fellow, Mineralogical Society of America
Society of Economic Geologists (Vice President, 1931; President, 1936)
American Chemical Society
National Academy of Sciences, elected 1937
American Academy of Arts and Sciences
American Institute of Mining, Metallurgical and Petroleum Engineers
American Association for the Advancement of Science
Tau Beta Pi
Sigma Xi
Phi Beta Kappa

AWARDS AND MEDALS

Distinguished Service Medal, United States Department of the Interior, 1952
Award, American Academy of Achievement, 1965
Honorary Doctor of Science, Lehigh University, 1942
Penrose Gold Medal, Society of Economic Geologists, 1956
Penrose Medal, Geological Society of America, 1964
Research Associate, California Institute of Technology, 1947–1954
Research Associate, Stanford University, 1957–1971

BIBLIOGRAPHY

KEY TO ABBREVIATIONS

Am. J. Sci. = American Journal of Science
Am. Mineralogist = American Mineralogist
Calif. Dept. Nat. Res. Div. Mines Bull. = California Department of Natural Resources, Division of Mines Bulletin
Econ. Geol. = Economic Geology
Eng. Mining J. Press = Engineering and Mining Journal Press
J. Wash. Acad. Sci. = Journal of the Washington Academy of Sciences
U.S. Geol. Surv. Bull. = United States Department of the Interior, Geological Survey, Bulletin
U.S. Geol. Surv. Mineral Res. of the U.S. = United States Department of the Interior, Geological Survey, Mineral Resources of the United States
U.S. Geol. Surv. Profess. Pap. = United States Department of the Interior, Geological Survey, Professional Papers

1912

A graphic method for dips on geologic sections. Econ. Geol., 7: 190–91.

1913

Sulphur deposits of the Sunlight Basin, Wyoming. U.S. Geol. Surv. Bull., No. 530, pp. 350–62.
Manganese and manganiferous ores. U.S. Geol. Surv. Mineral Res. of the U.S., 1912, Part 1, pp. 203–21.

1914

The ore deposits of Kirwin, Wyoming. U.S. Geol. Surv. Bull., No. 540, pp. 121–32.
Sulphur deposits in Park County, Wyoming. U.S. Geol. Surv. Bull., No. 540, pp. 477–80.
The Shoshone River section, Wyoming. U.S. Geol. Surv. Bull., No. 541, pp. 89–113.
With J. T. Pardee. Geology and mineral resources of the Sumpter Quadrangle, Oregon. Mineral Resources of Oregon, 1(6):3–128.

1916

Some manganese mines in Virginia and Maryland. U.S. Geol. Surv. Bull., No. 640, pp. 37–71.

1917

With C. T. Lupton. Anticlines in the Big Horn Basin, Wyoming. U.S. Geol. Surv. Bull., No. 656, 192 pp.

The origin of bentonite and the geologic range of related materials in the Big Horn Basin, Wyoming. J. Wash. Acad. Sci., 7:196–98.

Manganese. American Institute of Mining Engineers Bulletin, No. 129, pp. v–xiii.

1918

With others. Possibilities for manganese ore on certain undeveloped tracts in Shenandoah Valley, Virginia. U.S. Geol. Surv. Bull., No. 660, pp. 271–96.

1919

Manganese and manganiferous ores in 1917. U.S. Geol. Surv. Mineral Res. of the U.S., 1917, Part 1, pp. 665–96.

1920

The Heart Mountain overthrust, Wyoming. Journal of Geology, 28:536–57.

Manganese and manganiferous ores in 1918. U.S. Geol. Surv. Mineral Res. of the U.S., 1918, Part 1, pp. 607–56.

Measurements of folded beds. Econ. Geol., 15:367–85.

1921

With E. V. Shannon. Orientite, a new hydrous silicate of manganese and calcium from Cuba. Am. J. Sci., 1:491–506.

Manganese deposits near Bromide, Oklahoma. U.S. Geol. Surv. Bull., No. 725, pp. 311–29.

1923

Carnotite in southern Nevada. Eng. Mining J. Press, 115:232–35.

1924

Deposits of magnesia alum near Fallon, Nevada. U.S. Geol. Surv. Bull., No. 750, pp. 79–86.

1925

With W. T. Schaller. Hisingerite from Blaine County, Idaho. Am. J. Sci., 10:29–38.

Carnotite discovered near Aguila, Arizona. Eng. Mining J. Press, 120:19.

1926

Geology and oil and coal resources of the Oregon Basin, Meeteetse, and Grass Creek Basin quadrangles, Wyoming. U.S. Geol. Surv. Profess. Pap., No. 145, 111 pp.

1927

Late Tertiary thrust faults in the Mojave Desert, California. Proceedings of the National Academy of Sciences, 14:7–12.

1928

A manganese deposit of Pleistocene age in Bannock County, Idaho. U.S. Geol. Surv. Bull., No. 795, pp. 211–18.
Two Tertiary epochs of thrust faulting in the Mojave Desert, California. Bulletin of the Geological Society of America, 39:178–79.
With E. V. Shannon and F. A. Gonyer. Zeolites from Ritter Hot Spring, Grant County, Oregon. Proceedings of the U.S. National Museum, Vol. 73, Article 16, 18 pp.
Dolomitization and ore deposition. Econ. Geol., 23:821–63.

1929

Cycles in metal production. American Institute of Mining and Metallurgical Engineers Technical Publication, No. 183, 31 pp.

1930

With O. N. Rove. Occurrence and relations of alabandite. Econ. Geol., 25:35–56.
Genesis of iron–manganese carbonate concretions in central South Dakota. J. Wash. Acad. Sci., 20:243.

1931

Geology and ore deposits of the Goodsprings Quadrangle, Nevada. U.S. Geol. Surv. Profess. Pap., No. 162, 172 pp.
Zonal relations of the lodes of the Sumpter Quadrangle, eastern Oregon. American Institute of Mining and Metallurgical Engineers Transactions for 1931, pp. 305–46.
With B. N. Webber. Bedded deposits of manganese oxides near Las Vegas, Nevada. Nevada University Bulletin, Vol. 25, No. 6, 17 pp.

1932

Manganese sediments. In: *Treatise on Sedimentation,* by W. H. Twenhofel and others, pp. 562–81. Baltimore, Williams & Wilkins Company.

1933

Sedimentary manganese deposits. In: *Ore Deposits of the Western States* (Lindgren Volume), pp. 488–91. New York, American Institute of Mining & Metallurgical Engineers.

With J. T. Pardee. Manganese in western hydrothermal ore deposits. In: *Ore Deposits of the Western States* (Lindgren Volume), pp. 671–82. New York, American Institute of Mining & Metallurgical Engineers.

1936

With others. Mineral resources of the region around Boulder Dam. U.S. Geol. Surv. Bull., No. 871, 197 pp.

1937

With G. W. Crickmay. The Warm Springs of Georgia, their geologic relations and origin. United States Geological Survey Water-Supply Paper, No. 819, 40 pp.

With W. T. Schaller. Braunite from Mason County, Texas. Am. Mineralogist, 22:785–89.

Helvite from the Butte district, Montana. Am. Mineralogist, 22: 803–4.

1938

With H. D. Miser. The unweathered manganese deposits of the Batesville district, Arkansas. Econ. Geol., 32:1069.

1948

Iron deposits of the Kingston Range, San Bernardino County, California. Calif. Dept. Nat. Res. Div. Mines Bull., No. 129: Iron Resources of California, Part M, pp. 195–206.

1953

With J. J. Glass. Two uranium-bearing pegmatite bodies in San Bernardino County, California. Am. Mineralogist, 38:1040–50.

1954

General geology of the Mojave Desert region, California. Calif. Dept. Nat. Res. Div. Mines Bull., No. 170: Geology of Southern California, ed. by R. H. Jahns, Chapter 2, pp. 5–20.

A fault map of the Mojave Desert region, California. Calif. Dept. Nat. Res. Div. Mines Bull., No. 170: Geology of Southern California, ed. by R. H. Jahns, Chapter 4, pp. 15–18.

1955

Structural features of the Mojave Desert region, California. In: *Crust of the Earth*, ed. by A. Poldervaart, pp. 377–90. Geological Society of America Special Paper No. 62. (Symposium)

1956

Geology and mineral resources of the Ivanpah Quadrangle, California and Nevada. U.S. Geol. Surv. Profess. Pap., No. 275, 172 pp.

With others. Manganese deposits of the United States. In: *Symposium sobre yacimientos de manganeso*, ed. by J. Enaro González Reyna, Tome 3, pp. 169–75. 20th International Geological Congress, Mexico.

1960

With M. Fleischer. Deposits of the manganese oxides. Econ. Geol., 55:1–55.

1961

With others. Tephroite in California manganese deposits. Econ. Geol., 56:39–58.

1963

Manganese is a clue to deep base and precious metals. Mining World, 25:26–28.

With others. Deposits of the manganese oxides—supplement. Econ. Geol., 58:1–51.

1964

Veins of hypogene manganese oxide minerals in the southwestern United States. Econ. Geol., 59:1429–72.

1965

With others. Black calcite—a source of silver? Mining Congress Journal, 51:78.

1966

Stratified deposits of the oxides and carbonates of manganese. Econ. Geol., 61:431–61.

1967

With A. S. Radke. Silver-bearing black calcite in western mining districts. Econ. Geol., 62:1–21.
With others. Aurorite, argentian todorokite, and hydrous silver-bearing lead manganese oxide. Econ. Geol., 62:186–206.

1968

Silver in veins of hypogene manganese oxides. United States Geological Survey Circular, No. 553, 9 pp.

1969

With others. Hypogene veins of gibbsite, pyrolusite, and lithiophorite in Nye County, Nevada. Econ. Geol., 63:360–71.
With others. The ages of three uranium minerals, Mojave Desert, California. U.S. Geol. Surv. Profess. Pap., No. 650-B, pp. B84–B88.

1971

Coronadite—modes of occurrence and origin. Econ. Geol., 66:164–77.

1972

Manganite, housmannite, braunite: features, modes of origin. Econ. Geol., 67:103–110.

1954

General geology of the Mojave Desert region, California. Calif. Dept. Nat. Res. Div. Mines Bull., No. 170: Geology of Southern California, ed. by R. H. Jahns, Chapter 2, pp. 5–20.

A fault map of the Mojave Desert region, California. Calif. Dept. Nat. Res. Div. Mines Bull., No. 170: Geology of Southern California, ed. by R. H. Jahns, Chapter 4, pp. 15–18.

1955

Structural features of the Mojave Desert region, California. In: *Crust of the Earth,* ed. by A. Poldervaart, pp. 377–90. Geological Society of America Special Paper No. 62. (Symposium)

1956

Geology and mineral resources of the Ivanpah Quadrangle, California and Nevada. U.S. Geol. Surv. Profess. Pap., No. 275, 172 pp.

With others. Manganese deposits of the United States. In: *Symposium sobre yacimientos de manganeso,* ed. by J. Enaro González Reyna, Tome 3, pp. 169–75. 20th International Geological Congress, Mexico.

1960

With M. Fleischer. Deposits of the manganese oxides. Econ. Geol., 55:1–55.

1961

With others. Tephroite in California manganese deposits. Econ. Geol., 56:39–58.

1963

Manganese is a clue to deep base and precious metals. Mining World, 25:26–28.

With others. Deposits of the manganese oxides—supplement. Econ. Geol., 58:1–51.

1964

Veins of hypogene manganese oxide minerals in the southwestern United States. Econ. Geol., 59:1429–72.

1965

With others. Black calcite—a source of silver? Mining Congress Journal, 51:78.

1966

Stratified deposits of the oxides and carbonates of manganese. Econ. Geol., 61:431–61.

1967

With A. S. Radke. Silver-bearing black calcite in western mining districts. Econ. Geol., 62:1–21.
With others. Aurorite, argentian todorokite, and hydrous silver-bearing lead manganese oxide. Econ. Geol., 62:186–206.

1968

Silver in veins of hypogene manganese oxides. United States Geological Survey Circular, No. 553, 9 pp.

1969

With others. Hypogene veins of gibbsite, pyrolusite, and lithiophorite in Nye County, Nevada. Econ. Geol., 63:360–71.
With others. The ages of three uranium minerals, Mojave Desert, California. U.S. Geol. Surv. Profess. Pap., No. 650-B, pp. B84–B88.

1971

Coronadite—modes of occurrence and origin. Econ. Geol., 66:164–77.

1972

Manganite, housmannite, braunite: features, modes of origin. Econ. Geol., 67:103–110.

WILLIAM VERMILLION HOUSTON

January 19, 1900–August 22, 1968

BY KENNETH S. PITZER AND
HAROLD E. RORSCHACH, JR.

WILLIAM VERMILLION HOUSTON was an outstanding physicist who made major contributions to spectroscopy and solid-state physics. He was also an outstanding teacher and administrator who held positions of the highest responsibility in higher education, in scientific societies, and in governmental organizations.

Houston was born in Mount Gilead, Ohio, on January 19, 1900. His father was a Presbyterian minister, and he was brought up in an atmosphere that encouraged intellectual work. He attended elementary and secondary school in Columbus and obtained his baccalaureate degree in physics from The Ohio State University. He began his teaching career at the University of Dubuque, but after one year became convinced that his knowledge of physics was extremely limited. He entered the graduate school at the University of Chicago, where he obtained a master's degree, having taken courses with R. A. Millikan and A. A. Michelson. The stimulation of Millikan, with his enthusiasm for physics, and of Michelson, with his precision and attention to detail, was to have a strong influence on Houston's career. It was also at this time that he began his experimental work on the fine structure of hydrogen that led later to the discovery at Caltech of the anomalies in the spectra, which were eventually associated with quantum electrodynamic effects and measured precisely by W. E. Lamb and R. C. Retherford. Houston returned to Ohio State for his Ph.D. degree, which he received in 1925 for work in spectroscopy under the direction of Professor A. D. Cole.

Houston now went to the California Institute of Technology on a National Research Fellowship, largely because of Millikan, who had left Chicago for Caltech in 1922. There he began a career of teaching and research that would form the pattern for the rest of his life. At Caltech he continued his work on spectroscopy, making important improvements in the Fabry–Perot interferometer. For some ten years he continued a series of improvements in accuracy—from observing the well-known doublet, found many years earlier by Michelson, through slight disagreement with the Sommerfeld theory in the direction of the spinning-electron theory of G. E. Uhlenbeck and S. A. Goudsmit, and then from further minor disagreements with that theory to the interpretation by S. Pasternak in terms of a displaced s level, and the final interpretation in the work of Lamb and Retherford. Early in his career at Caltech, Houston taught a course from A. Sommerfeld's *Atombau und Spektrallinen.*

The award to Houston of a Guggenheim Fellowship in 1927 was naturally seized upon as an opportunity to go to Germany to study with Professor Sommerfeld. He had intended to study the theory of electron spin but was discouraged from this by Sommerfeld. Instead, Sommerfeld handed Houston the proof of his 1928 paper in which, following the lead of W. Pauli, he applied the Fermi statistics to phenomena in metals. He suggested that Houston look up the various treatments of the mean free path, because appropriate assumptions about the mean free path would give any necessary variation of resistance with temperature. It was in going over these proofs that Houston was led to the thought that one might take seriously the idea of the electron as a wave. He applied P. Debye's work on the thermal diffraction of x rays to a determination of the mean free path for electron waves and found a resistivity at high temperatures proportional to temperature. When Houston showed this work to Sommerfeld, they were both greatly pleased. Sommerfeld got up, paced back and forth across the room, and made a comment that Houston always remembered: "Die erste anständige Bearbeitung des Widerstandsgesetzes [the first decent treatment of the electrical resistance law]."

After spending the winter semester with Sommerfeld, Houston went to Leipzig to spend the spring with W. Heisenberg. Heisenberg suggested that he undertake the study of the spin-orbit interaction in two-electron spectra. Houston's work was successful, and he was able to show the transition from Russell-Saunders to j–j coupling in two-electron atoms and its influence on the Zeeman effect. He also followed with great interest Felix Bloch's work on the motion of an electron in a periodic potential, and they became close friends.

When he returned to Caltech, Houston took up again his experimental work on spectroscopy and continued his interest in the theory of electrons in atoms and solids. His precise measurements on the Zeeman effect resulted in a correction of ½ percent to the accepted value of e/m, and he gave great stimulation and impetus to R. T. Birge and J. W. M. Dumond to work up a consistent set of atomic constants with maximum precision. He made many other contributions to solid-state theory, among which were a treatment of the T^5 law for resistance at low temperature, a study of the surface photoeffect, and the first suggestion and analysis of the use of soft x rays to study the energy band structure of solids.

For many years at Caltech and later at Rice, Houston taught an introductory course on mathematical physics which was extremely effective and popular, not only among physics students but also with the more theoretically inclined chemists and engineers. The senior author of this memoir regarded it as one of the best-organized and best-presented courses in his entire experience.

During World War II, Houston's efforts were devoted to undersea warfare research, for which he was awarded the Navy Medal of Merit. The war years were especially long and strenuous, since Houston had supervisory responsibility for research pertaining to undersea warfare in a large number of institutions including installations at Harvard, San Diego, and Key West. Dr. Frank B. Jewett of the National Academy of Sciences persuaded Houston to enter undersea warfare work, not only because of his experience in physics but also because of his ability to stimulate others in the development of new ideas. Houston received the Medal of Merit ribbon, presented to him by the Secretary of the Navy for directing the building of the first homing missile and for supervising many of the scientific studies designed to improve the effectiveness of various weapons.

In 1946 Houston became the second president of Rice University, Houston, Texas. He served as president and professor of physics until 1961, and during this time he played a key role in the postwar expansion at Rice University and the establishment of new academic programs. These included the five-year program in engineering, in which students completed preparation in the humanities before taking specialized engineering courses; the lowering of the student:teacher ratio to 10:1; enlargement of the graduate school; and the creation of a closer relationship between students and faculty. The increase in the size and quality of the graduate program was perhaps his proudest achievement. The first year he was at Rice, one Ph.D. was graduated. The year he left, the number had grown to 35. He also initiated the development of a residential college system in the tradition of Oxford and Cambridge and more closely following the pattern at Yale, but adapted to the special needs of Rice.

Houston was a scientist, but he recognized the value of the humanities in a complete education, and the humanities program grew under his guidance. The aim of higher education, he said often, is to understand humanity as well as the material world.

After a serious illness in 1961, Houston retired as president of Rice, but he continued as professor of physics and devoted his full attention to teaching and to his graduate research students. He regained relatively good health and was very productive to the day of his death, which occurred in Edinburgh, Scotland, on August 22, 1968.

Houston received many honors that were tributes to his dedication to science, to his skill as a teacher, and to his ability to inspire others. Besides the fellowship of the Guggenheim Foundation for travel and study in Europe in 1927–1928, from 1925 to 1927 he held a National Research Council Fellowship at the California Institute of Technology.

He was elected a member of the National Academy of Sciences in 1943, and he served the Academy faithfully on important committees and on the Council (1959–1962).

He similarly served the American Physical Society in many important capacities culminating in its presidency in 1962.

He was a Fellow in the American Academy of Arts and Sciences and a member of the American Philosophical Society. By presidential appointment, he was a member of the board of the National Science Foundation for two terms and also served on the board of the Carnegie Foundation. He was granted the honorary degree of Doctor of Science by The Ohio State University in 1950 and the degree of Doctor of Laws by the University of California in 1956. He was a member of the Phi Beta Kappa Society and the Society of Sigma Xi.

Houston authored two books, *Principles of Mathematical Physics* and *Principles of Quantum Mechanics,* and over seventy scientific articles.

Rice University awarded him a medal of honor during its fiftieth anniversary celebration in 1962, and the Rice Alumni Association presented a Gold Medal Distinguished Service Award to him in 1967.

Houston was a serene man, never angry, good-natured, a man of dry, understated humor, and he made himself felt as a continuing influence for all that was kind and good in human relationships.

Houston married Mildred White in 1924, who survives him, as does one daughter, Mrs. Harold Coley of Houston, Texas, and a sister, Mrs. Burton Hollister, Glencoe, Illinois.

BIBLIOGRAPHY

KEY TO ABBREVIATIONS

Am. J. Phys. = American Journal of Physics
Am. Phys. Teacher = American Physics Teacher
Phys. Rev. = Physical Review
Phys. Today = Physics Today
Proc. Am. Phil. Soc. = Proceedings of the American Philosophical Society
Proc. Nat. Acad. Sci. = Proceedings of the National Academy of Sciences
Rice Inst. Pam. = Rice Institute Pamphlet
Z. Physik = Zeitschrift für Physik

1926

Fine structure and the wave lengths of the Balmer lines. Astrophysical Journal, 44:81–92.

Fine structure of the hydrogen lines. Nature, 117:590.

1927

A compound interferometer for fine structure work. Phys. Rev., 29:478–84.

A spectroscopic determination of e/m. Phys. Rev., 30:608–13.

The fine structure of the helium arc spectrum. Proc. Nat. Acad. Sci., 13:91–94.

1928

Die Elektronenemission kalter Metalle. Z. Physik, 47:33–37.

Elektrische Leitfahigkeit auf Grund der Wellenmechanik. Z. Physik, 48:449–68.

With George Moore. Transmission and reflection of gold and silver films. Journal of the Optical Society of America and Review of Scientific Instruments, 16:174–76.

1929

Some relationships between singlets and triplets in the spectra of two electron systems. Phys. Rev., 33:297–304.

Temperature dependence of electron emission under high fields. Phys. Rev., 33:361–63.

Temperature dependence of electric conductivity. Phys. Rev., 34:279–83.

1930

With L. D. Huff. Appearance of "forbidden lines" in spectra. Phys. Rev., 36:842–46.

1931

With C. M. Lewis. Rotational Raman spectrum of CO_2. Proc. Nat. Acad. Sci., 17:229–31.

Structure of soft x-ray lines. Phys. Rev., 38:1797–1801.

1932

With J. S. Campbell. New determination of e/m from the Zeeman effect. Phys. Rev., 39:601–15.

1933

With Charlton M. Lewis. Raman effect in ammonia and some other gases. Phys. Rev., 44:903–10.

1934

With L. E. Kinsler. The value of e/m from the Zeeman effect. Phys. Rev., 45:104–8.

With Y. M. Hsieh. The fine structure of the Balmer lines. Phys. Rev., 45:263–72.

With L. E. Kinsler. Zeeman effect in helium. Phys. Rev., 46:533–34. (L)

Principles of Mathematical Physics. New York, McGraw-Hill Book Co., Inc. xi + 265 pp. 2nd ed., xii + 363 pp. (1948).

The role of positrons and neutrons in modern physics. Am. Phys. Teacher, 2:53–62.

1935

The determination of e/m from the Zeeman effect. Zeeman Verhandelingen. The Hague, Martinus Nyhoff, N.V.

A nuclear model. Phys. Rev., 47:942–46.

1936

Higher education in science and engineering. In: *Journal of Proceedings and Addresses of the Thirty-eighth Annual Conference, Association of American Universities,* University of Texas, pp. 75–81. Chicago, University of Chicago Press.

1937

A new method of analysis of the structure of H_α and D_α. Phys. Rev., 51:446–49.
The viscosity of air. Phys. Rev., 52:751–57.
The surface photoelectric effect. Phys. Rev., 52:1047–53.
The philosophy of physics. Science, 85:413–19.
The physical content of quantum mechanics. Am. Phys. Teacher, 5:49–55.

1938

Resonance broadening of spectral lines. Phys. Rev., 54:884–88.

1939

Conservation of momentum in electrical conductivity. Phys. Rev., 55:1255–61.
Electrons in metals. Proc. Am. Phil. Soc., 81:525–32.
The laws of electromagnetic induction. Am. Phys. Teacher, 7:373–78.

1940

Acceleration of electrons in a crystal lattice. Phys. Rev., 57:184–86.
Nobel prize award in physics for 1939 to E. O. Lawrence. Scientific Monthly, 50:276–78.

1941

Electron theory of thermoelectric effects. Journal of Applied Physics, 12:519–29.

1945

Application of group theory to the normal vibrations of a cubic crystal. Rice Inst. Pam., 32:123–47.

1946

Trends of research in physics. Engineering and Science, 9:3, 16.
The influence of science on history. Rice Inst. Pam., 33:257–76.

1947

Can Engineering Be Taught in College? (Address delivered at Case Institute of Technology, July 2, 1947. Published independently.)

The electron. In: *Encyclopaedia Britannica*, Vol. 8, pp. 323–27. Chicago, Encyclopaedia Britannica, Inc.

1948

Lattice vibrations and specific heat of diamond. Zeitschrift für Naturforschung, 3a:607–11.
Normal vibrations of a crystal lattice. Reviews of Modern Physics, 20:161–65.

1949

With C. F. Squire. Electromagnetic induction in a superconductor. Phys. Rev., 76:685–86. (L)

1950

Electric and magnetic forces on superconductors. Proc. Am. Phil. Soc., 94:453–58.
With N. Muench. Electromagnetic forces on a superconductor. Phys. Rev., 79:967–70.
Physics for adventure. Phys. Today, 3 (6) :20–21.

1951

On the spirit of physics. Phys. Today, 4 (2) :9–10.
Principles of Quantum Mechanics. New York, McGraw-Hill Book Co., Inc. vii + 288 pp.

1952

Description of the physical world. In: *The Scientist Looks at His World*, pp. 5–32. Philadelphia, University of Pennsylvania Press.
With R. H. Pry and A. L. Lathrop. Gyromagnetic effect in a superconductor. Phys. Rev., 86:905–7.
Temperature dependence of electrical resistance. Phys. Rev., 88:1321–23.
Theory and practice in engineering. Phys. Today, 5 (9) :4–5.

1954

Robert Andrews Millikan. In: *The American Philosophical Society Year Book*, pp. 440–44. Philadelphia, The American Philosophical Society.

1955

Philosophy in the twentieth century. Proceedings of the Philosophical Society of Texas, 20:7–15.
With H. E. Rorschach. Motion of nuclei in liquid helium. Phys. Rev., 100:1003–7.
Physics in engineering. Am. J. Phys., 23:610–14.

1956

Objectives of engineering education. Journal of Petroleum Technology, 8:12–14, January.

1960

Waves and Particles. Columbus, Ohio State University Press. 18 pp. (First Annual Alpheus W. Smith Lecture.)
Electrons and nuclei in ideal crystals. In: *Modern Physics for the Engineer,* by L. N. Ridenour and W. A. Nierenberg, pp. 83–107. New York, McGraw-Hill Book Co., Inc.

1963

Some observations on the theory of electrons and atomic nuclei in solids. Phys. Today, 16:26–36.

1966

With D. R. Smith. Mechanical forces on a superconducting film. Physical Review Letters, 16:B552 1-2 and 2-2.
Are electrons real? Am. J. Phys., 34:351–57.
Particles and fields in physics. The Physics Teacher, 4:158–60.

1967

With D. R. Smith. Motion of magnetic flux in superconducting strips. Phys. Rev., 163:431–34.

HOWARD BISHOP LEWIS

November 8, 1887– March 7, 1954

BY WILLIAM C. ROSE AND MINOR J. COON

Howard bishop lewis died in Ann Arbor, Michigan, on March 7, 1954, after a prolonged illness. Thus ended the career of a dedicated and talented teacher, and a sound and skillful investigator. For thirty-two years he had served the University of Michigan with distinction as head of the Department of Biological Chemistry in the School of Medicine. In 1947, the University, in appreciation of his remarkable services and national reputation, conferred upon him a distinguished professorship entitled the John Jacob Abel University Professorship in Biological Chemistry. In addition to his departmental duties, Lewis was director of the College of Pharmacy from 1933 to 1947.

Lewis was born on a farm near Southington, Connecticut, on November 8, 1887, the son of Frederick A. and Charlotte R. (Parmelee) Lewis. Little information is available concerning his early life; he left no record of his boyhood, nor of the influences that motivated him in pursuing a scientific career. However, his scholarly temperament was revealed even before he entered college. Prior to his sixteenth birthday, he graduated from high school as valedictorian of his class. He had a special interest in the classics. During the year of waiting to meet the age requirement for admission to Yale, he mastered, by self-instruction, a two-year course in high school Greek. At Yale, he won the

Chamberlain Prize for the best entrance examination in the Greek language.

Lewis entered the freshman class of Yale College in 1904 and was awarded the Bachelor of Arts degree four years later. The record shows that his devotion to Greek and Latin persisted, though he graduated "with honors in physical sciences." He stood fourth in a class of three hundred and eighty. During his college years he was the recipient of prizes in Latin composition, chemistry, and calculus.

Most of the two years immediately following his graduation (1908–1910) was occupied in teaching at Hampton Institute, Hampton, Virginia, and at the Centenary Collegiate Institute, Hackettstown, New Jersey. During half of the second year, he began graduate study in chemistry at George Washington University. Apparently, Dr. Isaac K. Phelps, onetime member of the chemistry faculty at this institution, played an important role in encouraging Lewis to pursue his training in biochemistry. He, like Lewis, was a Yale graduate and a native son of Connecticut, and seems to have regarded biochemistry, a relatively new branch of chemistry at the time, as a particularly inviting field for a young scientist.

Lewis entered the Graduate School of Yale University in the fall of 1910. His program of training was directed by Professor Lafayette B. Mendel, a man of remarkable charm, pedagogic skill, and research acumen. During his last two years at Yale, Lewis served as Professor Mendel's laboratory assistant. He was awarded the degree of Doctor of Philosophy in 1913.

During much of his college career Lewis found it necessary to finance his training by tutoring and other extracurricular activities. During one summer, Professor Mendel obtained employment for him in the laboratories of the Connecticut State Hospital at Middletown. This was not an unusual experience for financially needy students in Mendel's laboratory. Several in turn were privileged to engage in such employment. The position paid a small stipend in addition to room and board. More importantly, it afforded an opportunity for the student to acquire valuable experience in clinical laboratory techniques, while leaving sufficient time for him to exercise his originality in the pursuit of an independent research project. Lewis used the occasion to study the nature of the antigen in the Wasserman reaction.

Following the completion of his training for the doctorate, Lewis accepted an instructorship in physiological chemistry in the School of Medicine of the University of Pennsylvania. He held this position for two years (1913–1915). Sometime during the latter year, he was invited to assume responsibility for the teaching and research programs of the Division of Physiological Chemistry * in the Chemistry Department of the University of Illinois. He accepted this challenge and began his new duties on the Urbana campus in the fall of 1915. There, single-handedly, except for the modicum of help received from a part-time student assistant, he organized and taught a general course in physiological chemistry and three graduate courses dealing with special topics. In addition, he attracted a number of students to work toward advanced degrees under his direction.

Between the Pennsylvania and Illinois assignments, Lewis married Mildred Lois Eaton, daughter of the late Dr. Edward Dwight Eaton, President of Beloit College from 1886 to 1917. She passed away in 1961. Two daughters, Charlotte Barber and Elizabeth Parmelee, survive.

Lewis remained at the University of Illinois until 1922, when he was called to head the Department of Physiological Chemistry † at the University of Michigan. There he continued to display his genius as a teacher, as an investigator, and as an administrator. But his influence did not stop at the borders of the campus. His wide knowledge of medical sciences and

---

* The name was later changed to the Division of Biochemistry.
† The name was later changed to the Department of Biological Chemistry.

medical education led many outside organizations to seek his services. For fifteen years he was a member of the National Board of Medical Examiners, a position which required an incredible amount of arduous labor. From 1936 until his final illness he was a member of the Council on Foods and Nutrition of the American Medical Association. From 1945 to 1948, he was a member of the Division of Medical Sciences of the National Research Council, and for five years he was chairman of the Michigan Nutrition Council.

As for organizations more closely associated with his specialty, Lewis was intimately involved in the activities of the American Institute of Nutrition as a councilor (1941–1942), vice president (1942–1943), and president (1943–1944). During the long period in which the American Society of Biological Chemists had no paid officials, Lewis, with rare skill and efficiency, performed the laborious task of being its secretary (1929–1933). Subsequently, he was elected to the offices of vice president (1933–1935), president (1935–1937), and councilor (1937–1940 and 1941–1942) of the Society. One of his greatest contributions to science was the dedicated manner in which, for many years, he managed the Placement Service of the Federation of American Societies for Experimental Biology. With a minimal allowance for secretarial help, he brought together many young scientists seeking employment and institutions seeking personnel. Partly because of these services, and partly because of his love of people, Howard Lewis probably knew personally more biochemists and related scientists than any other individual in this country.

At various times in his busy career, Lewis was a member of the editorial boards of five periodicals, namely, the *Journal of Biological Chemistry*, the *Journal of Nutrition*, *Chemical Reviews*, *Physiological Reviews*, and the *Proceedings of the Society for Experimental Biology and Medicine*. On several occasions he was honored by being chosen to deliver special lectures. In

1932, he was the Beaumont Lecturer of the Wayne County Medical Society; in 1941, he was Lecturer of the Harvey Society of New York; and in 1948, he was the Henry Russel Lecturer of the Research Club of the University of Michigan.

Membership in professional societies, other than those already mentioned, included the American Chemical Society, the American Physiological Society, the American Pharmaceutical Association, the American Association for the Advancement of Science (fellow), the Society for Experimental Biology and Medicine, and the American Medical Association (associate). In 1949 he was elected a member of the National Academy of Sciences. A review of Lewis's many outside activities leads one to wonder how he could have accomplished so much while successfully carrying the full-time responsibilities of a large and active department.

Despite his many professional duties, Lewis always seemed to find time for healthful recreation. He loved the out-of-doors. Whether his mood at the moment called for a game of tennis or a long walk in the country, he pursued the pastime with zeal and alacrity. One of his favorite hobbies was gardening. He seemed to take special delight in seeing plants grow. Perhaps this was an echo of earlier experiences as a boy on a Connecticut farm. He was an expert bridge player; and not the least important of his hobbies was his lifelong interest in philately. His knowledge of stamps is said to have amazed all who heard him talk about them. He lectured frequently to interested groups on such topics as "Pioneers in Philately"; "The Literature of Philately"; "The One Penny Black"; and "Some Early Charity Stamps." Sometimes the lectures were illustrated with slides. On one occasion he spoke on "Philately and Medicine" before the Detroit Academy of Surgeons. The next day, one of the physicians in the audience, who also was a Regent of the University, wrote in part as follows: "Your talk last night was a masterpiece. . . . I was actually thrilled. . . . It was an extremely interesting evening . . . such a refreshing, and altogether unusual evening."

Howard's knowledge and appreciation of music continued and grew throughout his career. As a young instructor in Philadelphia, he enjoyed the symphonies, the operas, and the other musical entertainments afforded by the city. One of his associates of that period describes this quality of Howard's character as follows:

"These were the years when grand opera was being first brought to Philadelphia. Our chief, Alonzo E. Taylor, as well as the rest of the laboratory family, were all enthusiastic devotees—Howard in particular. Assembling in the laboratory a morning after an evening of opera we were plunged immediately into a vigorous discussion of the opera in some detail. Howard had an amazing memory of all the plots and in particular of the musical themes in each. I relished these occasions, for my previous laboratory contacts had suggested that art and chemistry should not be too intimately mixed." *

Later, music became a common interest of the Lewis family. Each member, except Howard, acquired a proficiency in the use of one or more instruments. Thus a trio could be assembled and a delightful concert rendered at a moment's notice. Many happy hours were spent in this way, to the edification, not only of the instrumentalists themselves, but of their many friends who were privileged to hear the concerts.

Perhaps the secret of Howard Lewis's success in so many areas of human endeavor is to be found, not only in his inherent native ability, but also in the spirit which he displayed in the performance of every undertaking. Whether work or play was the object to which he was about to devote his seemingly inexhaustible store of energy, he approached it with enthusiasm and zest, as though its doing was a new adventure never before experienced. He gave his very best to every enterprise. Not only was he a hard worker; he was a hard player as well.

---

* From a letter to Mrs. Lewis from the late Dr. Wm. H. Adolph.

During the forty-one years of his professional career, Lewis participated in the training of many students. Sixty-six received the Doctor of Philosophy degree under his direction, and many others were awarded the Master of Science degree. As to undergraduates, one may conservatively estimate that in excess of five thousand were privileged to take one or more of his formal courses. The effect these trainees have had, and will continue to have, upon biochemical and medical progress is incalculable. In truth, Lewis's influence "marches on."

In research, Lewis displayed both originality and ingenuity. With the collaboration of his students and colleagues, he published an impressive list of scientific articles covering a broad range of topics and requiring the application of a multiplicity of technical skills in the successful elucidation of the topics covered. During the early years of his career, he became interested in the *in vivo* formation of hippuric acid following the administration of benzoic acid. He returned to this problem from time to time as new aspects of the conjugation occurred to him. He observed in man that, after doses of 6 to 10 g of sodium benzoate, the elimination of hippuric acid takes place rapidly, 85 to 90 percent of the theoretical yield being recovered in the urine within a period of five to six hours. In these tests, the output of urea was diminished, indicating the probability that the nitrogen of the hippuric acid had its origin largely in nitrogen that normally is excreted in the form of urea. In later investigations, a quantitatively less important peculiarity was noted by the author in human subjects, for which he had no satisfactory explanation. This was a marked decrease (50 to 70 percent) in the output of uric acid during the first four hours after administering the sodium benzoate, as compared with the excretion during the corresponding periods of the fore and after days.

Most of Lewis's experiments on the metabolic fate of benzoate were conducted on rabbits. The animals were maintained exclusively on a diet of milk, which has a very low glycine content. Despite the fact that this procedure largely deprived the subjects of exogenous glycine, the total amount of hippuric acid formed from a given dose of benzoate was not significantly diminished. Furthermore, even large doses of benzoate did not induce a noticeable increase in the output of total nitrogen. Thus the source of the glycine used in the conjugation is not to be found in an increased tissue decomposition. In a single experiment in which the bile was drained away from the intestine, the output of hippuric acid was not decreased. This appeared to exclude glycocholic acid as a significant source of the glycine. On the other hand, in all of the rabbit experiments, the distribution of nitrogen in the urine showed, as in the human subjects, a decrease in the output of urea. Evidently, in this species also, the nitrogen of the glycine used in the conjugation was derived from nitrogen that ordinarily is excreted as urea.

Studies of the *rate* of hippuric acid excretion afforded results of particular interest. The output during a six-hour period was greatly augmented when an abundant supply of glycine was given along with the benzoate. A similar, though less marked effect was induced by the simultaneous administration of DL-serine and benzoate. These results were interpreted by the author as indicating that serine can be rapidly converted into glycine for the purpose in question. Other amino acids and related compounds—alanine, cystine, leucine, aspartic acid, glycolic acid, glycolaldehyde, etc.—were found to be without effect upon the rate of synthesis of hippuric acid.

In other experiments, the administration of benzyl alcohol yielded hippuric acid at a rate only slightly less than that observed after the administration of an equivalent amount of sodium benzoate. Obviously, the alcohol is readily oxidized to the corresponding acid, at a rate which is at least as rapid as the conjugation of glycine and benzoate. That the liver may be the site of the conjugation was indicated when it was observed that animals poisoned with hydrazine, a substance known to exert detrimental effects upon the liver, excrete much less hippuric acid in a six-hour period than do normal animals receiving comparable doses of benzoate and glycine. Under these conditions, the diminished output of hippuric acid was shown not to be due to a slower rate of absorption of the components from the intestine, nor to an injurious effect of the hydrazine upon the kidneys.

Throughout his professional career, Lewis was much interested in the metabolic behavior of the physiologically important sulfur compounds, particularly the amino acids cystine and methionine. Among his many contributions to this topic, the following may be noted.

In extension of the observations of others, in which white rats were the experimental animals, Lewis found that cystine may be a limiting factor in the nutrition of dogs receiving a low protein diet. Thus the quality of a ration, as measured by its ability to maintain nitrogen equilibrium, may be enhanced by the addition of small amounts of cystine. Furthermore, the supplementing effects of proteins of different sources, when incorporated in the basal, low protein ration, were proportional to their cystine content. These findings in adult dogs, like the earlier investigations conducted in other laboratories upon growing rats, seemed to demonstrate that cystine is an indispensable dietary component. Later, the role of methionine, and the ability of cystine to replace it in part, were recognized.

Many of Lewis's investigations were concerned with the oxidation of cystine and its derivatives as measured by the distribution in the urine of inorganic sulfate, ethereal sulfate, and the so-called "unoxidized" sulfur compounds. Rabbits usually served as the subjects. Free cystine, as its sodium salt, was found to be oxidized to inorganic sulfate without increasing significantly the output of unoxidized sulfur compounds. This occurred rather rapidly, with 60 to 85 percent of the sulfate being recovered within 24 hours. When, however, moderate doses (0.5 to 1.0 g per kilogram of body weight) were administered *for several days* to either fasting or fed rabbits, renal casts and protein appeared in the urine accompanied by a diminution in the excretion of nonprotein nitrogen and creatinine. A further indication of renal injury was the marked rise in the nonprotein nitrogen of the blood. When the amino acid was administered subcutaneously, the results were variable. Oxidation largely to inorganic sulfate still occurred; but kidney damage, owing to the excretion of unchanged cystine, was observed in some cases. The degree of injury appeared to depend upon the rate at which the amino acid was absorbed from the site of injection.

Though cystine undergoes oxidation with considerable ease in the animal body, this is not true of certain derivatives of this amino acid. Thus, phenyluraminocystine is oxidized to a very limited extent, and increases markedly the output of unoxidized sulfur. This behavior of the compound was interpreted by Lewis as indicating the probability that deamination ordinarily precedes the oxidation of the amino acid. Furthermore, since phenyluraminocysteine was excreted after feeding phenyluraminocystine, the author suggests that perhaps the first step in the catabolism of cystine may be its conversion into cysteine. In line with this suggestion are the observations that thiolactic and thioglycolic acids are readily oxidized when fed to rabbits, or injected subcutaneously, whereas dithiodiglycolic acid is not. Perhaps, he says, only mercapto compounds, or substances readily converted into them, are oxidized with ease in the animal body. Lewis points out that such a generalization, if true, applies only to aliphatic compounds, since neither thiophenol nor thiocresol, in which, of course, the sulfhydryl group is attached directly to the benzene ring, is oxidized in the animal organism.

The fate of several other compounds related chemically to cystine was tested by Lewis and his colleagues. Definite, but variable, increases in the output of inorganic sulfate were observed following the oral administration of cysteic acid or taurine. Insofar as oxidation of these compounds occurred, it is believed to have been associated with the activity of the intestinal microflora. The accuracy of this conclusion is attested by the fact that, following the subcutaneous introduction of either cysteic acid or taurine, all extra sulfur appeared in the organic sulfur fraction of the urine. The excretion and distribution of the extra sulfur after the oral or subcutaneous administration of peptides containing glycine and either cysteic acid or taurine did not differ significantly from the findings with the free sulfonic acid. Neither S-carboxymethylcysteine, isocysteine, nor thiourea underwent oxidation when injected subcutaneously into rabbits. After the oral administration of S-carboxymethylcysteine, a slight increase in urinary sulfate was observed, which again is believed to have been due to activities of the intestinal flora. S-Benzyl derivatives of homocysteine and cysteine were not oxidized significantly. However, deamination probably occurred as shown by an increase in α-keto acids in the urines. Thus, deamination may take place even though further catabolic change is blocked by the presence of a nonlabile group.

In growth studies involving the use of young white rats, Lewis confirmed the observations made elsewhere, that taurine is not capable of improving the quality of rations known to be deficient in cystine and methionine. Also, cysteic acid, dibenzoylcystine, and the betaine of cystine are incapable of promoting the growth of animals upon such diets. On the other hand, diglycylcystine and dialanylcystine are readily utilized for growth purposes, while the dianhydride of dialanylcystine is not.

Lewis investigated the cystine content of hair from several species, and conducted experiments designed to determine the relationship of the sulfur-containing amino acids to the growth and composition of hair. It was observed that, within certain limits, the cystine and total sulfur content of the hair of white rats tended to vary with the content of the sulfur-containing amino acids in the diet, and to some extent with the age of the rats. Hair from young rats had a significantly lower cystine and total sulfur content than hair from adult animals. Hair from rats receiving a diet known to be deficient in cystine and methionine resembled in composition hair from young animals. However, retardation of growth per se, as illustrated by a lysine deficiency, did not produce hair low in cystine and total sulfur. In general, the cystine and methionine requirements for body growth seem to take precedence over the requirements for the production of hair. Later experiments demonstrated, as was to have been expected, that methionine is just as effective a supplement as cystine in inducing the growth and a normal cystine content of hair.

One would expect that the curious metabolic anomaly known as cystinuria would be of very special interest to one who had devoted so much time and energy in elucidating the biochemical behavior of sulfur compounds. And so it was. First, Lewis and his colleagues presented evidence indicating that cystinuria probably is not so rare a condition as had previously been thought. This conclusion was based upon the results of tests upon urine samples obtained from about 11,000 healthy young men and women. For the most part, the samples were procured in connection with the medical examinations given to entering students at the University of Michigan and at two neighboring institutions. The tests revealed four students whose urines regularly contained cystine crystals, and hence were intensely cystinuric. Samples from twenty-five additional individuals, though devoid of cystine crystals, consistently responded positively, in varying intensity, to color tests for the amino acid. Several individuals were subjected to extended investigation. The data obtained with one young man, who seemingly was in excellent health except for the excretion of cystine, showed that the output of cystine varied rather closely with the total nitrogen content of the urine, and not with the cystine content of the diet. Indeed, the subject could completely oxidize to sulfate doses of 2 to 3 g of cystine. Obviously, the excreted cystine must have been derived from endogenous sources.

Like results were obtained with other subjects. Invariably, the administration of cystine, whether isolated from hair, or derived from the patient's own urine, was without effect upon the cystine excretion, but induced a large increase in the sulfate content of the urine. A similar experiment in which cysteine hydrochloride was ingested led to increases in the output of both cystine and sulfate. When DL-methionine was given, much extra cystine appeared in the urine, accompanied by a moderate rise in sulfate. Strangely, less extra cystine was excreted after a given dose of methionine when the subject was consuming a high protein diet (124 g daily) than when he was ingesting a moderate protein intake (55–60 g daily). This suggested to Lewis the possibility that the utilization of the precursor of urinary cystine in cystinuria occurs more readily under conditions of a high level of protein metabolism. No evidence was obtained for the presence in the urine of a complex containing cystine. Furthermore, both in children and in adults, the loss of cystine in the urine did not alter the cystine content of the hair and nails. No cystine could be detected in the sweat of a patient with pronounced cystinuria.

Lewis's interest in amino acids was not restricted to cystine and methionine, though they seem to have been uppermost in his thoughts. His scientific curiosity included the origin, functions, and metabolic deportment of many amino acids. Extensive experiments were devised to determine the relative rates at which amino acids are absorbed from the alimentary tract, their influence on blood composition, and their effectiveness in the formation of glycogen. In studying absorption, use was made of the well-known technique devised by Cori. For this purpose, the amino acids, as their sodium salts, were administered by stomach tube to white rats. The extent of the absorption was measured in each case at the end of a period of three hours by killing the animal, removing its alimentary tract, and determining the amount of unabsorbed amino acid remaining in the tract. Incidentally, Lewis confirmed Cori's statement that the rate of absorption is independent of the absolute quantity and the concentration of the amino acid in the intestine.

The results obtained with each amino acid were expressed in terms of the "absorption coefficient" of the compound, which, by definition, is the milliequivalents absorbed per 100 g of body weight per hour. The figures are not reproduced here; it is sufficient to state that the absorption coefficients of the amino acids tested may be arranged in the following *descending* order: glycine, alanine, cystine (expressed as cysteine), glutamic acid, valine, methionine, leucine, isoleucine, and isovaline. Thus, of the above, glycine was absorbed most rapidly and isovaline least rapidly. No significant difference could be detected in the absorption coefficient of the natural L-form of an amino acid and that of its DL-counterpart.

In later experiments, attention was directed to the effects of structural changes on the rates of absorption of several amino acids, all of which were derivatives of propionic acid. The data revealed that α-alanine (natural L-alanine) is absorbed more rapidly than is β-alanine, and serine more rapidly than isoserine. These findings led Lewis to postulate that the rate of absorption is decreased as the amino group of a compound is moved away from the carboxyl. In like manner, a comparison of the absorption rates of alanine and serine on the one hand, and of β-alanine and isoserine on the other, seemed to indicate that the replacement of a hydrogen atom by a hydroxyl group diminished the rate of absorption. It would be interesting to know whether a similar relationship exists between structure and alimentary absorption in amino acids other than those derived from propionic acid.

Changes in the distribution of nonprotein nitrogenous constituents of the blood were determined following the administration of a number of amino acids. Rabbits were the experimental animals. The amino acids investigated were glycine; the L-forms of alanine, glutamic acid, arginine, and lysine; and the DL-forms of alanine and aspartic acid. Each amino acid was administered, usually orally, in an amount equivalent to 0.182 g of amino nitrogen per kilo of body weight. Blood samples were taken before the amino acid was given, and at intervals of 3, 6, 12, and usually 30 hours thereafter. Each sample was analyzed for nonprotein nitrogen, urea nitrogen, and amino acid nitrogen. From the nitrogen distribution values, it was evident that glycine and L-alanine are absorbed very rapidly, but that glycine undergoes deamination less rapidly than any of the other amino acids.

In studies of glycogen formation, the oral administration of either L- or DL-alanine to white rats which had been deprived of food for 24 hours resulted in a rapid deposition of glycogen in the liver. On the contrary, after administration of glycine or L-leucine, the hepatic glycogen values were similar to those of control animals. The monosodium salt of L-glutamic acid induced a slight increase in liver glycogen. In later experiments, the glycogenic effects of certain amino acids, after three-hour absorption periods, were found to proceed in the following *descending* order: DL- and L-alanine (essentially the same), DL-serine, D-alanine, and DL-isoserine. No glycogen formation could be detected after the administration of β-alanine.

Several of Lewis's papers dealt with the metabolism of phenylalanine. After the oral or subcutaneous administration of this amino acid to rabbits, significant amounts of phenylpyruvic acid appeared in the urine. However, no phenylpyruvic acid was excreted when the amino group was blocked by the formation of the ureido derivative of the amino acid. This observation was interpreted as indicating that oxidative deamination is a necessary step in the metabolism of phenylalanine and must occur prior to the opening of the benzene ring. No evidence was obtained for the excretion of p-hydroxyphenylpyruvic acid. In some experiments, after relatively large doses of phenylalanine, slight increases in the output of phenaceturic acid were observed. Apparently, under such conditions, part of the phenylpyruvic acid may be oxidized to phenylacetic acid, which is then conjugated with glycine and excreted without undergoing further oxidation.

Of particular interest was the observation that the daily administration of phenylalanine to white rats in doses exceeding 0.3 g per 100 g of body weight per day, and for considerable periods of time, led to the excretion of homogentisic acid. This appears to have been the first time that alcaptonuria has been consistently produced experimentally. The observation was interpreted by Lewis as lending support to a concept, which was controversial at the time but now is generally accepted, namely, that homogentisic acid is a normal intermediate in the metabolism of phenylalanine.

In experiments of a different kind, Lewis observed that N-methylglycine (carnosine) can undergo demethylation in the animal body, and thereby serve as a source of glycine for hippuric acid formation. On the other hand, a comparable reaction with N-ethylglycine does not occur.

In studies of histidine metabolism, five of eight rabbits that received large doses of this amino acid by mouth responded by excreting urocanic acid. However, no urocanic acid was excreted after the subcutaneous administration of like doses of histidine. Severe toxic manifestations were exhibited by every animal that excreted detectable amounts of urocanic acid, while those that failed to show the presence of this acid in the urine displayed no signs of intoxication. These findings led Lewis to question the assumption that urocanic acid is quantitatively an important intermediate in the normal metabolism of histidine. Doubtless he would have altered this opinion in the light of currently accumulated evidence.

Lewis verified the strange report in the literature that pregnant women frequently excrete histidine. Of the urine samples obtained from 169 pregnant females, 85 percent showed the presence of histidine in excess of the normal traces. In contrast, of the urine samples collected from 59 nonpregnant women and 50 men, only 9 percent showed the presence of excess histidine. No logical explanation is available to account for the excretion of this amino acid. The phenomenon does not occur until the third month of pregnancy, and consequently cannot be used as an early diagnostic aid.

Lewis and his colleagues were among the first to attempt the dietary replacement of an essential amino acid by a related compound for purposes of growth. As is well known, a diet containing 18 percent of gliadin as the chief source of nitrogen is incapable of supporting normal growth in young white rats. The factor limiting growth under such conditions is the low lysine content of the food. The addition of this amino acid to the basal ration greatly increases the rate of gain in body weight. It seemed reasonable to assume that some compound closely related to lysine might be transformed into the amino acid, and thereby improve the quality of the basal diet. With this possibility in mind, growth tests were made with several caproic acid derivatives as dietary supplements, namely, norleucine, α-hydroxycaproic acid, ϵ-hydroxycaproic acid, ϵ-aminocaproic acid, and α-hydroxy-ϵ-aminocaproic acid. All proved to be totally incapable of serving in place of the missing lysine, and consequently are not convertible into it. In the light of more recent investigations in other laboratories, in which the α-hydroxy analogues of several amino acids have been shown to be capable of serving in place of the corresponding amino acid, it seems very odd that α-hydroxy-ϵ-aminocaproic acid was not converted into lysine. The most likely explanation of the negative results is the probability that the test compound underwent catabolic changes, possibly involving the ϵ-amino group, before oxidation and amination could occur in the α-position.

Toward the end of his career, Lewis became interested in a toxemia known as lathyrism. This condition is associated with the prolonged consumption of large amounts of legumes of the genus *Lathyrus*. The toxemia is said to be rather common in India, in northern Africa, and in other areas where legumes of this genus constitute a high percentage of the daily diet. Those afflicted with the malady experience muscular weakness, lameness, and paralysis of the extremities. Lewis was able to induce the disease in young white rats (adult rats are more resistant) by feeding diets containing 50 percent of a finely ground meal prepared from decorticated sweet peas *(Lathyrus odoratus),* or from the seeds of certain other varieties of *Lathyrus*. Pathological examinations of the long bones of the leg revealed lesions similar to those observed in acute scurvy. However, the administration of ascorbic acid, which normally is synthesized by the rat, exerted no preventive effect.

The active principle was found to be readily extractable with cold water or 30 percent ethyl alcohol. From meal prepared from *Lathyrus sylvestris Wagneri,* the species having the greatest toxicity of the ten varieties tested, Lewis succeeded in concentrating the active agent about forty times. Since then, the possibility has been suggested that more than one deleterious compound may be present in *Lathyrus* legumes. One such component has been isolated and identified as β-(γ-L-glutamyl)-aminopropionitrile.

The above outline of some of Lewis's publications, though very incomplete, may give the reader an idea of the breadth of his research activities. Many aspects of protein metabolism, other than those described, were explored by him, as may be seen by examining his extensive bibliography. In addition, his interests included problems in carbohydrate metabolism, as illustrated by papers on the behavior of certain pentoses, mannose, and inulin in the animal organism. He investigated the metabolism of a number of branched-chain aliphatic acids, described new examples of β-oxidation, and conducted a series of studies on the hydrolysis of esters of dicarboxylic acids by liver lipase. Even the physiological effects and the metabolic fate of several toxic agents, notably hydrazine and its derivatives and selenium compounds, did not escape his attention. A multitude of miscellaneous topics, too numerous to be described in detail, came under his scientific scrutiny. Among the strikingly unique contributions may be mentioned a comparative biochemical study of the urine of the horned lizard, the nitrogenous components of the blood and urine of the turtle, and the nitrogenous metabolism of the earthworm. Truly, his versatility knew no bounds.

Shortly after his death, the Executive Faculty of the School of Medicine at the University of Michigan paid its respects to Howard Bishop Lewis by approving unanimously an appropriate testimonial to be recorded in its minutes and transmitted to his family. Excerpts from that expression of esteem, as phrased by his colleagues, may serve as a fitting conclusion to this survey of his life and work. It reads in part as follows:

"It is difficult to appraise the inspired work of Dr. Lewis, and to make a true evaluation of his vital years of service to the medical profession. To understand the magnitude of his influence, it is necessary to comprehend his remarkable ability and unusual skill in dealing with the training of his students and the administrative functions of his offices. . . . He taught the value of ideals and high standards of accomplishment, and gave to his pupils many guiding principles which have contributed to their enduring happiness and success in the profession of medicine and allied fields of science. . . .

"Dr. Lewis was as great and as honorable and as respected as the University he loved so much. May his students and colleagues reap the full benefit of the inspiration which he has left with us."

THE AUTHORS are deeply grateful to the late Mrs. H. B. Lewis for supplying much of the information herein recorded concerning her husband's early life and nonprofessional interests, and for permitting us to see and make use of the contents of letters written to her by close friends following Howard's death.

We are also indebted to Dr. A. A. Christman, a former student, friend, and colleague of Dr. Lewis, for supplying many of the scientific facts not otherwise available, and for rendering very substantial assistance in the preparation of the bibliography.

BIBLIOGRAPHY

KEY TO ABBREVIATIONS

Am. J. Pharm. Educ. = American Journal of Pharmaceutical Education
Am. J. Physiol. = American Journal of Physiology
Ann. Internal Med. = Annals of Internal Medicine
Ann. Rev. Biochem. = Annual Review of Biochemistry
Cyclo. Med., Surg., Specialties = Cyclopedia of Medicine, Surgery, and Specialties
J. Am. Chem. Soc. = Journal of the American Chemical Society
J. Am. Dietetic Assoc. = Journal of the American Dietetic Association
J. Am. Med. Assoc. = Journal of the American Medical Association
J. Biol. Chem. = Journal of Biological Chemistry
J. Mich. State Med. Soc. = Journal of the Michigan State Medical Society
J. Nutrition = Journal of Nutrition
J. Pharmacol. Exp. Therap. = Journal of Pharmacology and Experimental Therapeutics
Oral Surg., Oral Med., Oral Pathol. = Oral Surgery, Oral Medicine, and Oral Pathology
Proc. Soc. Exp. Biol. Med. = Proceedings of the Society for Experimental Biology and Medicine

1912

The behavior of some hydantoin derivatives in metabolism. I. Hydantoin and ethyl hydantoate. J. Biol. Chem., 13:347–56.
The value of inulin as a foodstuff. J. Am. Med. Assoc., 58:1176–77.

1913

The behavior of some hydantoin derivatives in metabolism. II. 2-Thiohydantoins. J. Biol. Chem., 14:245–56.
With B. H. Nicolet. The reaction of some purine, pyrimidine, and hydantoin derivatives with the uric acid and phenol reagents of Folin and Denis. J. Biol. Chem., 16:369–73.

1914

With E. M. Frankel. The influence of inulin on the output of glucose in phlorhizin diabetes. J. Biol. Chem., 17:365–67.
Studies on the synthesis of hippuric acid in the animal organism. I. The synthesis of hippuric acid in rabbits on a glycocoll-free diet. J. Biol. Chem., 17:503–8.
Studies in the synthesis of hippuric acid in the animal organism. II. The synthesis and rate of elimination of hippuric acid after benzoate ingestion in man. J. Biol. Chem., 18:225–31.

1915

With A. E. Taylor. A study of the protein metabolism under conditions of repeated hemorrhage. J. Biol. Chem., 22:71–75.
With A. E. Taylor. On the predominance of the liver in the formation of urea. J. Biol. Chem., 22:77–80.
The behavior of some hydantoin derivatives in metabolism. III. Parabanic acid. J. Biol. Chem., 23:281–86.

1916

With W. G. Karr. Studies in the synthesis of hippuric acid in the animal organism. III. The excretion of uric acid in man after ingestion of sodium benzoate. J. Biol. Chem., 25:13–20.
The metabolism of sulfur. I. The relative elimination of sulfur and nitrogen in the dog in inanition and subsequent feeding. J. Biol. Chem., 26:61–68.
With W. G. Karr. A comparative study of the distribution of urea in the blood and tissues of certain vertebrates with especial reference to the hen. J. Am. Chem. Soc., 38:1615–20.
With W. G. Karr. Changes in the urea content of blood and tissues of guinea pigs maintained on an exclusive oat diet. J. Biol. Chem., 28:17–25.

1917

The metabolism of sulfur. II. The influence of small amounts of cystine on the balance of nitrogen in dogs maintained on a low protein diet. J. Biol. Chem., 31:363–77.
With L. M. Smith. A study of the normal metabolism of the guinea pig. J. Am. Chem. Soc., 39:2231–39.
With W. G. Karr. The phenol excretion of guinea pigs maintained on an exclusive oat diet. Am. J. Physiol., 44:586–90.

1918

With M. E. Jewell. The occurrence of lichenase in the digestive tract of invertebrates. J. Biol. Chem., 33:161–67.
With E. A. Doisy. Studies in uric acid metabolism. I. The influence of high protein diets on the endogenous uric acid elimination. J. Biol. Chem., 36:1–7.
With M. S. Dunn and E. A. Doisy. Studies in uric acid metabolism.

II. Proteins and amino acids as factors in the stimulation of endogenous uric acid metabolism. J. Biol. Chem., 36:9–26.
Some analyses of the urine of reptiles. Science, 48:376.

1919

The antiscorbutic value of the banana. J. Biol. Chem., 40:91–101.

1920

The metabolism of sulfur. III. The relation between the cystine content of proteins and their efficiency in the maintenance of nitrogenous equilibrium in dogs. J. Biol. Chem., 42:289–96.
With L. E. Root. Amino acid synthesis in the animal organism. Can norleucine replace lysine for the nutritive requirements of the white rat? J. Biol. Chem., 43:79–87.

1921

Studies on the synthesis of hippuric acid in the animal organism. IV. A note on the synthesis of hippuric acid in the rabbit after exclusion of bile from the intestine. J. Biol. Chem., 46:73–75.
With A. A. Christman. Lipase studies. I. The hydrolysis of the esters of some dicarboxylic acids by the lipase of the liver. J. Biol. Chem., 47:495–505.
With M. S. Dunn. The action of nitrous acid on casein. J. Biol. Chem., 49:327–41.
With M. S. Dunn. A comparative study of the hydrolysis of casein and deaminized casein by proteolytic enzymes. J. Biol. Chem., 49:343–50.
With G. Stearns. Diet and sex as factors in the creatinuria of man. Am. J. Physiol., 56:60–71.

1922

With L. E. Root. The metabolism of sulfur. IV. The oxidation of cystine in the animal organism. J. Biol. Chem., 50:303–10.
With D. A. McGinty. The metabolism of sulfur. V. Cysteine as an intermediary product in the metabolism of cystine. J. Biol. Chem., 53:349–56.
With R. M. Hill. The hydrolysis of sucrose in the human stomach. Am. J. Physiol., 59:413–20.

1923

With R. C. Corley. Studies in uric acid metabolism. III. The influence of fats and carbohydrates on the endogenous uric acid elimination. J. Biol. Chem., 55:373–84.

With E. C. Hyde. Lipase studies. II. A comparison of the hydrolysis of the esters of the dicarboxylic acids by the lipase of the liver. J. Biol. Chem., 56: 7–15.

With H. Updegraff. The reaction between proteins and nitrous acid. The tyrosine content of deaminized casein. J. Biol. Chem., 56:405–14.

With W. H. Griffith. Studies in the synthesis of hippuric acid in the animal organism. V. The influence of amino acids and related substances on the synthesis and rate of elimination of hippuric acid after the administration of benzoate. J. Biol. Chem., 57:1–24.

With A. A. Christman. Biochemical studies on allantoin. I. The influence of amino acids on the excretion of allantoin by the rabbit. J. Biol. Chem., 57:379–95.

With W. H. Griffith. Studies in the synthesis of hippuric acid in the animal organism. VI. The influence of the protein of the diet on the synthesis and rate of elimination of hippuric acid after the administration of benzoate. J. Biol. Chem., 57:697–707.

1924

With H. Updegraff and D. A. McGinty. The metabolism of sulfur. VI. The oxidation of cystine in the animal organism. Second paper. J. Biol. Chem., 59:59–71.

With R. M. Hill. The metabolism of sulfur. VII. The oxidation of some sulfur compounds related to cystine in the animal organism. J. Biol. Chem., 59:557–67.

With R. M. Hill. The metabolism of sulfur. VIII. The behavior of thiophenol and thiocresol in the animal organism. J. Biol. Chem., 59:569–75.

With H. Updegraff. A quantitative study of some organic constitutents of the saliva. J. Biol. Chem., 61:633–48.

With D. A. McGinty and C. S. Marvel. Amino acid synthesis in the animal organism. The availability of some caproic acid derivatives for the synthesis of lysine. J. Biol. Chem., 62:75–92.

Sulfur metabolism. Physiological Reviews, 4:394–423.

1925

The metabolism of sulfur. IX. The effect of repeated administration of small amounts of cystine. J. Biol. Chem., 65:187–95.

Some contributions of chemistry to the art and science of medicine. J. Mich. State Med. Soc., 24:1–7.

Insulin. Annals of Clinical Medicine, 3:623–33.

1926

With D. A. McGinty. Lipase studies. III. The hydrolysis of the esters of the dicarboxylic acids by the lipase of the liver. J. Biol. Chem., 67:567–77.

With R. H. Wilson. The metabolism of sulfur. X. The determination of cystine in the urine. J. Biol. Chem., 69:125–31.

With G. T. Lewis. The metabolism of sulfur. XI. Can taurine replace cystine in the diet of the young white rat? J. Biol. Chem., 69:589–98.

With S. Izume. The influence of hydrazine and its derivatives on metabolism. I. The effect of substitution in the hydrazine molecule upon the hypoglycemic action of hydrazine. J. Pharmacol. Exp. Therap., 30:87–93.

With S. Izume. The influence of hydrazine and its derivatives on metabolism. II. Changes in the non-protein nitrogenous constituents of the blood and in the metabolism of injected glycine in hydrazine intoxication. J. Biol. Chem., 71:33–49.

With S. Izume. The influence of hydrazine and its derivatives on metabolism. III. The mechanism of hydrazine hypoglycemia. J. Biol. Chem., 71:51–66.

The role of the inorganic elements in nutrition. Dental Cosmos, 68:950–58.

1927

With G. T. Lewis. The metabolism of sulfur. XII. The value of diglycyl-cystine, dialanyl-cystine, and dialanyl-cystine dianhydride for the nutritive requirements of the white rat. J. Biol. Chem., 73:535–42.

With R. H. Wilson. The cystine content of hair and other epidermal tissues. J. Biol. Chem., 73:543–53.

With G. T. Lewis. The metabolism of sulfur. XIII. The effect of elementary sulfur on the growth of the young white rat. J. Biol. Chem., 74:515–23.

With M. G. Bodey and J. F. Huber. The absorption and utilization of inulin as evidenced by glycogen formation in the white rat. J. Biol. Chem., 75:715–23.
With F. H. Wiley. The distribution of nitrogen in the blood and urine of the turtle *(Chrysemys pinta)*. Am. J. Physiol., 81:692–95.

1928

With S. L. Diack. Studies in the synthesis of hippuric acid in the animal organism. VII. A comparison of the rate of elimination of hippuric acid after the ingestion of sodium benzoate, benzyl alcohol, and benzyl esters of succinic acid. J. Biol. Chem., 77:89–95.
Occurrence of cystine in sweat of cystinurics. Proc. Soc. Exp. Biol. Med., 26:69–70.
With P. Hodgson. Physical development and the excretion of creatine and creatinine by women. Am. J. Physiol., 87:288–92.
With M. W. Johnston. Comparative studies of the metabolism of amino acids. I. Changes in the non-protein nitrogenous constituents of the blood following administration of amino acids. J. Biol. Chem., 78:67–82.

1929

With S. A. Lough. The metabolism of sulfur. XIV. A metabolic study of a case of cystinuria. J. Biol. Chem., 81:285–97.
With H. D. Lightbody. The metabolism of sulfur. XV. The relation of the protein and cystine content of the diet to the growth of the hair in the white rat. J. Biol. Chem., 82:485–97.
With H. D. Lightbody. The metabolism of sulfur. XVI. Dietary factors in relation to the chemical composition of the hair of the young white rat. J. Biol. Chem., 82:663–71.
With R. H. Wilson. Comparative studies of the metabolism of amino acids. II. The rate of absorption of amino acids from the gastrointestinal tract of the white rat. J. Biol. Chem., 84: 511–31.
With L. F. Catron. The formation of glycogen in the liver of the young white rat after the oral administration of glycerol. J. Biol. Chem., 84:553–59.
With R. L. Grant and A. A. Christman. Exogenous arginine as the

precursor of creatine in the dog. Proc. Soc. Exp. Biol. Med., 27:231-33.

1930

With R. H. Wilson. Comparative studies of the metabolism of amino acids. III. The formation of glycogen after oral administration of amino acids to white rats. J. Biol. Chem., 85:559-69.
With G. Stearns. The metabolism of sulfur. XVII. The rate of oxidation of ingested cystine in the organism of the rabbit. J. Biol. Chem., 86:93-105.
With F. H. Wiley. The action of nitrous acid on casein. II. J. Biol. Chem., 86:511-28.

1931

With M. F. O'Connor. Cystinuria and tuberculosis. American Review of Tuberculosis, 23:134-38.
With M. M. Miller. Glycogen formation in the white rat after oral administration of xylose. Proc. Soc. Exp. Biol. Med., 28:448-49.
With N. F. Shambaugh and D. Tourtellotte. Comparative studies of the metabolism of the amino acids. IV. Phenylalanine and tyrosine. J. Biol. Chem., 92:499-511.

1932

With S. A. Lough. The metabolism of sulfur. XVIII. The distribution of urinary sulfur in the rabbit after the administration of monobromobenzene. J. Biol. Chem., 94:739-47.
With A. K. Silberman. The tyrosine content of cocoons of various species. J. Biol. Chem., 95:491-94.
With J. P. Chandler. Comparative studies of the metabolism of the amino acids. V. The oxidation of phenylalanine and phenylpyruvic acid in the organism of the rabbit. J. Biol. Chem., 96:619-36.
With M. M. Miller. Pentose metabolism. I. The rate of absorption of d-xylose and the formation of glycogen in the organism of the white rat after oral administration of d-xylose. J. Biol. Chem., 98:133-40.
With M. M. Miller. Pentose metabolism. II. The pentose content of the tissues of the white rat after the oral administration of d-xylose. J. Biol. Chem., 98:141-50.
With A. White. The metabolism of sulfur. XIX. The distribution

of urinary sulfur in the dog after the oral administration of monobromobenzene as influenced by the character of the dietary protein and by the feeding of L-cystine and DL-methionine. J. Biol. Chem., 98:607–24.

The occurrence of cystinuria in healthy young men and women. Ann. Internal Med., 6:183–92.

Cystinuria: a review of some recent investigations. Yale Journal of Biology and Medicine, 4:437–49.

The chemistry and metabolism of the compounds of sulfur. Ann. Rev. Biochem., 1:171–86.

The role of amino acids in the animal organism. I. Cystinuria and cystine calculi, a surgical and medical problem. J. Mich. State Med. Soc., 31:249–53.

The role of amino acids in the animal organism. II. The physiology of the amino acids. J. Mich. State Med. Soc., 31:307–13.

1933

With B. W. Chase. The metabolism of sulfur. XX. The rate of absorption of DL-methionine from the gastrointestinal tract of the white rat. J. Biol. Chem., 101:735–40.

With A. K. Silberman. Pentose metabolism. III. The rate of absorption of *l*-rhamnose and the formation of glycogen in the organism of the white rat after oral administration of *l*-rhamnose. J. Biol. Chem., 101:741–51.

With V. J. Tulane and A. A. Christman. Studies in the synthesis of hippuric acid in the animal organism. VIII. Hydrazine intoxication and hippuric acid synthesis in the rabbit. J. Biol. Chem., 103:141–50.

With V. J. Tulane. Studies in the synthesis of hippuric acid in the animal organism. IX. A comparative study of the rate of synthesis and excretion of hippuric and phenaceturic acids by the rabbit. J. Biol. Chem., 103:151–60.

With A. K. Silberman. Glycogen formation after oral administration of mannitol to white rats. Proc. Soc. Exp. Biol. Med., 31:253–55.

The chemistry and metabolism of the compounds of sulfur. Ann. Rev. Biochem., 2:95–108.

1934

With R. W. Virtue. The metabolism of sulfur. XXI. Comparative studies of the metabolism of L-cystine and DL-methionine in the rabbit. J. Biol. Chem., 104:59–67.

With R. W. Virtue. The iodometric determination of cystine in the urine. J. Biol. Chem., 104:415–21.

With S. A. Lough. The reaction of nitrous acid with cystine and related sulfur-containing compounds. J. Biol. Chem., 104:601–10.

With B. W. Chase. Comparative studies of the metabolism of amino acids. VI. The rate of absorption of leucine, valine, and their isomers from the gastrointestinal tract of the white rat. J. Biol. Chem., 106:315–21.

With W. C. Lee. The effect of fasting, refeeding, and of variations in the cystine content of the diet on the composition of the tissue proteins of the white rat. J. Biol. Chem., 107:649–59.

The progress of biochemistry. Review of Volume 3 of the Annual Review of Biochemistry. Science, 80:291–92.

1935

With R. L. Grant. Some products of partial hydrolysis of silk fibroin. J. Biol. Chem., 108:667–73.

With L. Frayser. The metabolism of sulfur. XXII. The cystine content of the hair and nails of cystinurics. J. Biol. Chem., 110:23–27.

With B. H. Brown. Specific rotation of cystine excreted in cystinuria. Proc. Soc. Exp. Biol. Med., 32:1100–2.

The chemistry and metabolism of the compounds of sulfur. Ann. Rev. Biochem., 4:149–68.

Editorial review. The chief sulfur compounds in nutrition. J. Nutrition, 10:99–116.

Sulfur. Cyclo. Med., Surg., Specialties, 8:922–29.

With A. Bendaña. The utilization of inulin for growth by the young white rat. J. Nutrition, 10:99–116.

1936

With B. H. Brown and F. R. White. The metabolism of sulfur. XXIII. The influence of the ingestion of cystine, cysteine, and methionine on the excretion of cystine in cystinuria. J. Biol. Chem., 114:171–84.

1937

With F. R. White and J. White. The metabolism of sulfur. XXIV. The metabolism of taurine, cysteic acid, cystine, and of some peptides containing these amino acids. J. Biol. Chem., 117: 663–71.

With B. H. Brown. Cystine in normal and cystinuric human blood. Proc. Soc. Exp. Biol. Med., 36:487–88.

1938

With E. V. Heard. The metabolism of sulfur. XXV. Dietary methionine as a factor related to the growth and composition of the hair of the young white rat. J. Biol. Chem., 123:203–10.

With E. Papageorge. Comparative studies of the metabolism of the amino acids. VII. Experimental alcaptonuria in the white rat. J. Biol. Chem., 123:211–20.

With E. T. Papageorge and M. M. Fröhlich. Excretion of homogentisic acid after oral administration of phenylalanine to alcaptonuric subjects. Proc. Soc. Exp. Biol. Med., 38:742–45.

With J. I. Routh. The enzymatic digestion of wool. J. Biol. Chem., 124:725–32.

With W. D. Block. The amino acid content of cow and chimpanzee hair. J. Biol. Chem., 125:561–70.

With P. C. Jen. Availability of dibenzoylcystine for growth of the young white rat. Proc. Soc. Exp. Biol. Med., 39:301–4.

1939

With P. C. Jen. The metabolism of sulfur. XXVI. The metabolism of the betaine of cystine. J. Biol. Chem., 127:97–103.

With R. A. Gortner, Jr. Quantitative determination of selenium in tissues and feces. Industrial and Engineering Chemistry, Analytical Edition, 11:198–200.

With S. F. Velick and J. White. The synthesis of dicholylcystine and cholylcysteic acid. J. Biol. Chem., 127:477–81.

Vitamins in theory and practice. Ann. Internal Med., 13:749–54.

With R. A. Gortner, Jr. The retention and excretion of selenium after the administration of sodium selenite to white rats. J. Pharmacol. Exp. Therap., 67:358–64.

With L. D. Abbott, Jr. Comparative studies of the metabolism of

the amino acids. VIII. Glycine precursors. Availability of N-methylglycine, N,N-dimethylglycine, and betaine for the synthesis of hippuric acid by the rabbit. J. Biol. Chem., 131:479–87.
Sulfur metabolism. Cyclo. Med., Surg., Specialties, 10:125–34.

1940

With J. Schultz and R. A. Gortner, Jr. Dietary protein and the toxicity of sodium selenite in the white rat. J. Pharmacol. Exp. Therap., 68:292–99.
With J. Schultz. The excretion of volatile selenium compounds after the administration of sodium selenite to white rats. J. Biol. Chem., 133:199–207.
With R. L. Garner. The metabolism of proteins and amino acids. Ann. Rev. Biochem., 9:277–302.

1941

The significance of the sulfur-containing amino acids in metabolism. Harvey Lectures, 36:159–87.
With L. D. Abbott, Jr. Comparative studies of the metabolism of the amino acids. IX. Glycine precursors. Availability of N-ethylglycine and glycolic acid for the synthesis of hippuric acid by the rabbit. J. Biol. Chem., 137:535–43.
With B. H. Brown. The metabolism of sulfur. XXVII. The distribution of sulfur in the ultrafiltrates of blood plasma. J. Biol. Chem., 138:705–16.
With B. H. Brown. The metabolism of sulfur. XXVIII. The cystine content and sulfur distribution of ultrafiltrates of plasma after the administration of L-cystine and DL-methionine to rabbits. J. Biol. Chem., 138:717–26.
Charles Wallis Edmunds. Am. J. Pharm. Educ., 5:245–48.
With F. R. Blood. The metabolism of sulfur. XXIX. S-Carboxymethylcysteine. J. Biol. Chem., 139:407–12.
With F. R. Blood. The metabolism of sulfur. XXX. Thiourea. J. Biol. Chem., 139:413–20.
End products of nitrogen metabolism in animals. Biological Symposia, 5:20–30.

1942

With W. J. Darby and J. R. Totter. The preparation of 4(5)-hydroxymethylimidazole. J. Am. Chem. Soc., 64:463–64.

Proteins in nutrition. J. Am. Med. Assoc., 120:198-204.
With W. J. Darby. Urocanic acid and the intermediary metabolism of histidine in the rabbit. J. Biol. Chem., 146:225-35.

1943

With M. B. Esterer. Experimental lathyrism in the white rat. Proc. Soc. Exp. Biol. Med., 53:263-64.
Trends in vitamin research. J. Am. Dietetic Assoc., 19:483-87.
With R. Eyles. The utilization of d-glucono-γ-lactone by the organism of the young white rat. J. Nutrition, 26:309-17.

1944

Natural toxicants and nutrition. Nutrition Reviews, 2:97-99.
With D. D. Dziewiatkowski. Glucuronic acid synthesis and the glycogen content of the liver of the rat. J. Biol. Chem., 153:49-52.
Russell Henry Chittenden (1856-1943). J. Biol. Chem., 153:339-42.
With L. Louis. The composition of the tissue proteins of the rabbit as influenced by inanition and the hepatotoxic agents, hydrazine and phosphorus. J. Biol. Chem., 153:381-86.
With S. Pedersen. The partition of urinary nitrogen after the oral administration of glutamic acid, pyrrolidonecarboxylic acid, proline, and hydroxyproline to rabbits. J. Biol. Chem., 154:705-12.

1945

With D. D. Dziewiatkowski. The metabolism of trimethylacetic (pivalic) and tertiarybutylacetic acids. New examples of conjugation with glucuronic acid. J. Biol. Chem., 158:77-87.

1946

O metabolismo intermediário e o papel nutritivo dos acidos aminados aromaticos e sulfurados da molecula proteica. Medicina, Cirurgia, Farmacia, 120:161-75.
Biochemistry, a basic pharmaceutical science. Am. J. Pharm. Educ., 10:352-54.
With C-W. Shen. The metabolism of sulfur. XXXI. The distribution of urinary sulfur and the excretion of keto acids after the

oral administration of some derivatives of cystine and methionine to the rabbit. J. Biol. Chem., 165:115–23.
With W. J. Wingo. The metabolism of sulfur. XXXII. Isocysteine. J. Biol. Chem., 165:339–46.

1947

Nutrition. Annals of the American Academy of Political and Social Science, 249:119–25.
Biochemistry in the pharmacy curriculum—optional or required subject. Am. J. Pharm. Educ., 11:119–25.
With S. Levey. The metabolism of phenoxyacetic acid, its homologues, and some monochlorophenoxyacetic acids. New examples of beta oxidation. J. Biol. Chem., 168:213–21.
With F. A. Schofield. A comparative study of the metabolism of α-alanine, β-alanine, serine, and isoserine. I. Absorption from the gastrointestinal tract. J. Biol. Chem., 168:439–45.
With F. A. Schofield. A comparative study of the metabolism of α-alanine, β-alanine, serine, and isoserine. II. Glycogen content of the liver after oral administration of the amino acids. J. Biol. Chem., 169:373–78.
The biochemical triumvirate in medicine. University of Tennessee Record, 50:80–83.

1948

With A. Venkataraman and P. R. Venkataraman. The metabolism of p-amino salicylic acid in the organism of the rabbit. J. Biol. Chem., 173:641–51.
Proteins in nutrition. J. Am. Med. Assoc., 138:207–13.
With R. S. Fajans, M. B. Esterer, C-W. Shen, and M. Oliphant. The nutritive value of some legumes. Lathyrism in the rat. The sweet pea *(Lathyrus odoratus)*, *Lathyrus sativus*, *Lathyrus cicera* and some other species of *Lathyrus*. J. Nutrition, 36:537–59.
With A. Y-H. Chu and A. A. Christman. Alkaline phosphatase of the serum in experimental lathyrism of the white rat. Proc. Soc. Exp. Biol. Med., 69:445–46.
Biologic functions of proteins. I. Functions of proteins in the living organism. Oral Surg., Oral Med., Oral Pathol., 1:221–25.
Biologic functions of proteins. II. The role of proteins in human nutrition. Oral Surg., Oral Med., Oral Pathol., 1:226–30.

1949

With D. D. Dziewiatkowski and A. Venkataraman. The metabolism of some branched chain aliphatic acids. J. Biol. Chem., 178: 169–77.

Protein metabolism in disease. Bulletin of the United States Army Medical Department, 9:364–74.

With A. R. Schulert. Experimental lathyrism in the white rat and mouse. Proc. Soc. Exp. Biol. Med., 71:440–41.

With S. Cohen. The nitrogenous metabolism of the earthworm (Lumbricus terrestris). J. Biol. Chem., 180:79–91.

1950

With D. R. Neuhaus and A. A. Christman. Biochemical studies on urokon (sodium 2,4,6-triiodo-3-acetylaminobenzoate), a new pyelographic medium. Journal of Laboratory and Clinical Medicine, 35:43–49.

With P. R. Venkataraman and A. Venkataraman. The metabolism of p-aminobenzoic acid in the rabbit. Archives of Biochemistry, 26:173–77.

With E. Roberts and G. B. Ramasarma. Amino acids of Bence-Jones protein. Proc. Soc. Exp. Biol. Med., 74:237–41.

With S. Cohen. The nitrogenous metabolism of the earthworm (Lumbricus terrestris). II. Arginase and urea synthesis. J. Biol. Chem., 184:479–84.

With E. P. Tyner and H. C. Eckstein. Niacin and the ability of cystine to augment deposition of liver fat. J. Biol. Chem., 187: 651–54.

1951

With R. S. Fajans. The supplemental value of cystine and methionine for low protein (casein) diets fed the young white rat. J. Nutrition, 44:399–411.

With G. S. Wells. The histidine content of the urine in pregnancy. American Journal of Obstetrics and Gynecology, 61:1123–28.

With D. Neuhaus and A. A. Christman. Evaluation of some iodine-containing organic compounds as x-ray contrast media. Proc. Soc. Exp. Biol. Med., 78:313–17.

1952

Fifty years of study of the role of protein in nutrition. J. Am. Dietetic Assoc., 28:701–6.

With A. R. Schulert. Experimental lathyrism. Proc. Soc. Exp. Biol. Med., 81:86–89.

1953

With A. Hainline, Jr. Synthesis of hippuric acid and benzoyl glucuronide by the rabbit. J. Biol. Chem., 201:673–81.

With R. C. Baldridge. Diet and the ergothioneine content of blood. J. Biol. Chem., 202:169–76.

ROBERT HARRY LOWIE

June 12, 1883–September 21, 1957

BY JULIAN H. STEWARD

ROBERT LOWIE was one of the key figures in the history of anthropology. His professional years spanned the first five decades of the present century. He entered anthropology not long after Franz Boas had established it as an academic discipline and had removed it from the rather philosophical study of the nineteenth century and placed it on an empirical, scientific basis. Although Lowie was initially employed for a few years by the American Museum of Natural History, his true niche was as a university scholar where his influence reached an increasing number of students as well as those who read his large number of publications.

Lowie's principal interests were in ethnological theory, including the history of such theory, and in social organization, especially kinship, marriage, the family, kinship terminology, men's and women's societies including age–grade societies, and political and social organization. He also made major contributions to the study of primitive religion and folklore. Lowie did not do original research on physical anthropology or archaeology, which were little developed during his active years, and he did not have a major interest in language.

There is a major fallacy, which seems to be shared by some members of the National Academy of Sciences, that archaeology is a "hard" science, thus ranking as more of a science than ethnology, because it deals with visible and measurable material objects. Lowie, however, directed ethnology by the most rigorous scientific criteria, which generally outstripped those formerly held by archaeology.

THE MAKING OF AN ETHNOLOGIST

Robert Lowie was born on June 12, 1883, in Vienna of a Hungarian father and a Viennese mother. His family came to New York City when he was ten years old where his father earned a living in merchandizing, but where Robert was reared in the German-Jewish intellectual tradition of lower Manhattan. Although he never adhered to Jewish orthodoxy, the ties of the Jewish family were so strong and Lowie was so close to his mother and sister that he did not marry until he had passed the age of forty. According to the cultural values of the community and family in which he was reared, Lowie always expected to make a career in the intellectual world. He attended the City College of New York and he resided among liberals in Greenwich Village. After graduation he engaged in school-teaching for several years but found this distasteful and, to his mind, largely futile. He had once considered a career in chemistry but abandoned it upon discovering that he was color-blind and also gave up any laboratory plans because of an extraordinary ineptitude in handling physical objects. Many years later he learned to drive an automobile but always drove at great peril, and all his confrontations with material objects of the simplest kind were major contests.

Lowie was attracted to anthropology because it represented intellectual fulfillment without the difficulties of physical manipulation of objects. He was also no doubt attracted to it because Boas represented a liberal point of view and had devoted himself to fighting the prejudices directed toward Jews and other ethnic and racial minorities as well as toward the teaching of anthropology. Lowie never became a political activist but his sympathies were definitely on the liberal side and he wrote extensively on racist problems.

Lowie taught in the New York public school system from 1901, when he was graduated from the City College of New York, until 1904, when he entered Columbia University as a graduate student to study anthropology under Franz Boas. He took his Ph.D. degree in 1907 and was appointed to the staff of the American Museum of Natural History.

At that time it was assumed that Boas's students should obtain their ethnological data from firsthand fieldwork rather than, as had been the case in previous decades, from secondary sources written by explorers, missionaries, and other nontrained people. It is remarkable that Lowie, city-bred and little experienced outside New York City, should have done so much of his fieldwork in areas that were extremely remote and extraordinarily difficult for one with urban habits to live in. His first fieldwork was done among the Lemhi Shoshoni of Idaho in 1906, and his second major field trip took him into Canada to study the Chipewayan Indians at Lake Athabaska in the Arctic drainage. In a little book entitled *Robert H. Lowie, Ethnologist: A Personal Record* (1959), Lowie recounts in detail the adventures of this trip. He traveled by train, then crossed the watershed downstream in fur traders' barges, and it was only through the kindly help of the trappers toward a person so obviously helpless in the face of the circumstances he encountered that he was able to survive the trip in reasonable safety. The final crisis came on his return trip when the railroad was surrounded and threatened by a forest fire, when again his fellow travelers guided him through his difficulties to safety.

Lowie did not pursue subarctic ethnology further, but in 1912 and 1915 he visited other Shoshonean tribes of the Great Basin, some of them so remote from the white settlers that he could not find English-speaking interpreters. His contributions to Great Basin Shoshonean ethnology, however, were the first, and for many years the only, sources on the area.

While he was associated with the American Museum of Natural History, his interests and fieldwork were largely directed by Clark Wissler, whose main area was the Indians of the Great Plains. Lowie visited and studied many of the tribes but his principal and lasting interest was the Crow, about whom he published a definitive book, *The Crow Indians* (1935).

During 1917–1918 Lowie was invited to become visiting lecturer in anthropology at the University of California at Berkeley by A. L. Kroeber, who had founded the department fifteen years earlier. In 1921, Lowie was appointed a permanent member of the staff at Berkeley and remained such until his retirement, although he held many visiting professorships and lectureships.

Lowie's interest in primitive peoples expanded in scope through voluminous reading, and his bibliography contains some 200 book reviews. His knowledge of South American Indians was stimulated by the visit to Berkeley in 1927 of Baron Erland Nordenskiöld, who until that time was virtually the only ethnologist to have worked with the South American Indians. A few years later, Lowie happened to discover a German-born resident of Brazil, Curt Nimuendajú. This remarkable man had visited some of the least known tribes in eastern Brazil, the Ge-speaking Indians, and had written extremely full manuscripts on their culture. Lowie translated these into English. His interest in the general area became a lasting one, such that he was a major contributor to, and editor of, the Tropical Forest volume of the *Handbook of South American Indians*.

During his life, he held office in many scientific societies and accepted appointments as visiting professor at many universities, including Ohio State, Yale, Columbia, Harvard, Washington, and Hamburg. He was granted honorary membership in such societies as the Royal Anthropological Institute of Great Britain, the Instituto do Cerara in Brazil, the American Philosophical Society, the New York Academy of Science, the Würtembergische Verein für Handelsgeographie, the Deutsche Gesellschaft für Völkerkund, the Société Suisse des Americanistes, and the Bavaria Academy of Science. He was awarded an honorary doctorate by the University of Chicago and received the Viking Medal. He was twice appointed editor of the *American Anthropologist* and served for a year as chairman of the Division of Anthropology and Psychology of the National Research Council. He was elected to the National Academy of Sciences in 1931.

ROBERT LOWIE'S SCIENTIFIC ACHIEVEMENTS

In order to understand the very great importance of Lowie's scientific work, it is necessary to consider the profound transition in anthropological thinking between the nineteenth and the twentieth centuries. After Darwin had liberated biology from the restrictions of the concept of the original creation of each species, anthropological studies soon adopted a kind of Darwinism for cultural origins. The concept was not entirely unique at this time, but it soon became formulated around the orthogenic and philosophical idea that cultures tended to progress from the simple to the complex through a series of worldwide stages that could be identified by specific criteria everywhere. The universal evolutionary scheme that became known as unilinear evolution was most completely expounded by Lewis H. Morgan in *Ancient Society*. Morgan classed all civilizations, including all surviving societies, into three principal stages and subdivisions thereof, known as savagery, barbarism, and civilization, the last epitomized by the achievements of the Victorian era. Specific criteria of material culture and society were alleged to characterize each of these stages.

Morgan's supporting data for his universal scheme were

drawn from miscellaneous sources rather than from direct fieldwork. When Franz Boas, Lowie's teacher, began his direct fieldwork in 1890 and after beginning his teaching at Columbia University at the turn of the century, he advocated an empirical approach to the question of the characteristics of each culture. Gradually, the nineteenth-century scheme was thrown into doubt, although James Frazer's *Golden Bough* perpetuated it into the 1920s. Lowie's outstanding contribution to anthropology, it seems to me, was to subject Morgan's scheme to minute empirical criticism based on the accumulated data of fieldwork, and in his *Primitive Society* (1920) he gave the entire idea the *coup de grâce*. I consider this to be Lowie's most important work, albeit a task that could not be repeated, because once an erroneous theory is demolished the job cannot and need not be repeated. At the same time Lowie thereby cleared the ground for new studies about the nature and origins of various traits of culture to which he himself contributed in large measure in *Primitive Society* and also in subsequent papers and books such as *The Origin of the State, Primitive Religion,* and studies on the origins of various forms of social organization.

Lowie pursued basic studies of kinship and fictitious kinship groups in his comparative research on clans, phratries, and moieties. In his theoretical treatment of these social divisions he avoided the general tendency of anthropologists of the early twentieth century to assume a single origin and diffusion, though his theory of multiple origins did not revert to the unilinear theory of the previous century.

In these studies he drew heavily upon the data of the Great Plains, whose tribes had been the subject of much of his own research as well as that of the American Museum of Natural History, and where men's societies were often arranged in age-grades. For comparative material he drew also upon the Hopi, among whom he had done fieldwork.

Lowie's research, which examined theoretical approaches to phenomena of social and political organization, led him to write a very useful little book called *The History of Ethnological Theory*, published in 1937.

Another of Lowie's major theoretical interests was treated in his book *The Origin of the State* (1927). The nineteenth-century evolutionists had sought reasons for the origin of various social and political phenomena, though few had subscribed to a universal or evolutionary scheme comparable in scope to that of L. H. Morgan. Lowie had suggested various theories concerning the origin of the family, kinship groups, and forms of society and had given them critical scrutiny. In *The Origin of the State* he did the same for this subject, repudiating the theory of a single cause of all origins and pointing to the complexity of the problem. Curiously, despite the subsequent interest in the development of states, there has been very little theoretical contribution to the subject.

Lowie was also greatly interested in legends and folklore, that is, in folk tales rather than in folklore in the European sense. His treatment of the varieties of religious experiences in his *Primitive Religion* (1924 and 1948) was not primarily critical of nineteenth-century thinking and for this reason, perhaps, had less impact on contemporary thought.

In his extraordinarily candid self-appraisal written for the National Academy of Sciences, Lowie pointed to his comparatively meager treatment of material culture, that is, technology and material manufactures, as a regrettable omission in his life's work. He was not uninformed about primitive technology and in fact eventually described it for the Plains Indians, especially his beloved Crow. This knowledge was incorporated finally in his book *The Crow Indians* (1935).

Over the years the American Museum of Natural History had issued a series of area-oriented handbooks that were intended primarily as guides to the museum exhibits. The

Plains Indian culture, with which the museum had been so greatly concerned under Clark Wissler, and for which Wissler had prepared the museum guide, was the subject of the handbook rewritten by Lowie in 1954.

During World War II and subsequently, anthropology became reoriented and enlarged its scope of interest. From primitive societies it first embraced acculturated people and finally societies of the contemporary world. Lowie had been little interested in Indian acculturation, though he had written occasionally on the subject, but his major contributions at this time were on German culture, which he knew very thoroughly through lifelong contacts with and frequent visits to Germany. He published a book called *The German People* in 1945 and another entitled *Toward Understanding Germany* in 1954. This abrupt departure from the conventional type of anthropology preceded by nearly twenty years comparable works by his colleagues that dealt with the modern world, and his books provided deep insights that only a person like Lowie could recognize.

Among Lowie's miscellaneous works was a book called *Are We Civilized?* published in 1929. This book, which was based upon many obscure sources dealing with European customs and practices of the last few centuries, was intended to draw attention to the artificiality of the concept that modern European cultures are intrinsically superior to those of primitive peoples. It was written in a humorous vein, though it did not, as Lowie had hoped, become a best-seller. This book illustrates the humorous strain in Lowie which was otherwise evident only when, to make a point in a lecture, he might perform a Crow war dance.

Many persons found Lowie somewhat difficult to approach, owing to a façade of apparent pomposity and possibly even conceit, but once his friendship was gained he was undeviatingly loyal and his generosity in giving of himself and offering encouragement was inexhaustible.

When a new anthropology building, which had been Kroeber's lifelong ambition, was finally built at the University of California at Berkeley, it was officially named the Robert H. Lowie Museum of Anthropology. This museum, together with the Museum of Art, was part of the A. L. Kroeber Hall, but the honor paid Lowie was especially significant in that Lowie was never identified with or personally attracted to museum work. His early connections with the American Museum of Natural History were mainly a means whereby he had the opportunity to do fieldwork under the direction of Clark Wissler, and he relinquished this job in 1921 to accept the more congenial role of Professor of Anthropology at the University of California.

Several appreciations of Lowie were published shortly after his death, which occurred on September 21, 1957. These are:

Paul Radin, *American Anthropologist*, 60 (1958):358–75.

A. L. Kroeber, *Year Book of the American Philosophical Society*, 1957:141–45, and *Sociologus*, 8 (1958):1–3.

Ermine Wheeler-Vogelin, *Journal of American Folklore*, 71 (1958):149–50.

In 1966 the Robert H. Lowie Museum of Anthropology published *The Complete Bibliography of Robert H. Lowie* with an introduction by Alan Dundes.

BIBLIOGRAPHY

KEY TO ABBREVIATIONS

Am. Anthropol. = American Anthropologist
Am. Antiquity = American Antiquity
Am. J. Psychiatry = American Journal of Psychiatry
Am. J. Sociol. = American Journal of Sociology
Am. Mercury = American Mercury
Am. Mus. J. = American Museum Journal
Anthropol. Linguistics = Anthropological Linguistics
Anthropol. Pap. Am. Mus. Nat. Hist. = Anthropological Papers of the American Museum of Natural History
Anthropol. Quart. = Anthropological Quarterly
Current Anthropol. Lit. = Current Anthropological Literature
J. Am. Folklore = Journal of American Folklore
Nat. Hist. = Natural History
New Repub. = New Republic
New Rev. = New Review
Proc. ———— Internat. Congr. Americanists = Proceedings of the ———— International Congress of Americanists
Psychol. Bull. = Psychological Bulletin
Sci. Monthly = Scientific Monthly
S.W. J. Anthropol. = Southwestern Journal of Anthropology
Univ. Calif. Publ. Am. Archaeol. Ethnol. = University of California Publications in American Archaeology and Ethnology
Z. Ethnol. = Zeitschrift für Ethnologie

Several bibliographies of Robert Lowie have been published, the most recent and fullest being *The Complete Bibliography of Robert H. Lowie,* with an Introduction by Alan Dundes, published by the Robert H. Lowie Museum of Anthropology, University of California, Berkeley, 1966. The present publications are taken from this, but do not include many items that were reprinted or that deal with nonanthropological subjects.

1907

With Livingston Farrand. Marriage. In: *Handbook of American Indians North of Mexico,* ed. by Frederick W. Hodge. Bureau of American Ethnology Bulletin 30, Vol. 1, pp. 808–10. Washington, U.S. Govt. Print. Off.

1908

Catchwords for mythological motives. J. Am. Folklore, 21:24–27.

The test-theme in North American mythology. J. Am. Folklore, 21:97–148.
Anthropological publications of the American Museum of Natural History for 1907–1908. Science, 28:522–24.

1909

The Northern Shoshone. Anthropol. Pap. Am. Mus. Nat. Hist., 2:165–306.
The Assiniboine. Anthropol. Pap. Am. Mus. Nat. Hist., 4:1–270.
Review. *Social Conditions, Beliefs, and Linguistic Relationships of the Tlingit Indians*, by John R. Swanton. J. Am. Folklore, 22:98–99.
Review. *Folklore as a Historical Science*, by George Lawrence Gomme. J. Am. Folklore, 22:99–101.
Editor, with H. H. St. Clair II. Shoshone and Comanche tales. J. Am. Folklore, 22:265–82.
Additional catchwords. J. Am. Folklore, 22:332–33.
Hero–trickster discussion. J. Am. Folklore, 22:431–33.
An ethnological trip to Lake Athabasca. Am. Mus. J., 9:10–15.
The Fijian collection. Am. Mus. J., 9:117–22.

1910

Notes concerning new collections. Anthropol. Pap. Am. Mus. Nat. Hist., 4:271–329.
With Clark Wissler. Anthropology. In: *New International Yearbook for 1909*, pp. 27–32. New York, Dodd, Mead & Co.
Review. *The Dawn of the World: Myths and Tales Told by the Mewan Indians of California*, by C. Hart Merriam. Am. Anthropol., 12:464–66.
Charms and amulets, American. In: *Encyclopedia of Religion and Ethics*, Vol. 3, pp. 401–9. New York, Charles Scribner's Sons.

1911

The methods of American ethnologists. Science, 34:604–5.
Review. *With a Prehistoric People, the Akikúyu of British East Africa*, by W. S. and K. Routledge. Am. Anthropol., 13:130–35.
A new conception of totemism. Am. Anthropol., 13:189–207.
Industry and art of the Negro race. Am. Mus. J., 11:12–19.
The new South Sea exhibit. Am. Mus. J., 11:53–56.

The Crow Indians of Montana. Am. Mus. J., 11:179–81.
A forgotten pragmatist: Ludwig Feuerbach. Journal of Philosophy, 8:128–29.
With Clark Wissler. Anthropology. In: *New International Yearbook for 1910*, pp. 34–40. New York, Dodd, Mead & Co.
Review. *Geschlachts—en Persoonsnamen der Piegans*, by C. C. Uhlenbeck. Am. Anthropol., 13:324–26.
Review. *The Origin of Civilisation and the Primitive Condition of Man*, by Lord Avebury. Am. Anthropol., 13:623.
Cosmogony and cosmology: Mexican and South American. In: *Encyclopedia of Religion and Ethics*, Vol. 4, pp. 168–74. New York, Charles Scribner's Sons.

1912

On the principle of convergence in ethnology. J. Am. Folklore, 25:24–42.
Some problems in the ethnology of the Crow and Village Indians. Am. Anthropol., 14:60–71.
American and English methods in ethnology. Am. Anthropol., 14:398–99.
Social life of the Crow Indians. Anthropol. Pap. Am. Mus. Nat. Hist., 9:179–248.
Chipewyan tales. Anthropol. Pap. Am. Mus. Nat. Hist., 10:171–200.
Crow Indian clowns. Am. Mus. J., 12:74.
Convergent evolution in ethnology. Am. Mus. J., 12:139–40.
Dr. Radosavljevich's critique of Professor Boas. Science, 35:537–40.
With Clark Wissler. Anthropology. In: *New International Yearbook for 1911*, pp. 46–50. New York, Dodd, Mead & Co.
Review. *Einleitung in die Philosophie*, by Hans Cornelius. Journal of Philosophy, Psychology, and Scientific Methods, 9:238–46.
Review. *The Baganda: An Account of Their Native Customs and Beliefs*. Current Anthropol. Lit., 1:34–37.
Review. *Deutsch Neu-Guinea*, by R. Neuhauss. Current Anthropol. Lit., 1:116–19.
Review. *Eine Forschungsreise im Bismarck-Archipel*, by Hans Vogel. Current Anthropol. Lit., 1:119.
Review. *Leitfaden der Völkerkunde*, by Karl Weule. Current Anthropol. Lit., 1:177–78.
Review. *In den Wildnissen Brasiliens*, by Fritz Krause. Current Anthropol. Lit., 1:199.

Review. *Ceremonial Bundles of the Blackfoot Indians,* by Clark Wissler. Current Anthropol. Lit., 1:286–88.

1913

Dance associations of the Eastern Dakota. Anthropol. Pap. Am. Mus. Nat. Hist., 11:101–42.
Societies of the Crow, Hidatsa and Mandan Indians. Anthropol. Pap. Am. Mus. Nat. Hist., 11:143–358.
The inferior races. New Rev., 1:934–42.
Review. *The Omaha Tribe,* by Alice C. Fletcher and Francis La Flesche. Science, 37:910–15.
Review. *Krückenruder,* by Fritz Graebner. Current Anthropol. Lit., 2:1–4.
Review. *Der Kaiserin-Agusta Fluss,* by Otto Reche. Current Anthropol. Lit., 2:19–20.
Review. *Und Afrika Sprach,* by Leo Frobenius. Current Anthropol. Lit., 2:87–91.
Review. *Man and His Forerunners,* by H. von Buttel-Reepen. Current Anthropol. Lit., 2:138.
Review. *The Childhood of the World: A Simple Account of Man's Origin and Early History,* by Edward Clodd. Current Anthropol. Lit., 2:227.
With Clark Wissler. Anthropology. In: *New International Yearbook for 1912,* pp. 30–35. New York, Dodd, Mead & Co.

1914

The Crow sun-dance. J. Am. Folklore, 27:94–96.
Social organization. Am. J. Sociol., 20:68–97.
Crow rapid-speech puzzles. J. Am. Folklore, 27:330–31.
Ceremonialism in North America. Am. Anthropol., 16:602–31.
International rivalry in science. New Repub., 1:15–16.
Ernst Haeckel. New Rev., 2:354–56.
Haeckel's Verhältnis zu Amerika. In: *Was wir Ernst Haeckel verdanken,* ed. by Heinrich Schmidt, Vol. II. pp. 404–7. Leipzig, Verlag Unesma G.M.B.H.
Some recent expressions of racial inferiority. New Rev., 2:542–46.
A pro-German view. New Rev., 2:642–44.
Reviews of anthropological literature. Psychol. Bull., 11:391–94. (This reference includes reviews on four publications: *The North American Indians of the Plains,* by Clark Wissler, 1912;

Kinship and Social Organization, by W. H. R. Rivers, 1914; *The Belief in Immortality and the Worship of the Dead.* Vol. 1: *The Belief among the Aborigines of Australia, the Torres Straits Islands, New Guinea and Melanesia,* by J. G. Frazer, 1913; Psychological interpretations of language, by A. M. Hocart, British Journal of Psychology, 5:267–79.)

With Clark Wissler. Anthropology. In: *New International Yearbook for 1913,* pp. 34–39. New York, Dodd, Mead & Co.

1915

Societies of the Arikara Indians. Anthropol. Pap. Am. Mus. Nat. Hist., 11:645–78.

Dances and societies of the Plains Shoshone. Anthropol. Pap. Am. Mus. Nat. Hist., 11:803–35.

The sun-dance of the Crow Indians. Anthropol. Pap. Am. Mus. Nat. Hist., 16:1–50.

The Crow Indian sun-dance. Am. Mus. J., 15:23–25.

Review. *Südsee, Urwald, Kannibalen,* by Felix Speiser. Am. Anthropol., 17:177–80.

Psychology and sociology. Am. J. Sociol., 21:217–29.

Review. *Some Fundamental Ideas of Chinese Culture,* by Berthold Laufer. Am. Anthropol., 17:350–52.

Review. *Native Tribes of the Northern Territory of Australia,* by Baldwin Spencer. Am. Anthropol., 17:354–55.

Review. *Ancient Hunters and Their Modern Representatives,* by W. J. Sollas. Am. Anthropol., 17:575–76.

Review. *The History of Melanesian Society,* by W. H. R. Rivers. Am. Anthropol., 17:588–91.

Oral tradition and history. Am. Anthropol., 17:597–99.

Exogamy and the classificatory systems of relationship. Proceedings of the National Academy of Sciences, 1:346–49.

American Indian dances. Am. Mus. J., 15:95–102.

The Crow Indians. Southern Workman, 44:605–12.

The sinking of the *Lusitania.* New Rev., 2:58–59.

Morgan's Ancient Society. New Rev., 3:101–4. Reprinted in Solidarität, 11:10–12.

Ceremonialism in North America. Reprinted in *Anthropology in North America,* by F. Boas and others, pp. 229–58. New York, G. E. Stechert & Co.

With Clark Wissler. Anthropology. In: *New International Yearbook for 1914,* pp. 35–39. New York, Dodd, Mead & Co.

1916

Historical and sociological interpretations of kinship terminologies. In: *Holmes Anniversary Volume,* ed. by Frederick Webb Hodge, pp. 269–77. Washington, J. W. Bryan Press.
Societies of the Kiowa. Anthropol. Pap. Am. Mus. Nat. Hist., 11:837–51.
Plains Indian age-societies: historical and comparative summary. Anthropol. Pap. Am. Mus. Nat. Hist., 11:877–92.
A note on Blackfoot relationship terms. Am. Anthropol., 18:148.
Ernst Mach: the messiah of scientific thought. New Repub., 6:335–37.
Theoretical ethnology. Psychol. Bull., 13:397–400.
A new Shakespeare. International, 10:246–47.
With Leta Hollingworth. Science and feminism. Sci. Monthly, 3:277–84.
With Clark Wissler. Anthropology. In: *New International Yearbook for 1915,* pp. 31–35. New York, Dodd, Mead & Co.
Review. *Alfred R. Wallace: Letters and Reminiscences,* by James Marchant. New Repub., 9:14–16.
Review. *The Turano-Ganowanian System and the Nations of North-East Asia,* by Leo Sternberg. Am. Anthropol., 18:287–89.
Review. *Ethnographisch Album van het Stroomgebied van den Congo,* by J. Marquart, J. D. E. Schmeltz, and J. P. B. de Josselin de Jong. Am. Anthropol., 18:436–37.
Review. *The Mythology of All Races. Vol. X: North American,* by Hartley Burr Alexander. Am. Anthropol., 18:563.
Review. *Inequality of Races,* by Arthur de Gobineau. New Rev., 4:166.

1917

Culture and Ethnology. New York, Douglas C. McMurtrie. 189 pp.
Notes on the social organization and customs of the Mandan, Hidatsa, and Crow Indians. Anthropol. Pap. Am. Mus. Nat. Hist., 21:1–99.
Oral tradition and history. J. Am. Folklore, 30:161–67.
The kinship systems of the Crow and Hidatsa. Proc. 19th Internat.

Congr. Americanists, ed. by F. W. Hodge, pp. 340–43. New York, Museum of the American Indian.
Review. *The Mythology of All Races. Vol. IX: Oceania,* by Roland B. Dixon. Am. Anthropol., 19:86–88.
Edward B. Tyler. Am. Anthropol., 19:262–68.
Ojibwa. In: *Encyclopedia of Religion and Ethics,* Vol. 9, pp. 454–58. New York, Charles Scribner's Sons.
Peyote rite. In: *Encyclopedia of Religion and Ethics,* Vol. 9, p. 815. New York, Charles Scribner's Sons.
Age societies of the Plains Indians. Am. Mus. J., 17:495–96.
Noted in Hopiland. Am. Mus. J., 17:568–73.
Review. *Heredity and Environment in the Development of Men,* by Edwin Grant Conklin. New Repub., 11:59–60.
Review. *The Birth Time of the World and Other Scientific Essays,* by J. Joly. New Repub., 12:196–97.
With Clark Wissler. Anthropology. In: *New International Yearbook for 1916,* pp. 31–36. New York, Dodd, Mead & Co.
Review. Kin, kinship, by W. H. R. Rivers. (*Encyclopaedia of Religion and Ethics,* Vol. 7, 1914, pp. 700–7.) Am. Anthropol., 19:269.
Review. *Marriage,* by W. H. R. Rivers. Am. Anthropol., 19:270–71.
Review. *Mother-Right,* by W. H. R. Rivers. Am. Anthropol., 19:272.
Review. *Harvard African Studies: Varia Africana I,* ed. by Oric Bates. Am. Anthropol., 19:546–47.
Review. *Eternity: World-War Thoughts on Life and Death, Religion, and the Theory of Evolution,* by Ernst Haeckel. The Masses, Vol. 9, No. 6, Issue No. 70.
The Universalist fallacy. New Repub., 13:4–6.

1918

Myths and traditions of the Crow Indians. Anthropol. Pap. Am. Mus. Nat. Hist., 25:1–308.
Age societies of the Plains Indians. Scientific American, 85:201.
More light: a rejoinder. Am. Anthropol., 20:229–30.
Survivals and the historical method. Am. J. Sociol., 24:529–35.
The true authority of science. Dial, 63:432–34.
Anthropology put to work. Dial, 65:98–100.

Review. *The Wonders of Instinct,* by Jean-Henri Fabre. Dial, 65:120.
With Clark Wissler. Anthropology. In: *New International Yearbook for 1917,* pp. 31–37. New York, Dodd, Mead & Co.
Review. *Aboriginal Siberia,* by A. M. Czaplicka. Am. Anthropol., 20:325–26.
Review. *Myths and Legends of the Sioux,* by Marie L. McLaughlin. Am. Anthropol., 20:451–53.
Review. *The Mythology of All Races, Vol. XIII: Egyptian,* by W. Max Muller; *Indo-Chinese,* by Sir James George Scott. New Repub., 16:113–14.
Review. *A Short History of Science,* by W. T. Sedgwick and H. W. Tyler. Dial, 65:157–58.

1919

The sun dance of the Shoshone, Ute, and Hidatsa. Anthropol. Pap. Am. Mus. Nat. Hist., 16:387–431.
The tobacco society of the Crow Indians. Anthropol. Pap. Am. Mus. Nat. Hist., 21:101–200.
The matrilineal complex. Univ. Calif. Publ. Am. Archaeol. Ethnol., 16:29–45.
Family and sib. Am. Anthropol., 21:28–40.
Biometrics. International Journal of Orthodontia and Oral Surgery, 5:219–27.
The economic interpretation of history, a footnote. Dial, 66:35–36.
Primitive ideas on numbers and systems of measurement. Nat. Hist., 19:110–12.
Ernst Haeckel and his work. Christian Science Monitor, 11:3.
Review. *The Mythology of All Races, Vol. III: Celtic,* by John Arnott Macculloch; *Slavic,* by Ján Máchal. New Repub., 18:29–30.
Biology and anthropology. New Repub., 20:3.
With Clark Wissler. Anthropology. In: *New International Yearbook for 1918,* pp. 37–41. New York, Dodd, Mead & Co.
Review. *Time Perspective in Aboriginal American Culture: A Study in Method,* by Edward Sapir. Am. Anthropol., 21:75–77.
Review. *Harvard African Studies II: Varia Africana II,* ed. by Oric Bates. Am. Anthropol., 21:208–10.
Review. *Neu-Caledonien und die Loyalty-inseln,* by Fritz Sarasin. Am. Anthropol., 21:311–15.

Review. *The Causes and Course of Organic Evolution,* by John M. Macfarlane. Dial, 66:48–49.
Review. *Men of the Old Stone Age,* by H. F. Osborn. Dial, 66:150.
Review. *Racial Factors in Democracy,* by P. A. Means. Dial, 67:32.

1920

Primitive Society. New York, Boni & Liveright. 463 pp.
Mysticism and science. Freeman, 1:63–64.
Applied psychology. Freeman, 1:91–92.
Herbert Spencer. Freeman, 1:219.
Review. *August Weismann,* by E. Gaupp. Freeman, 1:256–58.
Review. *The Autobiography of a Winnebago Indian,* by Paul Radin. Freeman, 1:334.
Review. *Psychology and Folk-Lore,* by R. R. Marett. Freeman, 1:453–54.
The father of eugenics. Freeman, 1:471–74.
An ethnologist's memories. Freeman, 1:517–18.
Review. *Science and Life,* by F. Soddy. Freeman, 2:20–21.
Wilhelm Wundt. Freeman, 2:42.
An ethnologist's memories (continued). Freeman, 2:85–86.
The divine right of lineage. Freeman, 2:179–81.
The people of unknown lands. Bookman, 52:156–60.
With Clark Wissler. Anthropology. In: *New International Yearbook for 1919,* pp. 42–48. New York, Dodd, Mead & Co.
Marriage and society among the Crow Indians. In: *Source Book in Anthropology,* by A. L. Kroeber and T. T. Waterman, pp. 349–54. Berkeley, University of California Press.
Review. *Die ethnologische Wirtschaftsforschung: Eine historisch-kritische Studie,* by W. Koppers. Am. Anthropol., 22:72–73.
Review. *Vorläufiger Bericht über Forschungen im Innern von Deutsch-Neu-Guinea,* by R. Thurnwald. Am. Anthropol., 22:80–81.
Review. *The Intellectuals and the Wage Workers: A Study in Educational Psychoanalysis,* by Herbert E. Cory. Am. Anthropol., 22:186.
Review. *Calendars of the Indians North of Mexico,* by Leona Cope. Am. Anthropol., 22:188.
Review. *Eine völkerkundliche Sammlung von den Europäischen Samojeden,* by A. Jacobi. Am. Anthropol., 22:189–90.

Review. *Messiahs: Christian and Pagan,* by W. D. Wallis. Am. Anthropol., 22:383.
Review. *The Principles of Sociology,* by Edward A. Ross. Nation, 111:418–19.
Review. *Life of Pasteur,* by R. Vallery-Radot; also *Pasteur: The History of a Mind,* by E. Duclaux. Freeman, 2:259–60.
Review. *Religion and Culture,* by F. Schleiter. New Repub., 21:364.
Review. *Unexplored New Guinea,* by Wilfred N. Beaver. New Repub., 23:26.
Review. *The Secrets of Animal Life,* by J. A. Thomson. New Repub., 23:260.

1921

Review. *Verebung und Auslese: Grundriss der Gesellschaftsbiologie und der Lehre vom Rassendienst,* by W. Schallmayer. Am. Anthropol., 23:77–78.
A note on aesthetics. Am. Anthropol., 23:170–74.
Review. *The Psychology of Insanity,* by Bernard Hart. Am. Anthropol., 23:215.
Review. *Source Book in Anthropology,* by A. L. Kroeber and T. T. Waterman. Am. Anthropol., 23:216–17.
Review. *The Northern d'Entrecasteaux,* by D. Jenness and A. Ballantyne. Am. Anthropol., 23:226–27.
Review. *My Life and Friends: A Psychologist's Memories,* by James Sully. Freeman, 2:524–25.
Review. *Recreations of a Psychologist,* by G. Stanley Hall. Freeman, 2:594–95.
Review. *Folk-lore in the Old Testament,* by J. G. Frazer. Freeman, 3:67–68.
Review. *When Buffalo Ran,* by G. B. Grinnell. Freeman, 3:141.
Review. *North American Indians of the Plains,* by Clark Wissler. Freeman, 3:190.
Review. *Eriebtes und Erkanntes,* by Wilhelm Wundt. Freeman, 3:260–61.
Review. In the beginning. (Discussion of *Primitive Society: The Beginnings of the Family and the Reckoning of Descent,* by Edwin Sidney Hartland, and *Die Anfänge des menschlichen Gemeinschaftslebens im Spiegel der neueren Völkerkunde,* by Wilhelm Koppers.) Freeman, 3:595–96.

The eugenicists' programme. Freeman, 4:129–30.
With Clark Wissler. Anthropology. In: *New International Yearbook for 1920*, pp. 41–46. New York, Dodd, Mead & Co.
Review. *The Origin of Man and His Superstitions*, by Carvath Read. New Repub., 28:80.
Review. *The New Stone Age in Northern Europe*, by John M. Tyler. New Repub., 28:223–24.

1922

The material culture of the Crow Indians. Anthropol. Pap. Am. Mus. Nat. Hist., 21:201–70.
Crow Indian art. Anthropol. Pap. Am. Mus. Nat. His., 21:27–332.
The religion of the Crow Indians. Anthropol. Pap. Am. Mus. Nat. Hist., 25:309–44.
The avunculate in patrilineal tribes. Am. Anthropol., 24:94–95.
Science. In: *Civilization in the United States*, ed. by Harold Stearns, pp. 151–61, New York, Harcourt, Brace & Company.
Takes-the-Pipe, a Crow warrior. In: *American Indian Life*, ed. by Elsie Clews Parsons, pp. 17–33. New York, B. W. Huebsch.
A Crow woman's tale. In: *American Indian Life*, ed. by Elsie Clews Parsons, pp. 35–40. New York, B. W. Huebsch.
A trial of shamans. In: *American Indian Life.*, ed. by Elsie Clews Parsons, pp. 41–43. New York, B. W. Huebsch.
Windigo, a Chipewyan story. In: *American Indian Life*, ed. by Elsie Clews Parsons, pp. 325–36. New York, B. W. Huebsch.
Review. *The Passing of the Great Race*, by Madison Grant. Freeman, 4:476–78.
Rejoinder to objector to review of Madison Grant. Freeman, 5:66.
Review. *The Origin and Evolution of the Human Race*, by Albert Churchward. Freeman, 5:190.
The Plains Indians. Freeman, 5:211–12.
The origin of the state. Freeman, 5:440–42; *ibid.*, 465–67.
Review. *The American Indian*, by Clark Wissler. Freeman, 5:547–48.
Review. *Lester F. Ward*, by Emily P. Cape. Freeman, 5:595–96.
Review. *Early Civilization: An Introduction to Anthropology*, by A. A. Goldenweiser. Freeman, 6:235–36.
Review. *Batouala*, by René Maran. Freeman, 6:284–85.
With Clark Wissler. Anthropology. In: *New International Yearbook for 1921*, pp. 43–47. New York, Dodd, Mead & Co.

Review. *Manhood of Humanity: The Science and Art of Human Engineering*, by Alfred Korzybski. New Repub., 29:313.
Review. *Readings in Evolution, Genetics and Eugenics*, by H. H. Newman. New Repub., 30:25–26.
Review. *Introduction to the Science of Sociology*, by R. E. Park and E. W. Burgess. Am. Anthropol., 24:215.

1923

The cultural connections of Californian and Plateau Shoshonean tribes. Univ. Calif. Publ. Am. Archaeol. Ethnol., 20:145–56.
The buffalo drive and an Old World hunting practice. Nat. Hist., 23:280–82.
Review. *Language*, by Edward Sapir. Am. Anthropol., 25:90–93.
Review. *Harvard African Studies III: Varia Africana III*, ed. by E. A. Hooten and Natica I. Bates. Am. Anthropol., 25:103–5.
Review. *The Evolution of Kinship: An African Study*, by Sidney Hartland. Am. Anthropol., 25:272–73.
A note on Kiowa kinship terms and usages. Am. Anthropol., 25:279–81.
Psychology, anthropology, and race. Am. Anthropol., 25:291–303.
Review. *Inheriting the Earth*, by O. W. von Engeln. Freeman, 6:572–73.
Review. *The Evolution of Man*, ed. by G. A. Bartsell. Freeman, 7:284–85.
Races and psychological tests. Freeman, 7:342–43.
Review. *The Golden Bough* (abridged). Freeman, 7:353–55.
Review. *Seneca Indian Myths*, by Jeremiah Curtin. Freeman, 7:380–81.
Review. *Social Change*, by W. F. Ogburn. Freeman, 7:431.
Review. *Man and Culture*, by Clark Wissler. Freeman, 8:93–94.
Review. *Letters to His Parents, 1852–1856: The Story of the Development of a Youth*, by Ernst Haeckel. Freeman, 8:164–65.
With Clark Wissler. Anthropology. In: *New International Yearbook for 1922*, pp. 43–48. New York, Dodd, Mead & Co.
Review. *The Evolution and Progress of Mankind*, by Hermann Klaatsch. New Repub., 35:268–69.
Review. *The Racial History of Mankind*, by R. B. Dixon. Nation, 116:698.
Review. *The Winnebago Tribe*, by Paul Radin. Occident, November, p. 43.

Review. *Psychologie des primitiven Menschen,* by R. Thurnwald. Am. Anthropol., 25:417–18.
Review. *Beothuk and Micmac,* by F. G. Speck. Am. Anthropol., 25:418–19.
Review. *The Andaman Islanders* by A. R. Brown. Am. Anthropol., 25:572–75.

1924

Primitive Religion. New York, Boni & Liveright. xix + 346 pp.
Shoshonean tales. J. Am. Folklore, 37:1–242.
Notes on Shoshonean ethnography. Anthropol. Pap. Am. Mus. Nat. Hist., 20:185–314.
The origin and spread of culture. Am. Mercury, 1:463–65.
Minor ceremonies of the Crow Indians. Anthropol. Pap. Am. Mus. Nat. Hist., 21:323–65.
With Clark Wissler. Anthropology. In: *New International Yearbook for 1923,* pp. 42–47. New York, Dodd, Mead & Co.
Review. *The Children of the Sun,* by W. J. Perry. Am. Anthropol., 26:86–90.
Review. *American Indians: Tribes of the Prairies and the East,* by Hermann Dengler. Am. Anthropol., 26:269.
Review. *Unter Feuerland-Indianern,* by Wilhelm Koppers. Am. Anthropol., 26:414–15.
Review. *The Toba Indians of the Bolivian Chaco,* by Rafael Karsten. Am. Anthropol., 26:538–40.
Review. *What Is Man?* by J. A. Thomson. New Repub., 41:18.

1925

The historical connection between certain Old World and New World beliefs. Proc. 21st Internat. Congr. Americanists, pp. 546–49.
Review. *Medicine, Magic and Religion,* by W. H. R. Rivers. Am. Anthropol., 27:457–58.
Review. *Monotheism among Primitive Peoples,* by Paul Radin. Am. Anthropol., 27:560–61.
Review. *Reallexikon der Vorgeschichte,* ed. by Max Ebert, Vols. 1 and 2. Am. Anthropol., 27:561–62.
Five as a mystic number. Am. Anthropol., 27:578.
A note on history and race. Am. Mercury, 4:342–43.
Is America so bad after all? Century Magazine, 109:723–29.

A women's ceremony among the Hopi. Nat. Hist., 25:178–83.
African ethnology. In: *New International Encyclopaedia,* 2d ed., Vol. 1, pp. 212–14. New York, Dodd, Mead & Co.

1926

Zur Verbreitung der Flutsagen. Anthropos, 21:615–16.
The banana in America. Nature, 117:517–18.
Review. *Kultur und Religion des primitiven Menschen,* by Theodor-Wilhelm Danzel. Am. Anthropol., 28:281–82.
Review. *Magie und Geheimwissenschaft in ihrer Bedeutung für Kultur und Kulturgeschichte,* by Theodor-Wilhelm Danzel. Am. Anthropol., 28:282–83.
Review. *Völker und Kulturen,* Erster Teil: *Gesellschaft und Wirtschaft der Völker,* by Wilhelm Schmidt and Wilhelm Koppers. Am. Anthropol., 28:283–85.
Review. *Social Origin and Social Continuities,* by A. M. Tozzer. Am. Anthropol., 28:285–86.
Review. *Les Récentes Découvertes pré-historiques in Indochine,* by M. R. Verneau. Am. Anthropol., 28:289, 424.
Review. *Unter den Zwergen von Malakka,* by Paul Schebesta. Am. Anthropol., 28:298–99.
Review. *Der diluviale Mensch in Europa,* by F. Birkner. Am. Anthropol., 28:420.
Review. *The Relation of Nature to Man in Aboriginal America,* by Clark Wissler. New Repub., 48:331–32.
Review. *Essai d'introduction critique à l'étude de l'économie primitive: Les Théories de K. Buecher et l'ethnologie moderne,* by Olivier Leroy. Am. Anthropol., 28:549.

1927

The Origin of the State. New York, Harcourt, Brace & Company. 117 pp.
Note on the history of anthropology. Science, 66:111.
Theoretische ethnologie in Amerika. Jahrbuch für Soziologie, 3:111–24.
Prestige among Indians. Am. Mercury, 12:446–48.
Anthropology and law. In: *The Social Sciences and Their Interrelations,* ed. by W. F. Ogburn and A. Goldenweiser, pp. 50–59. New York, Houghton Mifflin Company.

Review. *Illustrierte Völkerkunde (in zwei Bänden).* II: Zweiter Teil, ed. by Georg Buschan. Am. Anthropol., 29:112–13.
Review. *Reallexikon der Vorgeschichte,* ed. by Max Ebert, Vols. 3–7. Am. Anthropol., 29:332x–35x.
Review. *Archiv für Rassenbilder,* by E. Eickstedt. Am. Anthropol., 29:339.
Review. *Der Urspring der Gottesidee, I: Historischkritischer Teil,* by Wilhelm Schmidt. Am. Anthropol., 29:689–90.
Review. *The Diffusion of Culture,* by R. R. Marett. Am. Anthropol., 29:690–91.
Review. *The Peoples of Southern Nigeria,* by P. Amaury Talbot. Am. Anthropol., 29:715–17.
Review. *Downland Man,* by H. J. Massingham. New Repub., 51:234.
Review. *The Next Age of Man,* by Albert Edward Wiggam. New Repub., 51:261–62.
Review. *Myth in Primitive Religion* and *Sex and Repression in Savage Society,* by Bronislaw Malinowski. New Repub. (Winter Book Section), 53:115–16.
Review. *The Use of Stilts, Especially in Africa and America,* by K. G. Lindblom. Am. Anthropol., 30:157–58.
A note on relationship terminologies. Am. Anthropol., 30:263–67.
Individual differences and primitive culture. In: *Wilhelm Schmidt Festschrift,* ed. by W. Koppers, pp. 495–500. Vienna, Mechitaristen-Congregations-Buchdr.
Incorporeal property in primitive society. Yale Law Journal, 37:551–63.
Review. *Beziehungen und Beeinflussungen der Kunstgruppen in Paläolithikum* and *Alter und Bedeutung der nordafrikanischen Felszeichnungen,* by Herbert Kühn. Am. Anthropol., 30:327–28.
Edward S. Burgess, 1855–1928. Am. Anthropol., 30:481–82.
Word formation in the American Indian languages. Am. Mercury, 14:332–34.
Bathing through the ages. Am. Mercury, 15:62–64.
Aboriginal education in America. Am. Mercury, 15:192–96.
With E. W. Gifford. Notes on the Akwa'ala Indians. Univ. Calif. Publ. Am. Archaeol. Ethnol., 23:339–52.
Review. *Bei den Urwaldzwergen von Malaya,* by P. Schebesta. Am. Anthropol., 30:483–86.

Review. *The Yukaghir and the Yukaghirized Tungus*, by W. Jochelson. Am. Anthropol., 30:487–90.
Review. *Reallexikon der Vorgeschichte*, ed. by Max Ebert, Vols. 8 and 9. Am. Anthropol., 30:714–16.
Review. *Studies on the Origin of Cultivated Plants*, by N. Vavilov. Am. Anthropol., 30:716–19.

1929

Are We Civilized? Human Culture in Perspective. New York, Harcourt, Brace & Company. 306 pp.
Notes on Hopi clans. Anthropol. Pap. Am. Mus. Nat. His., 30:303–60.
Hopi kinship. Anthropol. Pap. Am. Mus. Nat. Hist., 30:361–88.
Culture and Ethnology. New York, Peter Smith. 189 pp.
Relationship terms. In: *Encyclopaedia Britannica*, 14th ed., Vol. 19, pp. 84–89. New York, Encyclopaedia Britannica, Inc.
Review. *The Yukaghir and the Yukaghirized Tungus* (continued), by W. Jochelson. Am. Anthropol., 31:163–65.
Review. *Instructions pour les voyageurs: Instructions d'enquête linguistique*, by Marcel Cohen. Am. Anthropol., 31:499.
Review. *Reallexikon der Vorgeschichte*, ed. by Max Ebert, Vols. 10 and 11. Am. Anthropol., 31:499–500, 780–85.
Review. *The Oriental Institute of the University of Chicago*, by J. W. Breasted; also *First Report of the Prehistoric Survey Expedition*, by K. S. Sandford and W. J. Arkell. Am. Anthropol., 31:501.
Review. *Pots and Pans: The History of Ceramics*, by H. S. Harrison. Am. Anthropol., 31:504–6.
Review. *Coming of Age in Samoa*, by Margaret Mead. Am. Anthropol., 31:532–34.

1930

Adoption, primitive. In: *Encyclopaedia of the Social Sciences*, Vol. 1, pp. 459–60. New York, The Macmillan Company.
Age societies. In: *Encyclopaedia of the Social Sciences*, Vol. 1, pp. 482–83. New York, The Macmillan Company.
Avoidance. In: *Encyclopaedia of the Social Sciences*, Vol. 2, pp. 369–70. New York, The Macmillan Company.
Ceremony, primitive. In: *Encyclopaedia of the Social Sciences*, Vol. 3, pp. 313–14. New York, The Macmillan Company.

Review. *In the Beginning: The Origin of Civilization,* by G. Elliot Smith; also *Gods and Men: The Attainment of Immortality,* by W. J. Perry. Am. Anthropol., 32:165–68.

Review. *Some Elements of Sexual Behavior in Primates,* by Gerrit S. Miller. Am. Anthropol., 32:168–69.

Review. *Ein Versuch zur Rettung des Evolutionismus,* by Wilhelm Schmidt. Am. Anthropol., 32:169–70.

Review. *Reallexikon der Vorgeschichte,* ed. by Max Ebert, Vol. 12. Am. Anthropol., 32:170–71.

Review. *Peoples of Asiatic Russia,* by Waldemar Jochelson; also *Adoption among the Gunantuna,* by Joseph Meier. Am. Anthropol., 32:178.

The kinship terminology of the Bannock Indians. Am. Anthropol., 32:294–99.

Review. *Reallexikon der Vorgeschichte,* ed. by Max Ebert, Vol. 13. Am. Anthropol., 32:300–1.

A Crow text, with grammatical notes. Univ. Calif. Publ. Am. Archaeol. Ethnol., 29:155–75.

"Freemasons" among North Dakota Indians. Am. Mercury, 19:192–96.

Literature and ethnography. Am. Mercury, 19:454–58.

American Indian cultures. Am. Mercury, 20:362–66.

Review. *Collected Essays in Ornamental Art,* by Hjalmar Stolpe. Am. Anthropol., 32:301–2.

Review. *The Relationship Systems of the Tlingit, Haida, and Tsimshian,* by T. M. Durlach. Am. Anthropol., 32:308–9.

Review. *Melanesian Shell Money,* by A. B. Lewis. Am. Anthropol., 32:312–13.

Review. The original home and mode of dispersal of the coconut, by Arthur W. Hill. Am. Anthropol., 32:320–21.

Review. *Der nordische Mensch: Die Merkmale der nordischen Rasse mit besonderer Berücksichtigung der rassischen Verhältnisse Norwegens,* by Halfdan Bryn. Am. Anthropol., 32:547.

Review. *The Savage as He Really Is,* by J. H. Driberg. Am. Anthropol., 32:557.

Review. *Ethnologischer Anzeiger,* by M. Heydrich. Am. Anthropol., 32:661.

1931

Hugo Obermaier's reconstruction of sequences among prehistoric

cultures in the Old World. In: *Methods in Social Science,* ed. by Stuart Rice, pp. 266-74. Chicago, University of Chicago Press.
Inventiveness of the American Indian. Am. Mercury, 24:90-93.
Indian theologians. Am. Mercury, 24:472-79.
Marriage and society among the Crow Indians. In: *Source Book in Anthropology,* ed. by A. L. Kroeber and T. T. Waterman, pp. 304-9. New York, Harcourt, Brace & Company.
Woman and religion. In: *The Making of Man,* ed. by V. F. Calverton, pp. 744-57. New York, The Modern Library, Inc.
Review. *An Introduction to Social Anthropology,* by Clark Wissler. Am. Anthropol., 33:111-12.
Review. *Tod und Unsterblichkeit im Glauben der Naturvölker,* by K. T. Preuss. Am. Anthropol., 33:626-27.
Review. *The Mothers: The Matriarchal Theory of Social Origins,* by Robert Briffault. Am. Anthropol., 33:630-31.
Review. *The Mound Builders,* by H. C. Shetrone. New Repub., 65:304-6.

1932

Kinship. In: *Encyclopaedia of the Social Sciences,* Vol. 8, pp. 568-72. New York, The Macmillan Company.
Marriage and family life among the Plains Indians. Sci. Monthly, 34:462-64.
Primitive points related to Aztecs. El Palacio, 32:82-83.
Development of family pattern. El Palacio, 32:191-92.
The Trocadero Museum. Am. Anthropol., 34:165.
Review. *American: The Life Story of a Great Indian,* by Frank B. Linderman. Am. Anthropol., 34:532-33.
Review. *The Narrative of a Southern Cheyenne Woman,* by Truman Michelson. Am. Anthropol., 34:534.
Review. *Old Man Coyote (Crow),* by Frank B. Linderman. Am. Anthropol., 34:717-18.
Proverbial expressions among the Crow Indians. Am. Anthropol., 34:739-40.

1933

Erland Nordenskiöld, with bibliography of his writings. Am. Anthropol., 35:158-64.
Review. *Die Verwandtschaftsorganisation der Urwaldstämme Südamerikas,* by Paul Kirchhoff. Am. Anthropol., 35:182-83.

Review. *Les Hommes-dieux chez les Chiriguano et dans l'Amérique du Sud*, by A. Métraux. Am. Anthropol., 35:183–84.
A Crow Indian medicine. Am. Anthropol., 35:207.
Queries. Am. Anthropol., 35: 288–96.
Review. *Die menschliche Gesellschaft*, by R. Thurnwald, Vols. 2 and 3. Am. Anthropol., 35:343–45.
Review. *Ethnologické materiálie z jihozápadu U.S.A.*, by F. Pospísil. Am. Anthropol., 35:359.
Review. *Flesh of the Wild Ox: A Riffian Chronicle of High Valleys and Long Rifles*, by Carleton S. Coon. Am. Anthropol., 35:372–73.
Review. *Notes d'ethnologie Néo-Calédonienne*, by M. Leenhardt. Am. Anthropol., 35:382.
Crow prayers. Am. Anthropol., 35:433–42.
Review. *Ethnology of Melanesia*, by A. B. Lewis. Am. Anthropol., 35:527.
Review. *Omaha Secret Societies*, by R. W. Fortune. Am. Anthropol., 35:529–33.
The family as a social unit. Papers of the Michigan Academy of Science, Arts, and Letters, 1932, 18:53–69. (Published also as appendix to the French translation of *Primitive Society*. See 1935.)
Land tenure, primitive societies. In: *Encyclopaedia of the Social Sciences*, Vol. 9, pp. 76–77. New York, The Macmillan Company.
Marriage. In: *Encyclopaedia of the Social Sciences*, Vol. 10, pp. 146–54. New York, The Macmillan Company.
Selk'nam kinship terms. Am. Anthropol., 35:546–48.
Primitive skeptics. Am. Mercury, 29:320–23.

1934

An Introduction to Cultural Anthropology. New York, Farrar and Rinehart. 365 pp.
Religious ideas and practices of the Eurasiatic and North American areas. In: *Essays Presnted to C. G. Seligman*, ed. by E. E. Evans-Pritchard and others, pp. 183–88. London, George Routledge & Sons, Ltd.
Review. *History, Psychology and Culture*, by Alexander Goldenweiser. Am. Anthropol., 36:114–15.
Schurtz, Heinrich (1863–1903). In: *Encyclopaedia of the Social Sciences*, Vol. 13, p. 587. New York, The Macmillan Company.

Social organization. In: *Encyclopaedia of the Social Sciences,* Vol. 14, pp. 141–48. New York, The Macmillan Company.
Review. *Red Mother,* by Frank B. Linderman. Am. Anthropol., 36:124–26.
Review. *Life in Lesu: The Study of a Melanesian Society in New Ireland,* by Hortense Powdermaker. Am. Anthropol., 36:129–30.
Some moot problems in social organization. Am. Anthropol., 36:321–30.
Review. *Bambuti, die Zwerge von Kongo,* by Paul Schebesta. Am. Anthropol., 36:469.
The Omaha and Crow kinship terminologies. In: Verhandlungen des XXIV. Internationalen Amerikanisten-Kongresses, Hamburg, 1930, ed. by R. Grossmann and G. Antze, pp. 102–8. Hamburg, Friederichsen, De Gruyter & Co. m.b.H.

1935

Eine kaukasisch-lappländische Parallele. Anthropos, 30:224–25.
The Crow Indians. New York, Farrar and Rinehart. 350 pp.
Waitz, Franz Theodor (1821–1864). In: *Encyclopaedia of the Social Sciences,* Vol. 15, p. 321. New York, The Macmillan Company.
Traité de sociologie humaine. (French translation of *Primitive Society,* translated by Alfred Métraux.) Paris, Payot. 460 pp.

1936

Cultural anthropology: a science. Am. J. Sociol., 42:301–20.
Manuel d'anthropologie culturelle. (French translation of *An Introduction to Cultural Anthropology,* translated by Alfred Métraux.) Paris, Payot. 390 pp.
Alfred L. Kroeber: professional appreciation. In: *Essay in Anthropology Presented to Alfred L. Kroeber,* ed. by R. H. Lowie, pp. xix–xxiii. Berkeley, University of California Press.
Lewis H. Morgan in historical perspective. In: *Essays in Anthropology Presented to Alfred L. Kroeber,* ed. by R. H. Lowie, pp. 169–81. Berkeley, University of California Press.
Bibliography of Alfred L. Kroeber. In: *Essays in Anthropology Presented to Alfred L. Kroeber,* ed. by R. H. Lowie, pp. 423–28. Berkeley, University of California Press.

Review. *Bei Bauern und Jägern in Inner-Angola*, by Lunda Baumann. Am. Anthropol., 38:118–20.
Review. *Die schwarze Frau im Wandel Afrikas: Eine soziologische Studie unter ostafrikanischen Stämmen*, by Hilde Thurnwald. Am. Anthropol., 38:120–21.
Review. *Introduction à la connaissance de l'île de Pâques*, by A. Métraux. Am. Anthropol., 38:126–27.

1937

The History of Ethnological Theory. New York, Farrar and Rinehart. 296 pp.
Review. *Schöpfung und Urzeit des Menschen im Mythus der afrikanischen Völker*, by Lunda Baumann. Am. Anthropol., 39:346–47.
Dr. Wissler on "The Crow Indians." Am. Anthropol., 39:366.
With Curt Nimuendajú. The dual organizations of the Ramkokamekra (Canella) of northern Brazil. Am. Anthropol., 39:565–82.
Translation. The Gamella Indians, by Curt Nimuendajú. Primitive Man, 10:58–72.
Introduction. In: *A Black Civilization*, by W. Lloyd Warner, pp. xiii–xvi. New York, Harper & Brothers.
Review. *Jabo Proverbs from Liberia*, by George Herzog and Charles G. Blooah. J. Am. Folklore, 50:198.

1938

Subsistence. In: *General Anthropology*, ed. by Franz Boas, pp. 282–326. Boston, D. C. Heath & Company.
A note on South American parallels to Maya and Aztec traits. Am. Antiquity, 4:157–59.
Translation. *The Social Structure of the Ramko-kamekra*, by Curt Nimuendajú. Am. Anthropol., 40:51–74, 760.
Review. *Handbuch der Methode der kulturhistorischen Ethnologie*, by Wilhelm Schmidt. Am. Anthropol., 40:142–44.
Review. *Primitive Behavior*, by W. I. Thomas. Am. Anthropol., 40:144.
The emergence hold and the foot-drum. Am. Anthropol., 40:174.
Review. *Blankets and Moccasins*, by G. D. Wagner and W. A. Allen. Am. Anthropol., 40:309.

Review. *Die Feuerland-Indianer; Band II: Die Yamana*, by Martin Gusinde. Am. Anthropol., 40:495–503.

1939

Ethnographic notes on the Washo. Univ. Calif. Publ. Am. Archaeol. Ethnol., 36:301–52.
With Curt Nimuendajú. The associations of the Šerente. Am. Anthropol., 41:408–15.
With Z. Harris and C. F. Voegelin. Hidatsa texts. Indiana Historical Society Prehistory Research Series, 1:169–239.
Translation. *The Apinaye'*, by Curt Nimuendajú. Catholic University of America Anthropological Series, No. 8. Washington, Catholic University of America. 189 pp.
Review. *Menschen der Südsee, Characktere und Schicksale*, by T. Thurnwald. J. Am. Folklore, 51:352–53.
An Introduction to Cultural Anthropology. New York, Farrar and Rinehart. 584 pp.
Native languages as ethnographic tools. Am. Anthropol., 42:81–89.
American culture history. Am. Anthropol., 42:409–28.
Translation. The Kupá, a cultivated plant of the Timbira of Brazil, by Curt Nimuendajú. In: Proceedings of the Sixth Congress of the Pacific Science Association, Berkeley, 1939, pp. 131–34. Berkeley, University of California Press.
Review. *Race, Culture and Language*, by Franz Boas. Science, 91: 598–99.

1941

Intellectual and cultural achievements of the human races. In: *Scientific Aspects of the Race Problem*, by H. S. Jennings *et al.*, pp. 189–249. Washington, Catholic University of America.
Note on the Gê tribes of Brazil. Am. Anthropol., 43:188–96.
Review. *Pioneers in American Anthropology: The Bandelier-Morgan Letters, 1873–1883*, ed. by Leslie A. White. Am. Antiquity, 7:196–97.

1942

The Crow language: grammatical sketch and analyzed text. Univ. Calif. Publ. Am. Archaeol. Ethnol., 39:1–141.
Studies in Plains Indian folklore. Univ. Calif. Publ. Am. Archaeol. Ethnol., 40:1–28.

The transition of civilizations in primitive society. Am. J. Sociol., 47:527–43.
Review. *The Social Life of Primitive Man*, by S. A. Sieber and F. H. Muller. Am. Anthropol., 44:313–14.
Review. *The Cheyenne Way*, by K. N. Llewellyn and E. A. Hoebel. Am. Anthropol., 44:478–79.
A marginal note to Professor Radcliffe-Brown's paper on "Social Structure." Am. Anthropol., 44:519–21.
The professor talks back. Antioch Review, 2:317–21.
Translation. *The Serente*, by Curt Nimuendajú. Publications of the F. W. Hodge Anniversary Publication Fund, Los Angeles, Vol. 4, 106 pp.
Review. *Smoke from Their Fires: The Life of a Kwakiutl Chief*, by C. S. Ford. To-morrow, 1:59–60.
Review. *Sun Chief*, by L. W. Simmons. To-morrow, 1:62–63.

1943

Property rights and coercive powers of Plains Indian military societies. Journal of Legal and Political Science, 1:59–71.
Soviet Russia and religion. To-morrow, 3:43–44.
Review. *Haddon: The Head Hunter*, by A. H. Quiggin. Am. Anthropol., 45:478–79.
A note on the social life of the Northern Kayapó. Am. Anthropol., 45:633–35.
Franz Boas, anthropologist. Sci. Monthly, 56:183–84.
Franz Boas: his predecessors and his contemporaries. Science, 97:202–3.

1944

Franz Boas (1858–1942). J. Am. Folklore, 57:59–64.
Bibliography of Franz Boas in folklore. J. Am. Folklore, 57:65–69.
American contributions to anthropology. Science, 100:321–27.
Jean Bassett Johnson. Am. Anthropol., 46:528–29.
South American messiahs. To-morrow, 4:68–70.
Translation. *Šerente Tales*, by Curt Nimuendajú. J. Am. Folklore, 57:181–87.

1945

The German People: A Social Portrait to 1914. New York, Farrar and Rinehart. 143 pp.

A note on Lapp culture history. S.W. J. Anthropol., 1:447–54.
Review. American Psychiatric Association, *One Hundred Years of American Psychiatry*. Am. J. Psychiatry, 102:138–41.
With Clyde Kluckhohn. The psychiatry–anthropology relationship. Am. J. Psychiatry, 102:414–16.

1946

A case of bilingualism. Word, 1:249–59.
Review. *A Scientific Theory of Culture and Other Essays,* by Bronislaw Malinowski. Am. Anthropol., 48:118–19.
Evolution in cultural anthropology: a reply to Leslie White. Am. Anthropol., 48:223–33.
Translation. *Social Organization and Beliefs of the Botocudo of Eastern Brazil,* by Curt Nimuendajú. S.W. J. Anthropol., 2:93–115.
Professor White and "anti-evolutionist" schools. S.W. J. Anthropol., 2:240–41.
Eastern Brazil: an introduction. In: *Handbook of South American Indians,* ed. by Julian H. Steward. Bureau of American Ethnology Bulletin 143, Vol. 1, pp. 381–97. Washington, U.S. Govt. Print Off.
The Bororo. In: *Handbook of South American Indians,* ed. by Julian H. Steward. Bureau of American Ethnology Bulletin 143, Vol. 1, pp. 419–34. Washington, U.S. Govt. Print. Off.
The Northwestern and Central Gê. In: *Handbook of South American Indians,* ed. by Julian H. Steward. Bureau of American Ethnology Bulletin 143, Vol. 1, pp. 477–517. Washington, U.S. Govt. Print. Off.
The Southern Cayapó. In: *Handbook of South American Indians,* ed. by Julian H. Steward. Bureau of American Ethnology Bulletin 143, Vol. 1, pp. 519–20. Washington, U.S. Govt. Print. Off.
The Tapuya; the Carirì; the Pancarurú; the Tarairiu; the Jeico; and the Guck. In: *Handbook of South American Indians,* ed. by Julian H. Steward. Bureau of American Ethnology Bulletin 143, Vol. 1, pp. 553–69. Washington, U.S. Govt. Print. Off.
With Louis C. Jones. New York Branch of the American Folklore Society. J. Am. Folklore, 59:489–91.
Historia de la Etnologia. (Spanish translation of *History of*

Ethnological Theory, translated by Paul Kirchhoff.) Fondo de Cultura economica, Mexico. 358 pp.

Translation. *The Eastern Timbira,* by Curt Nimuendajú. Univ. Calif. Publ. Am. Archaeol. Ethnol., 41:1–357.

1947

Franz Boas, 1858–1942. In: National Academy of Sciences, *Biographical Memoirs,* 24:303–22. New York, Columbia University Press.

Letters from Ernst Mach to Robert H. Lowie. Isis, 37:65–68.

Some problems in Plains Indian folklore. J. Am. Folklore, 60:401–3.

Primitive Society. 2d ed. New York, Liveright Publishing Corporation. xii + 463 pp.

1948

Social Organization. New York, Rinehart & Co., Inc. 465 pp.

Parochialism and historical instruction. In: *Learning and World Peace,* eighth symposium, ed. by Lyman Bryson and others, pp. 89–98. Conference on Science, Philosophy and Religion to the Democratic Way of Life, Philadelphia, 1947. New York, The Conference.

Some facts about Boas. S.W. J. Anthropol., 4:69–70.

Some aspects of political organization among the American Indians. Huxley Memorial Lecture for 1948, Royal Anthropological Institute, London, pp. 1–14.

The tropical rain forests: an introduction. In: *Handbook of South American Indians,* ed. by Julian H. Steward. Bureau of American Ethnology Bulletin 143, Vol. 3, pp. 1–56. Washington, U.S. Govt. Print. Off.

Review. *Geschichte der Kultur: Eine allgemeine Ethnologie,* by Kaj Birket-Smith. J. Am. Folklore, 61:401.

Primitive Religion. (Rev. ed.) New York, Liveright Publishing Corporation. xxiii + 382 pp.

1949

Supplementary facts about Clark Wissler. Am. Anthropol., 51:528.

John Montgomery Cooper, 1881–1949. Boletín bibliográfico de Antropología Americana, Mexico, D.F., 12:289–92.

Review. *Fatherland: A Study of Authoritarianism in the German Family,* by Bertram Schaffner. Man, 48:131.

Review. *The American People,* by Geoffrey Gorer. Man, 49:34.

1950

Observations on the literary style of the Crow Indian. In: *Beiträge zur Gesellungs- und Völkerwissenschaft* (Thurnwald Festschrift), pp. 271–83.

Social and political organization of the Tropical Forest and Marginal tribes. In: *Handbook of South American Indians,* ed. by Julian H. Steward. Bureau of American Ethnology Bulletin 143, Vol. 5, pp. 313–50. Washington, U.S. Govt. Print. Off.

Property among the Tropical Forest and Marginal tribes. In: *Handbook of South American Indians,* ed. by Julian H. Steward. Bureau of American Ethnology Bulletin 143, Vol. 5, pp. 351–67. Washington, U.S. Govt. Print. Off.

Review. *Gegenwarts-Probleme Berliner Familien: Eine soziologische Untersuchung an 498 Familien,* by Hilde Thurnwald. Am. Anthropol., 52:105–6.

Review. *Der Ursprung der Gottesidee,* Vol. 9, by Wilhelm Schmidt. Am. Anthropol., 52:519–21.

1951

Some problems of geographical distribution. In: *South Sea Studies,* pp. 11–26. Basel, Museum für Völkerkunde und Schweizerischen Museum für Volkskunde.

Beiträge zur Völkerkunde Nordamerikas. (Mitteilungen aus dem Museum für Völkerkunde in Hamburg.) Vol. XXIII, pp. 7–68, Hamburg.

Some aspects of political organization among American aborigines. Journal of the Royal Anthropological Institute of Great Britain and Ireland, 78:11–24.

Foreword. In: *Reality and Dream: Psychotherapy of a Plains Indian,* by George Devereux, pp. xiii–xiv. New York, International Universities Press.

1952

The heterogeneity of Marginal cultures. In: *Selected Papers of the XXIXth International Congress of Americanists,* ed. by Sol Tax, Vol. 3, pp. 1–7. Chicago, University of Chicago Press.

The Wenner-Gren Foundation International Symposium on Anthropology. Sociologus, 2:145–48.

Review. *Mythos und Kult bei Naturvölkern: Religions wissen-*

schaftliche Betrachtungen, by A. E. Jensen. J. Am. Folklore, 65:102–4.
Translation. *The Tukuna,* by Curt Nimuendajú. Univ. Calif. Publ. Am. Archaeol. Ethnol., 45:1–207.
Review. *Des Menschengeistes erwachen, wachsen, und irren,* by R. Thurnwald. Psyche, 4:50–52.
The song "Frohe Botschaft." J. Am. Folklore, 65:187.
Review. *Mythe, Mensch, und Umwelt: Beiträge zur Religion, Mythologie, und Kulturgeschichte,* ed. by A. E. Jensen. Am. Anthropol., 54:400–1.

1953

On historical and ethnographic techniques. Am. Anthropol., 55: 280.
Review. *Tupari,* by Franz Caspar. Am. Anthropol., 55:441–42.
Ethnography, cultural and social anthropology. Am. Anthropol., 55:527–34.
The relations between the Kiowa and the Crow Indians. Bulletin de la Société Suisse des Américanistes, 7:1–5.
The Comanche, a sample of acculturation. Sociologus, 3:122–27.
Alleged Kiowa–Crow affinities. S.W. J. Anthropol., 9:357–68.
Contemporary currents in American ethnology. Ethnological Research, 17:61–76. (Translated by I. Obayashi)
Review. *An Appraisal of Anthropology Today,* ed. by Sol Tax et al. Sociologus, 3:137–41.

1954

Indians of the Plains. New York, McGraw-Hill Book Co., Inc. 222 pp.
A Crow tale. Anthropol. Quart., 2:1–22.
Toward Understanding Germany. Chicago, University of Chicago Press. 396 pp.
Field research in South America. Man, 54:100.
Richard Thurnwald (1869–1954). Am. Anthropol., 56:863–67.
Review. *Allgemeine Völkerkunde: Formen und Entwicklung der Kultur,* by Kunz Dittmer. Am. Anthropol., 56:1114.
Review. *Miti e Leggende III: America Settentrionale,* by Raffaele Pettazzoni. Western Folklore, 13:218–20.
Review. *Franz Boas: The Science of Man in the Making,* by M. J. Herskovits. Sci. Monthly, 78:47.

1955

Reflections on the Plains Indians. Anthropol. Quart., 28:63–86.
Contemporary trends in American cultural anthropology. Sociologus, 5:113–21.
The military societies of the Plains Cree. Separata dos Anais do XXXI Congresso Internacional de Americanistes, pp. 1–9.
Review. *The Unwritten Law of Albania,* by Margaret Hasluck. Am. Anthropol., 57:1076.

1956

Boas once more. Am. Anthropol., 58:159–64.
Choosing reviewers. Man, 55:188.
Supernormal experiences of American Indians. To-morrow, 4:9–16.
Reminiscences of anthropological currents in America half a century ago. Am. Anthropol., 58:995–1016.
Notes on the Kiowa Indians. Tribus, 4:131–38.
Review. *The Hopi–Tewa of Arizona,* by Edward P. Dozier. Sociologus, 6:189–91.
Review. *Marriage, Authority, and Final Causes: A Study of Unilateral Cross-Cousin Marriage,* by George C. Homans and David M. Schneider. Am. Anthropol., 58:1144.

1957

Generalizations, field work, and materialism. Am. Anthropol., 59:884–85. (L)
Primitive messianism and an ethnological problem. Diogenes, 19:62–72.
With Luella Winifred Cole. *A Practical Handbook for Planning a Trip to Europe.* New York, Vantage Press, Inc. 206 pp.

POSTHUMOUS PUBLICATIONS

1958

The culture-area concept as applied to North and South America. Proc. 32d Internat. Congr. Americanists, Copenhagen, 1956, pp. 73–78. Copenhagen, Einar Munksgaard Forlag.
Individuum und Gesellschaft in der Religion der Naturvölker. Z. Ethnol., 83:161–69.

1959

The oral literature of the Crow Indians. J. Am. Folklore, 72:97–105.
A note on Crow curses. J. Am. Folklore, 72:105.
Robert H. Lowie, Ethnologist: A Personal Record. Berkeley, University of California Press. 198 pp.
Bemerkungen über die Rolle der Religion in Alltagsleben der Crow Indianer. Z. Ethnol., 84:1–4.
The development of ethnography as a science. In: *Men and Moments in the History of Science,* ed. by H. M. Evans, pp. 130–42. Seattle, University of Washington Press. 226 pp.

1960

Crow Texts: Collected, Translated and Edited by R. H. Lowie. Berkeley, University of California Press. 550 pp.
Crow Word Lists: Crow–English and English–Crow Vocabularies. Berkeley, University of California Press. 411 pp.
Empathy, or "seeing from within." In: *Culture in History: Essays in Honor of Paul Radin,* ed. by Stanley Diamond, pp. 145–59. New York, Columbia University Press.
A few Assiniboine texts, collected and translated by R. H. Lowie. Anthropol. Linguistics, 2:1–30.
My Crow interpreter. In: *In the Company of Man,* ed. by Joseph B. Casagrande, pp. 427–37. New York, Harper & Brothers.
The oral literature of the Crow Indians. Proceedings of the Third International Congress of Anthropological and Ethnological Sciences, Brussels, 1948, p. 133. Tervuren, The Congress.

1963

Compromise in primitive society. (Le Compromis dans la société primitive.) International Social Science Journal (Revue internationale des sciences sociales), 15:188–238.
Religion in human life. Am. Anthropol., 65:532–42.
Washo texts. Anthropol. Linguistics, 5:1–30.

1966

With Fred Eggan. Kinship terminology. In: *Encyclopaedia Britannica,* Vol. 13, pp. 377–81. Chicago, Encyclopaedia Britannica, Inc.

WINTHROP JOHN VANLEUVEN OSTERHOUT

August 2, 1871–April 9, 1964

BY L. R. BLINKS

WINTHROP JOHN VANLEUVEN OSTERHOUT was born in Brooklyn, New York, on August 2, 1871, a little over a century ago. He died in New York, April 9, 1964. Elected to the National Academy of Sciences in 1919, he lived to be one of its older members (aged ninety-two). He greatly influenced the course of biology in the United States, as it turned from a largely descriptive into an experimental and analytical science. He was one of the founders of the new discipline of general physiology, through his own work and through his editorship of the *Journal of General Physiology*, which he founded, with Jacques Loeb, in 1918. He remained an editor for over forty-five years, and trained many students who contributed to general physiology.

Winthrop Osterhout was the son of the Reverend John Vanleuven Osterhout and Annie Loranthe Beman Osterhout, the only child of Mr. and Mrs. R. Beman of Brooklyn. The mother's family were English; she lived in Baltimore before her marriage. The Osterhout family were Dutch, having come, as the name implies, from the town of Oosterhout (East Wood) south of the Rhine delta near Breda in the North Brabant province of the Netherlands. Jan Jansen van Osterhout and his wife, Annetje Gielis, came to New Amsterdam (later New York) before 1653, and lived first in Brooklyn; they moved up the Hudson, settling near Kingston. Later many family members lived in the vicinity of Ellensville, in Ulster County, and Winthrop's uncle William was a tanner in Tannersville, in the Catskills.

There seem to be no New England ancestors to account for the distinguished name of Winthrop, which may have been given for some good friend. At the time of Winthrop's birth his father was a Baptist minister in Webster, Massachusetts, his congregation consisting largely of working people of very small means. John Osterhout was an idealist who preferred to minister to poor people, rather than seek a position at a wealthier church. When Winthrop's mother and infant sister died of typhoid fever in 1873, the boy was left without a nurse. At first his father tried to care for the boy himself, and wrote that "Winnie is a good little traveller," when he took his son along wherever he went to preach. However, this arrangement proved too difficult, and young Winthrop was sent to live with his grandmother in Baltimore. This was apparently a happy time, since Grandmother was easygoing and gave him much freedom to play with boys of his own age on the street.

Meanwhile the elder Osterhout had remarried, but his second wife died very soon, and Winthrop never knew her. Finally, when he was eight years old, Winthrop moved to Providence, Rhode Island, where his father had again remarried; here he grew up under the care of his stepmother, who was good to him, although never very close; she was a somewhat formal person who always addressed her husband as Mr. Osterhout, or "Mr. O." However, Winthrop knew her as Mother; she lived into the third decade of the next century. The parents had bicycles and took trips on them, but the boy was not included, and in general did not enjoy athletics. He did not play games, not even tennis, and apparently did not have any close boyhood friends that he could remember. In later life his chief recreation was walking and rowing.

His father's church in Providence was also a poor one, and

the family never enjoyed affluence. Winthrop attended Bridgham Grammar School and Providence High School; when he was ten years old he got a job as errand boy in a bookstore, where he had a chance to get acquainted with books. His employer liked him and allowed him to read; from then on most of his leisure time was spent in reading. Finally, when he entered Brown University in 1889, he was entranced by the collection at the library. He at least glanced into every book on the shelves to see whether the contents interested him—a feat possible in 1890 but scarcely in any present university library! He was interested mainly in literature, and was elected class poet; he probably would have become a teacher of literature had not one of those chance happenings deflected him to science. In his junior year he met Professor H. C. Bumpus, who had recently come to Brown from Olivet (a small Congregational college in Michigan that had a remarkable succession of good biologists on its staff). Bumpus urged Osterhout to attend the botany course at nearby Woods Hole, in the summer of 1892; there the famous Marine Biological Laboratory, then only four years old, was just getting established. Here were such biologists as T. H. Morgan, E. G. Conklin, Frank Lillie, and Jacques Loeb, who later became a very close friend. The teacher of the botany course was W. A. Setchell, a recent Ph.D. of W. G. Farlow's at Harvard and then Instructor at Yale.

Osterhout and Setchell often went on collecting expeditions. Here began Osterhout's acquaintance with marine and freshwater algae—the organisms he was to exploit so successfully in later research. One day he actually found *Nitella* in Nobska Pond, though it was thirty years before its physiological advantages were recognized. (Fifty years later Osterhout was to write Setchell's biography for the American Philosophical Society.)

Osterhout made such an impression on Setchell that the latter invited him to assist in the course next summer, which he did, immediately after graduating. Now he was given the opportunity to do independent research, and discovered an interesting phenomenon in *Rhabdonia tenera* (now known as *Agardhiella*): four spores, each capable of forming a new plant, could also combine to form a single plant. This was the subject of Osterhout's first paper, in the *Annals of Botany*. He was also intrigued by plants living in brackish water, and tried some experiments that were the beginning of his later work on osmotic pressure and salt effects in algae.

Osterhout returned to Brown in the fall of 1893 as Instructor in Botany, remaining for two years while he studied for the M.A., which he took in 1894. He was able to spend the next year in Germany, where so many young American scientists then went for their graduate training. No doubt Setchell encouraged this move; in any case the young Osterhout chose Bonn, where Eduard Strasburger was then at the height of his fame as a plant cytologist. The great professor was very kind and helpful, and the atmosphere of the laboratory was congenial; Strasburger made the students his friends. Here Osterhout met other young Americans: R. A. Harper, who took his Ph.D. at Bonn that year and later taught at Wisconsin and Columbia; and David Fairchild, who became the famous "plant hunter" for the Bureau of Plant Introduction. (Curiously, in view of Osterhout's later utilization of *Valonia*, Fairchild went on from Bonn to Naples, where he investigated the cytology of that genus.)

At Bonn Osterhout worked on the cytology and reproduction of the freshwater red alga *Batrachospermum*. It was necessary to collect the plants at all hours of the day and night to find the proper stages—which led to some interesting conversations (in German) with farm dogs and also with the *Polizei*, who were suspicious of the collecting equipment: dark lantern and *gummischuhen!* These experiences no doubt contributed to Osterhout's good command of the German language, which he read easily and spoke well. He published several papers in German periodicals.

When the time came to return home in 1896, Osterhout had a position awaiting again at Brown, but chose instead to move west, to the University of California, then only 28 years old. Setchell had preceded him to Berkeley as Professor of Botany, and he appointed Osterhout as instructor in his department. At this grade the young man remained for five years while he completed his dissertation on the reproduction of *Rhabdonia*, the alga on which he began work in Woods Hole. He was awarded the Ph.D. degree in 1899 and was married the same year to Anna Maria Landstrom, Winthrop's father coming out from Providence to perform the ceremony. A daughter, Anna (Mrs. Theodore Edison), was born in 1901 and another (Mrs. Olga Osterhout Sears) four years later. Their aid in the preparation of this memoir is gratefully acknowledged.

Osterhout was promoted to Assistant Professor of Botany in 1901 and to Associate Professor in 1907. The years at Berkeley were exciting and influential ones. The university, up to that time an isolated and small institution, was beginning to take on the stature of greatness that it later assumed, partly because of the rapid growth of California, partly because of the competition of its new neighbor at Stanford, but mostly because of its remarkable president, Benjamin Ide Wheeler (another graduate of Brown). In a day of famous leaders, Wheeler was a great builder and stimulator. One of his notable innovations was the bringing of great scholars from Europe for a year; some of these arrivals in science were Arrhenius from Sweden, de Vries from Holland, and Ostwald from Germany (whose name meant the same thing as Osterhout). There also came to Berkeley for a period of eight years the brilliant physiologist Jacques Loeb, who influenced Osterhout very greatly. There exists a photograph taken in 1905 showing de Vries beside an *Oenothera* plant in the botanic garden, flanked with the portly Arrhenius and the ascetic slight figure of E. W. Hilgard, with Loeb smiling beside them, and Osterhout (in "bowler" hat) in the back row.

It was a fruitful and stimulating society for a young scientist, and it is not surprising that Osterhout's thoughts began turning from cytology and morphology to physiology and physical chemistry. These were the days of Loeb's interest in artificial parthenogenesis (experiments on which were carried out in the Herzstein Laboratory near Monterey), and "salt effects" were at the center of the physiology of the day. Osterhout began looking at algae from this point of view, noticing a perfectly natural experiment. He observed the plants on the hulls of river steamers going daily from the salt water of San Francisco Bay to the mountain-fresh water of Sacramento. Those plants which survived could obviously tolerate wide ranges of salinity. He also looked into the necessity of calcium to balance sodium, both in algae and in the roots of higher plants; these observations were the subject of several short papers. In addition, he wrote two books. A remarkable one, entitled *Experiments with Plants*, described simple, ingenious class exercises which could be performed with seeds, corks, and lamp chimneys. There was even included a homemade balance, sensitive to one-tenth of a gram, made from umbrella ribs! While this book was scorned by sophisticated colleagues who remembered Pfeffer's laboratory, its exercises were characteristic of Osterhout's "make-do" methods, and the book was still in use twenty years later in his Harvard elementary class. I found it very useful when I began to teach in a poorly equipped laboratory (ironically that of one of the scorners noted above). Apparently others did also, for it was translated into Dutch within two years, and later into Russian (by none other than the distinguished plant physiologist, N. A. Maximov). It might still be useful in underdeveloped countries. It contained some illustrations from Luther Burbank, whom Osterhout knew.

The other book, written in collaboration with the famous

agricultural and viticultural expert E. W. Hilgard, was entitled *Agriculture for Schools of the Pacific Slope*. While both books might be regarded as economic potboilers, they added greatly to the young botanist's reputation. At Berkeley, as his fame grew, Osterhout attracted increasing numbers of graduate students, among whom were A. A. Lawson, C. L. Williams, E. S. Byxbee, H. T. A. Hus, N. L. Gardner, and H. D. Densmore, the last a professor at Beloit College at the time of his work at Berkeley. All of these students worked on cytological problems: polar caps, spindle fibers, and the like. F. N. Magowan, however, studied the effects of salts on plants, reflecting Osterhout's own changing interests. Nathaniel L. Gardner, who was seven years older than Osterhout, became one of his most distinguished students, writing a large number of papers on Pacific Coast algae, many in collaboration with Osterhout's professor, Setchell. He and Osterhout went on collecting trips together—perhaps on the one from Monterey to Big Sur, aboard a very recalcitrant burro, which Osterhout recalled with amusement.

Berkeley had many charms—its genial climate, good times at the Bohemian Grove, friendship with colleagues, and the beginnings of the university's later greatness. But it was a long way from other centers; except at Stanford there was then little science west of Chicago, and the long trip east by train was wearisome and expensive. Osterhout had not visited Woods Hole for many years. Therefore it was not surprising that in 1909 when Harvard offered him an assistant professorship, he accepted, despite the step down in rank—and a "munificent" salary of $1500 per year (paid quarterly, moreover, which created financial problems on arrival in Cambridge). Loeb also left Berkeley the next year, to join the Rockefeller Institute for Medical Research in New York.

In Cambridge, Osterhout inherited the laboratories just vacated by G. L. Goodale—rooms in the "Agassiz Museum," that red-brick pile of New England mill architecture that still houses the Museum of Comparative Zoology, as well as the geological, anthropological, and some botanical collections, especially the "glass flowers" that attracted the tourists in flocks past Osterhout's office on the second floor. It is not surprising that later he carried on much of his research in a greenhouse in the Botanical Garden several blocks away. M. L. Fernald was in the Gray Herbarium; W. G. Farlow, Roland Thaxter, and E. C. Jeffrey in the Museum.

With such a collection of stars, life was not easy. Jeffrey in particular was soon in open enmity, even threatening to "shoot that damn Dutchman." However, there were many friendships as well, especially with George Howard Parker, the genial Professor of Zoology, who became probably Osterhout's best friend in Cambridge. With him, and those students who wished to attend, there were long walks on Sundays, often ending with a meal and red wine at the "Stella d'Italia" on the North Side of Boston. Osterhout became a member of two clubs, one consisting mostly of Harvard professors in Cambridge, the other (the Thursday Club) meeting in Boston and including prominent nonacademic people. President Lowell was always friendly. But still the salary remained low (Harvard then paying in the currency of prestige), and Osterhout had to eke out his earnings by teaching a course at Radcliffe as well as a Saturday morning extension course for teachers. He never owned an automobile, and he could be seen walking home to Buckingham Street in the evening, carrying a Harvard green baize bag full of papers and calculations, and lost in plans for the next day's experiments. About this time he taught himself mathematics, which now began to play an important part in his work.

Among his friends were the chemists G. P. Baxter, A. B. Lamb, and Theodore Richards, who was soon to be the first American to receive the Nobel Prize in chemistry. They appreciated his applications of chemistry to biology, and he established good "diplomatic relations" with them so that his students could quickly obtain advice in their work—an invaluable asset of being in a famous university.

In the summer of 1910 he returned to Woods Hole, where he worked almost every summer for the next dozen years. He was elected a trustee of the Marine Biological Laboratory in 1919, remaining on the board for thirty years. Now began a most fruitful period of research, when he employed a new organism for studying salt and other permeability effects, and a new technique (for biology) to measure them. The organism was the brown alga or kelp, *Laminaria;* the technique, electrical resistance of the tissue. The thin blade of the kelp was cut by a cork-borer into small disks and arranged in columns, like a pile of pennies, then inserted into a Kohlrausch bridge, such as was used for measuring the conductivity of electrolytes. The conductivity of the tissue was assumed to represent the permeability of its cells to the ions of the bathing solution. He was perhaps influenced in the choice of this technique by his friendship with Arrhenius, who had recently developed his theory of ionic dissociation. The current source was a tuning fork oscillator of 1000 Hertz, detected by a telephone. Of course, this circuit really measured *impedance,* but it was, because of the large number of cells in series, adequate for the purpose. His results were later confirmed with direct current resistance measurements by the writer.

Osterhout's procedure had the great advantage of giving quantitative measurements of changes in permeability from moment to moment, permitting the construction of time curves which could be used for calculation and prediction. It was found that the resistance remained high and constant in seawater, for long periods. On the other hand, a single salt, such as NaCl of the same conductivity, produced an immediate fall of resistance; if the exposure was continued for some hours, the fall was all the way to that of a dead tissue, completely permeable. Conversely, the resistance recovered if seawater was restored before the resistance had fallen all the way to the dead value. Thus injury and recovery were shown quantitatively.

Some divalent ions such as Ca, on the other hand, caused a rise of resistance at first, even to 60 or 70 percent above normal, which would be maintained for some time before falling, eventually to the dead value. Again there was recovery if the tissue was restored to seawater soon enough. However, if a mixture of the two salts (e.g., 97.5 percent Na, 2.5 percent Ca) was applied, each injurious *alone*, the tissue remained undamaged, the resistance maintaining its normal value, neither rising nor falling for long periods. Obviously a *balanced solution* had been attained between two ions (each separately injurious), and the principle of salt antagonism beautifully and quantitatively demonstrated. Varying mixtures of these salts, as well as others, were studied, as were the effects of acid and alkaline seawater, anesthetics, surface active substances, etc. The method was employed as well by several of Osterhout's students, and a great number of papers described the results, at first largely in *Science*, then in other journals. These studies were summarized in a series of Lowell Lectures, given in Boston in 1922, and assembled in a book entitled *Injury, Recovery and Death in Relation to Conductivity and Permeability*, published in a new series, "Monographs on Experimental Biology," of which Osterhout was an editor, along with Jacques Loeb and T. H. Morgan. It was one of Osterhout's best books, carefully written and demonstrating his facility in mathematics; but the assumptions used, a series of consecutive reactions in which a hypothetical substance M is formed by the reaction $A \to M$, and decomposed by the reaction $M \to B$, controlled by Ca and Na, respectively, were not directly demonstrated. This was the culmination of the *Laminaria* work, other matters now beginning to occupy Osterhout's attention. Indeed, only four or five more papers on these topics were published in the new periodical founded by Loeb and Osterhout, the *Journal of General Physiology,* of which the first number appeared in September 1918. Osterhout remained an editor for forty-five years. The journal was the main place of publication for him and his students and collaborators thereafter.

Volume I, No. 1 of *J.G.P.* contained a description of a new method of measuring respiration and photosynthesis, namely by the color changes produced in pH indicators by the production or utilization of CO_2. The first article (written with A. R. C. Haas) utilized this principle to study the "induction period" of photosynthesis; the second described an apparatus to circulate air from reaction chamber to indicator by means of a rubber bulb, with a soda lime tube to absorb CO_2. This apparatus was run with a motor and was dubbed the "Mills of the Gods"; it was the basis of a number of dissertations by students. Students doing their doctoral work on this or other problems were (as far as I can ascertain) W. T. Bovie, G. B. Reed, A. R. C. Haas, S. C. Brooks, M. M. Brooks, O. L. Inman, G. B. Ray, F. G. Gustafson, W. O. Fenn, Oran L. Raber, S. F. Cook, C. J. Lyon, P. A. Davies, and L. R. Blinks. This seems a small list for sixteen years, but Ph.D. factories were smaller in those days. Some half dozen of these students predeceased Osterhout; others went on to productive careers, two becoming members of the National Academy of Sciences.

Osterhout was promoted in 1913 to the rank of Professor, at the age of forty-two, four years after his arrival in Cambridge. For much of his Harvard career he was in charge of the elementary botany course, which he enlivened with simple but dramatic experiments, many of which could be demonstrated in lectures. He was a polished, effective speaker, who enjoyed making startling statements, and was not above showmanship when it could illustrate a point. He had to do this, he later explained, to keep the interest of Harvard's gilded youth, some of whom even brought bulldogs to class and aimed at the

Gentleman's C, in the days before the "Intellectual Renaissance" on the Charles. (Among his advisees was Vincent Astor, who was always accompanied by a bodyguard!) His advanced lectures, on the other hand, were serious, carefully studied efforts, filled with the latest research results, often freshly published in the newest *J.G.P.* Although his courses in plant physiology continued to bear the Pfefferian rubrics "Assimilation and Respiration," or "Growth, Irritability, and Reproduction," they were actually more and more concerned with the newest theories of enzyme action and of cellular permeability—in other words, general physiology. Indeed, for a long time his classes were the only place in Harvard College where practical work in biochemistry could be studied. L. J. Henderson, who taught biological chemistry, offered no laboratory; Otto Folin was at the Medical School, many miles away in Boston. Osterhout's courses consequently attracted many able students, not only in botany, but from zoology, and from the Bussey Institution, a dozen miles away. Through much of his stay in Harvard, Osterhout was faithfully assisted by Lee Morrison, who also performed many of the *Laminaria* experiments, and was addressed by some students as "Professor Morrison."

Around 1921 the emphasis changed to study of large coenocytic algae, at first *Nitella* and *Chara,* from each cell of which a drop of vacuolar sap could be drained, either for analysis of the sap (which was found to be very different from the surrounding solution), to follow its changes on injury, or to study the penetration of new substances from outside. Osterhout's first paper on *Nitella* dealt with the rate of loss of chloride ions under injury (e.g., by chloroform), determining chloride in the sap by microtitration. He also measured the fall of electrical impedance of *Nitella* under injury, but the method (at 1000 cycles) was not capable of showing very great changes, on account of the cell's high capacitance. (Direct current was later employed by the writer, with much higher resistance values demonstrable.) Beginning in 1922, a start was made on bioelectric measurements with *Nitella,* under a Carnegie Institution grant, which enabled E. S. Harris to assemble electronic equipment and literally *make* a string galvanometer. The study of dye penetration into *Nitella* also began at this time, in collaboration with Marian Irwin, a recent Ph.D. student of G. H. Parker.

In 1923 work with giant marine algal cells began. Years earlier, at Osterhout's suggestion, R. P. Wodehouse, then a Harvard graduate student, had gone to Bermuda in 1916 and studied the vacuolar sap of *Valonia macrophysa*. This is a coenocytic alga, the large cells of which can each yield one ml or more of sap with a minimum of contamination by seawater. Wodehouse found potassium to be abundant, while sulfate was absent, in the sap. W. J. Crozier in 1919 found the pH of the sap to be about 6, while that of the seawater was 8.1 or so. Crozier had also sent to Osterhout a large volume of sap from *Valonia* for careful chemical analysis by L. M. van der Pyl in Baxter's laboratory at Harvard. The analysis confirmed Wodehouse's qualitative findings. K was found to be 40 times as concentrated in the sap as in seawater, while Na was one-fifth to one-sixth as concentrated: K was accumulated, Na was partially excluded. Cl was a little higher in the sap than in seawater, while SO_4 was excluded (as was Mg).

The stage was now set for the study of *Valonia* at its place of growth; it was necessary to go to Bermuda for this. A grant (not at all common in those days) was obtained from the Rockefeller Institute, a sabbatical leave was arranged for the first term of the college year, and in the summer of 1923 Osterhout took the *Fort Victoria* of the Furness line to Bermuda. His assistant was Mr. M. J. Dorcas, from the Chemistry Department at Harvard; the writer joined the two in the autumn, and work began in earnest on *Valonia* at the Biological Station.

This year was possibly the happiest in Osterhout's life; he

had not been out of the United States since his student days in Germany, there were no interruptions, and he enjoyed the calm beauty of Bermuda (without automobiles then). His knee, injured in a mountain climb just before, prevented much walking, but there was the daily row back and forth between the Grasmere Hotel (where we lived) and Agar's Island (where we worked). Dorcas studied the entrance of CO_2 into the sap and later compared the saps of *Valonia macrophysa* with stranded "sea bottles" (then regarded as *V. ventricosa*). He found large differences, the latter cell not accumulating potassium at all. The anomaly was shifted to another genus when the writer identified the Bermuda "sea bottle" as a *Halicystis* (from a different natural order) and named it *H. Osterhoutii*. But the Pacific Coast *Halicystis* does accumulate K! In 1923, Osterhout made the first measurements of potential difference across the protoplasm of *Valonia*, using a Compton electrometer. The P.D. was small (five to ten millivolts), but could be greatly increased by immersing the cell in natural or artificial sap, indicating a pronounced asymmetry of the protoplasm. The cause of such asymmetry (found in several marine algae) is still not thoroughly understood fifty years later. It is formally explained, and in *Halicystis* demonstrated by vacuolar perfusion, that the cell's plasma membrane and its tonoplast differ in their relative permeability to ions.

Osterhout enjoyed the lively scene at the Hamilton waterfront market on Saturday nights; there were tropical fruits, brought in from the West Indies and exposed for sale under kerosene lamps, with haggling over price and condition often becoming intense. Such evenings might end in having a beer at the Windsor Palm Garden, but more often in listening to the Salvation Army songs and preaching. Perhaps these awoke boyhood memories of Baptist services (which left little other trace except a good fund of biblical quotations). At this time he also began taking black and white pictures of sunsets with a simple Brownie camera; some were quite spectacular. It was his only hobby. He was given a folding vest-pocket Kodak for Christmas that year, but he preferred the Brownie. He had a suspicion of complicated apparatus and always did experiments as simply as possible. He literally lived in his work; he kept a pad of paper beside his bed at night, on which he could write, in large flowing script, suggestions for the next day's experiments.

He had to return to Cambridge to offer his course shortly after Christmas; in February Jacques Loeb came to Bermuda on a holiday, only to die of a heart attack within a week. Loeb's death ended the friendship that began in 1892. But it created a vacancy in the Department of General Physiology at the Rockefeller Institute, to which Osterhout was called a year later. He accepted gladly, for although he had been a most successful teacher at Harvard, he had longed for time to do more research. The opportunity now presented, to attack the many problems posed by large algal cells, with adequate staff and fine equipment at the Institute, was irresistible. He gave his last class in the spring of 1925, turned over his three remaining graduate students to his successor, W. J. Crozier, and moved to New York that autumn. With him went E. S. Harris and Marian Irwin, to be joined by the writer in 1926. In Bermuda a branch laboratory was set up in the Grasmere Hotel, with E. B. Damon and W. C. Cooper, Jr., succeeding Dorcas.

Then began the most productive decade of Osterhout's life. The Institute was a scientific paradise, with full time available for research, and many associates, assistants, and technicians to help him. The electrical measurements begun at Harvard on *Nitella* were now pursued intensively by Harris, particularly with regard to the effects of salts on the potential. Osterhout discovered, in collaboration with Harris and the writer, that a "disturbance," a potential variation very like that of a nerve impulse, passed down the cell at a rate of about a centimeter per second, when the cell was stimulated in a variety of ways: electrical, chemical, thermal, etc. While this had been partially appreciated by Georg Hörmann in 1898, it had been unstudied until 1926 when amplifiers and faster recording instruments (Einthoven string galvanometer) allowed it to be followed in detail. (K. Umrath's papers began to appear three years later.) A large number of papers, too numerous to refer to individually, by Osterhout and Harris, later by Osterhout and S. E. Hill, exploited this discovery, and uncovered many interesting analogies to nerve: fatigue, block, alternans rhythm, as well as a most notable difference—conduction through a salt bridge to another cell. The mobilities of a number of ions in the cell surface were investigated, both under normal conditions and with seasonal alterations, effects of nonelectrolytes, and other agents. The bibliography during the decade 1930–1940 indicates the wide range of these studies.

Meanwhile, in Bermuda, Cooper was carrying on studies of the penetration of weak acids and bases, such as H_2S, H_2CO_3, and NH_3, into the vacuole of *Valonia*. It was found that these penetrated more rapidly as undissociated molecules than as charged ions and were therefore under control of the external pH value. Ammonia actually *accumulated* in the vacuole, e.g., up to 0.1 M NH_4Cl from 0.005 M in the seawater. This caused the *Valonia* cells to float and was a tempting analog to the accumulation of potassium. However, the latter was not under very great control by pH.

The laboratory next moved to an old part of "Undercliff," near the Grasmere, where E. B. Damon, A. G. Jacques, and L. L. Burgess worked on bioelectric and chemical properties of the cells. In New York, and later in Bermuda, the writer continued studies of the electrical resistance and capacity of *Valonia*, *Nitella*, and *Halicystis*, and Marian Irwin studied the penetration of vital dyes in cells and models. The latter two investigators published their results independently, the others usually collaborated with

Osterhout, who became more and more the writer of his assistants' results. Almost every weekend was spent in the country, writing or calculating; the load was heavy and the literary quality of the papers occasionally suffered. In the decade 1926–1936, some fifty joint papers appeared, as well as many by Osterhout alone. It is not surprising that important points were inserted as footnotes, often in proof. The result made for difficult reading, and since no book summing up this work has ever appeared, a great deal of important material is still buried in footnotes, remaining to be rediscovered by future workers.

A totally different research also developed along the line of ingenious models, by which the penetration of electrolytes into cells could be partially explained. Particularly striking was a mixture of p-cresol and guaiacol, separating two aqueous phases of different pH. Accumulation of salt occurred on the acid side (= "vacuole"), potassium being preferentially accumulated over sodium. In the research on such systems Osterhout was assisted by S. E. Kamerling, J. W. Murray, and W. M. Stanley (who was later to become a Nobel laureate and famous for "crystallizing" tobacco mosaic virus). Theodore Shedlovsky, Lewis Longsworth, and D. A. MacInnes were especially helpful in the physicochemical analysis of these models. One important concept developed from these studies was that of "carrier molecules," still a useful principle in discussions of cellular permeability.

Although Osterhout had not visited Europe since his student days in Bonn, he was now able to travel again, and attended the Botanical Congress at Cambridge, England, in 1930, saw the Passion Play at Oberammergau, and visited the French Colonial Exposition in Paris. He returned again in 1932 to France and Holland, seeing de Vries once more. He had earlier undergone an operation for glaucoma, saving one eye, but its sight deteriorated slowly henceforth. In the winter of 1933 came an attack of atrial fibrillation, when he was sixty-one. It was brought under control with digitalis and other drugs, but it appeared at the time that his activity must be greatly curtailed. He was actually to live more than thirty years longer, owing to expert medical care and devoted home nursing. He married Marian Irwin at this time. (His first marriage had ended in divorce the year before.)

His department began to break up; Damon and the writer departed to other positions, as did Hill later. Jacques was drowned in Bermuda in 1938, and the Bermuda laboratory was given up. Most of the work of the next two decades was carried on by Mrs. Osterhout and a number of technicians. It is remarkable that so much important research was still accomplished and so many papers written (fifteen in 1935 alone). In 1941 the whole volume of the *J.G.P.* was devoted to articles by friends and associates, in honor of his seventieth birthday. Osterhout never returned to Bermuda, but went regularly to Cold Spring Harbor or Woods Hole in the summers and attended the spring meetings of the National Academy of Sciences until about 1950. As his eyesight failed he kept in touch with developments by having others read to him, and he dictated papers after he could no longer see. Curiously, several of his later papers were on the egg of *Nereis,* a marine worm, his only work with animals. His last paper was a "summing up," written for the *Annual Review of Plant Physiology;* readers are referred to it for further details of his work.

In his last few years he was bedridden, but he retained clarity of intellect and dignity of bearing to the last. Winthrop Osterhout died peacefully in St. Barnabas Hospital in New York on April 9, 1964. His ashes are buried in the churchyard of St. James the Less in Philadelphia, along with those of Marian Irwin Osterhout, who died in 1973.

CHRONOLOGY

1871	Born Brooklyn, N.Y., August 2
1889	Graduated from Providence (R.I.) High School; entered Brown University
1892	Attended the Botany Course at the Marine Biological Laboratory, Woods Hole, Massachusetts
1893	A.B., Brown University
1893–1895	Instructor in Botany, Brown University
1894	M.A., Brown University
1894–1895	Instructor in Botany (summers), Marine Biological Laboratory, Woods Hole
1895–1896	Student of Eduard Strasburger, Bonn University
1896	First paper published, in *Annals of Botany*
1896–1901	Instructor in Botany, University of California
1899	Ph.D., University of California
	Married Anna Maria Landstrom, Berkeley, California
1901	Assistant Professor of Botany, University of California
1905	*Experiments with Plants* published
1907	Associate Professor, University of California
1909	Assistant Professor of Botany, Harvard University
1910	*Agriculture for Schools of the Pacific Slope* published (with E. W. Hilgard)
	Fellow, American Academy of Arts and Sciences
1913	Professor of Botany, Harvard University
1917	Member, American Philosophical Society
1918	*Journal of General Physiology* founded (with Jacques Loeb)
1919	Elected to National Academy of Sciences
	Trustee, Marine Biological Laboratory
	Hitchcock Lecturer, University of California
1920	Member, Board of Scientific Directors, Rockefeller Institute for Medical Research
1922	Colver Lecturer, Brown University
	Lowell Lecturer (Boston)
1923	Began work on *Valonia*, Bermuda Biological Station
1925	Sedgwick Lecturer, Massachusetts Institute of Technology
	D.Sc. (Hon.), Harvard University
	Member of the Rockefeller Institute

1926	D.Sc. (Hon.), Brown University
1929	Attended International Physiological Congress (Boston)
1930	Attended International Botanical Congress (Cambridge, England)
1933	Married (2d) Marian Irwin, New Castle, Delaware
1939	Member Emeritus, Rockefeller Institute
1957	Last paper published *(Annual Review of Plant Physiology)*
1964	Died, New York City, April 9

MEMBERSHIPS

Member, National Academy of Sciences

Corresponding Member, Botanical Society of Edinburgh; Kungliga Fysiografiska Sällskapet, Lund; Kaiserlich Leopold-Carolinische deutsche Akademie der Naturforscher (Halle); Academy of Natural Sciences (Philadelphia)

Member, Washington and New York Academies of Science, American Society of Plant Physiologists, Botanical Society of America, Society of General Physiologists, American Society of Naturalists, American Philosophical Society, American Chemical Society, American Physiological Society, Society for Experimental Biology and Medicine

Fellow, American Academy of Arts and Sciences, American Association for the Advancement of Science

WINTHROP JOHN VANLEUVEN OSTERHOUT 233

BIBLIOGRAPHY

This bibliography was greatly aided by one assembled by Nina Kobelt, Osterhout's secretary at the Rockefeller Institute.

KEY TO ABBREVIATIONS

Am. J. Botany = American Journal of Botany
Biol. Bull. = Biological Bulletin
Bot. Gaz. = Botanical Gazette
Bot. Rev. = Botanical Review
Cold Spring Harbor Symp. Quant. Biol. = Cold Spring Harbor Symposia on Quantitative Biology
Jahrb. wissensch. Bot. = Jahrbücher für wissenschaftliche Botanik
J. Biol. Chem. = Journal of Biological Chemistry
J.G.P. = Journal of General Physiology
Proc. Nat. Acad. Sci. = Proceedings of the National Academy of Sciences
Proc. Soc. Exp. Biol. Med. = Proceedings of the Society for Experimental Biology and Medicine
Univ. Calif. Publ. Bot. = University of California Publications in Botany

1896

On the life-history of *Rhabdonia tenera*, J. Ag. Annals of Botany, 10:403-27. 2 plates.
With W. A. Setchell. Some aqueous media for preserving algae for class material. Bot. Gaz., 21:140-41.
A simple freezing device. Bot. Gaz., 21:195.

1897

Über Entstehung der karyokinetischen Spindel bei *Equisetum*. Jahrb. wissensch. Bot., 30:159-65.

1898

Problems of heredity. University Chronicle (Berkeley), 1:311-15.

1900

Befruchtung bei *Batrachospermum*. Flora, 87:109-15.

1902

Cell studies. I. Spindle formation in *Agave*. Proceedings of the California Academy of Sciences, 2:255-65.

1904

Contributions to cytological technique. Univ. Calif. Publ. Bot., 2:73-75.

1905

Experiments with Plants. New York, The Macmillan Company. xix + 492 pp. (With many reprintings and at least two translations, one into Dutch, 1909, and one by N. A. Maximov in Russian, in the late 1920s.)

1906

The resistance of certain marine algae to changes in osmotic pressure and temperature. Univ. Calif. Publ. Bot., 2:227–28.

The role of osmotic pressure in marine plants. Univ. Calif. Publ. Bot., 2:229–30.

On the importance of physiologically balanced solutions for plants. Univ. Calif. Publ. Bot., 2:231–34.

The antitoxic action of potassium on magnesium. Univ. Calif. Publ. Bot., 2:235–36.

Extreme toxicity of sodium chloride and its prevention by other salts. J. Biol. Chem., 1:363–69.

On the importance of physiologically balanced solutions for plants. I. Marine plants. Bot. Gaz., 42:127–34.

1907

On the importance of physiologically balanced solutions for plants. II. Fresh-water and terrestrial plants. Bot. Gaz., 44:259–72.

On nutrient and balanced solutions. Univ. Calif. Publ. Bot., 2: 317–18.

1908

The antagonistic action of magnesium and potassium. Bot. Gaz., 45:117–24.

The value of sodium to plants by reason of its protective action. Univ. Calif. Publ. Bot., 3:331–37.

On the effects of certain poisonous gases on plants. Univ. Calif. Publ. Bot., 3:339–40.

On plasmolysis. Bot. Gaz., 46:53–55.

Weitere Untersuchungen über die Ubereinstimmung der Salzwirkungen bei Tieren und Pflanzen. Die Schützwirkung des Natriums für Pflanzen. Jahrb. wissensch. Bot., 46:121–36.

1909

Proeven met planten. Translated by S. J. Geerts-Ronner. The Netherlands.

The nature of balanced solutions. Bot. Gaz., 47:48–49.

On similarity in the behavior of sodium and potassium. Bot. Gaz., 48:98–104.

1910

With E. W. Hilgard. *Agriculture for Schools of the Pacific Slope.* New York, The Macmillan Company. xix + 428 pp.

On the penetration of inorganic salts into living protoplasm. Zeitschrift für physikalische Chemie, 70:408–13.

1911

The permeability of living cells to salts in pure and balanced solutions. Science, 34:187–89.

1912

The permeability of protoplasm to ions and the theory of antagonism. Science, 35:112–15.

Plants which require sodium. Bot. Gaz., 54:532–36.

Reversible changes in permeability produced by electrolytes. Science, 36:350–52.

Some chemical relations of plants and soil. Science, 36:571–76.

1913

The effect of anesthetics upon permeability. Science, 37:111–12. Also in Proceedings of the American Physiological Society (1911–12), 29:xi.

The organization of the cell with respect to permeability. Science, 38:408–9.

Protoplasmic contractions resembling plasmolysis which are caused by pure distilled water. Bot. Gaz., 55:446–51.

Some quantitative researches on the permeability of plant cells. Plant World, 16:129–44.

1914

The chemical dynamics of living protoplasm. Science, 39:544–46.

The effect of alkali on permeability. J. Biol. Chem., 19:335–43.

The effect of acid on permeability. J. Biol. Chem., 19:493–501.
Antagonism between acids and salts. J. Biol. Chem., 19:517–20.
Quantitative criteria of antagonism. Bot. Gaz., 58:178–86.
The measurement of antagonism. Bot. Gaz., 58:272–76.
The forms of antagonism curves as affected by concentration. Bot. Gaz., 58:367–71.
Stetige Änderungen in den Formen von Antagonismus-Kurven. Jahrb. wissensch. Bot., 54:645–50.
Über den Temperaturkoeffizienten des elektrischen Leitvermögens im lebenden und toten Gewebe. Biochemische Zeitschrift, 67:272–77.
Vitality and injury as quantitative conceptions. Science, 40:488–91.

1915

Extreme alterations of permeability without injury. Bot. Gaz., 59:242–53.
On the decrease of permeability due to certain bivalent kations. Bot. Gaz., 59:317–30.
The effects of some trivalent and tetravalent kations on permeability. Bot. Gaz., 59:464–73.
The determination of additive effects. Bot. Gaz., 60:228–34.
The measurement of toxicity. J. Biol. Chem., 23:67–70.
Normal and abnormal permeability. Am. J. Botany, 2:93–94.
On the nature of antagonism. Science, 41:255–56.

1916

The decrease of permeability produced by anesthetics. Bot. Gaz., 61:148–58.
A dynamical theory of antagonism. Proceedings of the American Philosophical Society, 55:533–53.
The dynamics of antagonism. Science, 43:721.
Eduard Strasburger (1844–1912). Proceedings of the American Academy of Arts and Sciences, Vol. 51, No. 14.
The nature of mechanical stimulation. Proc. Nat. Acad. Sci., 2:237–39.
Permeability and viscosity. Science, 43:857–59.
Antagonism and Weber's Law. Science, 44:318–20.
The penetration of balanced solutions and the theory of antagonism. Science, 44:395–96.
Specific action of barium. Am. J. Botany, 3:481–82.

1917

Antagonism and permeability. Science, 45:97–103.
The dynamics of the process of death. J. Biol. Chem., 31:585–89. Also in Science, 46:542.
Some aspects of the temperature coefficients of life processes. J. Biol. Chem., 32:23–27.
With A. R. C. Haas. An adaptation of Winkler's method to biological work. J. Biol. Chem., 32:141–46.
With A. R. C. Haas. The dynamics of photosynthesis. Science, 46:343.
The role of the nucleus in oxidation. Science, 46:367–69.
Similarity in the effects of potassium cyanide and of ether. Bot. Gaz., 63:77–80.
Tolerance of fresh water by marine plants and its relation to adaptation. Bot. Gaz., 63:146–49.
Does the temperature coefficient of permeability indicate that it is chemical in nature? Bot. Gaz., 63:317–20.

1918

The basis of measurement of antagonism. J. Biol. Chem., 34:363–68.
The determination of buffer effects in measuring respiration. J. Biol. Chem., 35:237–40.
Conductivity as a measurement of permeability. J. Biol. Chem., 36:485–88.
A demonstration of photosynthesis. Am. J. Botany, 5:105–11.
With A. R. C. Haas. Dynamical aspects of photosynthesis. Proc. Nat. Acad. Sci., 4:85–91.
Endurance of extreme conditions and its relation to the theory of adaptation. Am. J. Botany, 5:507–10.
With A. R. C. Haas. On the dynamics of photosynthesis. J.G.P., 1:1–16.
A method of studying respiration. J.G.P., 1:17–22.
An indicator method of measuring the consumption of oxygen. J.G.P., 1:167–69.
Note on the effect of diffusion upon the conductivity of living tissues. J. Biol. Chem., 36:489–90.
A method of measuring the electrical conductivity of living tissues. J. Biol. Chem., 36:557–68.

With A. R. C. Haas. A simple method of measuring photosynthesis. Science, 47:420–22.
Note on measuring the relative rates of life processes. Science, 48:172–74.
The nucleus as a center of oxidation. Brooklyn Botanical Garden Memoirs, 1:342–47.
A simple method of demonstrating the production of aldehyde by chlorophyll and by aniline dyes in the presence of sunlight. Am. J. Botany, 5:511–13.
Comparative studies of respiration. I. Introduction. J.G.P., 1:171–79.

1919

With A. R. C. Haas. The temperature coefficient of photosynthesis. J.G.P., 1:295–98.
A comparative study of permeability in plants. J.G.P., 1:299–304.
Decrease of permeability and antagonistic effects caused by bile salts. J.G.P., 1:405–8.
A comparison of permeability in plant and animal cells. J.G.P., 1:409–13.
Antagonism between alkaloids and salts in relation to permeability. J.G.P., 1:515–19.
Comparative studies on respiration. VII. Respiration and antagonism. Introductory note. J.G.P., 2:1–4.
Apparatus for the study of photosynthesis and respiration. Bot. Gaz., 68:60–62.

1920

The mechanism of injury and recovery. J.G.P., 3:15–20.
A theory of injury and recovery. I. Experiments with pure salts. J.G.P., 3:145–56.

1921

A theory of injury and recovery. II. Experiments with mixtures. J.G.P., 3:415–29.
A theory of injury and recovery. III. Repeated exposures to toxic solutions. J.G.P., 3:611–22.
Conductivity and permeability. J.G.P., 4:1–9.
The mechanism of injury and recovery of the cell. Science, 53:352–56.

1922

Direct and indirect determinations of permeability. J.G.P., 4:275–83.
Injury, recovery and death. American Journal of Physiology, 59:443.
Some aspects of selective absorption. J.G.P., 5:225–30.

1923

Exosmosis in relation to injury and permeability. J.G.P., 5:709–25.
Injury, Recovery and Death in Relation to Conductivity and Permeability. Monograph on experimental biology. Philadelphia, J. B. Lippincott Company. 259 pp. (Reviewed in J. Am. Chem. Soc., 45:1861.)
The mechanism of injury, recovery and death. Harvey Lectures, 17:174–200.
Continuation of investigations on permeability in cells. Carnegie Institution of Washington Year Book, 22:290.
The Nature of Life. New York, Henry Holt & Co. 117 pp. (Colver Lectures, Brown University, 1922.)

1924

Jacques Loeb, the scientist. Proc. Soc. Exp. Biol. Med., 21:iv; also in Science, 59:428.

1925

On the importance of maintaining certain differences between cell sap and external medium. J.G.P., 7:561–64.
With M. J. Dorcas. Contrasts in the cell sap of *Valonia* and the problem of flotation. J.G.P., 7:633–40.
Is living protoplasm permeable to ions? J.G.P., 8:131–46.
With M. J. Dorcas. The penetration of CO_2 into living protoplasm. J.G.P., 9:255–67.

1926

The behavior of electrolytes in *Valonia*. Proc. Soc. Exp. Biol. Med., 24:234–35.

1927

Some aspects of bioelectrical phenomena. J.G.P., 11:83–99.

With E. B. Damon and A. G. Jacques. Dissimilarity of inner and outer protoplasmic surfaces in *Valonia*. J.G.P., 11:193–205.

Some Fundamental Problems of Cellular Physiology. (3d William Thompson Sedgwick Memorial Lecture) New Haven, Yale University Press. 55 pp.

1928

Jacques Loeb. J.G.P., 8:ix–lix.

Jacques Loeb. Collecting Net, 25:7.

With E. S. Harris. Protoplasmic asymmetry in *Nitella* as shown by bioelectric measurements. J.G.P., 11:391–406.

With E. S. Harris. The death wave in *Nitella*. I. Application of like solutions. J.G.P., 12:167–86.

With A. G. Jacques. Internal vs. external toxicity in *Valonia*. J.G.P., 12:209–19.

With E. S. Harris. Reversible changes in living protoplasm. Proc. Soc. Exp. Biol. Med., 26:124–25.

Note on the penetration of electrolytes. Proc. Soc. Exp. Biol. Med., 26:192–97.

Some aspects of cellular physiology. In: *Lectures on Plant Pathology and Physiology in Relation to Man,* pp. 179–90 (Mayo Foundation Lectures, 1926–27). Philadelphia, W. B. Saunders Company.

1929

With E. S. Harris. The death wave in *Nitella*. II. Applications of unlike solutions. J.G.P., 12:355–61.

With W. C. Cooper, Jr., and M. J. Dorcas. The penetration of strong electrolytes. J.G.P., 12:427–33.

With E. S. Harris. The concentration effect in *Nitella*. J.G.P., 12:761–81.

With E. S. Harris. Note on the nature of the current of injury in tissues. J.G.P., 13:47–56.

With L. R. Blinks and E. S. Harris. Studies on stimulation in *Nitella*. Proc. Soc. Exp. Biol. Med., 26:836–38.

With E. S. Harris. Bioelectrical aspects of the all-or-none law. Proc. Soc. Exp. Biol. Med., 26:838–40.

Some aspects of permeability and bioelectrical phenomena. In: Molecular physics in relation to biology. Bulletin of the National Research Council, 69:170–228.

1930

With E. B. Damon. The concentration effect with *Valonia:* potential differences with concentrated and diluted sea water. J.G.P., 13:445–57.

With S. E. Hill. Negative variations in *Nitella* produced by chloroform and by potassium chloride. J.G.P., 13:459–67.

With S. E. Hill. Salt bridges and negative variations. J.G.P., 13:547–52.

With A. G. Jacques. The kinetics of penetration. II. The penetration of CO_2 into *Valonia.* J.G.P., 13:695–713.

Calculations of bioelectrical potentials. I. Effects of KCl and NaCl on *Nitella.* J.G.P., 13:715–32.

With W. C. Cooper, Jr. The accumulation of electrolytes. I. The entrance of ammonia into *Valonia macrophysa.* J.G.P., 14:117–25.

The kinetics of penetration. III. Equations for the exchange of ions. J.G.P., 14:277–84.

The accumulation of electrolytes. II. Suggestions as to the nature of accumulation in *Valonia.* J.G.P., 14:285–300.

With A. G. Jacques. The accumulation of electrolytes. III. Behavior of sodium, potassium and ammonium in *Valonia.* J.G.P., 14:301–14.

1931

Electrical phenomena in the living cell. Harvey Lectures, 25:169–85, 1929–30.

With S. E. Hill. The death wave in *Nitella.* III. Transmission. J.G.P., 14:385–92.

With S. E. Hill. Electrical variations due to mechanical transmission of stimuli. J.G.P., 14:473–85.

With S. E. Hill. The production and inhibition of action currents by alcohol. J.G.P., 14:611–16.

Physiological studies of single plant cells. Biological Reviews, 6:369–411.

1932

With A. G. Jacques. The accumulation of electrolytes. IV. Internal versus external concentrations of potassium. J.G.P., 15:537–50.

With W. M. Stanley. The accumulation of electrolytes. V. Models showing accumulation and a steady state. J.G.P., 15:667–89.

The kinetics of penetration. IV. Diffusion against a growing potential gradient in models. J.G.P., 16:157–63.
With W. M. Stanley. Models showing accumulation. Proc. Soc. Exp. Biol. Med., 29:577–78.
Studies on large plant cells. Australian Journal of Experimental Biology and Medical Science, 9:135–39.

1933

The kinetics of penetration. V. The kinetics of a model as related to the steady state. J.G.P., 16:529–57.
With S. E. Hill. Anesthesia produced by distilled water. J.G.P., 17:87–98.
Anesthesia in acid and alkaline solutions. J.G.P., 17:99–103.
The electrical behavior of large plant cells. Cold Spring Harbor Symp. Quant. Biol., 1:125–30. Also in Collecting Net, 8:213–14.
Osmotic pressure in relation to permeability in large plant cells and in models. Cold Spring Harbor Symp. Quant. Biol., 1:166–69.
Permeability in large plant cells and in models. Ergebnisse der Physiologie, 35:967–1021.
Some aspects of cell physiology. Annals of Internal Medicine, 7:396–400.
With S. E. Hill. Reversible loss of the potassium effect in distilled water. J.G.P., 17:105–8.

1934

With S. E. Kamerling and W. M. Stanley. The kinetics of penetration. VI. Some factors affecting penetration. J.G.P., 17:445–67.
With S. E. Kamerling and W. M. Stanley. The kinetics of penetration. VII. Molecular vs. ionic transport. J.G.P., 17:469–80.
With S. E. Kamerling. The kinetics of penetration. VIII. Temporary accumulation. J.G.P., 17:507–16.
With A. G. Jacques. The accumulation of electrolytes. VI. The effect of external pH. J.G.P., 17:727–50.
Nature of the action currents in *Nitella*. I. General considerations. J.G.P., 18:215–27.
With S. E. Kamerling. The kinetics of penetration. IX. Models of mature cells. J.G.P., 18:229–34.
With A. G. Jacques. Penetration of potassium into *Nitella*. Proc. Soc. Exp. Biol. Med., 31:1121–22.

1935

With S. E. Hill. Positive variations in *Nitella*. J.G.P., 18:369–75.
With S. E. Hill. Nature of the action current in *Nitella*. II. Special cases. J.G.P., 18:377–83.
With S. E. Hill. Nature of the action current in *Nitella*. Some additional features. J.G.P., 18:499–514.
With S. E. Hill. Restoration of the potassium effect by means of action currents. J.G.P., 18:681–86.
With S. E. Hill. Mechanical restoration of irritability and of the potassium effect. J.G.P., 18:687–94.
With A. G. Jacques. The kinetics of penetration. XI. Entrance of potassium into *Nitella*. J.G.P., 18:967–85.
Chemical restoration in *Nitella*. I. Ammonia and some of its compounds. J.G.P., 18:987–95.
With S. E. Kamerling. The accumulation of electrolytes. VIII. The accumulation of KCl in models. J.G.P., 19:167–78.
With S. E. Hill. Pacemakers in *Nitella*. I. Temporary local differences in rhythm. J.G.P., 19:307–9.
How do electrolytes enter the cell? Proc. Nat. Acad. Sci., 21:125–32.
How do electrolytes penetrate the cell? Collecting Net, 10:1–8.
With S. E. Hill. The role of ions in *Valonia* and *Nitella*. Biol. Bull., 69:329.
Some experimental modifications of the protoplasmic surface. Proc. Soc. Exp. Biol. Med., 32:715–16.
With S. E. Hill. Some aspects of anesthesia and irritability. Science, 81:418–19.
Mechanism of salt absorption by plant cells. Nature, 136:1034–35.

1936

Chemical restoration in *Nitella*. II. Restorative action of blood. J.G.P., 19:423–25.
Electrical phenomena in large plant cells. Physiological Reviews, 16:216–37.
The absorption of electrolytes in large plant cells. Bot. Rev., 2:283–315.
Über einige chemische und elektrische Eigenschaften von protoplasmaoberflächen. Kolloid-Zeitschrift, 77:373–85.
With S. E. Hill. Some ways to control bioelectrical behavior. Cold Spring Harbor Symp. Quant. Biol., 4:43–52.

Changes of apparent ionic mobilities in protoplasm. I. Effects of guaiacol on *Valonia*. J.G.P., 20:13–43.

1937

Changes of apparent ionic mobilities in protoplasm. II. The action of guaiacol as affected by pH. J.G.P., 20:685–93.

Electrochemical methods in the study of plant cells. Transactions of the Electrochemical Society, 71:93–99.

The protoplasmic surface in certain plant cells. Transactions of the Faraday Society, 33:997–1002.

1938

With S. E. Hill. Calculations of bioelectric potentials. II. The concentration potential of KCl in *Nitella*. J.G.P., 21:541–56.

Effects of potassium on the potential of *Halicystis*. J.G.P., 21:631–34.

With A. G. Jacques. The accumulation of electrolytes. X. Accumulation of iodine by *Halicystis* and *Valonia*. J.G.P., 21:687–93.

Changes of apparent ionic mobilities in protoplasm. III. Some effects of guaiacol on *Halicystis*. J.G.P., 21:707–20.

With A. G. Jacques. The accumulation of electrolytes. XI. Accumulation of nitrate by *Valonia* and *Halicystis*. J.G.P., 21:767–73.

With S. E. Hill. Nature of the action current in *Nitella*. IV. Production of quick action currents by exposure to NaCl. J.G.P., 22:91–106.

With S. E. Hill. Delayed potassium effect in *Nitella*. J.G.P., 22:107–13.

With S. E. Hill. Pacemakers in *Nitella*. II. Arrhythmia and block. J.G.P., 22:115–30.

With S. E. Hill. Calculations of bioelectric potentials. IV. Some effects of calcium on potentials in *Nitella*. J.G.P., 22:139–46.

With J. W. Murray. The movement of water from concentrated to dilute solutions through liquid membranes. Science, 87:430. (A)

With J. W. Murray. Movement of water against a gradient in models. Proc. Soc. Exp. Biol. Med., 38:468–70.

Potentials in *Halicystis* as affected by non-electrolytes. Proc. Nat. Acad. Sci., 24:75–76.

With S. E. Hill. Calculations of bioelectric potentials. III. Varia-

tion in partition coefficients and ion mobilities. Proc. Nat. Acad. Sci., 24:312–15.
With S. E. Hill. Reversal of the potassium effect in *Nitella*. Proc. Nat. Acad. Sci., 24:427–29.

1939

Changes of apparent ionic mobilities in protoplasm. IV. Influence of guaiacol on the effects of sodium and potassium in *Nitella*. J.G.P., 22:417–27.
Calculations of bioelectric potentials. V. Potentials in *Halicystis*. J.G.P., 23:53–57.
Calculations of bioelectric potentials. VI. Some effects of guaiacol on *Nitella*. J.G.P., 23:171–76.
With S. E. Hill. Chemical restoration in *Nitella*. III. Effects of inorganic salts. Proc. Nat. Acad. Sci., 25:3–5.
With J. W. Murray. Note on water in non-aqueous solutions. Science, 90:397–98.

1940

Alfred George Jacques. Science, 91:133–34.
With J. W. Murray. Behavior of water in certain heterogeneous systems. J.G.P., 23:365–90.
Some chemical aspects of the potassium effect. J.G.P., 23:429–32.
Effects of hexylresorcinol on *Nitella*. J.G.P., 23:569–73.
With S. E. Hill. Action curves with single peaks in *Nitella* in relation to the movement of potassium. J.G.P., 23:743–48.
Effects of guaiacol and hexylresorcinol in the presence of barium and calcium. J.G.P., 23:749–51.
Chemical restoration in *Nitella*. IV. Effects of guanidine. J.G.P., 24:7–8.
With S. E. Hill. The experimental production of double peaks in *Chara* action curves and their relation to the movement of potassium. J.G.P., 24:9–13.
Some models of protoplasmic surfaces. Cold Spring Harbor Symp. Quant. Biol., 8:51–52.

1941

Effects of hexylresorcinol on *Valonia*. J.G.P., 24:311–13.
Effects of nitrobenzene and benzene on *Valonia*. J.G.P., 24:699–702.
Positive potentials due to aniline and the antagonistic action of ammonia. Journal of Cellular and Comparative Physiology, 18:129–35.

1942

Increased irritability in *Nitella* due to guanidine. J.G.P., 26:65–73.

1943

Diffusion potentials in models and in living cells. J.G.P., 26:293–307.
Pacemakers in *Nitella*. III. Electrical alternans. J.G.P., 26:457–65.
Nature of the action current in *Nitella*. V. Partial response and the all-or-none law. J.G.P., 27:61–68.
A model of the potassium effect. J.G.P., 27:91–100.
Studies of the inner and outer surfaces of large plant cells. I. Plasmolysis due to salts. J.G.P., 27:139–42.
William Albert Setchell (1864–1943). American Philosophical Society Yearbook, pp. 431–32.

1944

Studies of the inner and outer protoplasmic surfaces of large plant cells. J.G.P., 28:17–22.
Differing rates of death at inner and outer surfaces of the protoplasm. I. Effects of formaldehyde on *Nitella*. J.G.P., 28:23–36.
Differing rates of death at inner and outer surfaces of the protoplasm. II. Negative potential in *Nitella* caused by formaldehyde. J.G.P., 28:37–41.
Differing rates of death at inner and outer surfaces of the protoplasm. III. Effects of mercuric chloride on *Nitella*. J.G.P., 28:343–47.

1945

Effects of hydroxyl on negative and positive cells of *Nitella*. J.G.P., 29:43–56.
Water relations in the cell. I. The chloroplasts of *Nitella* and of *Spirogyra*. J.G.P., 29:73–78.

1946

Some properties of protoplasmic gels. I. Tension in the chloroplast of *Spirogyra*. J.G.P., 29:181–92.
Nature of the action current in *Nitella*. VI. Simple and complex action patterns. J. G. P., 30:47–59.

1947

Some properties of protoplasmic gels. II. Contraction of chloroplasts in currents of water entering the cell and expansion in outgoing currents. J.G.P., 30:229–34.

The absorption of electrolytes in large plant cells. II. Bot. Rev., 13:194–215.

Some aspects of secretion. I. Secretion of water. J.G.P., 30:439–47.

1948

Abnormal protoplasmic patterns and death in slightly hypertonic solutions. J.G.P., 31:291–300.

Effects of hypertonic solutions on *Nereis* eggs. Biol. Bull., 95:269. (A)

Solubility of the vitelline membrane of *Nereis* eggs. Biol. Bull., 95:269. (A)

Experiments on chloroplasts and on photosynthesis. Biol. Bull., 95:270. (A)

1949

Movements of water in cells of *Nitella*. J.G.P., 32:553–58.

Transport of water from concentrated to dilute solutions in cells of *Nitella*. J.G.P., 32:559–66.

Some bioelectric problems. Proc. Nat. Acad. Sci., 35:548–58.

Extrusion of jelly by eggs of *Nereis limbata* under electrical stimulus. Biol. Bull., 97:260. (A)

1950

Higher permeability for water than for ethyl alcohol in *Nitella*. J.G.P., 33:275–84.

Effects of electrical currents on the absorption of water by eggs of *Nereis limbata*. J.G.P., 33:379–88.

Distant effects of toxic agents. J.G.P., 34:279–84.

The mechanism of accumulation. Biol. Bull., 99:308. (A)

Activation of *Nereis* eggs by a detergent. Biol. Bull., 99:362. (A)

Relative solubility of the components of the *Nereis* egg. Biol. Bull., 99:362. (A)

1951

Injury in relation to cell organization. J.G.P., 34:321–23.

Behavior of jelly in eggs of *Nereis limbata*. Biol. Bull., 101:226. (A)

Detergent action of sperm extract in *Nereis limbata*. Biol. Bull., 101:226. (A)

1952

Some aspects of protoplasmic motion. J.G.P., 35:519–27.

Mechanism of accumulation in living cells. J.G.P., 35:579–94.

Activation of eggs of *Nereis limbata* by a surface active extract of dead sperm. Biol. Bull., 103:305–6. (A)

Reversible contraction of protoplasmic structures by changes in pH values. Biol. Bull., 103:306. (A)

1953

Protamin in an extract of the sperm of *Nereis limbata*. Biol. Bull., 105:379–80. (A)

Surface active material obtained from *Nereis limbata*. Biol. Bull., 105:380. (A)

With Theodore Shedlovsky. Surface active properties of an extract of the sperm of *Nereis limbata*. Biol. Bull., 105:383–84. (A)

1954

Changes in resting potential due to a shift of electrolytes in the cell produced by non-electrolytes. J.G.P., 37:423–32.

Apparent violations of the all-or-none law in relation to potassium in the protoplasm. J.G.P., 37:813–24.

Note on the work of Jacques Loeb. In: *Ion Transport Across Membranes*, pp. 1–2. New York, Academic Press, Inc.

Reversible clotting in *Spirogyra*. Biol. Bull., 107:317. (A)

1955

Reversible shrinkage in *Chaetomorpha*. Biol. Bull., 109:366. (A)

Apparent violations of the all-or-none law in relation to potassium in the protoplasm. In: *Electrochemistry in Biology and Medicine*, ed. by T. Shedlovsky, pp. 213–24. New York, John Wiley & Sons, Inc.

1956

The role of water in protoplasmic permeability and in antagonism. J.G.P., 39:963–76.

Effect of electric current on the contraction of the chloroplasts of Spirogyra. Biol. Bull., 111:310. (A)

1957

The use of aquatic plants in the study of some fundamental problems. Annual Review of Plant Physiology, 8:1–10.

THEODORE WILLIAM RICHARDS

January 31, 1868–April 2, 1928

BY JAMES BRYANT CONANT

THEODORE WILLIAM RICHARDS was a precocious son of distinguished parents. He was born in Philadelphia on January 31, 1868, the third son and fifth child of William Trost Richards and Anna Matlack Richards, who had been married on June 30, 1856. As strict members of the Society of Friends, the Matlack family looked askance at a young man who earned his living painting pictures. Anna was "read out of meeting." The Quaker marriage ceremony took place in the house of a friend. The first months of the honeymoon were devoted to the composition and illustration of a manuscript volume of poems for the lady who had first brought the young couple together. A mutual interest in Browning and Tennyson had started an acquaintanceship which rapidly became a romance.

An old friend and fellow artist of Philadelphia reminiscing long after W. T. Richards had established his reputation as a landscape painter said, "He amazed me by getting married and resigning his position as designer [in a local firm manufacturing gas fixtures] in order to devote himself entirely to his art. I don't remember which event took place first but I thought the latter extremely unwise—and so it would have been with anyone else, but timidity had no place in his nature." Of the struggle of a largely self-taught artist to support a family in the Civil War years there is little record. By the time the third son,

Theodore, was conscious of his environment, the artist's family was comfortably settled in Germantown (a suburb of Philadelphia); the summers were spent in Newport, Rhode Island (after 1874).

Whether the father or the mother had the greater influence on young Theodore may be argued. But to anyone who examines the few personal documents that are left, there can be no doubt that the future chemist's career was molded at the outset by his two extraordinary parents. In an article prepared for a Swedish journal shortly after he was awarded the Nobel Prize in 1915, Theodore Richards paid tribute to his understanding mother and father:

"Although my parents had no experience with scientific investigation, their tastes and education having been of a very different kind, nevertheless they entered fully into the spirit of my desire to undertake it, and were wise enough to see that a possible future lay ahead for me in the path which so profoundly interested me. From that time my father always advised me to devote myself as much as possible to research. Moreover, he supported this advice in a very practical way (realizing that research in pure science is not a money-getting employment) and offered always to help me, out of his none too plentiful means, in case of a pinch, rather than to permit me to engage in the distracting task of making money by occupations outside of my main interest. Later after my marriage in 1896, when new cares presented themselves, and when he saw there was danger of my overworking, he placed into my hands a sum of money large enough to enable me to feel that I could take a year's rest from academic work, if that should prove necessary. The relief from worry, afforded by this sum in a savings bank, made the vacation unnecessary. There is no question that this generous and thoughtful confidence was a very important factor in the success of a not very optimistic and somewhat delicate young man, then entirely without any capital except his brains; and it would be impossible to exaggerate my feelings of gratitude."

Quite apart from the wise advice and the financial assistance, William T. Richards must have influenced his third son by his example. "There was nothing of the pose of his craft about him," writes his biographer, "the cast of keen observation in his face, and the easy grace of his carriage, denoted the man of original thought and unconstrained opinion, the artist who sees a little deeper into objective life than most people, and whose instincts are, therefore, less confined to convention. . . . He knew he could draw matchlessly, and yet there were elements in the portrayal of a breaking wave that he never achieved to his own satisfaction. If you pressed him with commendation on the side of drawing he would shield his modesty behind his struggles with that miracle of color under the curving wave. He had studied this for years. His son tells us that 'he stood for hours in the early days of Atlantic City or Cape May, with folded arms, studying the motion of the sea,—until people thought him insane. After days of gazing he made pencil notes of the action of the water. He even stood for hours in a bathing suit among the waves, trying to analyse the motion.' "

The words of the son which the father's biographer quotes demonstrate how much the patience and thoroughness of the artist bent on portraying nature had impressed the boy who so often stood by while the beginnings of a seascape were forming in the painter's mind. The link between the world of science and the world of art was a pride of both father and son in a capacity to take infinite pains. The chemist who was to become famous for the painstaking accuracy of his experimentations may well have received his inspiration from watching his father standing hour after hour in the surf.

If the influence of the father is largely a matter of conjecture, the role of Theodore's mother in his upbringing is definite and clear. She provided the formal education at home. Her experience with the schools in Germantown had been unsatisfactory. Therefore she decided to try the experiment of teaching the younger children herself.

"We used to have regular hours and school was not to be slighted," Theodore Richards reports in an autobiographical fragment. Continuing the description, he notes that "drawing and music were included in this home curriculum and so, of course, were reading, writing, arithmetic and geography as well as much more history than is usually taught to young children. . . . My mother's devotion was tireless and beyond praise. My debt to her (as well as to my father) is inestimable." He might well so write since not only had his mother's instruction prepared him for entry to the sophomore class at Haverford at the age of fourteen but her tutoring in Greek (which she learned for this purpose) a year later enabled him to enroll in the senior class at Harvard after graduation from Haverford.

A typescript composed two years before Richards died is entitled "Early Memories." He ends with an account of his leaving the summer home near Newport to head for college. He was "on his own for the first time," he writes. "With me in my pocket I carried two sonnets written for me by my mother (who was in many ways a very remarkable and brilliant woman)." Then follow the two sonnets, of which the opening lines of the second amount almost to a parental injunction:

> Fear not to go where fearless Science leads,
> Who holds the keys of God. What reigning light
> Thine eyes discern in that surrounding night
> Whence we have come, what law that supersedes
> The fiat of all oracles and creeds,
> Thy soul will never find that Wrong is Right;

At Christmas 1880, when Richards was not quite thirteen, chemistry had entered his life. He was given a large box containing materials and apparatus for 200 experiments "warranted to be safe and instructive." Richards has recorded his progress as a chemical student as follows: "Soon afterwards, when I had nearly blown off my head with this outfit, I was given Steele's *Fourteen Weeks in Chemistry* so that knowledge might diminish the risk; and when the somewhat limited scope of this book had been outspanned, I advanced to Eliot and Storer's *Elementary Chemistry* which contained a priceless fund of information. . . . Dr. John Marshall of the University of Pennsylvania Medical School was good enough to interest himself in the boy of thirteen who was so eager for sound chemical knowledge. He invited me to Professor Wormley's lectures at the University of Pennsylvania."

Such was Richards's memory in later years of his introduction to chemistry. At Haverford he first studied the subject with a serious purpose under Lyman B. Hall and decided to become a chemist. Looking back to that period in his life he recalls that "except for his somewhat defective eyesight he might have chosen to become an astronomer." At this point Josiah Parsons Cooke, Professor of Chemistry at Harvard, whom the family had come to know during the summers at Newport, Rhode Island, enters the story. He seems to have been instrumental in Richards's decision to spend another year of study and to take a second bachelor's degree at Harvard. Two years later Richards received the Ph.D. degree for important research on the atomic weights of oxygen and hydrogen accomplished under Professor Cooke's guidance. The results were reported in a paper published in 1888 as a joint communication. In the same year Richards printed three other papers based on his independent work on the atomic weights of copper and silver, as well as one dealing with the heat produced by the reaction of silver nitrate with solutions of metallic chlorides. Four publications and the young investigator was not yet twenty-one! Then followed a year abroad.

Two pieces of research were conducted in the chemical laboratory of Göttingen University, one in analytical chemistry under Paul Jannasch and one on vapor chemistry determination under Victor Meyer. In addition some weeks were spent in Munich and in Dresden studying special chemical methods. As a supplement to what Professor Cooke could teach him, these experiences seemed to place the young American chemist in the mainstream of current investigations. They formed an introduction to a far more important semester spent in Leipzig (with Wilhelm Ostwald) and in Göttingen (with Walther Nernst) in 1895. These two periods spent in German laboratories could be regarded as Richards's training in the then newly developing field of physical chemistry. At that period in history there were no centers of research in physical chemistry in either the United States or England. It is not much of an exaggeration to speak of Richards as a German-trained scientist. His outlook on life, however, was in no sense Germanic. In spite of his early and wide acquaintanceship among German chemists and a half year spent in Berlin in 1907, he seems to have found little to attract him in the empire ruled by the Kaiser. In England, on the other hand, he made lifelong friends. In the summer of 1889 he met one of the outstanding chemists, Sir Henry Roscoe (who was a friend of Professor Cooke), as well as Lord Rayleigh, who was soon to become an internationally famous physicist. With the English investigators he felt very much at home. He admired them and their way of life. It is altogether fitting that the definitive account of his life is the Theodore William Richards Memorial Lecture delivered by Sir Harold Hartley before the Chemical Society of London on April 25, 1929.

Richards was elected to the National Academy of Sciences in 1899. Of all the many honors he received, the award of the Faraday Medal of the Chemical Society of London must have pleased him as much as any. Together with his wife and three children he traveled to England in May 1911 for the occasion. Sir Harold Hartley refers to Richards's pleasure at Professor H. B. Dixon's allusion to him as the Faraday Lecturer who was fulfilling Canning's prophecy: "I look to the new world to redress the balance of the old." Honorary degrees from Oxford, Cambridge, and Manchester added to the delight of that summer. The Nobel Prize in chemistry awarded in November 1915 may be considered as the climax of Richards's public recognition. World War I, however, prevented his going to Sweden to receive the award at the time of its announcement. Later a projected trip had to be canceled because of the sudden illness of his oldest son, who was to have accompanied him to Stockholm.

As much as Richards loved England, and after the invasion of Belgium in 1914 despised all things German, his career as a teacher followed the pattern of Germany. Indeed, a call to the University of Göttingen in 1902 may be said to have assured his position at Harvard. President C. W. Eliot made him a full professor and agreed to the construction of new laboratory facilities if and when funds could be raised. (The Wolcott Gibbs Memorial Laboratory was built for Richards just before World War I.) Richards desired a few (but only a few) graduate students, the professorship of physical chemistry which involved giving a full course of lectures, and the privilege of continuing a half course of lectures on "Elementary Theoretical and Physical Chemistry, including the Historical Development of Chemical Theory." This course he had initiated in the 1890s when he was still an assistant professor. These teaching tasks Richards thoroughly enjoyed because he did them well. They were based on a full confidence in the lecture method, as it was employed in the German universities. As a young man Richards had been responsible for instruction in quantitative analysis. But by the time he was called to Göttingen he was ready to turn over concern with this phase of practical chemistry to junior professors whom he had trained. The arrangements which Richards entered into in 1902 at the age of thirty-four remained unaltered until his death. Though he became famous because of his many papers describing his researches, his performance as an excellent and devoted teacher was in itself worthy of high praise.

In 1896 Richards married Miriam Stuart Thayer, daughter of Joseph Henry Thayer, a professor at the Harvard Divinity School and outstanding New Testament scholar. Thanks to the generosity of his father, Richards was able to build a house not far from the Harvard College yard, in which the couple lived their entire married life. There were three children: Grace Thayer, who became the wife of the author of this memoir; William Theodore and Greenough Thayer, both of whom became professors, the one of chemistry at Princeton, the other of design at Virginia Polytechnic Institute. The summer months without fail were dedicated to a vacation, often on Mt. Desert Island in Maine. The health of both father and mother was somewhat precarious but the duties of the professor of physical chemistry were carried out without fail year after year. Only for half a year in 1907 did Richards absent himself from Cambridge in order to function as the Exchange Professor at Berlin. There were no leaves of absence for reasons of health, and Richards never availed himself of the privilege of taking a half year's sabbatical at full salary. He could not bear to be separated in term time from his graduate students whose experimentations he followed almost daily with a discerning yet sympathetic eye. The habit of attempting to forsee all possible contingencies, which was basic to his success as a scientific investigator, placed a heavy strain on his life as a husband and father. To worry about the smallest detail was to be a painstaking chemist setting new standards of accurate measurement. Yet to carry over to daily life the same attitude condemned the scientist to a total life of anxiety. As he approached sixty it became apparent to his close relatives that the nervous load Richards had been carrying for years was too much for the physical organism. Yet he continued his lectures and went to his laboratory on his regular schedule until within a few days of his death, which occurred on April 2, 1928. He went down with his colors flying as had been his wish.

RICHARDS'S SCIENTIFIC WORK

[Richards left an account of his scientific work up to the year 1914. The first portion of the document deals with his investigations of atomic weights. I have printed it as part of an article on "Theodore William Richards and the Periodic Table" (*Science*, Vol. 168, pp. 425–28, April 24, 1970). For the sake of completeness I reproduce it here and it constitutes the balance of the text of this memoir. The entire autobiographical fragment is written in the third person. The part which has not yet been published starts with his evaluation of his work on chemical thermodynamics. I have to thank my wife for making the manuscript available.]

The scientific work of Theodore W. Richards may be divided for convenience into five categories more or less closely interrelated. The first of these categories includes the study of atomic weights, the second, the investigation of various problems concerning chemical equilibrium, the third, original work upon chemical thermodynamics both practical and theoretical, the fourth, the study of various problems in electrochemistry, and the fifth both practical and theoretical work concerning the significance of atomic compressibility and the changes exhibited by atomic volumes under varying conditions.

During the past twenty-six years Richards has been directly concerned in the study of the atomic weights of twenty elements, and some of his pupils at Harvard have independently studied ten more. Thus far no one has been able to show that any one of the investigations concerning these thirty elements is seriously in error, and the results of all have been accepted as the best heretofore published by the International Committee on

Atomic Weights, which has no Harvard representative upon it. The elements investigated under the immediate direction of Richards or with his own hands are as follows: oxygen, copper, barium, strontium, zinc, magnesium, nickel, cobalt, iron, uranium, calcium, caesium, chlorine, bromine, silver, sodium, potassium, nitrogen, sulphur, and lithium.

The determination of the ratio of oxygen to hydrogen was taken up in collaboration with J. P. Cooke in 1886. They weighed hydrogen directly in large glass globes, and after having burnt it with copper oxide, determined the weight of water. The outcome gave a result for hydrogen only 0.0004 different from the value 1.0078 now generally accepted. This was the first direct determination showing that the ratio of hydrogen to oxygen is distinctly less than 1 is to 16, and the error in the result was one-half as large as the error that was previously considered as the best.

The behavior of copper oxide led Richards to suspect that the atomic weight of copper accepted at that time was in error, and accordingly he commenced an investigation of this element which lasted four years. He discovered that oxides of metals prepared from the nitrate always contain included gases, a circumstance which he found to vitiate the earlier work not only upon the atomic weight of copper but also those of a number of other elements. He showed also that the copper sulphate had much greater tendency to retain water than had been attributed to it, and by means of a number of new methods obtained a series of consistent results for the atomic weight of copper. The relation of copper to silver, of copper to bromine, and of copper to sulphuric acid were all determined with care, and all yielded essentially the same new value, thus leaving no doubt that the old value for copper was nearly one-half a percent too low.

The anomalous behavior of barium sulphate led Richards then to study the atomic weight of barium; both barium chloride and barium bromide were analyzed taking care to drive off all the water without decomposing the salts. Much time was spent upon the preparation of pure silver and every step of the analysis was tested taking great heed especially of the solubility of silver chloride. The result showed that barium was previously almost as unexact as copper. In this case as in the other not only were new results obtained but also the reasons for the deviations in the old ones were made clear.

Strontium, magnesium, zinc, nickel, cobalt, iron, uranium, and caesium were then taken up in succession, being studied by somewhat similar methods with the help of the experience gained in the earlier researches. In some of these Richards had the assistance of pupils. He was able to show that the old results on zinc and magnesium were in error because of the retention of gases on the oxides, and that most of the other values also had been vitiated by chemical imperfections in the methods employed. Richards not only employed and revised the old methods but devised new ones in the course of this work.

The investigation upon caesium marked the end of the first period of his investigations concerning atomic weights—the time during which the work of Stas had been considered impeccable. In 1904 the investigation of a large number of specimens of sodium bromide while verifying Stas's atomic weight for bromine seemed to indicate that this value for sodium was distinctly too high. Because the sodium bromide underwent transition from the dihydrate to the anhydrous salt at a perfectly definite point, it was evidently very pure. Hence its verdict could not be ignored and a new study of the atomic weight of sodium was undertaken. This investigation began a new period in Richards's work in which he was able to show the errors into which Stas had unwittingly fallen. He proved without question that not only was Stas's value for sodium too high but his value for chlorine was too low, and both of these conclusions have been verified by the subsequent work of others. Because Richards had previously chiefly used bromides, this discovery of the error in chlorine was not made during his earlier researches.

The discovery of error in two of Stas's most accurately determined results led to the natural suspicion that others also might need revision. Accordingly three determinations of potassium, of sulphur, and of nitrogen were undertaken with the help of able assistants, the last of the three investigations being conducted partly at the University of Berlin during the term of his exchange professorship there. Potassium chloride and bromide were both analyzed with all the care used in the case of sodium. Sulphur was approached by a new method involving the conversion of silver sulphate into the chloride, and nitrogen was attacked both by the synthesis of silver nitrate and by the analysis of ammonium chloride. The work on silver nitrate was in some ways the most convincing of all, because in this case it was possible to prove that the salt was essentially free from water, by decomposing it and passing the products of decomposition, suitably treated, through a phosphorus pentoxide tube. No more concordant results have ever been secured in the Harvard Laboratory than the six successive experiments by which the silver was converted into silver nitrate—the extreme variation between the results being less than one-thousandth of a percent. If any error existed in them, it was an error of amazing constancy.

The most recent finished problem with which he has been concerned was a study of the atomic weights of lithium, and silver. Not only was the ratio of lithium chloride to silver determined but also its ratio to silver chloride and besides this by a new method the amount of lithium chloride contained in lithium perchlorate was carefully determined. The ratio of silver to oxygen was thus directly obtained by this equation.

$$\frac{Ag}{LiCl} \times \frac{LiCl}{LiClO_4 - LiCl} = \frac{Ag}{O_4}$$

This was entirely a new procedure and for many reasons seems to give one of the very best means of determining the atomic weight of silver. Incidentally the atomic weight of lithium was found to be almost a whole percent less than that obtained by Stas. This seems to have been Stas's most grievous error, and came to pass only because all the defects in his process accumulated on the head of this lightest of all the metals.

Richards has himself said that "the secret of success in the study of atomic weights lies in carefully choosing the particular substances and processes employed, and in checking every operation by parallel experiments so that every unknown chemical and physical error will gradually be ferreted out of its hiding place. The most important causes of inaccuracy are: the solubility of precipitates and of the material of containing vessels; the occlusion of foreign substances by solids, and especially the presence of retained moisture in almost everything. Each of these disturbing circumstances varies with each individual case. Far more depends upon the intelligent choice of the conditions of experiment than upon the mere mechanical execution of the operations, although that too is important." In carrying out these suggestions he has brought into play all the powerful aid furnished by the new science of physical chemistry which has thrown so much light upon the mechanism of the establishment of chemical equilibrium. He has always heeded the advice given in the paragraph above, especially the series of errors caused by the unsuspected presence of water in the salts to be weighed. With this in mind there was evolved in the course of this work a remarkably simple device for driving off every trace of water from any salt, and then enclosing this salt in a bottle without exposure for an instant to the outside air so that it could be weighed without risk of attracting moisture. This device greatly helped his work as did also the nephelometer, an instrument for detecting minute traces of suspended precipitate by means of the light reflected by them. Both of these instruments were original with him. He has always pointed out very emphatically that the chemical difficulties in work of this kind greatly exceed the physical ones. The operation of weighing is far more easily controlled than the solubility of precipitates and the retention of foreign substances in the material to be weighed. For this reason he has preferred to use rather small quantities of material and to prepare these in a state of undoubted purity. As he has pointed out, there is no object in weighing 100 grams of material even to within 5 milligrams, if it contains as much as 0.01 percent of impurity. A much better result can be obtained by weighing 10 grams to within 0.1 of a milligram, provided that the material itself contains no more than 0.001 percent of impurity.

Richards's contributions to the science of chemical thermodynamics have been varied in nature, and, as in the other cases, they have had in part a practical interest and in part also primarily a theoretical one; his first published paper was a brief study of the constant heat of precipitations of argentic chloride, now so well explained by Arrhenius's theory. Subsequently he has studied a wide variety of thermochemical phenomena with unusual precision, having devised entirely a new method of calorimetry for this purpose. This method, first put in practice by him, consists in causing the environment of the calorimeter to change in temperature at precisely the same rate as the calorimeter itself. Thus at one stroke the various corrections for cooling, and for the lag of the thermometer, are wholly eliminated, and a more satisfactory thermochemical result is obtained than can be reached in any other way. With the help of pupils, he has applied this method to the determination of the specific heats of solids at low temperatures, the specific heats of liquids, the heats of solution of metals in acids, and the heats of combustion of organic substances, having obtained a great variety of data upon these various topics, many already published and many awaiting publication. He has been able to show in most cases that others have made greater or less important errors in their work, for example, in the case of the determination of specific heats of solids when corrected for the heat loss or gain during transfer by running parallel experiments with a hollow vessel of the same bulk and same material as the sold piece of metal to be measured, thus making possible by mere subtraction the accurate correction for this error. He was also able to prove that Julius Thomsen's methods for correcting the results with concentrated solutions to those with dilute solutions was incorrect in detail.

In his study of the specific heats of the elements at low temperatures he emphasized especially the rapid falling off of the specific heat with the temperature in many cases, a phenomenon recently taken up more in detail and at even lower temperatures by Walther Nernst. His study of heat capacities, however, was not limited to the practical laboratory work. In a paper, which deserves especial mention because it has been frequently overlooked, he pointed out on the basis of such data as were available at that time that the change of heat capacity of a reacting system was in all probability connected with the difference between the total energy change and the free energy change in that reaction. He was the first to point out that in all probability the two latter quantities are equal to one another in case no change of heat capacity occurs during the reaction, and he also pointed out that in all probability an increase in heat capacity during a reaction signifies that the total energy change is less than the free energy change, whereas, on the other hand, a decrease in the heat capacity during the reaction probably causes the total energy change to be greater than the free energy change. These statements clearly made in 1902 are without question the basis of Nernst's subsequent mathematical treatment of the subject. Richards' data were rather inadequate and his paper tentative, but the essential ideas involved are unquestionably outlined in this paper, although not treated there in full detail.

Electrical problems were first attacked by Richards in his effort to discover if the electrochemical equivalents are precisely equal to the corresponding chemical equivalents, as the atomic theory would lead one to expect. He studied therefore in great detail the copper and the silver voltameter (or coulometer, as he more appropriately named the instrument). He was able to trace the error in the former due to the formation of cuprous sulphate, and a very elaborate study of the silver coulometer led him to discover the chief causes of error in the instrument as used up to that time, and then to propose several methods of obtaining accurate results. The difficulty of the work seems to be indicated by the discussion which has since been raised by the subsequent work of others in the light of the recent investigations conducted at the Bureau of Standards at Washington as well as by G. A. Hulett, but there can be no question that every point made in Richards's papers was correct.

He was able to show in these researches not only that Faraday's law of electrolysis holds with great exactness, but also that this exactness is fully equalled by the behavior of fused salts when subjected to electrolysis. He proved also that electrostenolytic effects are likewise without influence upon Faraday's law. These investigations taken together constitute the most striking evidence as yet obtained of the accuracy of this fundamental generalization. They place it among the very few laws which seem to be as exact as far as our very careful observation can show.

His electrochemical work has also included the determination of single potential differences as well as of the electromotive forces exhibited by dilute and concentrated liquid amalgams. The most interesting contribution to the former class of phenomena is that concerning the electromotive force of iron under varying conditions and the effect of occluded hydrogen. In this research he not only for the first time discovered the true single potential difference exhibited by iron, but explained the reasons for the low results obtained by others and threw new light upon the nature of hydrogen occluded by iron and the mechanism of overvoltage. All his results on this subject have subsequently been confirmed by Förster in a monograph published by the Bunsen Gesellschaft. With regard to his work upon electromotive forces produced by dilute amalgams, it is enough to say that with the help of pupils he has studied amalgams of cadmium, zinc, thallium, indium, lead, tin, copper, and lithium, in many cases using very concentrated solutions of the metal in mercury, and these varied data were made the basis not only for a striking verification of the exactness of the law of concentration-effect at great dilution but also a basis for a thermodynamic analysis of the cases of the deviations exhibited by concentrated solutions.

The work upon the significance of changing atomic volume and atomic compressibility which has occupied much of Professor Richards's time during the last thirteen years has both a practical and a theoretical aspect. His views concerning the nature of the liquid and solid state have led him to make a large number of determinations of compressibility, of surface tension, and heat of evaporation, which have enriched considerably our knowledge upon this subject, and which cannot but be of lasting value, even independent of any hypothesis. Prominent among these data are the determinations of the compressibilities of the elements. In a series of investigations using an entirely new method, devised by himself, for determining compressibility, he determined the relative compressibilities of thirty-five liquid or solid elements, so distributed as to depict for the first time clearly the periodic nature of this property.

The close correspondence between compressibilities of the solid elements and their atomic volumes is shown by the two curves in the accompanying diagram, cut from one of his publications.*

In addition to these data concerning the elements he has, with the help as before of a number of pupils, determined the compressibilities of a variety of simple compounds, such as the halides of lithium, sodium, potassium, and thallium, on the one hand, and hydrocarbons, alcohols, esters, amines, and organic halides, on the other hand. These data, many of them entirely new, afford a basis for a variety of interesting theoretical conclusions concerning the mechanism of the compression of solids and liquids. His work on surface tension and heat of evaporation, which was undertaken in order to test his hypothesis concerning the relation of these properties, has never yet been fully published, and therefore cannot be fully discussed at present, but enough has appeared in print to show the importance of the work.

As has been stated, all these investigations were suggested or inspired by Richards's theory of atomic compressibility which differs radically from the current kinetic conception of the structure of solid and liquid bodies. His hypothesis first arose in his mind from the consideration of the behavior of gases, and the now generally accepted variability of the quantity b in the equation of van der Waals. He reasoned that if b is changeable, the actual size of the molecules to which b is probably nearly related must also be changeable. This implies molecular compressibility, and if molecules are compressible, they must be much compressed by the great forces of cohesion and chemical affinity which exist in solid and liquid substances. Accordingly he immediately sought for evidence of the compressing effect of chemical affinity and cohesion, and promptly found it in the rediscovery of the general but not invariable rule;—greater affinity usually causes greater contraction on combination. This

* This diagram is not reproduced here.

idea has been suggested by Davy one hundred years ago, and several others since have revived it; but the idea nevertheless made no impression upon chemical literature as a whole, and was entirely overlooked by Richards until after the publication of his first papers. It must be said, however, that the oversight was perhaps more fortunate than not, because the entirely new approach to the subject led Richards to penetrate much more fundamentally into it than those who had preceded him. He has been able to show without much room for doubt that the reasons for the occasional deviations from the general rule, deviations which probably destroyed earlier confidence in the whole matter, are almost certainly due to the concomitant action of both chemical affinity and cohesion; in other words he by approximate quantitative evidence was able to show that not only the combination of atoms to make molecules causes compression, as the affinity is greater, but also that the molecules in cohering to one another in order to form a liquid or a solid compress one another in this process also. Hence the total volume of a liquid or solid appears according to his hypothesis to be the result of these varying and very different affinity-pressures.

He has been able to show that in a great many cases this hypothesis which has led him to consider atoms and molecules as closely packed without spaces between them in liquids and solids is consistent with a great variety of widely different phenomena both physical and chemical. For example, it gives entirely a new insight into the tenacity, ductility, hardness, brittleness, and surface tension; it gives a new and easily conceivable interpretation of the critical point; the peculiar relations of material and light, such as magnetic rotation, fluorescence, partial absorption, etc., may be referred to the modified vibrations of compressed atoms. He has pointed out also that the theory gives a very plausible explanation to the reason why as a rule among isomers the denser isomer is less volatile, less compressible, and possesses a greater surface tension than the less dense isomer.

A clear kinetic picture of the asymmetric carbon and in general the mechanism of the actual chemical affinities of any two atoms may be based upon this hypothesis. As he has said in the Faraday Lecture: "The satisfying of each valence of an atom would cause a depression on the atomic surface, owing to the pressure exerted by the affinity in that spot. The stronger the affinity, the greater should be this distortion. Evidently this conception gives a new picture of the asymmetric carbon atom, which combined with four other different atoms, would have upon its surface depressions of four unequal magnitudes, and be twisted into an unsymmetrical tetrahedron. The combining atoms would be held on the faces of the tetrahedron thus formed, instead of impossibly perching upon the several peaks. According to this hypothesis, the carbon atom need not be imagined as a tetrahedron in the first place; it would assume the tetrahedral shape when combined with the other four atoms. One can easily image that the development of each new valence would change the affinities previously exercised, somewhat as a second depression in the side of a rubber ball will modify a forcibly caused dimple in some other part. Thus a part of the effect which each new atom has on the affinities of the other atoms already present may be explained."

He has published a number of papers upon the subject of atomic compressibility; the whole matter is summed up briefly in his Faraday Lecture of 1911. During the twelve years since his first publication upon the subject, no one seems to have been able to advance a first-rate argument against this theory of compressible atoms, and if it continues to gain ground, as it has during this period, one may safely predict that before long it is bound to cause nothing short of a revolution in the kinetic point of view concerning the nature of equilibrium and change in solid and liquid substances as well as a better understanding of the deviations of gases from the exact gas law.

BIBLIOGRAPHY

Note: As was customary in the last century, Richards usually published the results of his researches in both English and German scientific journals. To list all of Richards's papers would be to expand this bibliography unnecessarily. Therefore only one explicit reference is listed below for the report of an investigation.

KEY TO ABBREVIATIONS

Am. Chem. J. = American Chemical Journal
Am. J. Sci. = American Journal of Science
Ber. = Berichte der Deutschen chemischen Gesellschaft (later, Chemische Berichte)
Carnegie Inst. Wash. Publ. = Carnegie Institution of Washington Publication
Carnegie Inst. Wash. Year Book = Carnegie Institution of Washington Year Book
Chem. News = Chemical News and Journal of Physical Science (later, Chemical Products and the Chemical News)
Chem. Rev. = Chemical Reviews
J. Am. Chem. Soc. = Journal of the American Chemical Society
J. Franklin Inst. = Journal of the Franklin Institute
J. Phys. Chem. = Journal of Physical Chemistry
Orig. Com. 8th Internat. Congr. Appl. Chem. = Original Communications of the 8th International Congress of Applied Chemistry
Proc. Am. Acad. Arts Sci. = Proceedings of the American Academy of Arts and Sciences (later, Daedalus)
Proc. Nat. Acad. Sci. = Proceedings of the National Academy of Sciences
Z. anorg. Chem. = Zeitschrift für anorganische Chemie (later, Zeitschrift für anorganische und allgemeine Chemie)
Z. physik. Chem. = Zeitschrift für physikalische Chemie, Stochiometrie und Verwandtschaftslehre (later, Zeitschrift für physikalische Chemie)

1888

On the constancy in the heat produced by the reaction of argentic nitrate on solutions of metallic chlorides. Chem. News, 57:16–17.

With Josiah Parsons Cooke. The relative values of the atomic weights of hydrogen and oxygen. Am. Chem. J., 10:81–110.

A determination of the relation of the atomic weights of copper and silver. Am. Chem. J., 10:182–87.

Further investigation on the atomic weight of copper. Am. Chem. J., 10:187–91.

1889

A method of vapour density determination. Chem. News, 59:87–88.

With P. Jannasch. The determination of sulphuric acid in presence of iron. Chem. News, 60:19–20.

1890

Ueber cupriammoniumbromide. Ber., 23:3790–91.

1891

The analysis of cupric bromide and the atomic weight of copper. Chem. News, 63:20–23, 34–36, 43–44.

1892

A revision of the atomic weight of copper. Chem. News, 65:236–37, 244–45, 260–61, 265–68, 281–82, 293, 302–3.
A revision of the atomic weight of copper. Chem. News, 66:7, 20–21, 29–31, 47–48, 57–58, 74, 82–83.

1893

With Elliot Folger Rogers. On the occlusion of gases by the oxides of metals. Am. Chem. J., 15:567–78.
With Hubert Grover Shaw. Cupriammonium double salts. Am. Chem. J., 15:642–53.
A revision of the atomic weight of barium. First paper. The analysis of baric bromide. Proc. Am. Acad. Arts Sci., 28:1–30; Z. anorg. Chem., 3:441–71.
A revision of the atomic weight of barium. Second paper. The analysis of baric chloride. Proc. Am. Acad. Arts Sci., 29:55–91; Z. anorg. Chem., 6:89–127, 1894.

1894

A revision of the atomic weight of strontium. First paper. The analysis of strontic bromide. Proc. Am. Acad. Arts Sci., 30:369–89; Z. anorg. Chem., 8:253–73, 1895.
With H. George Parker. On the occlusion of baric chloride by baric sulphate. Proc. Am. Acad. Arts Sci., 31:67–77; Z. anorg. Chem., 8:413–23, 1895.

1895

With Andrew Henderson Whitridge. On the cupriammonium double salts. Am. Chem. J., 17:145–54.
With George Oenslager. On the cupriammonium double salts. Am. Chem. J., 17:297–305.

With Elliot Folger Rogers. A revision of the atomic weight of zinc. First paper. The analysis of zincic bromide. Proc. Am. Acad. Arts Sci., 31:158–80; Z. anorg. Chem., 10:1–24.

1896

With H. George Parker. A revision of the atomic weight of magnesium. Proc. Am. Acad. Arts Sci., 32:55–73; Z. anorg. Chem., 13:81–100.

1897

With John Trowbridge. The spectra of argon. Am. J. Sci., 4S.3:15–20.
With John Trowbridge. The multiple spectra of gases. Am. J. Sci., 4S.3:117–20.
With John Trowbridge. The effect of great current strength on the conductivity of electrolytes. Philosophical Magazine, 43:376–78.
On the temperature coefficient of the potential of the calomel electrode, with several different supernatant electrolytes. Proc. Am. Acad. Arts Sci., 33:3–20; Z. physik. Chem., 24:39–54.
Note on the rate of dehydration of crystallized salts. Proc. Am. Acad. Arts Sci., 33:21–27; Z. anorg. Chem., 17:165–69, 1898.
With Allerton Seward Cushman. A revision of the atomic weight of nickel. First paper. The analysis of nickelous bromide. Proc. Am. Acad. Arts Sci., 33:97–111; Z. anorg. Chem., 16:167–83, 1898.
With Gregory Paul Baxter. A revision of the atomic weight of cobalt. First paper. The analysis of cobaltous bromide. Proc. Am. Acad. Arts Sci., 33:115–28; Z. anorg. Chem., 16:362–76, 1898.
With Benjamin Shores Merigold. On the cuprosammonium bromides and the cupriammonium sulphocyanates. Proc. Am. Acad. Arts Sci., 33:131–38; Z. anorg. Chem., 17:245–52, 1898.

1898

The relation of the taste of acids to their degree of dissociation. Am. Chem. J., 20:121–26.
A convenient gas generator, and device for dissolving solids. Am. Chem. J., 20:189–95.
A table of atomic weights. Am. Chem. J., 20:543–54.
On the cause of the retention and release of gases occluded by the oxides of metals. Am. Chem. J., 20:701–32.
With J. B. Churchill. The transition temperature of sodic sulphate,

a new fixed point in thermometry. Chem. News, 78:229, 238–39; Z. physik. Chem., 26:691–98.

With Wentworth Lewis Harrington. Boiling point of mixed solutions. I. Z. physik. Chem., 27:421–25.

With Gilbert Newton Lewis. Some electrochemical and thermochemical relations of zinc and cadmium amalgams. Proc. Am. Acad. Arts Sci., 34:87–99; Z. physik Chem., 28:1–12, 1899.

1899

With Henry Burnell Faber. On the solubility of argentic bromide and chloride in solutions of sodic thiosulphate. Am. Chem. J., 21:167–72.

Note on the spectra of hydrogen. Am. Chem. J., 21:172–74.

With Allerton Seward Cushman. A revision of the atomic weight of nickel. Second paper. The determination of the nickel in nickelous bromide. Proc. Am. Acad. Arts Sci., 34:327–48; Z. anorg. Chem., 20:352–76.

With Gregory Paul Baxter. A revision of the atomic weight of cobalt. Second paper. The determination of the cobalt in cobaltous bromide. Proc. Am. Acad. Arts Sci., 34:351–69; Z. anorg. Chem., 21:250–72.

With Edward Collins and George W. Heimrod. The electrochemical equivalents of copper and silver. Proc. Am. Acad. Arts Sci., 35:123–50; Z. physik. Chem., 32:321–47, 1900.

1900

Note on a method of standardizing weights. J. Am. Chem. Soc., 22:144–49.

The driving tendency of physico-chemical reaction, and its temperature coefficient. J. Phys. Chem., 4:383–93.

With Gregory Paul Baxter. A revision of the atomic weight of iron. Preliminary paper. Proc. Am. Acad. Arts Sci., 35:253–60; Z. anorg. Chem., 23:245–54.

On the determination of sulphuric acid in the presence of iron; a note upon solid solutions. Proc. Am. Acad. Arts Sci., 35:377–83; Z. anorg. Chem., 23:383–90.

1901

With E. H. Archibald. A study of growing crystals by instantaneous photomicrography. Am. Chem. J., 26:61–74.

With Frank Roy Fraprie. The solubility of manganous sulphate. Am. Chem. J., 26:75–80.
With Charles F. McCaffrey and Harold Bisbee. The occlusion of magnesic oxalate by calcic oxalate, and the solubility of calcic oxalate. Proc. Am. Acad. Arts Sci., 36:377–93; Z. anorg. Chem., 28:71–89.
The possible significance of changing atomic volume. Proc. Am. Acad. Arts Sci., 37:3–17; Z. physik. Chem., 40:169–84, 1902.

1902

With Sidney Kent Singer. The quantitative separation of hydrochloric and hydrocyanic acids. Am. Chem. J., 27:205–9.
With B. Shores Merigold. A new investigation concerning the atomic weight of uranium. Chem. News, 85:177–78, 186–88, 201, 207–9, 222–24, 229–30, 249.
A redetermination of the atomic weight of calcium. Preliminary paper. J. Am. Chem. Soc., 24:374–77.
With Ebenezer Henry Archibald. The decomposition of mercurous chloride by dissolved chlorides: a contribution to the study of concentrated solutions. Proc. Am. Acad. Arts Sci., 37:347–61; Z. physik. Chem., 40:385–98.
The significance of changing atomic volume. II. The probable source of the heat of chemical combination, and a new atomic hypothesis. Proc. Am. Acad. Arts Sci., 37:399–411; Z. physik. Chem., 40:597–610.
With George William Heimrod. On the accuracy of the improved voltameter. Proc. Am. Acad. Arts Sci., 37:415–43; Z. physik. Chem., 41:302–30.
The significance of changing atomic volume. III. The relation of changing heat capacity to change of free energy, heat of reaction, change of volume, and chemical affinity. Proc. Am. Acad. Arts Sci., 38:293–317; Z. physik. Chem., 42:129–54.
With Wilfred Newsome Stull. The speed and nature of the reaction of bromine upon oxalic acid. Proc. Am. Acad. Arts Sci., 38:321–37; Z. physik. Chem., 41:544–59.
With Wilfred Newsome Stull. The universally exact application of Faraday's Law. Proc. Am. Acad. Arts Sci., 38:409–13; Z. physik. Chem., 42:621–25, 1903.
With Kenneth Lamartine Mark. An apparatus for the measurement of the expansion of gases by heat under constant pressure.

Proc. Am. Acad. Arts Sci., 38:417–28; Z. physik. Chem., 43:475–86, 1903.

1903

Note concerning the calculation of thermochemical results. J. Am. Chem. Soc., 25:209–14.
The freezing-points of dilute solutions. J. Am. Chem. Soc., 25:291–98.
With Ebenezer Henry Archibald. A revision of the atomic weight of caesium. Proc. Am. Acad. Arts Sci., 38:443–70; Z. anorg. Chem., 34:353–82.
With Frederic Bonnet, Jr. The changeable hydrolytic equilibrium of dissolved chromic sulphate. Proc. Am. Acad. Arts Sci., 39:3–30; Z. physik. Chem., 47:29–51, 1904.
The inclusion and occlusion of solvent in crystals. Proceedings of the American Philosophical Society, 42:28–36; Z. physik. Chem., 46:189–96.

1904

With Sidney Kent Singer. Note on a method of determining small quantities of mercury. J. Am. Chem. Soc., 26:300–2.
With Wilfred Newsome Stull. New method of determining compressibility, with application to bromine, iodine, chloroform, bromoform, carbon tetrachloride, phosphorus, water and glass. J. Am. Chem. Soc., 26:399–412.
The significance of changing atomic volume. IV. The effects of chemical and cohesive internal pressure. Proc. Am. Acad. Arts Sci., 39:581–604; Z. physik. Chem., 49:15–40.
With Harold Bisbee. A rapid and convenient method for the quantitative electrolytic precipitation of copper. J. Am. Chem. Soc., 26:530–36.

1905

Note on the efficiency of centrifugal purification. J. Am. Chem. Soc., 27:104–11.
With Burritt S. Lacy. Electrostenolysis and Faraday's Law. J. Am. Chem. Soc., 27:232–33.
With Roger Clark Wells. A revision of the atomic weights of sodium and chlorine. J. Am. Chem. Soc., 27:459–529.
A revision of the atomic weight of strontium. Second paper. The

analysis of strontic chloride. Proc. Am. Acad. Arts Sci., 40:603–7; Z. anorg. Chem., 47:145–50.

1906

With George Shannon Forbes. Energy changes involved in the dilution of zinc and cadmium amalgams. Carnegie Inst. Wash. Publ., 56, iii + 68 pp.

With Roger C. Wells. The transition temperature of sodic bromide: a new fixed point in thermometry. Proc. Am. Acad. Arts Sci., 41:435–48; Z. physik. Chem., 56:348–61.

With Frederick G. Jackson. A new method of standardizing thermometers below 0° C. Proc. Am. Acad. Arts Sci., 41:451–54; Z. physik. Chem., 56:362–65.

1907

Neuere Untersuchungen über die Atomgewichte. Ber., 40:2767–79.

With Arthur Staehler, G. Shannon Forbes, Edward Mueller, and Grinnell Jones. Further researches concerning the atomic weights of potassium, silver, chlorine, bromine, nitrogen, and sulphur. Carnegie Inst. Wash. Publ., 69:7–88.

With W. N. Stull, F. N. Brink, and F. Bonnet, Jr. The compressibilities of the elements and their periodic relations. Carnegie Inst. Wash. Publ., 76:7–67.

Investigations concerning the values of the atomic weights and other physico-chemical constants. Carnegie Inst. Wash. Year Book, 6:193.

Bemerkungen zum Gebrauch von Zentrifugen. Chemiker Zeitung, 31:1251.

With F. N. Brink. Densities of lithium, sodium, potassium, rubidium, and caesium. J. Am. Chem. Soc., 29:117–27.

With Lawrence J. Henderson and Harry L. Frevert. Concerning the adiabatic determination of the heats of combustion of organic substances, especially sugar and benzol. Proc. Am. Acad. Arts Sci., 42:573–93; Z. physik. Chem., 59:532–52.

With F. Wrede. The transition temperature of manganous chloride: a new fixed point in thermometry. Proc. Am. Acad. Arts Sci., 43:343–50.

1908

Investigation of the values of atomic weights and other fundamental

physico-chemical constants. Carnegie Inst. Wash. Year Book, 7:201–3.
With J. Howard Mathews. The relation between compressibility, surface tension, and other properties of material. J. Am. Chem. Soc., 30:8–13.
With A. W. Rowe. A new method for the determination of the specific heats of liquids. Proc. Am. Acad. Arts Sci., 43:475–88.
With J. Howard Mathews. Concerning the use of electrical heating in fractional distillation. Proc. Am. Acad. Arts Sci., 43:521–24.
Note concerning the silver coulometer. Proc. Am. Acad. Arts Sci., 44:91–94.
Les travaux de l'Université de Harvard sur les poids atomiques. Journal de Chimie Physique, 6:92–136.

1909

Modern chemistry and medicine. Atlantic Monthly, 103:39–43.
Wolcott Gibbs. Ber., 42:5037–54.
With J. Hunt Wilson and R. N. Garrod-Thomas. Electrochemical investigation of liquid amalgams of thallium, indium, tin, zinc, cadmium, lead, copper, and lithium. Carnegie Inst. Wash. Publ., 118:1–72; I. Z. physik. Chem., 72:129–64; II. *Ibid.*, 72: 165–201, 1910.
Extended investigations of precise values of atomic weights; and a study of volume and energy relative to material in relation to the new hypothesis of compressible atoms. Carnegie Inst. Wash. Year Book, 8:219–21.
With Paul Köthner and Erich Tiede. Further investigation of the atomic weights of nitrogen and silver. J. Am. Chem. Soc., 31:6–20.
With W. N. Stull, F. N. Brink, and F. Bonnet, Jr. The compressibilities of the elements and their periodic relations. J. Am. Chem. Soc., 31:154–58.
With G. Jones. The compressibilities of the chlorides, bromides, and iodides of sodium, potassium, silver, and thallium. J. Am. Chem. Soc., 31:158–91.
A modified form of Gooch crucible. J. Am. Chem. Soc., 31:1146.
With J. Howard Mathews. Further note concerning the efficiency of fractional distillation by heat generated electrically. J. Am. Chem. Soc., 31:1200–2.

Recent investigations in thermochemistry. J. Am. Chem. Soc., 31:1275–83.
Experimentelle Untersuchungen über die Atomgewichte, 1887–1908. Hamburg and Leipzig, Leopold Voss. 890 pp.

1910

With Hobart Hurd Willard. Further investigation concerning the atomic weights of silver, lithium and chlorine. J. Am. Chem. Soc., 32:4–49.
With Richard Henry Jesse, Jr. The heats of combustion of the octanes and xylenes. J. Am. Chem. Soc., 32:268–98.
With Laurie Lorne Burgess. The adiabatic determination of heats of solution of metals in acids. J. Am. Chem. Soc., 32:431–60.
With Gregory P. Baxter. Concerning the correction of the apparent weight of a salt to the vacuum standard. J. Am. Chem. Soc., 32:507–12.
With Allan W. Rowe and L. L. Burgess. The adiabatic determination of heats of solution of metals in acids. J. Am. Chem. Soc., 32:1176–86.
With Otto Hönigschmid. A revision of the atomic weight of calcium. I. Analysis of calcium bromide. J. Am. Chem. Soc., 32:1577–90.
With F. G. Jackson. The specific heat of the elements at low temperatures. Z. physik. Chem., 70:414–51.
With Gregory P. Baxter and Bruce Wyman. Henry Augustus Torrey. Science, 32:50–51.

1911

With Otto Hönigschmid. Revision of the atomic weight of calcium. Second paper. Analysis of calcium chloride. J. Am. Chem. Soc., 33:28–35.
With George Leslie Kelly. The transition temperatures of sodium chromate as convenient fixed points in thermometry. J. Am. Chem. Soc., 33:847–63.
With J. Howard Mathews. A method for determining heat of evaporation as applied to water. J. Am. Chem. Soc., 33:863–88.
The possible solid solution of water in crystals. J. Am. Chem. Soc., 33:888–93.
The fundamental properties of the elements. (Faraday Lecture.) Journal of the Chemical Society, 99:1201–18.

1912

With John W. Shipley. A new method for the quantitative analysis of solutions by precise thermometry. J. Am. Chem. Soc., 34:599–603.

Atomic weights. J. Am. Chem. Soc., 34:959–71.

With W. N. Stull, J. H. Mathews, and C. L. Speyers. Compressibilities of certain hydrocarbons, alcohols, esters, amines, and organic halides. J. Am. Chem. Soc., 34:971–93.

The control of temperature in the operations of analytical chemistry. Orig. Com. 8th Internat. Congr. Appl. Chem., 1:403–9.

The measurement of temperature in the operations of analytical chemistry. Orig. Com. 8th Internat. Congr. Appl. Chem., 1:411–21.

Nephelometry. Orig. Com. 8th Internat. Congr. Appl. Chem., 1:423–27.

1913

The chemical significance of the crystallin form. J. Am. Chem. Soc., 35:381–96.

With A. W. Rowe. An improved method for determining specific heats of liquids, with data concerning dilute hydrochloric, hydrobromic, hydriodic, nitric, and perchloric acids and lithium, sodium, and potassium hydroxides. Proc. Am. Acad. Arts Sci., 49:173–99.

1914

With John W. Shipley. A convenient method for calibrating thermometers by means of floating equilibrium. J. Am. Chem. Soc., 36:1–10.

With Augustus H. Fiske. On the transition temperatures of the hydrates of sodium carbonate as fixed points in thermometry. J. Am. Chem. Soc., 36:485–90.

The critical point, and the significance of the quantity b in the equation of van der Waals. J. Am. Chem. Soc., 36:617–34.

With Marshall W. Cox. The purity of fused lithium perchlorate, and its bearing upon the atomic weight of silver. J. Am. Chem. Soc., 36:819–28.

Further remarks concerning the chemical significance of crystalline form. J. Am. Chem. Soc., 36:1686–95.

With Max E. Lembert. The atomic weight of lead of radioactive origin. J. Am. Chem. Soc., 36:1329-44.
With Clarence L. Speyers. The compressibility of ice. J. Am. Chem. Soc., 36:491-94.
The present aspect of the hypothesis of compressible atoms. J. Am. Chem. Soc., 36:2417-39.

1915

With F. O. Anderegg. The inclusion of electrolyte by the deposit in the silver voltameter. J. Am. Chem. Soc., 37:7-23.
With Charles R. Hoover. Molecular weight of sodium carbonate and the atomic weight of carbon referred to silver and bromide. J. Am. Chem. Soc., 37:95-108.
With Charles R. Hoover. Molecular weight of sodium sulfate and the atomic weight of sulfur. J. Am. Chem. Soc., 37:108-13.
With Edward P. Bartlett. Compressibilities of mercury, copper, lead, molybdenum, tantalum, tungsten and silver bromide. J. Am. Chem. Soc., 37:470-81.
With F. O. Anderegg. The complications at the anode in the silver coulometer (voltameter). J. Am. Chem. Soc., 37:675-93.
With Frederick Barry. The heats of combustion of aromatic hydrocarbons and hexamethylene. J. Am. Chem. Soc., 37:993-1020.
Concerning the compressibilities of the elements and their relations to other properties. J. Am. Chem. Soc., 37:1643-56.
With Leslie B. Coombs. Surface tensions of water, methyl, ethyl, and isobutyl alcohols, ethyl butyrate, benzene and toluene. J. Am. Chem. Soc., 37:1656-76.

1916

With Charles Wadsworth 3d. The density of lead from radioactive minerals. J. Am. Chem. Soc., 38:221-27.
Suggestion concerning the statement of the phase rule. J. Am. Chem. Soc., 38:983-89.
With J. W. Shipley. Compressibility of certain typical hydrocarbons, alcohols and ketones. J. Am. Chem. Soc., 38:989-99.
With C. Wadsworth 3d. Density of radio-lead from pure Norwegian cleveite. J. Am. Chem. Soc., 38:1658-60.

The essential attributes of the elements. J. Franklin Inst., 182:78–86.

Ideals of chemical investigation. Science, 44:37–45.

1917

With H. W. Richter. On the absence of thermal hysteresis in the copper-constantin thermoelement between 30° and 100°. J. Am. Chem. Soc., 39:231–35.

With Norris F. Hall. Attempt to separate the isotopic forms of lead by fractional crystallization. J. Am. Chem. Soc., 39:531–41.

With W. Buell Meldrum. Melting points of the chlorides of lithium, rubidium and cesium, and the freezing points of binary and ternary mixtures of these salts, including also potassium and sodium chloride. J. Am. Chem. Soc., 39:1816–28.

With Harold S. Davis. Improvements in calorimetric combustion, and the heat of combustion of toluene. Proc. Nat. Acad. Sci., 3:50–58.

1918

With Victor Yngve. The transition temperatures of strontium chloride and strontium bromide as fixed points in thermometry. J. Am. Chem. Soc., 40:89–96.

With V. Yngve. The solubility of sodium sulfate as a means of determining temperature. J. Am. Chem. Soc., 40:164–74.

With Walter C. Schumb. The refractive index and solubilities of the nitrates of lead isotopes. J. Am. Chem. Soc., 40:1403–9.

1919

With Sven Palitzsch. Compressibility of aqueous solutions, especially of urethane, and the polymerization of water. J. Am. Chem. Soc., 41:59–69.

With W. M. Craig and J. Sameshima. The purification by sublimation and the analysis of gallium chloride. J. Am. Chem. Soc., 41:131–32.

With Sylvester Boyer. The purification of gallium by electrolysis, and the compressibility and density of gallium. J. Am. Chem. Soc., 41:133–34.

With Farrington Daniels. Concentrated thallium amalgams: their electrochemical and thermochemical behavior, densities and freezing points. J. Am. Chem. Soc., 41:1732–68.

With J. W. Shipley. The dielectric constants of typical aliphatic

and aromatic hydrocarbons, cyclohexane, cyclohexanone, and cyclohexanol. J. Am. Chem. Soc., 41:2002–12.
With Emmett K. Carver and Walter C. Schumb. Effect of pressure and of dissolved air and water on the melting point of benzene. J. Am. Chem. Soc., 41:2019–28.
The problem of radioactive lead. Science, 49:1–11.

1920

With Jitsusaburo Sameshima. The compressibility of indium. J. Am. Chem. Soc., 42:49–54.
With Jitsusaburo Sameshima. The atomic weight of lead from a Japanese radioactive mineral. J. Am. Chem. Soc., 42:928–30.
With Setsuro Tamaru. A calorimetric method for standardizing thermometers by electrical energy. J. Am. Chem. Soc., 42:1374–77.
With Norris F. Hall. The melting points and thermoelectric behavior of lead isotopes. J. Am. Chem. Soc., 42:1550–56.
With Harold S. Davis. The heats of combustion of benzene, toluene, aliphatic alcohols, cyclohexanol, and other carbon compounds. J. Am. Chem. Soc., 42:1599–1617.
With Allan W. Rowe. An indirect method of determining the specific heat of dilute solutions, with preliminary data concerning hydrochloric acid. J. Am. Chem. Soc., 42:1621–35.
With Henry Krepelka. A revision of the atomic weight of aluminum. The analysis of aluminum bromide. Preliminary paper. J. Am. Chem. Soc., 42:2221–32.

1921

With Sylvester Boyer. Further studies concerning gallium. Its electrolytic behavior, purification, melting point, density, coefficient of expansion, compressibility, surface tension and latent heat of fusion. J. Am. Chem. Soc., 43:274–94.
With A. W. Rowe. The heats of dilution and the specific heats of dilute solutions of nitric acid and of hydroxides and chlorides and nitrates of lithium, sodium, potassium, and cesium. J. Am. Chem. Soc., 43:770–96.
With Emmett K. Carver. A critical study of the capillary rise method of determining surface tension, with data for water, benzene, toluene, chloroform, carbon tetrachloride, ether and dimethyl aniline. J. Am. Chem. Soc., 43:827–47.
With Edward P. Bartlett and James H. Hodges. The compres-

sibility of benzene, liquid and solid. J. Am. Chem. Soc., 43: 1538–42.
With W. Buell Meldrum. The existence of tetrahydrated sodium sulfate in mix-crystals with sodium chromate. J. Am. Chem. Soc., 43:1543–45.
The magnitudes of atoms. J. Am. Chem. Soc., 43:1584–91.

1922

With Charles P. Smyth. Solid thallium amalgams and the electrode potential of pure thallium. J. Am. Chem. Soc., 44:524–45.
With James Bryant Conant. The electrochemical behavior of liquid sodium amalgams. J. Am. Chem. Soc., 44:601–11.
With Theodore Dunham, Jr. The effect of changing hydrogen-ion concentration on the potential of the zinc electrode. J. Am. Chem. Soc., 44:678–84.
With Allan W. Rowe. The heats of neutralization of potassium, sodium and lithium hydroxides with hydrochloric, hydrobromic, hydriodic and nitric acids, at various dilutions. J. Am. Chem. Soc., 44:684–707.
With Thorbergur T. Thorvaldson. The heat of solution of zinc in hydrochloric acid. J. Am. Chem. Soc., 44:1051–60.
With Setsuro Tamaru. The heat of solution of cadmium in hydrochloric acid. J. Am. Chem. Soc., 44:1060–66.

1923

Compressibility, internal pressure and atomic magnitudes. J. Am. Chem. Soc., 45:422–37.
With William M. Craig. The atomic weight of gallium. J. Am. Chem. Soc., 45:1155–67.
With Charles P. Smyth. The heat of solution of thallium in dilute thallium amalgams. J. Am. Chem. Soc., 45:1455–60.

1924

Atomic weights and isotopes. Chem. Rev., 1:1–40.
With William T. Richards. The effect of a magnetic field on the potential of hydrogen occluded in iron. J. Am. Chem. Soc., 46:89–104.
With Edouard P. R. Saerens. The compressibilities of the chlorides, bromides, and iodides of lithium, rubidium and cesium. J. Am. Chem. Soc., 46:934–52.

With Clarence L. Speyers and Emmett K. Carver. The determination of surface tension with very small volumes of liquid, and the surface tensions of octanes and xylenes at several temperatures. J. Am. Chem. Soc., 46:1196–1207.
The internal pressure of solids. J. Am. Chem. Soc., 46:1419–36.
Compressibility, internal pressure and change of atomic volume. J. Franklin Inst., 198:1–27.
With William T. Richards. Preliminary attempt to measure gravimetrically the distance-effect of chemical affinity. Proc. Nat. Acad. Sci., 9:379–83.

1925

A brief history of the investigation of internal pressures. Chem. Rev., 2:315–48.
Internal pressures produced by chemical affinity. J. Am. Chem. Soc., 47:731–42.
With Frank T. Gucker, Jr. An improved differential method for the exact determination of specific heats of aqueous solutions; including results for various salts and organic acids. J. Am. Chem. Soc., 47:1876–93.
With Harris Marshall Chadwell. The densities and compressibilities of several organic liquids and solutions, and the polymerization of water. J. Am. Chem. Soc., 47:2283–2302.

1926

With Harold S. King and Lawrence P. Hall. Attempts to fractionate mixed isotopes of lead, and the atomic weight of this metal. J. Am. Chem. Soc., 48:1530–43.
Further evidence concerning the magnitude of internal pressures, especially that of mercury. J. Am. Chem. Soc., 48:3063–80.

1927

With Alfred L. Loomis. The chemical effects of high frequency sound waves. I. A preliminary survey. J. Am. Chem. Soc., 49:3086–3100.

1928

With Harry L. Frevert and Charles E. Teeter, Jr. A thermochemical contribution to the study of the system cadmium-mercury. J. Am. Chem. Soc., 50:1293–1302.

With Marcel Françon. The atomic weight of cesium. J. Am. Chem. Soc., 50:2162–66.
With Joseph D. White. The compressibility of thallium, indium, and lead. J. Am. Chem. Soc., 50:3290–3303.
With L. P. Hall and B. J. Mair. The compressibility of sodium, barium, and beryllium. J. Am. Chem. Soc., 50:3304–10.

1929

With Arthur W. Phillips. The atomic weight of copper from the Lake Superior region and from Chile. J. Am. Chem. Soc., 51:400–10.
With Lawrence P. Hall. Specific heats of sodium and potassium hydroxide solutions. J. Am. Chem. Soc., 51:707–12.
With Frank T. Gucker. The heats of dilution of sodium hydroxide, acetic acid and sodium acetate, and their bearing on heat capacities and heat of neutralization. J. Am. Chem. Soc., 51:712–27.
With B. J. Mair and L. P. Hall. Heats of dilution and heat capacities of hydrochloric acid solutions. J. Am. Chem. Soc., 51:727–30.
With Lawrence P. Hall. Further studies on the thermochemical behavior of sodium hydroxide solutions. J. Am. Chem. Soc., 51:731–36.
With Beveridge J. Mair. The heats of neutralization of acetic acid. J. Am. Chem. Soc., 51:737–40.
With Beveridge J. Mair. A study of the thermochemical behavior of weak electrolytes. J. Am. Chem. Soc., 51:740–48.
With Malcolm Dole. The heats of dilution and specific heats of barium and calcium chloride solutions. J. Am. Chem. Soc., 51:794–802.
Ideals of chemical investigation. Journal of Chemical Education, 6:2239–45.
With Marcel Françon. The decomposition of mercurous chloride in concentrated solutions of other chlorides. J. Phys. Chem., 33:936–50.

Rudolf Ruedemann

RUDOLF RUEDEMANN

October 16, 1864–June 18, 1956

BY JOHN RODGERS

RUDOLF RUEDEMANN was born in Georgenthal, Saxe-Coburg-Gotha, the son of Albert and Franziska (Seebach) Ruedemann. His paternal ancestors had been Lutheran ministers for nearly 300 years, but his father was a grocer in a small town in the Thüringerwald. Both father and mother were enthusiastic amateur naturalists and, abetted also by a helpful science teacher in the Progymnasium, Ruedemann early acquired an interest in botany. At the University of Jena, however, he changed to geology (petrology at first), and in 1887 he received the degree of doctor of philosophy.

He then took a position as assistant in stratigraphy and paleontology at the University of Strassburg and earned a second doctor's degree. It was here that he met his wife, Elizabeth Heitzmann, whom he married on October 17, 1890. To eke out the family income, he secured a license to teach in secondary schools, and then, judging his chances of obtaining a higher university post in Germany very small, he emigrated to the United States in 1892.

Very soon after his arrival, he obtained a position teaching science in the high school at Lowville, New York; a year later he moved to a similar position at Dolgeville, New York. It was in the years at Dolgeville that he took up the study of fossil graptolites (a fairly large class of extinct animals *incertae sedis*), being stirred to it by some extraordinarily well-preserved material showing the complete ontogeny of *Diplograptus*, the first such material to be described in detail.

His studies of these and other fossils brought him into contact with James Hall and John M. Clarke at the State Museum in Albany, New York, which Hall had made one of the major centers of paleontologic research in North America. After Hall's death in 1898, Clarke, who succeeded Hall as State Paleontologist, urged Ruedemann to stand for the examination for Assistant State Paleontologist; he was appointed to this post in March 1899 and he held it until 1926, when he succeeded Clarke as State Paleontologist. He retired in 1937 but worked actively at the Museum until 1942. He continued to live in Albany until his death in 1956; he was survived by his wife, seven children (four with doctor's degrees), 16 grandchildren, and 19 great-grandchildren.

Although Dr. Ruedemann's paleontologic and stratigraphic interests were broad (he made significant studies of corals, conularids, cephalopods, trilobites, and eurypterids), his central interest remained the graptolites, of which he was for decades the outstanding specialist in North America. In his earlier years at Albany, he specialized in the Ordovician graptolites of eastern New York State, and soon he showed that they could be readily zoned and that the black shale facies in which they mainly occur represents a far longer time span than had been realized. In particular, by 1912 he had used his findings to demonstrate a major lateral facies change from limestone eastward through black shale into graywacke (we would now say flysch), one of the very first demonstrations of large-scale facies changes in American geology. (His appreciation of the significance of such changes he probably owed to his contact with Johannes Walther at Jena.) Part of this change takes place in the flat-lying strata of east-central New York, but part in the badly deformed rocks at the west edge of the Appalachian orogenic belt, and Ruedemann's work played an important part in the unraveling of that deformation; in particular, he was one of the first, if not the first, to suggest (in 1909) the allochthonous or klippe hypothesis for the so-called Taconic slate, a hypothesis by now very widely accepted.

As a result of his acknowledged preeminence in the study of graptolites, graptolite collections from all over North America were sent to him at Albany for specific determination and stratigraphic control, and he thus became thoroughly familiar with the graptolite faunas of the whole continent. Two major works developed from this familiarity. One of these (in the 1930s) was a detailed study of the other fossils associated with the graptolites, which he showed to represent not a benthonic but a planktonic fauna, and he further concluded that the graptolitic black shale and associated strata were deposited in large part in deep water; this idea was not well received at the time, but the recognition of the role of turbidity currents in the deeper ocean about 1950 showed that Ruedemann had been quite right. The other major work was his monumental memoir on the graptolites of North America, his last published work.

During his long career, Ruedemann concerned himself with many other geological topics. Some of these interests were ephemeral, and nothing came of them, but more than once he was a pioneer; for example, already in 1897 he used the orientation of fossil graptolites to deduce the direction of former oceanic currents, and in 1928 he contributed substantially to the recognition that the Capitan limestone (Permian of West Texas) is a fossil reef.

Dr. Ruedemann was widely and favorably known among paleontologists and geologists all over the world. He was elected president of the Paleontological Society in 1916 and a member of the National Academy of Sciences in 1928, as well as corresponding or honorary member of several European societies. But he was always a very informal person, especially cordial and helpful to beginning students, as the present writer can attest, and he was always willing to relate, in a German accent that seemed to thicken with the years, a string of delightful anecdotes, often funny and irreverent, but often pertinent and revealing.

In her memorial to him, the late Dr. Winifred Goldring, his successor as State Paleontologist of New York, summed up his life as follows:

"There were just two important interests in Doctor Ruedemann's life, his scientific work and his family. He often remarked that he judged all women by comparison with his wife; and he relied greatly upon her good sense and judgment, realizing that she was more practical than he. In spite of the fact that he pursued his work at home as well as in the office, he still found time to be with his children when they were young; and he spoke many times of the long Sunday hikes he had with them. In later years he took deep satisfaction in their successes. He was very proud of his family and rightly so. During the course of a conversation in his last years, Doctor Ruedemann remarked that he had been happy in his work and had enjoyed seeing it in print, that he had been happy with his family, notwithstanding the difficult years, that his life as a whole had been a satisfaction to him and he had no regrets—a wonderful way to feel at the end of a long life."

BIBLIOGRAPHY

KEY TO ABBREVIATIONS

Am. Geologist = American Geologist
Am. J. Sci. = American Journal of Science
Am. Naturalist = American Naturalist
Bull. Geol. Soc. Am. = Bulletin of the Geological Society of America
Geol. Soc. Am. Mem. = Geological Society of America Memoir
J. Paleontol. = Journal of Paleontology
N.Y. State Geol. Ann. Rept. = New York State Geologist Annual Report
N.Y. State Mus. Ann. Rept. = New York State Museum Annual Report
N.Y. State Mus. Bull. = New York State Museum Bulletin
N.Y. State Mus. Mem. = New York State Museum Memoir
Pan-Am. Geol. = Pan-American Geologist
Proc. Am. Phil. Soc. = Proceedings of the American Philosophical Society
Proc. Geol. Soc. Am. = Proceedings of the Geological Society of America
Proc. Nat. Acad. Sci. = Proceedings of the National Academy of Sciences
Proc. U.S. Nat. Mus. = Proceedings of the U.S. National Museum
Smithsonian Inst. Misc. Coll. = Smithsonian Institution Miscellaneous Collections
Univ. Tex. Bull. = University of Texas Bulletin

1887

Die Contacterscheinungen am Granit der Reuth bei Gefrees. Inaugural dissertation, Neues Jahrbuch für Mineralogie, Geologie und Paläontologie, Beilage-band V, pp. 641–76.

1895

Vorläufige Mittheilung über Bau von *Diplograptus*. Berichte der Naturforschende Gesellschaft zu Freiburg I/B, Band IX, pp. 174–75.
Synopsis of the mode of growth and development of *Diplograptus*. Am. J. Sci., 49:453–55.
Development and mode of growth of *Diplograptus* M'Coy. N.Y. State Geol. Ann. Rept. 14 (for 1894), pp. 217–49; N.Y. State Mus. Ann. Rept. 48, Vol. 2 (for 1894), pp. 217–49.

1896

Note on the discovery of a sessile *Conularia*, Article I. Am. Geologist, 17:157–66.
Note on the discovery of a sessile *Conularia*, Article II. Am. Geologist, 18:65–71.

1897

Evidence of current action in the Ordovician of New York. Am. Geologist, 19:367–91.
The discovery of a sessile *Conularia*. N.Y. State Geol. Ann. Rept. 15 (for 1895), pp. 699–728.

1898

Synopsis of recent progress in the study of graptolites. Am. Naturalist, 22:1–16.
Additional note on the oceanic current in the Utica epoch. Am. Geologist, 21:75–81.
The discovery of a sessile *Conularia*. N.Y. State Mus. Ann. Rept. 49, Vol. 2 (for 1895), pp. 699–728.
On the development of *Tetradium cellulosum* Hall sp. Am. Geologist, 22:15–25.

1901

Hudson River beds near Albany and their taxonomic equivalents. N.Y. State Mus. Bull., 42:485–587.
Trenton conglomerate of Rysedorph Hill, Rensselaer County, N.Y., and its fauna. N.Y. State Mus. Bull., 49:3–114.

1902

With J. M. Clarke. Contact lines of Upper Siluric formations on the Brockport and Medina quadrangles. N.Y. State Mus. Bull., 52:517–23.
The graptolite (Levis) facies of the Beekmantown formation in Rensselaer County, N.Y. N.Y. State Mus. Bull., 52:546–75.
Mode of growth and development of *Goniograptus thureaui* M'Coy. N.Y. State Mus. Bull., 52:576–92.

1903

With J. M. Clarke. Catalogue of type specimens of Paleozoic fossils in the New York State Museum. N.Y. State Mus. Bull. 65, 847 pp.
The Cambric *Dictyonema* fauna of the slate belt of eastern New York. N.Y. State Mus. Bull., 69:934–58.
Noetling on the morphology of the pelecypods. Am. Geologist, 31:33–40.

Professor Jaeckel's thesis on the mode of existence of *Orthoceras* and other cephalopods. Am. Geologist, 31:199–217.
With J. M. Clarke. Guelph fauna in the State of New York. N.Y. State Mus. Mem. 5, 195 pp.

1904

Graptolites of New York, Part 1: Graptolites of the lower beds. N.Y. State Mus. Mem. 7, 349 pp.

1905

The structure of some primitive cephalopods. N.Y. State Mus. Bull., 80:296–341.

1906

Cephalopods of the Beekmantown and Chazy formations of the Champlain basin. N.Y. State Mus. Bull. 90, 223 pp.

1908

Graptolites of New York, Part 2: Graptolites of the higher beds. N.Y. State Mus. Mem. 11, 583 pp.
Note on *Dictyonema websteri* Dawson *(D. retiforme)*. Nova Scotian Institute of Science Proceedings and Transactions, Vol. 11, Part 4, p. 47.

1909

Types of inliers observed in New York. N.Y. State Mus. Bull., 133:164–93.
Some marine algae from the Trenton limestone of New York. N.Y. State Mus. Bull., 133:194–216.

1910

With J. F. Kemp. Geology of the Elizabethtown and Port Henry quadrangles. (Chapters 5–8 by Ruedemann.) N.Y. State Mus. Bull. 138, 165 pp.
On the symmetric arrangement in the elements of the Paleozoic platform of North America. N.Y. State Mus. Bull., 140:141–49; also in Am. J. Sci., 30:403–11.
With H. P. Cushing, H. Fairchild, and C. H. Smythe. Geology of the Thousand Islands region. N.Y. State Mus. Bull. 145, 194 pp.

Anatomy and physiology in invertebrate extinct organisms. Popular Science Monthly, 77:142–45.

1911

Stratigraphic significance of the wide distribution of graptolites. Bull. Geol. Soc. Am., 22:231–37.

1912

Note on a specimen of *Plectoceras jasoni* (Billings). N.Y. State Mus. Bull., 158:141–42.
With J. M. Clarke. The Eurypterida of New York. N.Y. State Mus. Mem. 14, Vol. 1, 439 pp.; Vol. 2, 190 pp.
The Lower Siluric shales of the Mohawk Valley. N.Y. State Mus. Bull. 162, 151 pp.

1913

Graptoloidea. Chapter in: *Text-Book of Paleontology,* by K. A. von Zittel, ed. by C. R. Eastman, pp. 125–33. New York, The Macmillan Co.

1914

With H. P. Cushing. Geology of Saratoga Springs and vicinity. N.Y. State Mus. Bull. 169, 177 pp.

1916

Bather's studies in Edrioasteroidea. Science, 43:244.
On the presence of a median eye in trilobites. Proc. Nat. Acad. Sci., 2:234–37.
Account of some new or little known species of fossils, mostly from the Paleozoic rocks of New York. N.Y. State Mus. Bull., 189:7–112.
Note on the habitat of the eurypterids. N.Y. State Mus. Bull., 189:113–15.
Two new starfishes from the Silurian of Argentina. N.Y. State Mus. Bull., 189:116–20.
The presence of a median eye in trilobites. N.Y. State Mus. Bull., 189:127–43.
The cephalic suture lines of *Cryptolithus (Trinucleus* auct.). N.Y. State Mus. Bull., 189:144–48.

1917

The paleontology of arrested evolution. N.Y. State Mus. Bull., 196:105–34. (Presidential address, 1916 meeting of the Paleontological Society.)

1918

The phylogeny of the acorn barnacles. Proc. Nat. Acad. Sci., 4:382–84.

1919

On some fundamentals of pre-Cambrian paleogeography. Proc. Nat. Acad. Sci., 5:1–6.

1920

A recurrent Pittsford (Salina) fauna. N.Y. State Mus. Bull., 219–20:205–22.

1921

Observations on the mode of life of primitive cephalopods. Bull. Geol. Soc. Am., 32:315–20.
Homeomorphic development of so-called species and genera of graptolites in separate regions. N.Y. State Mus. Bull., 227–28:63–68.
On sex distinction of fossil cephalopods. N.Y. State Mus. Bull., 227–28:68–70.
On some cases of reversion of trilobites. N.Y. State Mus. Bull., 227–28:70–79.
On color bands in *Orthoceras*. N.Y. State Mus. Bull., 227–28:79–88.
A new eurypterid from the Devonian of New York. N.Y. State Mus. Bull., 227–28:88–92.
Preservation of alimentary canal in an eurypterid. N.Y. State Mus. Bull., 227–28:92–95.
Note on *Caryocaris* Salter. N.Y. State Mus. Bull., 227–28:95–100.
Fauna of Dolgeville beds. N.Y. State Mus. Bull., 227–28:100–1.
Additions to the Snake Hill and Canajoharie faunas. N.Y. State Mus. Bull., 227–28:101–8.
The age of the black shales of the Lake Champlain region. N.Y. State Mus. Bull., 227–28:108–16.

The graptolite zones of the Ordovician shales of New York. N.Y. State Mus. Bull., 227-28:116-30.
Report on fossils from the so-called Trenton and Utica beds of Grand Isle, Vermont. State Geologist, Vermont, Report for 1919-1920, pp. 90-100.
With J. M. Clarke and C. H. Smythe. Henry Platt Cushing. Science, 53:510-52.
With E. O. Ulrich and R. S. Bassler. Notes on the ventral appendages of *Neolenus serratus*. Smithsonian Inst. Misc. Coll., 67:366-68.

1922

Additional studies in arrested evolution. Proc. Nat. Acad. Sci., 8:54-55.
The existence and configuration of pre-Cambrian continents. N.Y. State Mus. Bull., 239-40:65-151.
On the occurrence of an *Apus* in the Permian of Oklahoma. Journal of Geology, 30:311-18.
Further notes on the paleontology of arrested evolution. Am. Naturalist, 56:256-72.
Positions of the ancient continents. Pan-Am. Geol., 38:367-77.

1923

Fundamental lines of North American geologic structures. Am. J. Sci., 6:1-10.

1924

Recent publications on the origin and habitat of the Eurypterida. Am. J. Sci., 7:227-32.
An ancestral acorn barnacle. N.Y. State Mus. Bull., 251:93-104.
With G. M. Ehlers. Occurrence of the Collingwood formation in Michigan. Michigan University Museum of Geology Contributions, 2:13-18.
Notes on graptolites. In: A new graptolite locality in central Maine, by E. H. Perkins. Am. J. Sci., 8:223-27.
The phylogeny of the Cirripedia. Annals and Magazine of Natural History, 14(83):533-44.
Report on graptolites. In: Geological formations of Beaverfoot-Brisco-Stanford Range, by C. D. Walcott. Cambrian Geology and Paleontology V. Smithsonian Inst. Misc. Coll., 75:12-13, 15.

1925

The Utica and Lorraine formations of New York. Part 1, Stratigraphy. N.Y. State Mus. Bull. 258, 175 pp.
Fundamental lines of North American geologic structure. N.Y. State Mus. Bull., 260:71–80.
The Utica and Lorraine formations of New York. Part 2, Systematic paleontology, No. 1: Plants, sponges, corals, graptolites, crinoids, worms, bryozoans, brachiopods. N.Y. State Mus. Bull. 262, 171 pp.
Some Silurian (Ontarian) faunas of New York. N.Y. State Mus. Bull. 265, 134 pp.
With C. Schuchert. John Mason Clarke, 1857–1925. Science, 62: 117–21.
Siluric faunal facies in juxtaposition. Pan-Am. Geol., 44:309–12.
Geological history of the Hudson River. New York State Waterways Association Annual Report 16, pp. 76–82.

1926

Report on paleontology and paleobotany. N.Y. State Mus. Bull., 267:32–33.
Faunal facies differences of the Utica and Lorraine shales. N.Y. State Mus. Bull., 267:61–77.
A Devonian starfish from Gaspé. N.Y. State Mus. Bull., 276:79.
The Utica and Lorraine formations of New York. Part 2, Systematic paleontology, No. 2: Mollusks, crustaceans and eurypterids. N.Y. State Mus. Bull. 272, 227 pp.
Report on graptolites. In: Geology and mineral deposits of Windermere Map Area, British Columbia, by J. F. Walker. Geological Survey of Canada Memoir No. 148, pp. 25–31.
Hunting marine fossils in New York State. Natural History, 26: 505–14.
Neuere amerikanische Theorien über die Entstehung der Kontinente und Ozeane. Geologische Rundschau, Band 17a (Gustav Steinmann Festschrift), pp. 49–61.

1927

"Singing" earthworms. Science, 65:163.

1928

Reef character of Capitan limestone. Letter to P. B. King in: The Pennsylvanian and Permian stratigraphy of the Glass Mountains, by P. B. and R. E. King. Univ. Tex. Bull., 2801:139.

1929

With Winifred Goldring. Making fossils popular in the New York State Museum. N.Y. State Mus. Bull., 279:47–51.

Neuere Beobachtungen an Graptolithen-schiefern in Amerika. Leopoldina, Amerikaband, K. Leopoldinischen deutschen Akademie der Naturforscher zu Halle, Berichte, Band 4, pp. 7–12.

Note on *Oldhamia (Murchisonites) occidens* (Walcott). N.Y. State Mus. Bull., 281:47–50.

Coralline algae, Guadalupe Mountains. American Association of Petroleum Geologists Bulletin, 13:1079–80.

Alternating oscillatory movement in the Chazy and Levis troughs of the Appalachian geosyncline. Bull. Geol. Soc. Am., 40:409–16.

Fossils from the Permian tillite of São Paulo, Brazil, and their bearing on the origin of tillite. Bull. Geol. Soc. Am., 40:417–26.

Description of *Climacograptus innuatus* var. *brasiliensis* and other fossils. In: Una zona de Graptolitos do Llandovery inferior no Rio Trombetas, Estado do Para, Brazil, by C. J. Maury. Serviço Geológico e Mineralógico do Brazil, Monografia, Vol. 7, pp. 21–24, 27–29, 47–53.

Lists of Silurian graptolites of southeastern Alaska and Ordovician graptolites of Prince of Wales Island. In: Geology and mineral deposits of southeastern Alaska, by A. F. Buddington and T. Chapin. United States Geological Survey Bulletin, 800:76, 81.

1930

A study of fossils. New York State Education, 17:612–15.

A graptolite from the Chushina formation. Am. J. Sci., 20:308–11.

Geology of the Capital District (Albany, Cohoes, Troy and Schenectady quadrangles), with a chapter on glacial geology by John H. Cook. N.Y. State Mus. Bull. 285, 218 pp.

1931

Age and origin of the siderite and limonite of the Burden iron mines

near Hudson, New York. N.Y. State Mus. Bull., 286:135-52.
With E. O. Ulrich. Are the graptolites bryozoans? Bull. Geol. Soc. Am., 42:589-603.
With Winifred Goldring. Some museum methods developed in the New York State Museum. N.Y. State Mus. Bull., 288:71-83.
Tangential master streams of the Adirondack drainage. Am. J. Sci., 22:431-40.
Some new Middle Cambrian fossils from British Columbia. Proc. U.S. Nat. Mus., Vol. 79, Article 27, 18 pp.

1932

Development of the drainage of the Catskills. Am. J. Sci., 23:337-49.
Guide to the fossil exhibits of the New York State Museum. New York State Museum Circular, No. 9, 53 pp.
Utica to Albany, New York. In: Paleozoic Stratigraphy of New York, by D. H. Newland and others. XVI International Geological Congress Guidebook 4, pp. 121-36.
Interior markings of *Colpocaris elytroides*. In: A crustacean fauna from the Woodford formation of Oklahoma, by C. L. Cooper. J. Paleontol., 6:348.

1933

Paleozoic planktonic faunas of North America. Proc. Nat. Acad. Sci., 19:157-59.
Camptostroma, a Lower Cambrian floating hydrozoan. Proc. U.S. Nat. Mus., 82:1-8.
Albany to Lake George, New York. In: Eastern New York and Western New England, by C. R. Longwell and others. XVI International Geological Congress Guidebook 1, pp. 14-20.
Ordovician graptolites from the Marathon and Solitario regions, Texas. In: The geology of Texas, by E. H. Sellard, W. S. Adkins, and F. B. Plummer. Univ. Tex. Bull. 3232, Plate 4, with explanation.
The Cambrian of the Upper Mississippi Valley. Part 3, Graptolitoidea. Milwaukee Public Museum Bulletin, Vol. 12, No. 3, pp. 307-48.
Graptolites. In: Brisco-Dogtooth Map Area, British Columbia, by C. S. Evans. Geological Survey of Canada Summary Report 1932, Part AII, pp. 137 AII-138 AII.

With C. E. Decker. Graptolites of the Viola limestone. Pan-Am. Geol., 50:237.

1934

Vorweltliche Meerestiere in lebenden Bildern: "Aquarien der Vorwelt." Natur und Volk, Band 64, pp. 9–14.
Eurypterids from the Lower Devonian of Beartooth Butte, Wyoming. Proc. Am. Phil. Soc., 73:163–67.
Eurypterids in graptolite shales. Am. J. Sci., 27:374–85.
Cambrian graptolites. Science, 80:15.
With C. E. Decker. The graptolites of the Viola limestone. J. Paleontol., 8:303–27.
Paleozoic plankton of North America. Geol. Soc. Am. Mem. 2, 141 pp.
Paleozoic rocks of the Lowville Quadrangle. N.Y. State Mus. Bull., 296:193–94.

1935

Ecology of black mud shales in eastern New York. J. Paleontol., 9:79–91.
With J. W. Laverdière. Notes sur quelques graptolites nouveaux des environs de Québec (1). Le Naturaliste Canadien, Sér. 3, Vol. 6 (Vol. LXII), pp. 6–12.
A review of the eurypterid rami of the genus *Pterygotus* with descriptions of two new Devonian species. Carnegie Museum Annals, Vol. XXIV, Serial 164, pp. 69–72.
With G. H. Chadwick. Ordovician shales of New York. Science, 81:400.
Silurian phyllocarid crustaceans from Oklahoma. J. Paleontol., 9:447–48.
The eurypterids of Beartooth Butte. Proc. Am. Phil. Soc., 75:129–41.
With E. S. C. Smith. The Ordovician in Maine. Am. J. Sci., 30:353–55.

1936

Ordovician graptolites from Quebec and Tennessee. J. Paleontol., 10:385–87.
The dates of publication of the earlier New York State Museum reports. Science, 84:373–74.

Memorial to Charles Henry Richardson. Proc. Geol. Soc. Am., 1935, pp. 301-5.
With T. Y. Wilson. Eastern New York Ordovician cherts. Bull. Geol. Soc. Am., 47:1535-86.
Eastern New York Ordovician cherts, supplementary notes. Bull. Geol. Soc. Am., 47:2016-17.

1937

A new North American (Quebec) graptolite faunule. Am. J. Sci., 33:57-62.
Observation on excitation on fireflies by explosives. Science, 85: 222-23.
With D. H. Newland. Brief sketch of the geological work of the State Museum. N.Y. State Mus. Bull., 313:89-92.
Different views held on the origin of the Saratoga mineral waters. Science, 86:531-32.

1938

Graptolites from Silurian shale at Galena Creek, tributary of Prairie River, 14½ miles east of gates of South Nahanni River, Northwest Territories. Canadian Field-Naturalist, 52:18-21.
With W. J. Schoonmaker. Beaver dams as geologic agents. Science, 88:523-25.

1939

With R. R. Shrock. A new Wisconsin Upper Cambrian foraminifer. Am. J. Sci., 237:66-71.
The Hudson River. Hudson River Magazine, 2:19-23.
Editor, with Robert Balk. *Geology of North America,* Vol. 1: Introductory chapters and geology of the stable areas. *(Geologie der Erde,* ed. by Erich Krenkel.) Berlin, Gebrüder Borntraeger. 643 pp.
Graptolithina. Unit 1 in: *Type Invertebrate Fossils of North America (Devonian).* Philadelphia, Wagner Free Institute of Science. 13 cards.
Xiphosura (Eurypterids). Unit 11 in: *Type Invertebrate Fossils of North America (Devonian).* Philadelphia, Wagner Free Institute of Science. 17 cards.

1942

Oldhamia and the Rensselaer grit problem. N.Y. State Mus. Bull., 327:5–13.
Cambrian and Ordovician fossils. N.Y. State Mus. Bull., 327:19–30.
Notes on Ordovician Machaeridia of New York. N.Y. State Mus. Bull., 327:33–44.
Notes on Ordovician plankton and radiolarian chert of New York. N.Y. State Mus. Bull., 327:45–71.
With Christina Lochman. Graptolites from the Englewood formation (Mississippian) of the Black Hills, South Dakota. J. Paleontol., 16:657–59.

1944

With B. F. Howell. Impression of a worm on the test of a Cambrian trilobite. J. Paleontol., 18:96.
With Winifred Goldring. Memorial to David H. Newland. Proc. Geol. Soc. Am., 1943, pp. 209–16.
The Hudson Valley belt of graptolite shales and negative anomalies of gravity. Am. J. Sci., 242:391–96.

1945

Geology of the Catskill and Kaaterskill quadrangles, Part I: Cambrian and Ordovician geology of the Catskill Quadrangle, N.Y. (With chapter on glacial geology by J. H. Cook; on economic geology by D. H. Newland.) N.Y. State Mus. Bull. 331, 188 pp. (1942); geological map (1945).
An Ordovician *Ceratiocaris*. American Midland Naturalist, 34:547–48.

1947

Memorial to Edward Oscar Ulrich, 1857–1944. National Academy of Sciences, *Biographical Memoirs,* 24:259–80. Washington, National Academy of Sciences.
Graptolites of North America. Geol. Soc. Am. Mem. 19, 652 pp.

EDWARD ARTHUR STEINHAUS

November 7, 1914–October 20, 1969

BY E. F. KNIPLING

FEW MEN have had a comparable record of dedicated service and achievement for the betterment of society than did Dr. Edward Arthur Steinhaus, one of the nation's outstanding biological scientists. As a pioneer scientist working in the field of pathology of invertebrate pests, Dr. Steinhaus had an extraordinarily productive career during his fifty-four years of life. He was an outstanding research scientist in the fields of insect microbiology and insect pathology, an inspiring teacher of many of the world's leading insect pathologists, an able educator who was instrumental in the formation of the innovative "new biology" curricula, the author of a great body of scientific publications, and the organizer of the new scientific discipline of invertebrate pathology. All this he accomplished in spite of severe multiple congenital health handicaps, knowledge of which he determinedly and successfully kept from all except his family and closest associates.

Dr. Steinhaus was a man who looked at life "whole" and attacked the "specific." He was deeply and sensitively concerned over man's relationship to man, man's relationship to his environment, and man's relationship to science. It was these concerns in a broad sense which perhaps led him to his many specific contributions to mankind, which in turn earned for him recognition as a leading scientist of the twentieth century.

Central to all his work were two basic concerns: "What goes wrong with life?" and the need to recognize the interrelationships of man, nature, and science.

Recognized by the scientific community as the "father of insect pathology," Dr. Steinhaus founded a new field of science that can provide acceptable biological means of dealing with many insect and other invertebrate pest problems. His work in this capacity will continue to have an impact on scientific thought and technological advances for many years to come. The world is now in an era when there is universal concern over the adverse effects of the use of nonselective chemical pesticides on the quality of the environment. Thus, the role that pathogenic insect microbes might play as effective and safe ways to control destructive pests is a subject now under intensive investigation by insect pathologists the world over.

Edward Arthur Steinhaus, who became known merely as "Ed" to his family, close friends, and associates, was born in Max, North Dakota, on November 7, 1914. The influence of a proud, talented, and industrious family, combined with his early life and experiences in the small economically depressed rural community of Max, had much to do with Ed's choice of a career, as well as with his concern for his fellow men, especially those who might be underprivileged. In North Dakota Ed became painfully aware of the dilemma of man when he is not in a position to cope with the destructive forces of nature.

Of German extraction, Ed's grandfather came to America in 1857; he first settled in Wisconsin and later moved to Minnesota. Ed's father, Arthur A. Steinhaus, moved from Minnesota to central North Dakota in 1906 at the age of twenty-five. Limited in formal education, Arthur first worked as a tinsmith. Later, together with his brother, he established a general merchandise store to service the people of the community of Max. He also operated a farm, as did most of the people in the rural community.

In 1910, Alice Blanche Rhinehart, a beautiful auburn-haired

young lady, came to Max from the nearby town of Sheldon, North Dakota, to teach elementary school. Arthur Steinhaus married Alice in January 1914. They had four sons: Ralph, John, James, and Edward, Ed being the oldest. Alice Steinhaus's father was Pennsylvania Dutch, and her mother was of English–Scottish descent. She established, after considerable effort, that one of her ancestors, Richard Warren of London, came to America on the *Mayflower*.

Ed Steinhaus had varying duties to perform as a youngster. He did odd jobs on the farm, but most of his time was devoted to clerking in his father's store. He had learned to operate a printing press, and among his duties he printed handbills and did other printing work for the store. In addition, he edited and printed a small local news bulletin. This interest in writing, editing, and publishing remained with him throughout his life. Work in his father's store brought Ed into close association with all segments of the people in the community—farmers, farm workers, business people, and town "intellectuals" among others. The opportunity to know people in all walks of life and to obtain their views on subjects relating to religion, politics, and social problems gave Ed an insight about people and their problems that governed his philosophy of life and motivated him to serve mankind. Ed often told of the lively discussions on religious, political, and social issues that took place around the large coal stove in the back of the store during cold winter days.

Ed's own writings reveal that his mother had a major influence on his interests, personality, and general philosophy of life. She introduced him to the joys of reading. Ed especially enjoyed books by Huxley and Darwin, which stimulated his interest in science. He himself related that his interest in science was raised to "white heat" by Paul de Kruif's *Microbe Hunters*. His interest was also intensified by his high school science teacher, Miss Alice Paulsen.

While scientific subjects seemed to be Ed's primary concern, he had almost equal enthusiasm for other kinds of literature, including poetry. Had he not elected to follow science as a career, it is almost certain that journalism and the business of editing and publishing would have become his lifetime pursuit. In actual fact, however, his interest in journalism and his ability to write so well explain in large measure why he was able to make such great and lasting contributions to science.

Even though he was not a student of music and painting, Ed had a deep appreciation for these arts. His liking for singing, music, and painting could also be attributed to his mother. She was an accomplished amateur pianist who reportedly could play virtually any tune. Moreover, at the age of seventy, Ed's mother took up painting as a diversion and won local prizes for her work. Ed's opinion: "She was as good as Grandma Moses ever was."

The years of the depression, coupled with a serious drought in the thirties, made a deep imprint on Dr. Steinhaus's outlook on life. It is probable that the hardships experienced by people of the farming and business community of Max during this trying period were the motivating forces behind Ed's strong desire to help the oppressed. The economy of the community was affected not only by the general depression and droughts but by a fire which destroyed most of the business section of Max. When relating the effects of the depression and natural disasters on the people, Dr. Steinhaus stated, "The 'Grapes of Wrath' were evident all about them." He marveled that his father was able to keep the general store open during the years when farmers profited little from their crops and could not pay bills. His father eventually had to "write off" thousands of dollars owed him for clothing, farm machinery, general supplies, and other items. Yet he continued to extend credit even though the chances for payment were nil.

Steinhaus entered the North Dakota Agricultural College (now called North Dakota State University) in 1932. For a time he had difficulty deciding whether to major in entomology or bacteriology, but finally elected the latter. Later, as a graduate student, he consolidated his interest in both subjects when he recognized the opportunities for new research on the interrelationship of insects and their associated microbes.

In 1936, after graduation from the Agricultural College, Dr. Steinhaus was granted an assistantship in bacteriology at the Ohio State University. His requirements for a Ph.D. degree were completed in 1939, with a major in bacteriology and a minor in entomology.

Dr. Steinhaus's decision to enter into a career of scientific investigation of the microbes of insects was made in 1939 after winning a postdoctoral Muelhaupt Scholarship. I had occasion to hear him speak of the difficulty he had in deciding to enter a field of study that most members of the scientific community felt was of little practical consequence. Yet, his interest and vision prevailed, with some encouragement from Dr. Alvah Peterson, Professor Emeritus of The Ohio State University and one of the leading teachers of entomology of our era.

In this period of growing worldwide concern over the deterioration of our overpopulated and misused environment, all of those who are engaged in dealing with pest problems and who, at the same time, are striving to alleviate environmental pollution caused by pesticides can appreciate fully the good fortune of fate that made Dr. Steinhaus elect to undertake a career investigating insect pathogens. This line of investigation, which only a few years ago seemed so inconsequential, is now recognized as one of the great hopes for the eventual development of safer alternative means of dealing with many insect pest problems. Moreover, the increasing need for food, fiber, and other essential agricultural crops to feed the ever-expanding world population will demand the availability of effective as well as safe ways to control insect pests—man's greatest competitor for the food that the environment is capable of producing.

During the days of Ed's initial research in the early forties, certainly no one, including Ed, could have foreseen the breadth and scope of the interrelationship of microbes and insects. Yet, when we consider that insects exceed all other animals of the world and that every insect will no doubt be found to harbor microbes, either for their benefit or as deterrents to their welfare, one begins to appreciate the scope of the scientific field that Dr. Steinhaus brought to the forefront. Previous to his time, a few investigators had carried out superficial studies of the microbes associated with insects and other invertebrate animals. In this effort, several largely abortive attempts had been made to utilize pathogenic organisms to control insects, but these generally had failed. Considerable success had been achieved by investigators with the U.S. Department of Agriculture in the control of the Japanese beetle with a microorganism. But, as Ed himself stated, research in the general field of insect pathology was a "lonely field" in the early years, since there were so few scientists to talk to who were knowledgeable and interested in research on insect microbes.

Dr. Steinhaus began his investigation by undertaking a systematic compilation of the microbes reported to be associated with insects. In 1940 he published an article reviewing his work. He continued compiling information and making observations in his own studies, and his efforts led to a compendium of microorganisms associated with insects which was published in 1946 as a book entitled *Insect Microbiology*. In 1940 Dr. Steinhaus joined the U.S. Public Health Service staff at Hamilton, Montana, where he carried out research on diseases affecting man and on vaccines for controlling those diseases.

The year 1940 was also the beginning of a new phase in the personal life of Ed Steinhaus. This is the year he married Mabry Clark. Mabry was born and grew up in Mississippi and graduated from Mississippi State University. She entered graduate school at The Ohio State University and while there met Ed. After receiving her master's degree in bacteriology, she taught at North Dakota State University, Ed's alma mater, for a year and a half before marrying Dr. Steinhaus. During their marriage, Mabry devoted most of her time to caring for the home and their three children: Margaret Ann, now Mrs. Steve Goetz, Timothy Clark, and Cynthia Alice. In addition, however, she worked professionally outside the home as a bacteriologist for a few years and inside the home as Ed's "nonprofessional" research assistant. Her activities such as searching literature, proofreading, and indexing for Dr. Steinhaus helped him to record his many important contributions in the field of insect pathology. She is continuing to bring together writings of Dr. Steinhaus that are to be published in the future. Having the understanding, support, and able assistance of one so close to and so familiar with his interests and goals must have added immeasurably to Ed's many achievements.

One of Dr. Steinhaus's great disappointments in life came in 1942 when he was unsuccessful in his persistent efforts to enlist in the armed forces. His general philosophy concerning wars was definitely antimilitaristic and he deplored the United States involvement in Vietnam. But he viewed the defense of our country when under direct attack in a different light and was anxious to help defend it. It was during his half-dozen attempts to enlist in one or the other of the three branches of the armed forces that the seriousness of Dr. Steinhaus's physical defects was revealed. The series of rather thorough physical fitness examinations revealed a large number of serious internal physical defects, any one of which could have disqualified him for military duty. Subsequently, more detailed and refined medical examinations were made in attempts to offer the explanation for his many health problems which surfaced over the years. The true complete explanation did not come, however, until the year of his death. He was born with a damaged and nonfunctional hypothalamus on the left side. This accounted for missing or abnormal organs, including the absence of one kidney, incompletely formed baselar vertebra, a shortened leg, and an upside-down stomach. The physician who finally diagnosed the cause of his many ills expressed wonderment over the fact that Dr. Steinhaus had lived so long and could not even imagine how any man could have been so creative and productive with so many defects. It is equally amazing to others that a person could so effectively submerge his discomforts and pains, yet carry on with enthusiasm, vigor, and efficiency many scientific activities day after day, month after month, and year after year. One can imagine that even Ed himself, not knowing what it was like to be well and healthy, did not know the extent of his defects. This situation magnifies the stature of a man who earned the admiration and respect of so many people even in the absence of knowledge of the obstacles with which he had to contend each day of his life.

Dr. Steinhaus's eminence as a scientist and pioneer research worker, which earned him recognition as the "father of insect pathology," emerged at the University of California, Berkeley. There he received an appointment in the Department of Bacteriology in 1944 and was soon transferred to the College of Agriculture and the Agricultural Experiment Station as Assistant Professor of Insect Pathology and Assistant Insect Pathologist, respectively. His advancement to higher positions came steadily. By 1954, he had become Professor of Insect Pathology with the University and Insect Pathologist with the Experiment Station. He organized and directed the Laboratory of Insect Pathology, the first in the world. Later, in 1960, this small laboratory was elevated to the position of Department of Insect Pathology. In 1963 the Department became the Division of Invertebrate Pathology within the Department of Entomology and Parasitology.

With the establishment of the University of California, Irvine, in 1963, Chancellor Daniel G. Aldrich prevailed upon Dr. Steinhaus to organize the School of Biological Sciences and become its first Dean. In relating the selection of Dr. Steinhaus for this post, Dr. Aldrich stated: "He was my first appointment (to the new University), and what an example he set for us! He was a tireless administrator, an indefatigable researcher, and a concerned and understanding teacher, admired by undergraduates and graduates alike. Dean Steinhaus organized, staffed, and developed a program in the biological sciences that is unique in this country today."

Dean Steinhaus trained and developed most of the senior insect pathologists of the world today. His graduate students came from all parts of the globe. The number was limited only by the available facilities and resources. After completing their training, the students returned to their countries or accepted posts in other parts of the world to establish new centers for teaching or research in a new scientific discipline. It is evident from the many sincere and eloquently stated letters of condolence received by Mrs. Mabry Steinhaus that Dr. Steinhaus's former students had an intense love, admiration, and respect for him, not only as a teacher, but also as a personal adviser and counselor. Dr. Steinhaus demanded of his students thoroughness, accuracy, and efficiency, but he had seemingly unlimited patience in considering their problems. His secretary was instructed by Ed to budget his time so that he could give primary consideration to the needs and problems of his students. He made himself available for counseling with students even during his busiest times.

Ed, a prolific and articulate writer of scientific publications, was described by his secretary as a scientific writer with "soul." His bibliography consisted of more than 150 technical articles and books. It contains research papers on bacterial, viral, fungal, and protozoan diseases of insects. In his research dealing primarily with insect viruses, he found that two different types of viruses occur in insects—the granulosis and the noninclusion viruses. In his research on viruses he recorded or described fifty new viruses in insects. In addition to the many individual articles, he authored two books, *Insect Microbiology*, published in 1946, and *Principles of Insect Pathology*, published in 1949. At the time of his death, he was writing a book on the history of insect pathology and its development in North America. He had planned a book on "invertebrate pathology." Dr. Steinhaus also edited and contributed substantially to a two-volume work entitled *Insect Pathology: An Advanced Treatise*.

In addition to his many publications, Dr. Steinhaus founded and edited the *Journal of Invertebrate Pathology*, initially called the *Journal of Insect Pathology*. Moreover, he organized the Society for Invertebrate Pathology and served as its first president in 1967 and 1968. His contributions to entomology were not limited to insect pathology; it was largely through his efforts that the *Annual Review of Entomology* was established in 1955, and he was its co-editor for the first six years. This is now regarded as the world's most important serial publication dealing with all aspects of the subject of entomology, to which hundreds of leading entomologists and associated scientists have contributed.

Even though Dr. Steinhaus modestly expressed regret in not contributing more to applied insect pathology, he was the first to demonstrate that an insect could be controlled under field conditions by the use of a virus spray containing the nuclear polyhedral virus of the alfalfa caterpillar. Although the insect pathogen *Bacillus thuringiensis* was known for years, he recognized its potential for controlling insects and investigated its pathogenic characteristics, including the associated endotoxin. His study of this organism included field tests which demonstrated the effectiveness of the organism for the control of several economic insect pests. Such results stimulated further work by other investigators and by industrial firms. This biological organism is now produced and marketed as a highly selective biological insecticide for controlling a number of insect pests.

Few scientists have attained the high level of admiration and respect of associates and peers so early in their professional careers as did Dr. Steinhaus. In 1959 he was among the first of the entomologists to receive the Founders' Memorial Award given each year by the Entomological Society of America for outstanding contributions to this field of science. In 1963 he served as the president of this society. His recognition as an outstanding entomologist was not limited to his associates in the United States. It was worldwide, as attested by his election to the Entomological Society of the USSR and several other foreign or international organizations.

Recognition of his ability and stature in the field of science grew steadily, as evidenced by the demands for Dr. Steinhaus's services and by the many honors he received. His alma mater, North Dakota State University, awarded him an honorary Sc.D. degree in 1962. He served as visiting lecturer at a number of universities and declined many more invitations. In 1963 he delivered the principal address at the Second International Congress of Insect Pathology, held in Paris. He was a Fellow of the Entomological Society of America, the American Association for the Advancement of Science, and the American Academy of Microbiology; in addition, he was an honorary member of the Society of Science and Technology, India, and the Entomological Society of the USSR. Members of the National Academy of Sciences (Applied Biology Section) elected him to membership in 1968.

In addition to his many contributions to scientific societies, Dr. Steinhaus contributed much of his time and talent to the advancement of science by serving on many national and international committees and as a consultant to many scientific institutions and organizations, including the Public Health Service, Pacific Science Board, National Research Council, World Health Organization, Office of Science and Technology, and U.S. Department of Agriculture.

Dr. Steinhaus recognized the importance, and encouraged the exchange, of ideas and viewpoints among scientists as a means of advancing scientific developments. His role in the establishment of the *Journal of Invertebrate Pathology* and in organizing the Society for Invertebrate Pathology has been cited. However, he was also the leading force in the establishment of a recognized new scientific discipline, invertebrate pathology. Quoting from his own statement, Dr. Steinhaus brought together "loose strings of scattered thrusts in the study of diseases of insects and other invertebrates, molding it into a discipline called invertebrate pathology." This molding of a new scientific discipline was accomplished in the span of less than a dozen years. It is apparent that his next goal was to develop closer interrelationships between scientific disciplines. As he advanced to positions of greater responsibility, his obvious goal was to create a "new biology" that could deal with scientific problems on a broader, more solid front and thereby contribute even more to science and human welfare. This he did as Dean of the School of Biological Sciences at the University of California, Irvine. He organized the school into departments concerned with "organismic biology," "population and environmental biology," "molecular and cell biology," and "psychobiology."

Also, while serving as Dean of the School of Biological Sciences, he continued his interest in invertebrate pathology, establishing and later electing to direct a new center for pathobiology. In establishing the center, he had in mind a program of study encompassing diseases of all forms of life. At the core was his lifelong interest in determining "what goes wrong with life." A manuscript by his colleagues entitled "In Memorium" states, "The formation of the Center for Pathobiology in 1968, with Professor Steinhaus as its first Director, was the culmination of a lifelong aspiration to centralize information and research facilities dedicated to the advancement of the understanding of disease in all forms of life. Confirmed by the University of California as a new development in biology, the Center for Pathobiology will grow as a memorial to Edward A. Steinhaus."

Emphasis thus far has been given to Dr. Steinhaus's contributions to science per se and to the development of scientists, rather than to how he himself was more concerned with science as a means of benefiting the welfare of man in every aspect of life. He expressed concern over the lack of appreciation of the close interrelationships of science and other developments. Some of his last written words in his unpublished autobiographical manuscript were ". . . society has been led by our institutions—educational, religious, communications . . . into wrong relationships with the natural world. Considerations of culture have been separated too greatly from nature, and the idea that man's relations to nature is a moral one has often been forgotten." He went on to say that he believed with Albert Schweitzer that "the great fault of all ethics hitherto has been that they believed themselves to have to deal only with the relations of man to man." Concerned with the relation man has with nature, Dr. Steinhaus also wrote that he viewed "the pollution of the air, soil, water with the wastes of man's technological advances as nothing less than a sin, in the classical meaning of the word." He also regarded as sin and poor economics "the indiscriminate use of chemical insecticides, the destruction of animal species to a point where they either have or are about to disappear from the Earth, the cutting of forests without reforestation, the attempts to dam and flood parts of the Grand Canyon—a creation of God's which cannot be duplicated."

The plight of the underprivileged was a matter of grave concern to Dr. Steinhaus. He himself wondered whether he "was miscast as a scientist" and should not have been a social worker. He believed that the social sciences were not keeping pace with the "hard sciences" and expressed the feeling that technical ills could be corrected "if only the political scientist, the economist, the social scientist, and the humanist concerned with communication would do his share in leading the way."

A biographical account of an individual of Dr. Steinhaus's stature would be incomplete without some reference to his religious philosophy. He regarded himself as a religious man, but not necessarily in the classical sense. To him religion should be a way of life and not just a way of believing. As a youth he was exposed to the traditional concepts of religion existing in a Protestant community consisting principally of German Lutherans, the denomination to which his father belonged. His mother was originally a Presbyterian but after marriage became affiliated with the Lutheran church. One of his brothers became a Lutheran minister after serving as a navigator in World War II. After reaching adulthood, Dr. Steinhaus became affiliated with several different denominations, but eventually joined the Congregational faith.

His views on religion were liberal and he was strongly in favor of freedom of religion. He had little patience for the pomp often attendant upon religious ceremonies and was more interested in the basic principles of religion. This is perhaps why he admired the practical approach to religion of the Salvation Army.

Dr. Steinhaus had no difficulty in compromising his basic concepts of science and religion. Once when asked by a graduate student why he believed in a supreme intelligence or a God, Dr. Steinhaus replied, "Just look out of the window—why, He's all over the place—in the trees, the grass, the people, here in these bacterial cultures, here in the insects, in the molecules and atoms of this chemical, and out there in infinite space—it's all God." Characteristically, it was his view that people should not dwell on conflicts between religion and science but rather that the two philosophies should team up in their approach to a solution of "what goes wrong" in the world. His viewpoint on this subject was in keeping with his philosophy of life that motivated him to accomplish so much through science and education for the welfare of mankind.

IN PREPARING this biographical memoir, I am especially indebted to Mabry C. Steinhaus for providing me with reference material not otherwise available. This was largely in the nature of manuscripts of biographies written by others, including those prepared by E. Gorton Linsley and Ray F. Smith of the University of California, Berkeley; James L. McGaugh, Howard A. Schneiderman, and John E. Smith of the University of California, Irvine; John D. Briggs, Ohio State University, and Mauro Martignoni and Ken Hughes of the U.S. Forestry Sciences Laboratory, Oregon State University, Corvallis. I also drew from biographical information obtained from the National Academy of Sciences. An unpublished document prepared by E. A. Steinhaus himself contained most valuable autobiographical information, which was kindly included in the material supplied by Mrs. Steinhaus. I wish also to express my appreciation for the assistance by my daughter, Edwina, in the organization and editing of the biographical memoir.

BIBLIOGRAPHY

KEY TO ABBREVIATIONS

Bacteriol. Rev. = Bacteriological Reviews
Bull. Entomol. Soc. Am. = Bulletin of the Entomological Society of America
Calif. Agr. = California Agriculture
J. Bacteriol. = Journal of Bacteriology
J. Econ. Entomol. = Journal of Economic Entomology
J. Insect Pathol. = Journal of Insect Pathology
J. Invert. Pathol. = Journal of Invertebrate Pathology
J. Parasitol. = Journal of Parasitology
Public Health Rept. = Public Health Reports

1936

The effect of *Escherichia coli* on the growth of *Bacillus subtilis* when grown in mixed cultures. North Dakota State College Thesis (B.S.), Fargo, North Dakota. 31 pp.

1938

With J. M. Birkeland. "Cannibalism" among bacteria. J. Bacteriol., 36:216. (A)

1939

With J. M. Birkeland. Selective bacteriostatic action of sodium lauryl sulfate and of "Dreft." Proceedings of the Society of Experimental Biology and Medicine, 40:86–88.
With J. M. Birkeland. Studies on the life and death of bacteria. I. The senescent phase in aging cultures and the probable mechanisms involved. J. Bacteriol., 38:249–61.

1940

Studies on the life and death of bacteria. Abstracts of Doctoral Dissertations, No. 31, pp. 325–31. Columbus, Ohio State University Press.
A discussion of the microbial flora of insects. J. Bacteriol., 40:161–62. (A)
The microbiology of insects with special reference to the biologic relationships between bacteria and insects. Bacteriol. Rev., 4:17–57.

1941

A study of the bacteria associated with thirty species of insects. J. Bacteriol., 42:757–89.

1942

Note on a toxic principle in eggs of the tick, *Dermacentor andersoni* Stiles. Public Health Rept., 57:1310–12.
Rickettsia-like organism from normal *Dermacentor andersoni* Stiles. Public Health Rept., 57:1375–77.
The microbial flora of the Rocky Mountain wood tick, *Dermacentor andersoni* Stiles. J. Bacteriol., 43:91–92. (A)
The microbial flora of the Rocky Mountain wood tick, *Dermacentor andersoni* Stiles. J. Bacteriol., 44:397–404.
With G. M. Kohls. Isolation of an acid-fast bacillus from a hawk. Journal of the American Veterinary Medical Association, 51:502.
Catalogue of Bacteria Associated Extracellularly with Insects and Ticks. Minneapolis, Burgess Publishing Company. 206 pp.

1943

With R. R. Parker and G. M. Kohls. Tularemia in beavers and muskrats and contamination of natural waters and mud by *Pasteurella tularensis* in the northwestern United States. J. Bacteriol., 45:56–57.
A new bacterium, *Corynebacterium lipoptenae*, associated with the louse fly, *Lipoptena depressa* Say. J. Parasitol., 29:80.
With R. R. Parker. Rocky Mountain spotted fever: duration of potency of tick-tissue vaccine. Public Health Rept., 58:230–32.
With R. R. Parker. Experimental Rocky Mountain spotted fever: results of treatment with certain drugs. Public Health Rept., 58:351–52.
With R. R. Parker and G. M. Kohls. *Amblyomma americanum* a vector of Rocky Mountain spotted fever. Public Health Rept., 58:491.
With R. R. Parker. American and Australian Q fevers: persistence of the infectious agents in guinea pig tissues after defervescence. Public Health Rept., 58:523–27.
With R. R. Parker and G. M. Kohls. Rocky Mountain spotted fever: spontaneous infection in the tick *Amblyomma americanum*. Public Health Rept., 58:721–29.
With G. M. Kohls. Tularemia: spontaneous occurrence in shrews. Public Health Rept., 58:842.
With R. R. Parker. *Salmonella enteritidis:* experimental transmission by the Rocky Mountain wood tick *Dermacentor andersoni* Stiles. Public Health Rept., 58:1010–12.

With H. B. Foote, W. L. Jellison, and G. M. Kohls. Effect of chlorination on *Pasteurella tularensis* in aqueous suspension. Journal of the American Water Works Association, 35:902–10.

1944

With R. R. Parker and M. T. McKee. Cultivation of *Pasteurella tularensis* in a liquid medium. Public Health Rept., 59:78–79.
With R. R. Parker. The isolation of a filter-passing agent from the rabbit tick *Haemaphysalis leporis-palustris* Packard. Public Health Rept., 59:1528–29.
With T. L. Perrin. Pathologic reaction in guinea pigs to Humphreys' virus strain. Public Health Rept., 59:1603–9.

1945

Insect pathology and biological control. J. Econ. Entomol., 38:591–96.
Bacterial infections of potato tuber moth larvae in an insectary. J. Econ. Entomol., 38:718–19.

1946

Insect Microbiology. Ithaca, Comstock Pub. Co., Inc. 763 pp.
An orientation with respect to members of the genus *Bacillus* pathogenic for insects. Bacteriol. Rev., 10:51–61.

1947

With L. E. Hughes. Isolation of an unidentified spirochete from hen's eggs after inoculation with liver tissue from hens. Public Health Rept., 62:309–11.
A new disease of the variegated cutworm, *Peridroma margaritosa* (Haw). Science, 106:323.
Control of insect pests by means of disease agents. Calif. Agr., 1:2.
A coccidian parasite of *Ephestia kühniella* Zeller and of *Plodia interpunctella* (Hbn.) (Lepidoptera, Phycitidae). J. Parasitol., 33:29–32.

1948

Polyhedrosis ("wilt disease") of the alfalfa caterpillar. J. Econ. Entomol., 41:859–65.
With Albert Abdel-Malek. Invasion route of *Nosema* sp. in the potato tuberworm, as determined by ligaturing. J. Parasitol., 34:452–53.

1949

With K. M. Hughes. Two newly described species of Microsporidia from the potato tuberworm, *Gnorimoschema operculella* (Zeller) (Lepidoptera, Gelechiidae). J. Parasitol., 35:67–75.
With K. M. Hughes and H. B. Wasser. Demonstration of the granulosis virus of the variegated cutworm. J. Bacteriol., 57:219–24.
With C. G. Thompson. Alfalfa caterpillar tests; biological control by artificial spread of virus disease. Calif. Agr., 3:5–6.
With C. G. Thompson. Preliminary field tests using a polyhedrosis virus to control the alfalfa caterpillar. J. Econ. Entomol., 42:301–5.
Insect pathology: the field concerned, training required, and opportunities possible. Canadian Entomologist, 81:53–57.
Principles of Insect Pathology. New York, McGraw-Hill Book Co., Inc. 757 pp.
With C. G. Thompson. Granulosis disease in the buckeye caterpillar, *Junonia coenia* Hübner. Science, 110:276–78.
Nomenclature and classification of insect viruses. Bacteriol. Rev., 13:203–23.

1950

With C. G. Thompson. Further tests using a polyhedrosis virus to control the alfalfa caterpillar. Hilgardia, 19:411–45.
With C. G. Thompson. Alfalfa caterpillar control; treatment of fields by airplane application of spray advances destruction of pest. Calif. Agr., 4:8, 16.
Diagnoses of insect diseases; microbial infections in insects diagnosed as part of the research in developing new ways of controlling crop pests. Calif. Agr., 4:11, 15.

1951

Possible use of *Bacillus thuringiensis* Berliner as an aid in the biological control of the alfalfa caterpillar. Hilgardia, 20:359–81.
Report on diagnoses of diseased insects, 1944–1950. Hilgardia, 20:629–78.
With R. R. Parker, G. M. Kohls, and W. L. Jellison. Contamination of natural waters and mud with *Pasteurella tularensis* and tularemia in beavers and muskrats in the northwestern United States. National Institutes of Health Bulletin, No. 193. Washington, U.S. Govt. Print. Off. 61 pp.

With H. B. Wasser. Isolation of a virus causing granulosis in the red-banded leaf roller. Virginia Journal of Science, 2:91–93.
Pest control by bacteria; alfalfa caterpillar in field reduced to subeconomic levels within two days by bacillus applied as spray. Calif. Agr., 5:5.

1952

Microbial infections in European corn borer larvae held in the laboratory. J. Econ. Entomol., 45:48–51.
With K. M. Hughes. A granulosis of the western grape leaf skeletonizer. J. Econ. Entomol., 45:744–45.
The susceptibility of two species of *Colias* to the same virus. J. Econ. Entomol., 45:897–99.
Infectious diseases of insects. In: *Insects* (Yearbook of Agriculture, 1952), ed. by Alfred Stefferud, pp. 388–94. Washington, U.S. Govt. Print. Off.

1953

Taxonomy of insect viruses. Annals of the New York Academy of Sciences, 56:517–37.
With C. Ritchie Bell. The effect of certain microorganisms and antibiotics on stored-grain insects. J. Econ. Entomol., 46:582–98.
Diseases of insects reared in the laboratory or insectary. University of California, College of Agriculture, Leaflet No. 9. 26 pp.

1954

With E. A. Jerrel. Further observations on *Bacillus thuringiensis* Berliner and other spore-forming bacteria. Hilgardia, 23:1–23.
The effects of disease on insect populations. Hilgardia, 23:197–261.
Insects on stamps. Weekly Philatelic Gossip, 58:172–75.
Duration of infectivity of the virus of silkworm jaundice. Science, 120:186–87.

1955

Observations on the symbiotes of certain Coccidae. Hilgardia, 24:185–206.

1956

With M. M. Batey and C. L. Boerke. Bacterial symbiotes from the caeca of certain Heteroptera. Hilgardia, 24:495–518.

Microbial control—the emergence of an idea. Hilgardia, 26:107–60.
Editor, with R. F. Smith. Annual Review of Entomology, Vol. 1. Stanford, California, Annual Reviews, Inc. 466 pp. (Beginning with Vol. 2, 1957, place of publishers: Palo Alto, California). Vol. 2, 1957, 407 pp.; Vol. 3, 1958, 520 pp.; Vol. 4, 1959, 467 pp.; Vol. 5, 1960, 451 pp.; Vol. 6, 1961, 470 pp.; Vol. 7, 1962, 536 pp.
Living insecticides. Scientific American, 195:96–104.
Potentialities for microbial control of insects. Journal of Agricultural and Food Chemistry, 4:676–80.

1957

New records of insect-virus diseases. Hilgardia, 26:417–30.
With Robert L. Rabb and Frank E. Guthrie. Preliminary tests using *Bacillus thuringiensis* Berliner against hornworms. J. Econ. Entomol., 50:259–62.
Concerning the harmlessness of insect pathogens and the standardization of microbial control products. J. Econ. Entomol., 50:715–20.
Microbial diseases of insects. Annual Review of Microbiology, 11:165–82.
List of insects and their susceptibility to *Bacillus thuringiensis* Berliner and closely related bacteria. Mimeographed Series, 4:1–24. Laboratory of Insect Pathology, University of California, Berkeley.
With F. J. Brinley. Some relationships between bacteria and certain sewage-inhabiting insects. Mosquito News, 17:299–302.
New horizons in insect pathology. Journal of the New York Entomological Society, 65:113–21.

1958

Stress as a factor in insect disease. Proceedings of the Xth International Congress on Entomology, Montreal, 1956, Vol. 4, pp. 725–30. Ottawa, The Congress, Science Service Building.
Crowding as a possible stress factor in insect disease. Ecology, 39:503–14.

1959

Serratia marcescens Bizio as an insect pathogen. Hilgardia, 28:351–80.
Granuloses in two Alaskan insects. J. Econ. Entomol., 52:350–52.

On the improbability of *Bacillus thuringiensis* Berliner mutating to forms pathogenic for vertebrates. J. Econ. Entomol., 52:506–8.

With J. P. Dineen. A cytoplasmic polyhedrosis of the alfalfa caterpillar. J. Insect Pathol., 1:171–83.

With J. Lipa. *Nosema hippodamiae* n. sp., a microsporidian parasite of *Hippodamia convergens* Guérin (Coleoptera, Coccinellidae). J. Insect Pathol., 1:304–8.

Possible virus disease in European red mite. J. Insect Pathol., 1:435–37.

Insect pathology and microbial control. Pest Control Review, University of California Agricultural Extension Service, February, pp. 1–3.

Insect pathology and microbial control. Excerpts from press conference. University of California Division of Agricultural Sciences. Berkeley, University of California Press. 15 pp. (Special leaflet.)

Bacteria as microbial control agents. Transactions of the 1st International Conference on Insect Pathology and Biological Control, Prague, August 1958, pp. 37–50.

1960

With G. H. Bergold, K. Aizawa, K. M. Smith, and C. Vago. The present status of insect virus nomenclature and classification. International Bulletin of Bacteriological Nomenclature and Taxonomy, 10:259–62.

With J. P. Dineen. Observations on the role of stress in a granulosis of the variegated cutworm. J. Insect Pathol., 2:55–65.

With G. A. Marsh. Granulosis of the granulate cutworm. J. Insect Pathol., 2:115–17.

The duration of viability and infectivity of certain insect pathogens. J. Insect Pathol., 2:225–29.

Notes on polyhedroses in *Periodroma, Prodenia, Colias, Heliothis,* and other Lepidoptera. J. Insect Pathol., 2:327–33.

With Gertraude Wittig and Joyce P. Dineen. Further studies of the cytoplasmic polyhedrosis virus of the alfalfa caterpillar. J. Insect Pathol., 2:334–45.

Bacterial and viral diseases of insects of medical importance (and other excerpts from *Report of Conference on the Biological Control of Insects of Medical Importance,* Washington, D.C., February 1960, pp. 21–27). Washington, D.C., American Institute of Biological Sciences.

Insect control, biological. In: *McGraw-Hill Encyclopedia of Science and Technology*, Vol. 7, p. 122. New York, McGraw-Hill Book Co., Inc.

Insect pathology. In: *McGraw-Hill Encyclopedia of Science and Technology*, Vol. 7, pp. 122a–h. New York, McGraw-Hill Book Co., Inc.

Insect pathology: challenge, achievement, and promise. Bull. Entomol. Soc. Am., 6:9–16. (1959 Entomological Society of America Memorial Lecture.)

The importance of environmental factors in the insect-microbe ecosystem. Bacteriol. Rev., 24:365–73.

Some developments in insect pathology and microbial control in the United States. Proceedings of the Society for Study of Plant Protection, 2:151–53. (Translation into Chinese of talk given at National Taiwan University.)

1961

With M. E. Martignoni. *Laboratory Exercises in Insect Microbiology and Insect Pathology*. Minneapolis, Burgess Publishing Company. 75 pp.

On the correct author of *Bacillus sotto*. J. Insect Pathol., 3:97–100.

1962

With J. Lipa. Further report on identifications of protozoa pathogenic for insects. Acta Parasitologica Polonica, 10:165–75.

Noninfectious disease: an area of neglect in insect pathology. J. Insect Pathol., 4:i–viii.

With G. A. Marsh. Report of diagnoses of diseased insects, 1951–61. Hilgardia, 33:349–490.

1963

Introduction. Chapter 1 in: *Insect Pathology: An Advanced Treatise*, Vol. I, pp. 1–27. New York, Academic Press, Inc.

Background for the diagnosis of insect diseases. Chapter 16 in: *Insect Pathology: An Advanced Treatise*, Vol. II, pp. 549–89. New York, Academic Press, Inc.

Editor. *Insect Pathology: An Advanced Treatise*. New York, Academic Press, Inc. Vol. I, 661 pp.; Vol. II, 689 pp.

Insect pathology and biomedical research. J. Insect Pathol., 5:i–iv.
With Ruth Leutenegger. Icosahedral virus from a scarab *(Sericesthis).* J. Insect Pathol., 5:266–70.

1964

Microbial diseases of insects. Chapter 18 in: *Biological Control of Insect Pests and Weeds,* ed. by Paul DeBach and E. I. Schlinger, pp. 515–47. London, Chapman & Hall, Ltd.
Pathology, a biological science. J. Insect Pathol., 6:i–v.
The day is at hand. Bull. Entomol. Soc. Am., 10:3–7. (Entomological Society of America Presidential Address.)
When an insect dies. Bull. Entomol. Soc. Am., 10:183–89.
Diagnosis: a central pillar of insect pathology. Colloque international sur la pathologie des insectes et la lutte microbiologique, Paris, October 1962. Entomophaga Memoire No. 2, pp. 7–21.

1965

A new name but the same goals. J. Invert. Pathol., 7:i.
External signs of disease and abnormality in the insect egg. J. Invert. Pathol., 7:ii–x.
Symposium on microbial insecticides. IV. Diseases of invertebrates other than insects. Bacteriol. Rev., 29:388–96.

1966

Greater scholarship in pathology. J. Invert. Pathol., 8:i–ii.
With R. D. Zeikus. Observations on a previously undescribed type of cellular degeneration in hydra. J. Invert. Pathol., 8:14–34.
Insect control, biological. In: *McGraw-Hill Encyclopedia of Science and Technology,* Vol. 7, p. 122. New York, McGraw-Hill Book Co., Inc.
Insect pathology. In: *McGraw-Hill Encyclopedia of Science and Technology,* Vol. 7, pp. 122–122h. New York, McGraw-Hill Book Co., Inc.

1967

Microbial control—a comment on its present status in the United States. Bull. Entomol. Soc. Am., 13:104–8.
A guide to the biological sciences. Division of Biological Sciences, University of California, Irvine. 48 pp. (Previous editions: 1965, 1966.)
On the importance of invertebrate pathology in comparative pathol-

ogy. Revue de Pathologie Comparée, 67:139–42.
With G. A. Marsh. Previously unreported accessions for diagnosis and new records. J. Invert. Pathol., 9:436–38.
With M. E. Martignoni. An abridged glossary of terms used in invertebrate pathology. Pacific Northwest Forest and Range Experiment Station. U.S. Department of Agriculture, Forest Service. 22 pp.

1968

Immunity to infectious diseases in beneficial insects. Abstracts of papers from the XIIIth International Congress of Entomology, Moscow, USSR, p. 258.
Hungry people and invertebrate pathology. J. Invert. Pathol., 10:i–iii.
Microbial control is not all. Proceedings of the Joint U.S.-Japan Seminar on Microbial Control of Insect Pests, Fukuoka, Kyushu, April 1967, pp. 40–48.
With R. D. Zeikus. Teratology of the beetle *Tenebrio molitor*. I. Gross morphology of certain abnormality types. J. Invert. Pathol., 10:190–210.
Centers for pathobiology. J. Invert. Pathol., 11:i–iv.
With R. D. Zeikus. Teratology of the beetle *Tenebrio molitor*. II. The development and gross description of the pupal-winged adult. J. Invert. Pathol., 11:8–24.
With R. D. Zeikus. Teratology of the beetle *Tenebrio molitor*. III. Ultrastructural alterations in the flight musculature of the pupal-winged adult. J. Invert. Pathol., 12:40–52.
With R. D. Zeikus. An unusual structural layer in the foregut of the beetle *Tenebrio molitor*. Submitted for publication in Journal of Ultrastructure Research.

1969

With R. D. Zeikus. Teratology of the beetle *Tenebrio molitor*. IV. Ultrastructure of the necrotic fat body and foregut associated with the pupal-winged adult. J. Invert. Pathol., 13:337–44.
With R. D. Zeikus. Teratology of the beetle *Tenebrio molitor*. V. Ultrastructural changes and viruslike particles in the foregut epithelium of pupal-winged adults. J. Invert. Pathol., 14:115–21.
Invertebrates as models for the study of diseases of man. Federation Proceedings, 28:1810–14.

CHESTER HAMLIN WERKMAN

June 17, 1893–September 10, 1962

BY RUSSELL W. BROWN

CHESTER HAMLIN WERKMAN broadly conceived of his sphere of scientific interest as physiological microbiology. His career, which extended over a period of approximately forty years (1921–1962) was spent for the most part in the investigation of the intermediate steps by which microorganisms accomplished the biochemical transformations which enabled them to obtain energy for their essential role in nature. During that time he was one of a relatively small group of microbiologists in the United States and in Western Europe whose primary concerns were to understand and reconstruct the specific enzymatic pathways involved in metabolic processes. The anaerobic and microaerophilic bacteria were of immediate interest because their chemical transformations were more readily quantitated and expressed by carbon and oxidation–reduction balances of the products. With these organisms it was possible generally to conduct experiments in which known quantities of substrates were converted to intermediate and end products which were determined quantitatively. A variety of quantitative methods and experimental procedures were developed which made it possible to greatly expand the knowledge of the biochemistry of microorganisms. Werkman and his students at Iowa State University and a group at the University of Wisconsin were perhaps the most productive investigators in the field of microbial biochemistry in the United States during the 1930s when work elsewhere was oriented primarily toward the morphology and the pathogenic activities of microorganisms. There were, concurrently, the well-known investigations of A. J. Kluyver and his associates in Holland and of a number of other outstanding biochemists and microbial physiologists in Europe, including such names as G. Embden, H. von Euler, H. A. Krebs, Fritz Lipmann, Otto Meyerhof, Carl Neuberg, J. H. Quastel, Marjorie Stephenson, T. Thunberg, A. I. Virtanen, Otto Warburg, H. Wieland, and others. Present-day cell biology, and more specifically molecular biology, is concerned with the interrelationships of a multiplicity of substances within the cell. Moreover, in more recent years methods and procedures have advanced tremendously beyond those that were in use during Werkman's life. Nevertheless, the investigative approach employed by Werkman and his contemporaries was in large measure the foundation upon which the present-day concepts of bacterial metabolism were built.

To some extent, fortuitous circumstances may have played an important role in the life of Chester Hamlin Werkman. He was a graduate student at Iowa State University during the early twenties under Dr. Robert Earle Buchanan, who had already achieved national and international recognition in the systematic and general aspects of microbiology. When Werkman became associated with the university, the Department of Bacteriology in the Division of Science was making a concerted effort in developing a research program; he entered, therefore, an academic situation in which the climate was favorable for a person of unusual energy and aptitude for research. His career was launched during a period when some investigators were beginning to examine with vigor the biochemical aspects of microbial activity. His undergraduate concentration in organic chemistry enabled him to view the microbe, not as the ultimate object of interest, but rather as a versatile tool for the investigation of the chemical activities of living organisms. It can be said with certainty, however, that fortuitous circumstances were not the most important factors in the career which he achieved; perhaps more than anything else his entire life was motivated by a strong desire to be involved at the frontier of his field, and this ambition was reinforced by an unusual store of energy and personal drive.

Werkman was born in Fort Wayne, Indiana, June 17, 1893, and died in Ames, Iowa, September 10, 1962. He is survived by his wife, Mrs. Cecile Werkman, and their son, Robert, who has been a resident for a number of years of Bartlesville, Oklahoma, as well as by a sister, Mrs. Iona Werkman Leonard, of Fort Wayne, Indiana. Very little information of record is available regarding Werkman's early life. He did not have much inclination to discuss his boyhood with family and friends and on only very rare occasions did he reminisce about his elementary and high school experiences in Fort Wayne and later as an undergraduate student at Purdue University. Nevertheless, the following information, resulting primarily from Mrs. Werkman's recollections, gives some knowledge of the period when Werkman, as a young boy, found it necessary to assume responsibility for his livelihood and to chart his own future without the aid of strong family ties. These recollections offer some insight certainly into the nature and quality of the motivations which shaped his character and personal outlook, and which doubtless were responsible for his ambition to achieve recognition as a scientist in later years. The statements which follow have resulted also from recollections by Dr. Buchanan of conversations with Werkman, both during the period when the latter was a graduate student and during the subsequent years of their association at Iowa State.

Werkman's parents were of English, German, and Dutch descent; his mother was a schoolteacher before she was married; his father operated a barbering establishment and was active in the affairs of the barber's union in Fort Wayne. Werkman's mother died when he was age fourteen or fifteen and the author is uncertain when his father died; it is assumed, however, that this event occurred perhaps about the time of Werkman's first year as an undergraduate student at Purdue University.

Werkman attended secondary school at Fort Wayne, where he excelled in his studies. His performance in chemistry was especially outstanding and during his senior year he served as laboratory assistant to the instructor. He was permitted to do independent experimentation and promptly had an explosion, thus learning the hard way some of the hazards involved in the chemical laboratory. As a consequence of this accident he was unable to attend the graduation party because of burned hands. After graduation from high school he was employed by the Pennsylvania Railroad at Fort Wayne, Indiana; interestingly, his superintendent in this job was influential in persuading him to attend college.

He had saved some money from working and he entered Purdue University as an undergraduate. His undergraduate major was organic chemistry and the academic record which he made at Purdue was of the highest order; his grades were all A's except for one B. He applied himself diligently in the formal class and laboratory with a tenacious desire to excel; he despised being second best in anything. During the summer between his junior and senior years at Purdue, he worked for the federal government in what is now called the Pure Food and Drug Administration in the Department of Agriculture and was involved in the inspection of carloads of eggs for contamination and spoilage.

After his graduation from Purdue University in 1919, Werkman moved to Philadelphia where he continued, for a brief period, the job of inspection of food products as an employee in the Department of Agriculture. He was unhappy, however, with the routine nature of this assignment and, after a very few months, he accepted a position as an instructor in chemistry at the University of Idaho. While there, he published his first research paper with W. M. Gibbs, "Tuberculosis of poultry," *Idaho Agr. Exp. Sta. Bull.* 126, 1921, which marked the beginning of a long list of scientific publications. Moreover, it is significant that during his brief stay at the University of Idaho, a second paper which he co-authored with Gibbs was published— "Effect of tree products on bacteriological activities in soil. I. Ammonification and nitrification," *"Soil Science,* 13:303-22, 1922. But the insight which he had gained into the nature and structure of the university made him aware that graduate study, with the attainment of the doctoral degree, was essential for his advancement in the academic community. He therefore began to investigate immediately the opportunities for a graduate fellowship. As a result of several applications he received awards from the University of Chicago, Iowa State University, and the University of California—Los Angeles. He decided to accept the fellowship at Iowa State, primarily because he thought that living expenses would be less in Ames than in the urban centers of Chicago and Los Angeles. He entered the graduate school at Iowa State in September 1920 in the Department of Bacteriology, with Dr. Robert E. Buchanan as his major professor.

The desire to excel was as much the driving force for Werkman's success as a graduate student at Iowa State as it had been during his undergraduate years at Purdue. He applied himself diligently and his background training in organic chemistry served him well in investigations in the field of immunology. He completed the requirements for the Doctor of Philosophy degree in the spring of 1923 and his thesis, entitled "Immunologic Significance of Vitamins," was published in the *Journal of Infectious Diseases* in 1923 in three parts:

Immunologic significance of vitamins. I. Influence of the lack of vitamins on the production of specific agglutinins, precipitins, hemolysins and bacteriolysins in the rat, rabbit and pigeon;

II. Influence of lack of vitamins on resistance of rat, rabbit and pigeon to bacterial infection;

III. Influence of the lack of vitamins on the leukocytes and on phagocytosis.

Subsequently, two additional publications appeared in this initial series:

Werkman, C. H., V. E. Nelson, and E. I. Fulmer. Immunologic significance of vitamins. IV. Influence of lack of vitamin C on resistance of the guinea-pig to bacterial infection, on production of specific agglutinins, and on opsonic activity. *J. Infect. Diseases,* 34:447–53, 1924.

Werkman, C. H., F. M. Baldwin, and V. E. Nelson. Immunologic significance of vitamins. V. Resistance of the avitamic albino rat to diphtheria toxin; production of antitoxin and blood pressure effects. *J. Infect. Diseases,* 35:549–56, 1924.

After receiving the Ph.D. degree, Werkman was still influenced by a restless urge to find an academic situation where he believed his desires and ambitions could be realized with some degree of dispatch. He remained with Dr. Buchanan at Iowa State during the academic year 1923–1924, and then he accepted a faculty position at the University of Massachusetts for one year, 1924–1925; but in the fall of 1925 he returned to Iowa State, where he became involved with the biochemical and physiological aspects of microbiology until his death in 1962.

Perhaps it can be said that Werkman's professional career had its real beginning in 1925 when he made the decision to return, once again, to Ames, Iowa. This move initiated his permanent association with the Department of Bacteriology at Iowa State and with Dr. Buchanan and another member of the department, Dr. Max Levine, who already was achieving recognition for his work in sanitary bacteriology. One of Werkman's early assignments was to assist Dr. Levine with routine water analysis and the bacteriological analysis of specimens from the college hospital.

During the period 1925–1930, Werkman developed an interest in the relatively unexplored field of the biochemistry of bacteria and began to stake out his own scientific domain. He often remarked that he did not envision as promising the conventional approach to the study of microorganisms which was mostly morphological and otherwise descriptive. He felt that the science had too long adhered to the conventional methods of the botanists and zoologists with not enough attention being given to the more complex biochemical role of microorganisms in nature. Werkman viewed bacteria primarily as the least complicated models for the study of the basic chemical transformations involved in living processes. He became interested in certain groups of bacteria because of their unusual fermentative activity, the end-products of their metabolic processes, and the mechanisms by which these products were produced from an initial substrate. For example, the genus *Propionibacterium* constituted one of his early interests, which he pursued for a number of years along with many other types of fermentative bacteria. The fact that the members of the genus *Propionibacterium* were responsible for the specific flavor and aroma of Swiss cheese was of little consequence; he was intrigued by the chemical sequence involving the quantitative transformation of glucose to propionic and acetic acids and carbon dioxide. As will be seen later, this particular brand of scientific curiosity led Werkman and his graduate students in numerous directions but always in pursuit of some aspect of the processes initiated by enzymatic activity.

In all fairness, it must be recorded that Werkman was endowed with an unusual capacity and perhaps an instinct for originality and innovation; he was in search constantly for a "new angle," either a completely new idea regarding the chemical activities of microorganisms or at least a novel approach to the most significant things being done at the moment by the most progressive investigators in other laboratories. Not only did he consider it essential to be active in the "mainstream" of bacteriological research, preferably enzymatic research, but it was most important that he and his students be in the vanguard. Moreover, Werkman had a very uncommon fascination for scientific equipment; a new and sophisticated item was not merely a research tool, it was also a thing of beauty. He was exceedingly adventuresome in his eagerness to undertake a novel approach to a particular research project, and he was especially interested in developing new research methods and procedures and in the further refinement of methods developed by other investigators. He was actually a gadgeteer in many respects. It frequently developed that new items of equipment were built in his laboratory long before they became available commercially.

Having had his basic training essentially in the field of organic chemistry, Werkman utilized consistently the chemical approach to the study of microbiological processes. He was concerned almost exclusively with the nature and mode of action of the enzymatic systems that enabled microorganisms to perform their role in nature. He viewed microorganisms as intriguing systems of enzymes capable of a multiplicity of chemical transformations, but with relative similarity in their basic biochemical behavior. His thinking was always foremost in the biochemical vein; he was most at home with chemists; and when he sought collaboration in research outside of his own laboratory at Iowa State, a review of his publications reveals that he almost invariably involved members of the faculty in the Department of Chemistry. Werkman had virtually no contact with undergraduate students, since he very rarely offered a course to undergraduate majors in bacteriology, and his graduate students, with few exceptions, had majored in chemistry as undergraduates. He was known to comment on numerous occasions that the student best qualified to pursue the doctoral program in his laboratory was one with basic training in chemistry, and that such a student could acquire the necessary acquaintance with microorganisms as they became useful to him in his biochemical investigations.

Publications bearing Werkman's name during the period 1920–1930 exhibit a variety of unrelated research efforts and suggest that he was searching for an area that would become his primary focus. These early adventures in research included items such as tuberculosis infection in poultry, ammonification and nitrification in soils, coli-aerogenes organisms in swimming pools, immunologic significance of vitamins, dye utilization in bacteriological media, continuous reproduction of microorganisms, accessory growth factors for microorganisms, bacterial spoilage of canned vegetables, synthesis of vitamins by microorganisms, and factors influencing the death rates of microorganisms. In 1922, however, two papers ("The production of propionic acid from pentoses by *Propionibacterium pentosaceum*," and "Physiological behavior of the propionic acid group of bacteria"), presented at a meeting of the Iowa Academy of Sciences, can be said, in retrospect, to represent the essential direction of his subsequent research interests.

Although he focused his attention on the chemical activities of many types of organisms, Werkman was interested also in their identification by the products of fermentation and the relationship of the several species of bacteria within a generic grouping. However, the bacteria of the genus *Propionibacterium* and the members of the genus *Clostridium* that produce butyl and isopropyl alcohols and acetone were the most thoroughly investigated by him. These bacterial species were examined systematically by the conventional procedures for classification, but more importantly they became the subjects of a long-range program of biochemical investigations.

The classification of the propionic acid group of bacteria was investigated extensively by C. B. van Niel during the period when he was associated with Professor A. J. Kluyver at Delft, Holland, and is described in his doctoral dissertation, *The Propionic Acid Bacteria*, published in 1928. Subsequently, studies of these bacteria were conducted in Werkman's laboratory resulting in some extensions and modifications of van Niel's classification and nomenclature and in the proposal for the establishment of the additional specific designation of *Propionibacterium raffinosaceum* (Werkman and Sara Kendall, 1931, "The propionic acid bacteria. I. Classification and nomenclature"). This work was based upon the conventional methods and criteria employed in the systematic study of nonpathogenic bacteria. At this time, eleven species had been recognized and Werkman was not satisfied that the classification of the genus *Propionibacterium* had been firmly established. It was his nature to be intrigued with the novelty in research methods and he encouraged one of his graduate students to apply serological procedures to the study of the propionic acid bacteria (Werkman and R. W. Brown, 1933, "The propionic acid bacteria. II. Classification"). This investigation of the genus *Propionibacterium* is perhaps the first instance in which serological procedures were employed in the study of nonpathogenic microorganisms, and it confirmed the genetic relationship of the several species of the propionic acid bacteria.

In directing his attention to the physiology of microorganisms, Werkman undoubtedly was influenced to a considerable extent by the work of Dr. Kluyver and his associates in the Delft laboratory. He developed great admiration for Kluyver; they visited each other's laboratories and they eventually became warm friends. Moreover, Werkman's interest in the propionic acid bacteria, as well as in other fermentative types of microorganisms, was stimulated further by the work of van Niel and other European investigators who at that time were making important advances in this highly specialized area of science.

During the decade 1930–1940, the involvement of Werkman and his graduate students in the mechanisms of bacterial fermentations was clearly established, and it was during this period that the Werkman laboratory made its initial impact as an important contributor in the field of microbial physiology. Attention was focused first on the quantitative determination of the end-products of the fermentation of carbohydrate substrates by various fermentative microorganisms including propionic acid, lactic acid, butyric acid–butyl alcohol, and coliform bacteria. In this endeavor it was considered essential to render an accurate account of the fate of the carbon substrate in the tradition of the quantitative organic chemist. Since many of the known procedures were not of sufficient accuracy, it was necessary to direct much of the effort of the laboratory toward developing more highly refined qualitative and quantitative methods. In 1930 Werkman applied the partition method in the determination of mixtures of fatty acids, and for several years thereafter he and his graduate students made significant advances in the development and refinement of quantitative methods. Especially noteworthy were the contributions of O. L. Osburn, Harland G. Wood, and Grant L. Stahly in the refinement and extension of the partition method, as well as the application of other quantitative procedures in the determination of a variety of the products of bacterial fermentations. These methods were concerned primarily with mixtures of compounds such as ethyl, isopropyl, and butyl alcohols; acetaldehyde, acetone, formic, acetic, propionic, lactic, pyruvic, and butyric acids, trimethylene glycol, 2,3-butylene glycol, acetylmethylcarbinol, diacetyl, carbon dioxide, and hydrogen.

During this period some of the research in Werkman's laboratory was sponsored in part by grants from industry, particularly corporations utilizing agricultural products in the production of the so-called organic solvents. It would be appropriate to list these corporations, but unfortunately accurate data are not available. Werkman made a specific effort to cultivate the acquaintance of research and administrative personnel in the fermentation industry and to enlist their interest in his program of research at Iowa State. While his personal commitment was to fundamental research mainly, he exerted considerable effort in applied research, including such things as: the fermentation of pentosans from cornstalks, production of acetic acid from cornstalks by thermophilic bacteria, production of trimethylene glycol by fermentation, lactic acid fermentation of malt sprouts, the utilization of agricultural byproducts in the production of propionic acid, fermentation of artichokes, determination of the furfural-yielding constituents of plant materials, and the utilization of agricultural products and wastes for production of butyl and isopropyl alcohols. He served as a consultant to several corporations in the fermentation industry and occasionally would assign some of his graduate students to stort-term exploration of some specific problem encountered in the industry.

Gradually, however, the research became increasingly more sophisticated in an effort to elucidate the intermediate mechanisms of microbial fermentations. The role of pyruvic acid as an intermediate was investigated extensively in a variety of types of fermentations and likewise the intermediate roles of various fatty acids, such as the condensation of two molecules of acetic acid to form butyric acid and the degradation of the four-carbon butyric acid to form acetone and carbon dioxide in the butyl alcohol fermentation. These investigations and others similar in nature projected Werkman and his students into the "mainstream" of scientific endeavor.

Perhaps it can be said that the early recognition of Werkman and his students came as a result of the innovations in their approach to investigations in microbial physiology. Although van Niel in 1928 postulated that pyruvic acid was formed during the fermentation of glucose by the propionic acid bacteria, it was not established as an intermediate product in the propionic acid fermentation until it was isolated and identified by Wood and Werkman and reported in 1934. This was accomplished by fixation of the keto-acid with sodium bisulfite, using the procedures devised by Neuberg to isolate acetaldehyde. Fixation with bisulfite was applied also in investigations of the intermediate roles of acetaldehyde and pyruvic acid in the fermentation of glycerol by bacteria belonging to the coli-aerogenes group, and the presence of formaldehyde as an intermediate compound in the fermentation of glucose by certain members of the genus *Propionibacterium* was detected by fixation with dimethyldehydroresorcinol (dimedon).

In 1933, G. Embden, H. J. Denticke, and G. Kraft, and Otto Meyerhof and W. Kiessling proposed phosphoglyceric acid as the key intermediate in yeast and muscle glucolysis, thus replacing methylglyoxal as an intermediate. Werkman and his students, being particularly alert to developments by the German investigators, became very interested in the intermediary role of phosphoglyceric acid. In a series of publications, R. W. Stone and Werkman *(Iowa State Col. J. Sci.*, 10:341–43, 1936; 11:1–3, 1936; *Biochem. J.*, 31:1516–23, 1937), Werkman, E. A. Zoellner, Henry Gilman, and Howard Reynolds (*J. Bacteriol.*, 31:5, 1936), and W. P. Wiggert and Werkman (*Biochem. J.*, 32:101–7, 1938) reported on the formation of phosphoglyceric acid and related intermediary compounds in the dissimilation of glucose by a variety of heterotrophic microorganisms, including *Citrobacter freundii, Escherichia coli, Propionibacterium arabinosum, P. pentosaceum, Aerobacter indologenes, Lactobacillus pentoaceticus, L. plantarum, Bacillus subtilis, B. mycoides, Azotobacter vinelandii, Streptococcus paracitrovorus, Staphylococcus albus,* and *Aerobacter aerogenes.* Although Neuberg and

M. Kobel (*Biochem. Z.*, 264:456, 1933) had shown that phosphoglyceric acid was converted to pyruvic acid and phosphoric acid by *Lactobacillus delbruckii;* Werkman, Zoellner, Gilman, and Reynolds (1936) were the first to isolate phosphoglyceric acid from bacteria. Moreover, it was Stone and Werkman (1936–1937) who demonstrated the general occurrence of phosphoric esters among members of the order *Eubacteriales*.

Perhaps the most important contribution which came from Werkman's laboratory was the demonstration in 1936 of the utilization of carbon dioxide in the dissimilation of glycerol by the propionic acid bacteria. While the research was done under Werkman's direction, it was the alertness of his associate and former student, Harland Wood, in interpreting the quantitative data obtained which demonstrated the utilization of CO_2 by heterotrophic bacteria, a supposition which Werkman was reluctant at first to accept. However, after the data were more carefully examined he readily supported Wood's interpretation that CO_2 was indeed utilized in the fermentation of glycerol by propionic acid bacteria. This demonstration of the synthetic use of carbon dioxide by heterotrophic bacteria gained for Harland Wood the Eli Lilly Award in 1942 and the focus of national and international attention on the research of the Werkman laboratory. In presenting their experimental results Wood and Werkman stated:

"The most significant fact shown by the data is the apparent utilisation of CO_2 by the propionic acid bacteria. This was evident, since the CO_2 at the conclusion of the fermentation was not equivalent to that of the original medium in the form of $CaCO_3$. This observation has been substantiated by two types of calculation of especial value, i.e., carbon recovery and redox index. If CO_2 is utilised, and is in turn (after synthesis) dissimilated, then calculations based on the assumption that glycerol is the sole source of carbon, should show an excess of products, i.e., the calculated recovery of carbon will exceed 100 per cent. The data presented show that this occurred and that calculations based on glycerol *plus* CO_2 are acceptable. The calculation of carbon recovery is not in all cases entirely satisfactory proof of CO_2 utilisation, but the oxidation–reduction balance is convincing. CO_2 contains but one carbon and requires a large utilisation to show a detectable change in the carbon balance; in the oxidation–reduction balance the CO_2 is highly oxidised and therefore has a marked effect. The data show that results calculated on the basis of glycerol *plus* CO_2 are reasonable and acceptable. The fact that the chemical analysis shows a decrease of CO_2 is perhaps proof enough of CO_2 utilisation. However, the carbon and oxidation–reduction balances furnish additional evidence.

"One important problem, which requires consideration in relation to the data presented, is the mechanism of succinic acid formation. A number of investigators working particularly with yeast and fungi (Butkewitsch and Federoff in 1930; Wieland and Sonderhoff in 1933) have reported that succinic acid is formed by a condensation of two molecules of acetic acid. Virtanen in 1925, and Virtanen and Karstrom in 1931, however, have suggested that the propionic acid bacteria produce succinic acid from glucose by a 4- and 2-carbon cleavage of the hexose molecule. Virtanen's proposal was prompted by the observation that the propionic acid bacteria in the presence of toluene form succinic and acetic acids from glucose with no gas. This observation appeared incompatible with schemes involving a 3-carbon cleavage and the formation of 2-carbon compounds by a 2- and 1-carbon cleavage. The absence of CO_2 or other 1-carbon compounds appeared conclusive proof against such a scheme. However, the present evidence of the utilisation of CO_2 by the propionic acid bacteria leaves no reason to assume that the 1-carbon compounds should equal the sum of the

2-carbon compounds. It is necessary in the light of our present knowledge to leave open the possibility of a 4- and 2-carbon cleavage."

Following the appearance of the publication by Wood and Werkman in 1936, it was not surprising that other investigators questioned the evidence for this "physiologically important phenomenon." For example, van Niel in 1937 made the significant statement that "Wood and Werkman claim that carbon dioxide is reduced during the fermentation of glycerol by propionic acid bacteria. The published results cannot, however, be considered conclusive, although the data do seem to favor their claim." A challenge of this nature issued by van Niel and others was an important stimulus to Wood and Werkman to present more experimental data in support of the utilization of carbon dioxide by heterotrophic bacteria. Werkman and Wood and their associates further extended investigations of the role of carbon dioxide in the dissimilation of carbon compounds by heterotrophic bacteria, and it was mainly through their efforts that the utilization of carbon dioxide became firmly established as an important component of biochemistry.

It has been inferred earlier that Werkman was fascinated by the most advanced and sophisticated equipment and he could always be depended upon to secure the funds necessary for new equipment, especially if the item was of such recent concept that it was not available commercially. Moreover, he was searching constantly for new and improved techniques for investigating the intermediate pathways of microbial fermentations. It was fortunate, therefore, that Alfred O. Nier in the Department of Physics, University of Minnesota, published the description of "a mass spectrometer for routine isotope abundance measurements" *(Rev. Sci. Instruments* 11:212–16, 1940) and suggested that the apparatus was sufficiently accurate to measure the $^{13}C/^{12}C$ ratio if separated ^{13}C was used as a tracer in biological investigations.

Measurements of the stable carbon isotopes by means of the mass spectrometer had revealed that 1.09 percent of the carbon in nature was ^{13}C, and in 1941 A. O. Nier and J. Bardeen published a paper on "the production of concentrated carbon (13) by thermal diffusion" *(J. Chem. Physics,* 9:690–92, 1941). They adapted the thermal diffusion method of K. Clusius and G. Dickel *(Naturwissenschaften,* 26:546, 1938; 27:148, 1939) for the concentration of $^{13}CH_4$ by constructing a 72-foot diffusion column broken into two parts in an available vertical space of approximately 36 feet. With this column it was possible to increase the ^{13}C content of methane from 1.09 to 11.5 percent.

In 1941, after consultation with Nier, Harland Wood supervised and assisted in the construction of a 72-foot thermal diffusion column in the elevator shaft of Science Hall and a mass spectrometer in the basement section of Werkman's laboratory. Both of these equipment items were constructed essentially in accordance with Nier's specifications and with the participation of the graduate students who were with Werkman at that time. This was a very substantial undertaking for a group with relatively little experience in the construction of scientific equipment, and this accomplishment placed Werkman's group in a very advantageous position by providing them with the immediate use of such highly sophisticated research tools. With the assistance of personnel in the Department of Chemistry, various ^{13}C-labeled compounds were synthesized and utilized as substrates in the study of metabolism.

The first detailed publications from Werkman's laboratory reporting the use of ^{13}C-labeled compounds appeared in the *Journal of Biological Chemistry,* 139, 1941. The authors of these papers were H. G. Wood, C. H. Werkman, Allen Hemingway, and A. O. Nier, and the articles represented a joint publication between the Bacteriology Section, Agricultural Experiment Station, Iowa State College, Ames, Iowa, and the Departments of Physiological Chemistry and Physics, University of Minnesota, Minneapolis. The first paper, entitled "Heavy carbon as a tracer in heterotrophic carbon dioxide assimilation" (1941), gave further confirmation to the earlier work of Wood and Werkman by demonstrating that $^{13}CO_2$ fixed in fermentations of galactose, pyruvic acid, or citric acid by *Escherichia coli* occurs exclusively in the succinic and formic acids, and that in the fermentation of glucose and glycerol by *Propionibacterium pentosaceum* the fixed carbon dioxide is in the succinic acid, propionic acid, and propyl alcohol. Moreover, "the data obtained by determination of the fixed ^{13}C are in agreement with the suggestion that succinic acid is formed by union of a 3-carbon compound and carbon dioxide and the propionic acid by decarboxylation of a symmetrical dicarboxylic acid containing fixed carbon dioxide in only one carboxyl group." Further evidence for the mechanism of succinic acid synthesis was presented in the second paper, which showed by degradation of succinic acid synthesized by *E. coli* and *P. pentosaceum* that the fixed carbon dioxide, which had been labeled with ^{13}C, occurred exclusively in the carboxyl groups of the acid. This finding was in agreement with the author's proposal that carbon dioxide is fixed by union with pyruvic acid. The same authors published a report *(J. Biol. Chem.,* 142:31–45, 1942) on the "fixation of carbon dioxide by pigeon liver in the dissimilation of pyruvic acid." These investigators had presented evidence earlier that in the case of a number of bacteria the initial reaction in the fixation of carbon dioxide proceeded as follows:

$$CO_2 + CH_3 \cdot CO \cdot COOH = COOH \cdot CH_2CO \cdot COOH$$

It was presumed that the oxalacetate was converted to other 4-carbon dicarboxylic acids, and it was of interest to determine whether animal tissues fix carbon dioxide by this reaction. The method employed was essentially a system by which "pyruvate was dissimilated by ground pigeon liver in a medium containing $NaHCO_3$ enriched with ^{13}C." In summarizing the experiments with pigeon liver the authors stated that "the dissimilation of pyruvate by pigeon liver occurs with accompanying fixation of carbon dioxide. By use of $^{13}CO_2$ the fixed carbon has been shown to be exclusively in the carboxyl groups of the 4-carbon dicarboxylic acids (malate, fumarate, and succinate), the carboxyl adjacent to the carbonyl of α-ketoglutarate, and the carboxyl of lactate. Aerobically in the presence of malonate succinate is formed which contains little or no fixed carbon. It is proposed that the 4-carbon dicarboxylic acids are formed by two mechanisms, one reductive through the carbon fixation reaction, the other oxidative by a tentative and modified Krebs cycle which does not involve citric acid.* The scheme accounts for the observed positions of the fixed carbon and the aerobic formation in the presence of malonate of succinate not containing fixed carbon." The results provided strong support for Krebs's proposed cycle.

H. D. Slade, Wood, Nier, A. Hemingway, and Werkman (*J. Biol. Chem.*, 143:133–45, 1942) investigated the extent to which other heterotrophic bacteria were capable of carbon dioxide fixation. They reported that "fixation of CO_2 by C_3 and C_1 addition is apparently a very general reaction," as demonstrated with several genera of heterotrophic bacteria, including *Aerobacter, Proteus, Staphylococcus, Streptococcus,* and *Clostridium.* In summary, they stated that "the assimilation of CO_2 is established as a general phenomenon among heterotrophic bacteria. It is shown by the use of heavy carbon, ^{13}C, as a tracer, that the fixed carbon is located in the carboxyl groups of succinic, lactic, and acetic acids. The assimilated CO_2 is distributed as follows: *Aerobacter indologenes,* acetate, lactate, and succinate; *Proteus vulgaris, Streptococcus paracitrovorus,* and *Staphylococcus can-*

* This conclusion was in error and was based on the idea that citrate is a symmetrical molecule and therefore the ketoglutarate formed from citrate was expected to be labeled in both carboxyl groups. Only when Ogston (Ogston, A. G., *Nature,* 162:4129, 1948) explained that an enzyme can distinguish between the primary carboxyl of citrate did this incorrect conclusion become clarified.

didus, lactate and succinate; *Clostridium welchii,* acetate and lactate; *Clostridium acetobutylicum,* lactate."

A heat-labile enzyme prepared from *Micrococcus lysodeikticus* was described by L. O. Krampitz and Werkman (*Biochem. J.* 35:595–602, 1941) which catalyzed the decarboxylation of oxalacetate with the formation of pyruvic acid and carbon dioxide, suggesting that the enzyme is involved in the reverse process of carboxylation, as was proposed by Wood and Werkman in CO_2 utilization. Subsequently, in experiments using $NaH^{13}CO_3$, Krampitz, Wood and Werkman (*J. Biol. Chem.* 147: 243–53, 1943) reported that "the exchange of $^{13}CO_2$ with the carboxyl groups of oxalacetic acid during spontaneous decarboxylation was found to be insignficant. The exchange, however, was increased significantly during the enzymatic decarboxylation of the acid. The exchange occurred exclusively in the carboxyl group adjacent to the methylene group." They concluded that "these results are further evidence of the validity of the fixation reaction as proposed by Wood and Werkman."

In the presence of glucose, washed cell suspensions of *Aerobacter indologenes,* which had been grown in nutrient medium containing peptone, glucose, and inorganic salts, were shown to condense two molecules of ^{13}C-labeled acetic to succinic acid with the carbon-to-carbon linkage occurring at the position of the methyl group of acetic acid (Slade and Werkman, *Arch. Biochem.,* 2:97–111, 1943). Although they thought that this occurred by direct condensation of two moles of acetate, it is now known that this conversion occurs by the malate synthetase reaction involving acetyl-COA and glyoxalate.

Werkman and his graduate students had a long-term interest in the physiology of the butyric acid–butyl alcohol bacteria. With the availability of the heavy carbon isotope and the mass spectrometer it was, therefore, a natural consequence that these investigative tools would be employed in the study of these bacteria. In further investigation of the mechanism of the butyl alcohol fermentation (Wood et al., J. Am. Chem. Soc., 66:1812–18, 1944) they stated that "for an understanding of the mechanism of formation of butyl alcohol, it was necessary to know not only the position of the heavy carbon in the carbon chain but also the concentration of heavy carbon in each position. Such information is essential in deciding whether two molecules of acetic acid unite, for example, as follows:

$$2CH_3 \cdot {}^{13}COOH \rightarrow CH_3 \cdot {}^{13}CO \cdot CH_2 \cdot {}^{13}COOH + H_2O$$
$$CH_3 \cdot {}^{13}CO \cdot CH_2 \cdot {}^{13}COOH + 8H \rightarrow$$
$$CH_3 \cdot {}^{13}CH_2 \cdot CH_2 \cdot {}^{13}CH_2OH + 2H_2O$$

or, whether the acetic acid units with an intermediate compound from the corn starch. In this latter case, probably only one position in the molecule would contain a concentration of heavy carbon in excess of the normal, since that portion of the molecule arising from the starch would have a normal concentration of ^{13}C." In order to determine precisely the location of the heavy carbon atoms, it was necessary to develop a method of degrading butyric acid to achieve selective isolation of fragments of the carbon chain. This was accomplished by a modification of the hydrogen peroxide oxidation procedure of R. H. Allen and E. J. Witzemann (J. Am. Chem. Soc., 63:1922–27, 1941). The oxidation products, which included carbon dioxide, acetic acid, acetone, acetaldehyde, propionaldehyde, and an unidentified non-volatile compound, were determined quantitatively and their ^{13}C contents were measured. The degradation of butyric acid and the determination of the location of ^{13}C atoms in the oxidation products are excellent examples of the technical precision characteristic of Werkman's laboratory.

With the exception of the Booth-Green mill, the work of W. P. Wiggert, Milton Silverman, M. F. Utter, and Werkman (Iowa State Coll. J. Sci., 14:179–86, 1940) was the first to show that extracts could be prepared from bacteria (as had been done with yeast and muscle) which dissimilate carbohydrates. The availability of these enzyme preparations permitted some of the first studies of glycolytic enzymes in bacteria, especially by Utter and Werkman (*J. Bacteriol.*, 41:5, 1940; *J. Bacteriol.*, 42:665–76, 1941; *Biochem. J.*, 36:485–93, 1942). These studies demonstrated that bacteria have fermentative pathways involving many of the same reactions as yeast and muscle.

G. Kalnitsky and Werkman (*J. Bacteriol.*, 44:256–57, 1942, and *Arch. Biochem.*, 2:113–24, 1943) employed a cell-free enzyme preparation obtained by grinding a mass of *Escherichia coli* cells with powdered glass, with subsequent extraction using phosphate buffer (Wiggert and Werkman's method), in the anaerobic dissimilation of pyruvic acid; the result was the formation of acetic, formic, and succinic acids and carbon dioxide, and with a trace of lactic acid. The enzyme preparation contained very active formic dehydrogenase and hydrogenase activity. $^{13}CO_2$ was fixed in formic and succinic acids. The quantity of $^{13}CO_2$ in formic acid suggested that it was formed from the pyruvic acid. The formation of succinic acid from pyruvate and carbon dioxide, with the ^{13}C in the carboxyl group, indicated the fixation of CO_2 with the formation of a carbon-to-carbon linkage.

During his extended career Werkman and his associates investigated a relatively wide range of the biochemical activities of bacteria. It is appropriate to mention briefly some of the other investigations which have not been treated more extensively in this paper. Helen J. Weaver (1927) was perhaps Werkman's first graduate student; she was involved in the study of the bacteriological spoilage of canned vegetables. Shortly thereafter, Gertrude Sunderlin (1928) studied the synthesis of vitamins by microorganisms. Sara Kendall (1931) made a systematic study of the propionic acid bacteria; G. Gillen (1932) studied the production of trimethylene glycol by bacteria; Roger Patrick (1933) studied the xylan-fermenting bacteria; C. A. Johnson and H. D. Coile (1933) devised an electron tube potentiometer for the determination of oxidation–reduction potentials; and Carl Erb (1936) participated in the design of both a multiple-cup micro- and multiple-cup macro-respirometer, which he employed in studying the aerobic dissimilation of lactic acid by the propionic acid bacteria and which were used in many subsequent investigations by Werkman and his students. Milton Silverman (1938, 1939) was among the first to demonstrate the role of vitamin B_1 and cocarboxylase in bacterial metabolism; A. A. Andersen (1940) studied the growth factor and amino acid requirements of bacteria and described a dextro-lactic acid-forming organism of the genus *Bacillus;* Milo N. Mickelson (1940) investigated the mechanism of the dissimilation of glycerol and the formation of trimethylene glycol by organisms related to the coli-aerogenes group of bacteria; and M. E. Nelson (1940) studied the dissimilation of levulose and other substrates in the lactic acid fermentation. Carl Brewer (1939, 1940) investigated the aerobic and anaerobic dissimilation of citric acid by the coliform bacteria, W. S. Waring (1944) the function of iron in microbial metabolism, David Paretsky (1947, 1950) the mechanism for the conversion of 2,3-butylene glycol to acetylmethylcarbinol in bacterial fermentation, and Noel Gross (1947) the isotopic composition of acetylmethylcarbinol produced by yeast juice from ^{13}C-labeled acetaldehyde and pyruvate. A. G. C. White (1947) investigated the assimilation of acetate by yeast and the use of fatty acids in fat synthesis; Samuel Ajl (1948, 1949) studied the mechanism of carbon dioxide replacement by dicarboxylic acids, which by amination, transamination, or similar reactions serve as substitutes for carbon dioxide; and G. E. Wessman (1950) demonstrated the inhibition of carbon dioxide fixation by avidin.

During the period of about 1950 until his death in 1962, it is not unlikely that Werkman found it somewhat difficult to maintain the cohesiveness of his research program and the momentum which his laboratory had experienced in earlier years. His energy and scientific drive were curtailed measurably by a chronic illness which worsened progressively, but nevertheless he was active with his students and in the affairs of the Department of Bacteriology almost to the very end. It is evident from the publications coming from his laboratory that he attempted to continue work on carbon dioxide fixation as well as to develop some new directions. Examples of the research of his students during this period are as follows: dismutative assimilation of carbon dioxide (Dean Watt, 1950–1954), bacterial synthesis of purines (W. B. Sutton, 1951–1953), bacterial synthesis of amino acids (Eric Fowler, 1952) bacterial metabolism of amino acids (Mitchell Korzenovsky, 1953), mechanism of aerobic dissimilation of glucose (C. A. Claridge, 1954), formation of adenosine by cell-free bacterial extracts (John Ott, 1954), the role of transamination in bacterial metabolism (D. H. Hug, 1958), chemoautotrophic fixation of carbon dioxide by bacteria of the genus *Mycobacterium* (T. Myoda, 1960), carbon dioxide fixation by heterotrophic and photosynthetic bacteria (D. S. Bates and C. L. Baugh, 1960), and fatty acid carboxylation by cell-free bacterial extracts (G. W. Claus, 1961–1962).

Seldom does an individual scientist stand alone in his contributions to the body of knowledge; more often than not his reputation and recognition result from the force of his leadership compounded with the efforts of his graduate students and his younger associates in research, and this was certainly true in regard to C. H. Werkman. In any attempt to review his accomplishments as a distinguished American scientist it would be impossible to dissociate his individual work from that of the numerous younger scientists who were associated with him over a period of several decades. This fact is recognized here, and it should be emphasized, moreover, that in a memoir of this nature it is not possible to record specifically the extensive basic contributions to the reputation of the Werkman laboratory which were made by his many students. The impressive bibliography attached to this paper must be viewed as the composite contribution of Werkman and his associates, and the research reports cited specifically should serve only to illustrate some of the directions of the research effort stimulated by Werkman as the leader of his laboratory.

Werkman was a member of the faculty of Iowa State University in the Department of Bacteriology continuously from 1925 until his death in 1962. He served as Assistant Professor, 1925–1927, and Associate Professor, 1927–1933. He attained the rank of Professor in 1933, became department head in 1945, and continued in this capacity until his death. He served as major professor for more than fifty graduate students, of whom thirty-six received the Doctor of Philosophy degree; he was author and co-author of at least 275 publications in scientific journals. For various periods he served as an editor of the following scientific journals: *Archives of Biochemistry, Advances in Enzymology, Proceedings of the Society for Experimental Biology and Medicine, Enzymologia* (assistant editor), *Biotek Publications* (assistant editor), and *Iowa State College Journal of Science*. In 1944 Werkman received the degree of Doctor of Science *honoris causa* from Purdue University, and in 1951 he received the Pasteur Award.

Dr. Werkman was elected to the National Academy of Sciences in 1946; he also held membership in the following organizations: American Society for Microbiology, American Chemical Society, Society of American Biological Chemists, Biochemical Society of Great Britain, American Association for the Advancement of Science (Fellow), Society of Experimental Biology and Medicine, Iowa Academy of Science, Society of the Sigma Xi, Phi Kappa Phi, Phi Lambda Upsilon, and Kappa Delta Pi. In 1958 he was the recipient of the Iowa State University Faculty Citation. He served as a member of the Board of Trustees of the Carver Research Foundation of Tuskegee Institute.

BIBLIOGRAPHY

KEY TO ABBREVIATIONS

Antonie van Leeuwenhoek J. Microbiol. Serol. = Antonie van Leeuwenhoek Journal of Microbiology and Serology
Arch. Biochem. = Archives of Biochemistry
Arch. Biochem. Biophys. = Archives of Biochemistry and Biophysics
Biochem. J. = Biochemical Journal
Ind. Eng. Chem. = Industrial and Engineering Chemistry
Ind. Eng. Chem., Anal. Ed. = Industrial and Engineering Chemistry, Analytical Edition
Iowa Agr. Exp. Sta. Res. Bull. = Iowa Agricultural Experiment Station Research Bulletin
Iowa State Coll. J. Sci. = Iowa State College Journal of Science
J. Agr. Res. = Journal of Agricultural Research
J. Am. Chem. Soc. = Journal of the American Chemical Society
J. Bacteriol. = Journal of Bacteriology
J. Biol. Chem. = Journal of Biological Chemistry
J. Infect. Diseases = Journal of Infectious Diseases
Proc. Iowa Acad. Sci. = Proceedings of the Iowa Academy of Science
Proc. Nat. Acad. Sci. = Proceedings of the National Academy of Sciences
Proc. Soc. Exp. Biol. Med. = Proceedings of the Society for Experimental Biology and Medicine

1921

With William M. Gibbs. Tuberculosis of poultry. Idaho Agricultural Experiment Station Bulletin 126.

1922

With W. M. Gibbs. Effect of tree products on bacteriological activities in soil. I. Ammonification and nitrification. Soil Science, 13:303–22.

1923

Immunologic significance of vitamins. I. Influence of the lack of vitamins on the production of specific agglutinins, precipitins, hemolysins and bacteriolysins in the rat, rabbit and pigeon. J. Infect. Diseases, 32:247–54.

Immunologic significance of vitamins. II. Influence of lack of vitamins on resistance of rat, rabbit and pigeon to bacterial infection. J. Infect. Diseases, 32:255–62.

Immunologic significance of vitamins. III. Influence of the lack of vitamins on the leukocytes and on phagocytosis. J. Infect. Diseases, 32:263–69.

With Max Levine. *Bacterium coli* and *Bacterium aerogenes* in swimming pools. Journal of the American Water Works Association, 10:620–22.

1924

Theory of dye utilization in bacterial media. J. Bacteriol., 8:295–97.
With V. E. Nelson and E. I. Fulmer. Immunologic significance of vitamins. IV. Influence of lack of vitamin C on resistance of the guinea-pig to bacterial infection, on production of specific agglutinins, and an opsonic activity. J. Infect. Diseases, 34:447–53.
With F. M. Baldwin and V. E. Nelson. Immunologic significance of vitamins. V. Resistance of the avitamic albino rat to diphtheria toxin; production of antitoxin and blood pressure effects. J. Infect. Diseases, 35:549–56.

1925

Continuous reproduction of microorganisms. Science, 62:115–16.

1926

The role of accessory food factors in the physiology of microorganisms. J. Bacteriol., 11:86–87.

1927

Microbiological death rates. Proc. Iowa Acad. Sci., 34:85–87.
Vitamin effects in the physiology of microorganisms. J. Bacteriol., 14:335–47.
With H. J. Weaver. Studies in the bacteriology of sulphur stinker spoilage of canned sweet corn. Iowa State Coll. J. Sci., 2:57–67.
With Helen Weaver. Bacterial blackening of canned vegetables. Proc. Iowa Acad. Sci., 34:92–93.

1928

Factors influencing the death time of microorganisms. Proc. Iowa Acad. Sci., 35:97.
With Gertrude Sunderlin. Synthesis of vitamin B by microorganisms. J. Bacteriol., 16:17–33.

1929

Bacteriological studies on sulfid spoilage of canned vegetables. Iowa Agr. Exp. Sta. Res. Bull. 117.

1930

An improved technic for the Voges-Proskauer test. J. Bacteriol., 20:121–25.

Determination of organic acids in mixtures. I. Determination of fatty acids in mixtures by partition between isopropyl ether and water. Ind. Eng. Chem., 2:302–4.

Determination of organic acids. II. Determination of mixtures of two fatty acids by partition between ethyl ether and water. Iowa State Coll. J. Sci., 4:459–64.

Determination of organic acids. III. Note on the use of the isoamyl ether–water system in the partition method. Iowa State Coll. J. Sci., 5:1–3.

With R. H. Carter. Factors influencing the production of acetic acid from corn stalks by thermophilic bacteria. Proc. Iowa Acad. Sci., 37:51–52.

Dimethyl-alpha-naphthylamine for the determination of bacterial reduction of nitrates. Proc. Iowa Acad. Sci., 37:53–55.

With E. I. Fulmer. *An Index to the Chemical Action of Microorganisms on the Non-Nitrogenous Organic Compounds.* Springfield, Charles C. Thomas, Publisher. xiii + 198 pp.

With O. L. Osburn. Determination of butyl and ethyl alcohols in fermentation mixtures. Proc. Soc. Exp. Biol. Med., 28:241–42.

With Roger Patrick. Notes on the bacterial flora of the snake. Proc. Iowa Acad. Sci., 37:57–58.

1931

Determination of organic acids. IV. A method for the provisional identification and quantitative determination of two fatty acids in a mixture. Iowa State Coll. J. Sci., 5:121–25.

With O. L. Osburn. A method for the determination of ethyl and butyl alcohols in fermentation mixtures. J. Bacteriol., 21:20–21.

With E. I. Fulmer and A. L. Williams. The effect of sterilization of media upon their growth promoting properties toward bacteria. J. Bacteriol., 21:299–303.

With E. I. Fulmer and A. L. Williams. Production of bacterial growth stimulants by heating the medium under pressure. Proc. Soc. Exp. Biol. Med., 28:462.

With Sara Kendall. The propionic acid bacteria. I. Classification and nomenclature. Iowa State Coll. J. Sci., 6:17–32.

With O. L. Osburn. Determination of organic acids. V. Application of partition method to quantitative determination of acetic, propionic and butyric acids in mixture. Ind. Eng. Chem., Anal. Ed., 3:264.
With O. L. Osburn. Determination of butyl and ethyl alcohols in mixtures. Ind. Eng. Chem., 3:387–89.

1932

With Charles Davis. Apparatus for continuous fractional vacuum distillation. Chemist-Analyst, 21:20–21.
With G. F. Gillen. Bacteria producing trimethylene glycol. J. Bacteriol., 23:167–82.
With O. L. Osburn. Determination of carbon in fermented liquors. Ind. Eng. Chem., 4:1–6.
With Roger Patrick. A new species of Actinomyces pathogenic in man. Proc. Iowa Acad. Sci., 39:49–51.
With O. L. Osburn. Comparative dissimilation of xylose and glucose by *Escherichia coli* and *Citrobacter anindolcium*. Proc. Iowa Acad. Sci., 39:134–35.
With O. L. Osburn and H. G. Wood. Determination of formic, acetic and propionic acids in fermenting mixtures. Proc. Soc. Exp. Biol. Med., 29:294–95.

1933

With M. C. Brockmann. Determination of 2,3-butylene glycol in fermentations. Ind. Eng. Chem., 5:206–7.
With M. C. Brockmann. Oxidation–reduction studies on the 2,3-butylene glycol–acetylmethylcarbinol system in a fermentation. Proc. Soc. Exp. Biol. Med., 30:1146–48.
With C. S. McCleskey and Howard Reynolds. Physiology of *Shigella paradysenteriae* var. *Sonnei*. Proc. Soc. Exp. Biol. Med., 30:1050–51.
With C. W. Davis and C. A. Tarnutzer. Notes on the trimethylene glycol fermentation. J. Bacteriol., 24:33.
With R. W. Brown. The propionic acid bacteria. II. Classification. J. Bacteriol., 26: 393–417.
With Roger Patrick. Bacterial fermenting xylan. Iowa State Coll. J. Sci., 4:407–18.
With H. Reynolds and O. L. Osburn. Determination of the furfural yielding constituents of plant materials. Iowa State Coll. J. Sci., 4:443–51.

With G. L. Stahly. Physiological studies of the butyl–acetone group of bacteria. I. Gelatinolysis. Iowa State Coll. J. Sci., 7:93–109.

With C. A. Johnson and H. D. Coile. Electron tube potentiometer for the determination of redox potentials. Iowa State Coll. J. Sci., 7:163–75.

With O. L. Osburn and H. G. Wood. Determination of formic, acetic and propionic acids in mixture. Ind. Eng. Chem., Anal. Ed., 5:247–50.

With H. Reynolds and C. S. McCleskey. Sugar dissimilation by *Shigella paradysenteriae* var. *Sonnei*. Proc. Iowa Acad. Sci., 11:81–82.

1934

With H. Reynolds and H. D. Coile. The butyl–acetone fermentation in sugar media. Iowa State Coll. J. Sci., 7:415–26.

With D. B. Charlton and M. E. Nelson. Physiology of *Lactobacillus fructivorans* sp. nov., isolated from spoiled salad dressing. Iowa State Coll. J. Sci., 9:1–12.

With H. Reynolds. Fermentation of artichokes. Proc. Iowa Acad. Sci., 41:75–78.

With H. Reynolds and C. S. McClesky. Dissimilation of sucrose by *Shigella paradysenteriae* var. *Sonnei*. J. Infect. Diseases, 55:207–19.

With G. L. Stahly and O. L. Osburn. Quantitative determination of acetone and ethyl, butyl and isopropyl alcohols in fermentation liquors. Analyst, 59:319–25.

With H. G. Wood. The utilization of agricultural by-products in the production of propionic acid by fermentation. J. Agr. Res., 49:1017–24.

With H. G. Wood. Intermediate products of the propionic acid fermentation. Proc. Soc. Exp. Biol. Med., 31:938–40.

With H. G. Wood. Pyruvic acid in the dissimilation of glucose by the propionic acid bacteria. Biochem. J., 28:745–47.

With H. G. Wood. The propionic acid bacteria. On the mechanism of glucose dissimilation. J. Biol. Chem., 105:63–72.

1935

With B. W. Hammer, G. L. Stahly, and M. B. Michaelian. Reduction of acetylmethylcarbinol and diacetyl to 2,3-butylene glycol

by the citric acid fermenting streptococci of butter cultures. Iowa Agr. Exp. Sta. Res. Bull. 191.
With M. E. Nelson. Dissimilation of glucose by heterofermentative lactic acid bacteria. J. Bacteriol., 30:547–58.
With M. E. Nelson. Dissimilation of pyruvic acid by *Lactobacillus lycopersici*. Proc. Soc. Exp. Biol. Med., 32:1622–23.
With O. L. Osburn and J. Stritar. The thermophilic fermentation of beet pulp. J. Agr. Res., 50:165–72.
With O. L. Osburn. Utilization of agricultural wastes. II. Influence of nitrogenous substrate on production of butyl and isopropyl alcohols by *Clostridium butylicum*. Ind. Eng. Chem., 27:416–19.
With H. Reynolds. Fermentation of artichokes. Proc. Iowa Acad. Sci., 41:75–78.
With G. L. Stahly, B. W. Hammer, and M. B. Michaelian. The fate of acetylmethylcarbinol and diacetyl in dairy products. Proc. Iowa Acad. Sci., 42:73–76.
With R. W. Stone and H. G. Wood. Activation of the lower fatty acids by propionic acid bacteria. J. Bacteriol., 30:652–53.

1936

With E. A. Zoellner, Henry Gilman, and H. Reynolds. Phosphoglyceric acid in the dissimilation of glucose by *Citrobacter freundii*. J. Bacteriol., 31:5.
With Carl Erb and H. G. Wood. The aerobic dissimilation of lactic acid by the propionic acid bacteria. J. Bacteriol., 31:595–602.
With R. W. Stone and Carl Erb. Respiratory behavior of the propionic acid bacteria. Proc. Soc. Exp. Biol. Med., 33:483–84.
With Milo Mickelson and H. Reynolds. Fermentation of pyruvic acid by bacteria of the colon aerogenes group. Proc. Soc. Exp. Biol. Med., 34:748–50.
With M. E. Nelson. Diversion of the normal heterolactic dissimilation by the addition of hydrogen acceptors. J. Bacteriol., 31:603–10.
With M. E. Nelson. The dissimilation of pyruvic acid by *Lactobacillus lycopersici*. Iowa State Coll. J. Sci., 10:141–44.
With O. L. Osburn and H. G. Wood. Determination of volatile fatty acids by the partition method. Ind. Eng. Chem., 28:270–75.

With G. L. Stahly. Determination of acetylmethylcarbinol in fermentation liquors. Iowa State Coll. J. Sci., 10:205–11.
With H. G. Wood and Carl Erb. A macro-respirometer for the study of aerobic bacterial dissimilation. Iowa State Coll. J. Sci., 10:295–302.
With R. W. Stone. Role of phosphoglyceric acid in the dissimilation of glucose by the propionic acid bacteria. Iowa State Coll. J. Sci., 10:341–43.
With R. W. Stone. The role of phosphoglyceric acid in the dissimilation of glucose by bacteria of the *Escherichia–Aerobacter* group. Iowa State Coll. J. Sci., 11:1–3.
With H. G. Wood. The utilization of CO_2 in the dissimilation of glycerol by the propionic acid bacteria. Biochem. J., 30:48–53.
With H. G. Wood. Mechanism of glucose dissimilation by propionic acid bacteria. Biochem. J., 30:618–23.
With R. W. Stone and H. G. Wood. Activation of the lower fatty acids by propionic acid bacteria. Biochem. J., 30:624–28.

1937

With R. W. Brown and O. L. Osburn. Dissimilation of pyruvic acid by *Clostridium butylicum*. Proc. Soc. Exp. Biol. Med., 36:203–5.
With O. L. Osburn and R. W. Brown. The butyl alcohol–isopropyl alcohol fermentation. J. Biol. Chem., 121:685–95.
With H. G. Wood and Carl Erb. Dissimilation of pyruvic acid by the propionic acid bacteria. Iowa State Coll. J. Sci., 11:287–92.
With H. Reynolds. The fermentation of xylose by the colon-aerogenes group of bacteria. Iowa State Coll. J. Sci., 11:373–78.
With H. Reynolds. The intermediate dissimilation of glucose by *Aerobacter indologenes*. J. Bacteriol., 33:603–14.
With H. Reynolds. Carboligatic activity of *Escherichia coli*. Archiv für Mikrobiologie, 8:149–52.
With H. Reynolds and B. J. Jacobsson. The dissimilation of organic acids by *Aerobacter indologenes*. J. Bacteriol., 34:15–20.
With H. G. Wood and R. W. Stone. The intermediate metabolism of the propionic acid bacteria. Biochem. J., 31:349–59.
With R. W. Stone. The occurrence of phosphoglyceric acid in the bacterial dissimilation of glucose. Biochem. J., 31:1516–23.
With R. W. Stone and H. G. Wood. The dissimilation of phos-

phate esters by the propionic acid bacteria. Enzymologia, 4: 24–30.
With H. G. Wood and A. A. Andersen. Growth factors for propionic and lactic acid bacteria. Proc. Soc. Exp. Biol. Med., 36:217–19.

1938

With C. R. Brewer, M. B. Michaelian, and B. W. Hammer. Effect of aeration under pressure on diacetyl production in butter cultures. Iowa Agr. Exp. Sta. Res. Bull. 233.
With R. W. Brown and G. L. Stahly. Behavior of butyric acid–butyl alcohol bacteria toward acetylmethylcarbinol and asparagin. Iowa State Coll. J. Sci., 12:245–51.
With Milo Mickelson. Influence of pH on the dissimilation of glucose by *Aerobacter indologenes*. J. Bacteriol., 36:67–76.
With O. L. Osburn and R. W. Brown. Dissimilation of intermediary compounds in the butyl–isopropyl alcohol fermentation. Iowa State Coll. J. Sci., 12:275–84.
With M. Silverman. Vitamin B_1 in bacterial metabolism. Proc. Soc. Exp. Biol. Med., 38:823–27.
With W. P. Wiggert. Phosphorylation by the living bacterial cell. Biochem. J., 32:101–7.
With H. G. Wood. The utilization of CO_2 by the propionic acid bacteria. Biochem. J., 32:1262–71.
With H. G. Wood and A. A. Andersen. Nutrition of the propionic acid bacteria. J. Bacteriol., 36:201–14.
With H. G. Wood and W. P. Wiggert. The fermentation of phosphate esters by the propionic acid bacteria. Enzymologia, 2: 373–76.

1939

Bacterial dissimilation of carbohydrates. Bacteriological Reviews, 3:187–227.
With M. Silverman. Bacterial synthesis of co-carboxylase. Enzymologia, 5:385–87. Also in Proc. Soc. Exp. Biol. Med., 40: 369–72.
With C. R. Brewer. The anaerobic dissimilation of citric acid by *Aerobacter indologenes*. Enzymologia, 6:273–81.
With C. R. Brewer. The oxidation of citric acid by coli-aerogenes bacteria. Proc. Soc. Exp. Biol. Med., 41:185–88.

With M. N. Mickelson. Effect of aldehydes and fatty acids as added hydrogen acceptors on the fermentation of glucose by *Aerobacter indologenes*. J. Bacteriol., 37:619–27.

With M. Silverman. Adaptation of the propionic acid bacteria to vitamin B_1 synthesis including a method of assay. J. Bacteriol., 38:25–32.

With W. P. Wiggert, M. Silverman, and M. F. Utter. Note on the preparation of active cell-free juice from bacteria. J. Bacteriol., 38:111.

With R. W. Brown and H. G. Wood. Nutrient requirements of butyric acid–butyl alcohol bacteria. J. Bacteriol., 38:631–40.

With M. Silverman. Function of vitamin B_1 in anaerobic bacterial metabolism. Iowa State Coll. J. Sci., 13:107–13.

With M. N. Mickelson. Pressure–aeration effects on the dissimilation of glucose by *Aerobacter indologenes*. Iowa State Coll. J. Sci., 13:157–60.

With H. Reynolds and W. M. Hoehn. Occurrence of acrolein as an intermediate during the fermentation of glycerol by the coli-aerogenes bacteria. Iowa State Coll. J. Sci., 13:275–77.

With M. Silverman. Thiamin effects in bacterial metabolism. Iowa State Coll. J. Sci., 13:365–68.

With W. P. Wiggert. Fluoride sensitivity of *Propionibacterium pentosaceum* as a function of growth conditions. Biochem. J., 33:1061–69.

1940

Further biochemical methods. In: *Pure Culture Study of Bacteria: Manual of Methods,* Leaflet VI. 8th ed. Committee on Bacteriological Technic of the Society of American Bacteriologists. Geneva, N.Y., Biotech Publications.

With W. P. Wiggert, M. Silverman, and M. F. Utter. Preparation of an active juice from bacteria. Iowa State Coll. J. Sci., 14:179–86.

With A. A. Andersen. Description of a dextro lactic acid forming organism of the genus *Bacillus*. Iowa State Coll. J. Sci., 14:187–94.

With C. R. Brewer. Dissimilation of citric acid by *Streptococcus paracitrovorus*. Antonie van Leeuwenhoek J. Microbiol. Serol., 6:110–20.

With M. N. Mickelson. Formation of trimethyleneglycol from glycerol by *Aerobacter*. Enzymologia, 8:252–56.
With H. G. Wood, C. R. Brewer, and M. N. Mickelson. A macrorespirometer for the study of the aerobic metabolism of microorganisms. Enzymologia, 8:314–17.
With C. R. Brewer. The aerobic dissimilation of citric acid by coliform bacteria. Enzymologia, 8:318–26.
With C. R. Brewer. Anaerobic dissimilation of citric acid by coliform bacteria. Enzymologia, 9:236–40.
With M. N. Mickelson. The dissimilation of glycerol by coli-aerogenes intermediates. J. Bacteriol., 39:709–15.
With M. Silverman. The acetylmethylcarbinol enzyme system of *Aerobacter aerogenes*. Proc. Soc. Exp. Biol. Med., 43:777–78.
With M. F. Utter. Occurrence of the aldolase equilibrium in bacterial metabolism. J. Bacteriol., 41:5.
With H. G. Wood. The fixation of CO_2 by cell suspensions of *Propionibacterium pentosaceum*. Biochem. J., 34:7–14.
With H. G. Wood. The relationship of bacterial utilization of CO_2 to succinic acid formation. Biochem. J., 34:129–38.
With R. W. Stone and M. N. Mickelson. The dissimilation of phosphoglyceric acid and hexosediphosphate by *Aerobacter indologenes*. Iowa State Coll. J. Sci., 14:253–60.
With M. E. Nelson. The dissimilation of levulose by heterofermentative lactic acid bacteria. Iowa State Coll. J. Sci., 14:359–65.
With H. G. Wood and C. Geiger. Accessory growth factor and amino acid requirements of heterofermentative lactic acid bacteria. Iowa State Coll. J. Sci., 14:367–78.
With H. G. Wood. The utilization of carbon dioxide by bacteria. In: *Third International Congress for Microbiology*, ed. by M. Henry Dawson, pp. 246–47. Held in New York, September 1939. New York, The Congress. (A)

1941

With L. O. Krampitz. The enzymic decarboxylation of oxaloacetate. Biochem. J., 35:595–602.
With M. Silverman. The formation of acetylmethylcarbinol from pyruvic acid by a bacterial enzyme preparation. J. Biol. Chem., 138:35–48.

With H. D. Slade. The anaerobic dissimilation of citric acid by cell suspensions of *Streptococcus paracitrovorus.* J. Bacteriol., 41: 675–83.
With H. G. Wood, A. Hemingway, and A. O. Nier. Note on the degradation of propionic acid synthesized by *Propionibacterium.* Iowa State Coll. J. Sci., 15:213–14.
With H. D. Slade, H. G. Wood, A. O. Nier, and A. Hemingway. Note on the utilization of carbon dioxide by heterotrophic bacteria. Iowa State Coll. J. Sci., 15:339–41.
With M. F. Utter. Occurrence of the aldolase and isomerase equilibria in bacterial metabolism. J. Bacteriol., 42:665–76.
With H. G. Wood, A. Hemingway, and A. O. Nier. Heavy carbon as a tracer in heterotrophic carbon dioxide assimilation. J. Biol. Chem., 139:365–76.
With H. G. Wood, A. Hemingway, and A. O. Nier. Position of the carbon dioxide-carbon in propionic acid synthesized by *Propionibacterium.* Proc. Soc. Exp. Biol. Med., 46:313–16.
With H. G. Wood, A Hemingway, and A. O. Nier. The position of carbon dioxide-carbon in succinic acid synthesized by heterotrophic bacteria. J. Biol. Chem., 139:377–81.
With H. G. Wood, A. Hemingway, A. O. Nier, and C. G. Stuckwisch. Reliability of reactions used to locate assimilated carbon in propionic acid. J. Am. Chem. Soc., 63:2140–42.
With H. G. Wood, A. Hemingway, and A. O. Nier. Mechanism of fixation of carbon dioxide in the Krebs cycle. J. Biol. Chem., 139:483–84.

1942

Mechanisms for the complete oxidation of carbohydrates by aerobic bacteria. In: *Symposium on Respiratory Enzymes,* pp. 258–61. Madison, University of Wisconsin Press.
With H. D. Slade. Intermediary metabolism of certain heterotrophic bacteria particularly *Streptococcus paracitrovorus* and *Aerobacter indologenes.* Iowa State Coll. J. Sci., 17:123–25.
With H. D. Slade. Bacterial assimilation of acetic and succinic acids containing heavy carbon by *Aerobacter indologenes.* Proc. Soc. Exp. Biol. Med., 51:65–66.
With H. G. Wood, A. Hemingway, and A. O. Nier. Fixation of carbon dioxide by pigeon liver in the dissimilation of pyruvic acid. J. Biol. Chem., 142:31–45.

With H. D. Slade, A. O. Nier, H. G. Wood, and A. Hemingway. Assimilation of heavy carbon dioxide by heterotrophic bacteria. J. Biol. Chem., 143:133–45.
With M. F. Utter. Dissimilation of phosphoglyceric acid by *Escherichia coli*. Biochem. J., 36:485–93.
With G. L. Stahly. The origin and relationship of acetylmethylcarbinol and 2,3-butylene glycol in bacterial fermentation. Biochem. J., 36:575–81.
With M. F. Utter. Effect of metal ions on the reactions of phosphopyruvate in *Escherichia coli*. J. Biol. Chem., 146:289–300.
With W. S. Waring. Growth of bacteria in an iron-free medium. Arch. Biochem., 1:303–10.
With H. G. Wood. On the metabolism of bacteria. Botanical Review, 8:1–68.
With H. G. Wood. Heterotrophic assimilation of carbon dioxide. Advances in Enzymology, 2:135–82.
With G. Kalnitsky. Fixation of CO_2 by a cell-free extract of *Escherichia coli*. J. Bacteriol., 44:256–57.

1943

With W. S. Waring. Iron requirements of heterotrophic bacteria. Arch. Biochem., 1:425–33.
With H. D. Slade. Assimilation of acetic and succinic acids containing heavy carbon by *Aerobacter indologenes*. Arch. Biochem., 2:97–111.
With G. Kalnitsky. Anaerobic dissimilation of pyruvate by a cell-free extract of *Escherichia coli*. Arch. Biochem., 2:113–24.
With G. Kalnitsky and H. G. Wood. CO_2-fixation and succinic acid formation by a cell-free enzyme preparation of *Escherichia coli*. Arch. Biochem., 2:269–81.
With M. F. Utter. Role of phosphate in the anaerobic dissimilation of pyruvic acid. Arch. Biochem., 2:491–92.
With G. Kalnitsky. Enzymatic decarboxylation of oxalacetate and carboxylation of pyruvate. Arch. Biochem., 4:25–40.
With L. O. Krampitz and H. G. Wood. Enzymatic fixation of carbon dioxide in oxalacetate. J. Biol. Chem., 147:243–53.
With A. G. Norman. The use of the nitrogen isotope N^{15} in determining nitrogen recovery from plant materials decomposing in soil. Journal of the American Society of Agronomy, 35:1023–25.

1944

With S. Waring. Iron deficiency in bacterial metabolism. Arch. Biochem., 4:75–87.
With M. F. Utter. Formation and reactions of acetyl phosphate in *Escherichia coli*. Arch. Biochem., 5:413–22.
With R. W. Brown and H. G. Wood. Fixation of carbon dioxide in lactic acid by *Clostridium butylicum*. Arch. Biochem., 5:423–33.
With M. F. Utter and F. Lipmann. Reversibility of the phosphoroclastic split of pyruvate. J. Biol. Chem., 154:723–24.
With H. G. Wood, R. W. Brown, and C. G. Stuckwisch. The degradation of heavy carbon butyric acid from the butyl alcohol fermentation. J. Am. Chem. Soc., 66:1812–18.

1945

With G. Kalnitsky and M. F. Utter. Active enzyme preparations from bacteria. J. Bacteriol., 49:595–602.
With M. F. Utter and F. Lipmann. Reversibility of the phosphoroclastic split of pyruvate. J. Biol. Chem., 158:521–31.
With H. G. Wood and R. W. Brown. Mechanism of the butyl alcohol fermentation with heavy carbon acetic and butyric acids and acetone. Arch. Biochem., 6:243–60.
With A. G. C. White and L. O. Krampitz. On a synthetic medium for the production of penicillin. Arch. Biochem., 8:303–9.

1946

The mechanism of alcoholic fermentation. Chapter 10 in: *Enzymes and Their Role in Wheat Technology*, Vol. 1. New York, Interscience Publishers, Inc.
With A. G. C. White and L. O. Krampitz. Method for the direct determination of diacetyl in tissue and bacterial filtrates. Arch. Biochem., 9:229–34.
With M. F. Utter and L. O. Krampitz. Oxidation of acetyl phosphate and other substrates by *Micrococcus lysodeikticus*. Arch. Biochem., 9:285–300.
With M. F. Utter and G. Kalnitsky. Enzymatic nature of cell-free extracts from bacteria. Arch. Biochem., 9:407–17.

1947

With L. O. Krampitz. On the mode of action of penicillin. Arch. Biochem., 12:57–67.

With A. G. C. White. Assimilation of acetate by yeast. Arch. Biochem., 13:27–32.
With D. Paretsky. The conversion of 2,3-butylene glycol to acetylmethylcarbinol in bacterial fermentations. Arch. Biochem., 14:11–16.
With T. Wiken, D. Watt, and A. G. C. White. Reversibility of pyruvate dismutation. Arch. Biochem., 14:478.
With N. H. Gross. Isotopic composition of acetylmethylcarbinol formed by yeast juice. Arch. Biochem., 15:125–31.
With C. R. Brewer and M. N. Mickelson. Effect of growth substrate on enzymic constitution of *Aerobacter indologenes*. Arch. Biochem., 15:379–87.
With N. H. Gross. Fixation of heavy carbon acetaldehyde by active juices. Antonie van Leeuwenhoek J. Microbiol. Serol., 12:17–25.

1948

With A. G. C. White. Fat synthesis in yeast. Arch. Biochem., 17:475–82.
With S. J. Ajl. Replacement of CO_2 in heterotrophic metabolism. Arch. Biochem., 19:483–92.
With S. J. Ajl. Enzymatic fixation of carbon dioxide in α-ketoglutaric acid. Proc. Nat. Acad. Sci., 34:491–98.
With J. Wilson. Reversibility of a phosphoroclastic reaction. Biochem. J., 42:598–600.

1949

Heterotrophic assimilation of carbon dioxide. In: *Fourth International Congress for Microbiology*, ed. by Mogens Bjørneboe, pp. 43–57. Held in Copenhagen, July 1947. Waltham, Mass., Chronica Botanica Company.
With S. J. Ajl. Anaerobic replacement of carbon dioxide. Proc. Soc. Exp. Biol. Med., 70:522–24.
With S. J. Ajl. On the mechanism of carbon dioxide replacement in heterotrophic metabolism. J. Bacteriol., 57:579–93.

1950

With S. J. Ajl. On the oxidative decarboxylation of α-ketoglutaric acid. Iowa State Coll. J. Sci., 24:279–86.
With S. J. Ajl and W. R. Hart. Biotin in succinic acid oxidation. Enzymologia, 14:1–7.
With W. V. Bartholomew and L. B. Nelson. The use of the nitro-

gen isotope N^{15} in field studies with oats. Agronomy Journal, 42:100–103.
With D. Paretsky. The bacterial metabolism of glycine. Arch. Biochem., 25:288–98.
With G. E. Wessman. Biotin in the assimilation of heavy carbon in oxalacetate. Arch. Biochem., 26:214–18.
With D. Watt. Dismutative assimilation of carbon dioxide. Arch. Biochem., 28:30–35.

1951

With E. B. Fowler and C. S. Stringer. A dual purpose titrimeter and dispenser. Iowa State Coll. J. Sci., 25:599–605.
With D. Watt. Modification of the enzyme system of *Micrococcus pyogenes*. Arch. Biochem. Biophys., 31:383–90.
With W. B. Sutton and F. Schlenk. Glycine as a precursor of bacterial purines. Arch. Biochem. Biophys., 32:85–88.

1952

With E. B. Fowler. Role of CO_2 in bacterial synthesis of aspartate. Arch. Biochem. Biophys., 36:365–70.
With E. B. Fowler. The bacterial synthesis of alanine and glutamate. Arch. Biochem. Biophys., 41:42–47.
With Mitchell Korzenovsky. Bacterial metabolism of arginine. Arch. Biochem. Biophys., 41:233.

1953

With Mitchell Korzenovsky. Conversion of citrulline to ornithine by cell-free extracts of *Streptococcus lactis*. Arch. Biochem. Biophys., 46:174–85.
With W. B. Sutton. The carbon and nitrogen precursors of bacterial purines. Arch. Biochem. Biophys., 47:1–7.
With C. A. Claridge. Formation of 2-ketogluconate from glucose by a cell-free preparation of *Pseudomonas aeruginosa*. Arch. Biochem. Biophys., 47:99–105.

1954

With J. L. Ott. Formation of adenosine by cell-free extracts of *Escherichia coli*. Arch. Biochem. Biophys., 48:483–84.
With D. D. Watt. Inhibition of anaerobic dissimilation of pyruvate by phenylpyruvate. Arch. Biochem. Biophys., 50:64–70.

With C. A. Claridge. Intermediates of the aerobic dissimilation of 2-ketogluconate by *Pseudomonas aeruginosa*. Arch. Biochem. Biophys., 51:395–401.
With G. E. Wessman and L. P. Allen. The biotin requirement of *Micrococcus lysodeikticus*. J. Bacteriol., 67:554–58.
With C. A. Claridge. Evidence for alternate pathways for the oxidation of glucose by *Pseudomonas aeruginosa*. J. Bacteriol., 68:77–79.
With Mitchell Korzenovsky. Stochiometry of the citrulline phosphorylase reaction of *Streptococcus lactis*. Biochem. J., 57:343–47.

1955

With E. B. Fowler. Synthesis of amino acids by *Aerobacter aerogenes*. Arch. Biochem. Biophys., 56:22–27.
With J. L. Ott. Bacterial formation of adenosine properties of cell-free enzyme system in *Escherichia coli*. Suomalainen Tiedeakatemia–Toimituksia Annales Academia Scientiarum Fennica, Series A, 60:174–80.

1957

With J. L. Ott. Coupled nucleoside phosphorylase reactions in *Escherichia coli*. Arch. Biochem. Biophys., 69:264–76.
With D. H. Hug. Transamination in *Rhodospirillum rubrum*. Arch. Biochem. Biophys., 72:369–75.
With J. L. Ott. Enzymic transfer of the ribosyl group from inosine to adenine. Biochem. J., 65:609–11.

1958

With R. W. Kinney. Transamination in *Propionibacterium jensenii*. Iowa State Coll. J. Sci., 32:455–61.
With I. Suzuki. Chemoautotrophic fixation of carbon dioxide by *Thiobacillus thiooxidans*. Iowa State Coll. J. Sci., 32:475–83.
With I. Suzuki. Chemautotrophic carbon dioxide fixation by extracts of *Thiobacillus thiooxidans*. I. Formation of oxalacetic acid. Arch. Biochem. Biophys., 76:103–11.
With I. Suzuki. Chemoautotrophic carbon dioxide fixation by extracts of *Thiobacillus thiooxidans*. II. Formation of phosphoglyceric acid. Arch. Biochem. Biophys., 77:112–23.

1959

With C. L. Baugh, T. Myoda, and D. S. Bates. Mechanisms of carbon dioxide fixation by cell-free extracts of heterotrophic and photosynthetic bacteria. Iowa State Coll. J. Sci., 34:113–18.

With I. Suzuki. Glutathione and sulfur oxidation by *Thiobacillus thiooxidans*. Proc. Nat. Acad. Sci., 45:239–44.

1960

With D. S. Bates. Nucleotide-dependent carbon dioxide fixation in *Rhodospirillum rubrum*. Iowa State Coll. J. Sci., 35:41–48.

With C. L. Baugh and G. W. Claus. Heterotrophic fixation of carbon dioxide by extracts of *Nocardia corallina*. Arch. Biochem. Biophys., 86:255–59.

With R. W. Kinney. *Brevibacterium leucinophagum* spec. nov. International Bulletin of Bacteriological Nomenclature and Taxonomy, 10:213–17.

With T. Myoda. Carbon dioxide fixation by the genus *Mycobacterium*. Iowa State Coll. J. Sci., 35:73–88.

With R. W. Kinney. Evidence for a tricarboxylic acid cycle in *Brevibacterium leucinophagum*. Iowa State Coll. J. Sci., 35:89–96.

1961

With C. L. Baugh, D. S. Bates, and G. W. Claus. Propionate carboxylation by *Nocardia corallina*. Enzymologia, 23:225–30.

With T. Myoda. Carbon dioxide fixing systems in *Mycobacterium phlei* grown in a simple chemically defined medium. Iowa State Coll. J. Sci., 35:463–72.

1962

With C. L. Baugh, D. S. Bates, and G. W. Claus. Fatty acid carboxylation by extracts of *Nocardia corallina*. Iowa State Coll. J. Sci., 37:23–28.

ACKNOWLEDGMENTS FOR THE PHOTOGRAPHS

Photograph of Charles Haskell Danforth
by Peter Hughes

Photograph of Thomas Francis, Jr.
by Fabian Bachrach

Photograph of William Vermillion Houston
by Howard A. Thompson
The Rice Institute

Photograph of Howard Bishop Lewis
by Dey Studio

Photograph of Robert Harry Lowie
courtesy of Lowie Museum of Anthropology
University of California, Berkeley

Winthrop John Vanleuven Osterhout
by Louis Schmidt

Theodore William Richards
by Fotograv. Gen. Stab. Lit. Anst.

Photograph of Rudolf Ruedemann
by Pach Bros.

Photograph of Edward Arthur Steinhaus
courtesy of Center for Pathobiology
University of California, Irvine

Photograph of Chester Hamlin Werkman
by Hill's Studio